TRANSWORLD PUBLISHERS
61–63 Uxbridge Road, London W5 5SA
www.penguin.co.uk

Transworld is part of the Penguin Random House group of companies whose addresses can be found at global.penguinrandomhouse.com

First published in Great Britain in 2016 by Bantam Press
an imprint of Transworld Publishers
Bantam edition published 2017

A CIP catalogue record for this book
is available from the British Library.

ISBN
9780553818666

Typeset in 9/13.25pt ITC Stone Serif by Jouve (UK), Milton Keynes.
Printed and bound by Clays Ltd, St Ives plc.

Penguin Random House is committed to a sustainable future for our business, our readers and our planet. This book is made from Forest Stewardship Council® certified paper.

1 3 5 7 9 10 8 6 4 2

Too Important for the Generals

How Britain nearly lost the First World War

Allan Mallinson

BANTAM BOOKS

LONDON · TORONTO · SYDNEY · AUCKLAND · JOHANNESBURG

La guerre! C'est une chose trop grave pour la confier à des militaires.

(War is too serious a matter to entrust to military men,
usually rendered as
War is too important to be left to the generals.)

Georges Clemenceau,
Prime Minister of France November 1917 to January 1920,
quoted in Georges Suarez, *Soixante années d'histoire française* (1932)

At no time, so far as I know, did it ever cross our minds that we could possibly not win the war, and we never knew how near we came to not winning it.

Guy Chapman MC,
Royal Fusiliers 1914–20,
in *Vain Glory: A Miscellany of the Great War 1914–1918* (1937)

CONTENTS

CONTENTS

MAPS

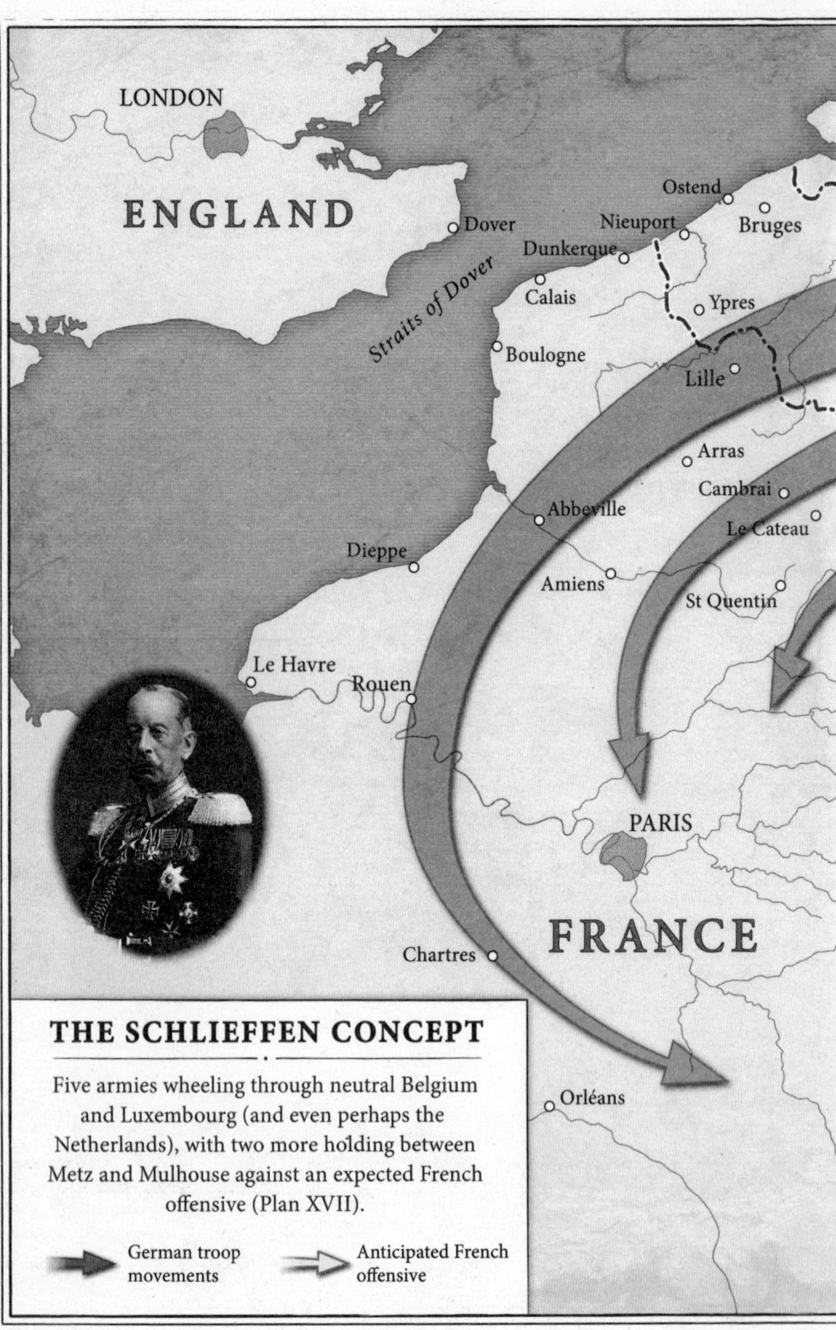

THE SCHLIEFFEN CONCEPT

Five armies wheeling through neutral Belgium and Luxembourg (and even perhaps the Netherlands), with two more holding between Metz and Mulhouse against an expected French offensive (Plan XVII).

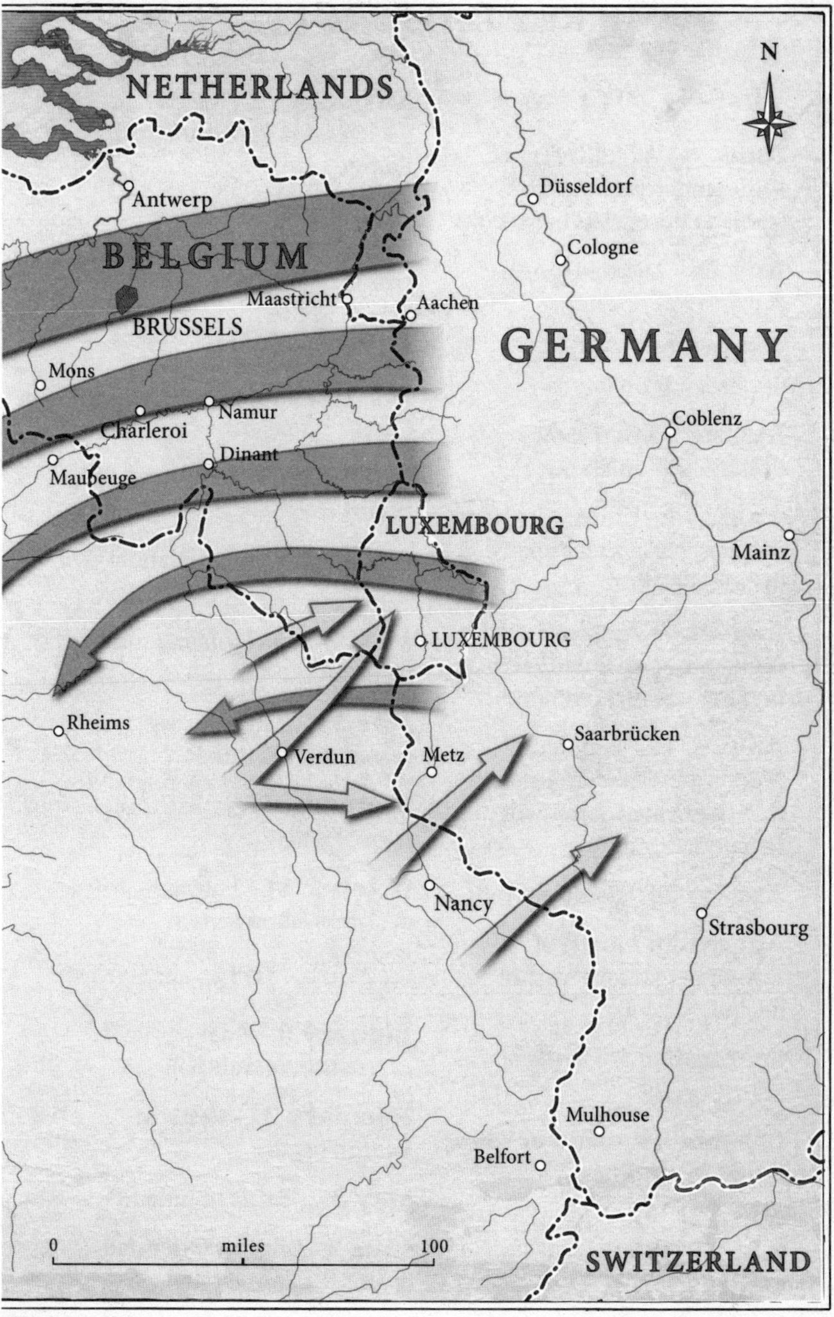
N
NETHERLANDS
Antwerp
BELGIUM
BRUSSELS
Maastricht
Aachen
Düsseldorf
Cologne
GERMANY
Mons
Charleroi
Namur
Maubeuge
Dinant
Coblenz
LUXEMBOURG
Mainz
LUXEMBOURG
Rheims
Verdun
Metz
Saarbrücken
Nancy
Strasbourg
Mulhouse
Belfort
0
miles
100
SWITZERLAND

SOME KEY DATES 1914–1918

1914

June 28 – Archduke Franz Ferdinand assassinated by Serbian nationalists in Sarajevo

July 28 – Austria-Hungary declares war on Serbia

August 1 – Germany declares war on Russia

August 3 – Germany declares war on France

August 4 – United Kingdom declares war after Germany invades Belgium

August 6 – Austria-Hungary declares war on Russia, Serbia declares war on Germany

August 19 – President Woodrow Wilson announces that the United States will remain neutral

August 23 – Battle of Mons

August 26 – Battle of Tannenberg (East Prussia) begins

September 5 – Battle of the Marne begins

October 19 – Battle of Ypres begins ('First Ypres')

October 29 – Turkish fleet bombards Russian Black Sea coast

November 1 – Russia declares war on Ottoman Empire

November 5 – France and Britain declare war on Ottoman Empire

1915

February 19 – Dardanelles Campaign begins

April 22 – 'Second Ypres' begins

April 25 – Gallipoli landings begin

May 7 – RMS *Lusitania* sunk by U-20

May 23 – Italy joins war on side of the Entente

September 25 – Battle of Loos begins

October 14 – Bulgaria declares war on Serbia

1916

January 9 – Final evacuation of Gallipoli

February 21 – Battle of Verdun begins

May 31 – Battle of Jutland

June 4 – Brusilov Offensive begins (Eastern Front)

July 1 – Battle of the Somme begins (15 September, first use of tanks)

August 6 – Sixth Battle of the Isonzo (Italian Front) begins

August 27 – Romania declares war on Central Powers

1917

February 1 – Germans declare unrestricted submarine warfare

March 1 – British troops enter Baghdad

March 15 – Russian Tsar Nicholas II abdicates

April 6 – United States declares war on Germany

April 16 – Nivelle Offensive begins (including Battle of Arras)

June 28 – Greece officially declares war on Central Powers

July 31 – 'Third Ypres' begins (Passchendaele)

October 24 – Battle of Caporetto (Italian Front) begins

November 7 – Bolsheviks overthrow Russian government

December 11 – General Allenby enters Jerusalem

December 17 – Russo-German Armistice begins

1918

March 3 – Russia signs (peace) Treaty of Brest Litovsk

March 21 – Germany launches Spring Offensive

July 15 – Second Battle of Marne begins

August 8 – Battle of Amiens ('the black day of the German Army') – 'The Hundred Days' allied counter-offensive begins

October 24 – Battle of Vittorio Veneto (Italian Front) begins

October 30 – Turks sign Armistice (throughout Middle East); Bulgarians sign Armistice (fighting on Macedonian Front effectively ceases)

November 3 – Austria-Hungary signs Armistice (Italian Front)

November 9 – Kaiser Wilhelm II abdicates and flees Germany

November 11 – Germany signs Armistice at Compiègne

Preface

> For we have a peculiar power of thinking before we act, and of acting, too, whereas other men are courageous from ignorance but hesitate upon reflection.
>
> Pericles, Funeral oration at the end of the first year of the Peloponnesian War, 430 BC

In July 2013, following the lead set by the government, the British army issued instructions laying out its approach to the First World War centenary commemorations – 'Operation Reflect'. Its aim was (and remains, until 11 November 2018) to 'mark the centenary of the First World War in an appropriate manner in order to commemorate the sacrifice of our forebears, learn enduring lessons, and educate ourselves and others'.

This was something of a departure for the army. Hitherto it had steered clear of the First World War, perhaps because four years of stalemate seemed irrelevant to modern conflict. On the face of it, the campaigns of Marlborough and Wellington and the battles of the Second World War looked more likely to yield lessons in strategy and 'the operational art', while counter-insurgency campaigns such as those in Malaya, Kenya and Cyprus were the obvious places to seek inspiration in the 'war on terror'.

The army launched Operation Reflect with a conference in London in July 2014, followed in September by a week's 'staff ride'* in France and Belgium in which 150 hand-picked British and French captains and majors, led by the general officer commanding the 3rd (UK) Division and attended by the chief of the general staff, his French opposite number and several German officers, studied the course of the war on the Western Front on the ground over which it had been fought. It was all very high-powered, with just about every 'name' in the book of British military historians taking part in one event or the other.

The captains and majors, fresh from Afghanistan, and in many cases with previous service in Iraq, were soon in awe of the sheer size of the problem that the British army had faced in the Great War, expanding as it had from a relatively small expeditionary force in August 1914 to some two million by 1918, 90 per cent of whom had never been in uniform before.

The London conference, the staff ride and the 'exploitation' conference at Sandhurst which followed two months later were not designed to answer the questions about British generalship posed by entertainments such as *Oh! What a Lovely War* and *Blackadder Goes Forth*. Even so, it seemed to me that professional sympathy for the magnitude of the generals' task, with much talk about 'the learning curve' (in truth, a flat line for far too long), made for a sort of fatalism among the officers taking part which was not unlike that prevailing in the army of 1916–18 – something along the lines of: 'Although things should never have got to this pass, the war is where it is and can only be won by destroying the German army on the Western Front, and in the process, come what may, huge numbers of men are going to be killed.'

Indeed, this seems to be the growing consensus among historians. In one of the most recent and purportedly authoritative studies of modern warfare, Professor David Woodward of Marshall

* Originally carried out (as the term suggests) on horseback, this was a technique pioneered by the Prussian *Generalstab* to take officers over the ground of a past campaign or battle to study its leadership and the decisions taken, and to consider whether alternatives could have been employed.

University, West Virginia, writes baldly of 'a cruel truth' that costly frontal offensives were the only way to win the war.*

I profoundly disagree.

As I have recently explained,† personal and institutional failures – both political and military – marked Britain's preparations for the war, and its early conduct. There were two literally vital elements missing: strategy and generalship. In fact, personal and institutional failures marked the next four years just as much, the want of strategy and generalship exacting a terrible tactical price – not least in casualties – that still taints the ultimate allied victory of November 1918.

Whether and when Clemenceau actually said that war is too important to be left to the generals is unimportant; it is what he thought, and the words have force. While aphorisms can be trite, at the time of their coining they have not of course been dulled by use. One of the problems in writing about the First World War, a conflict unsurpassed in the variety and volume of its literature, is language. Of some words and phrases there is now no common understanding: used often and indiscriminately, they no longer have meaning. Yet this is not to deny their original aptness. Clarify the language – 'strategy', 'attrition', 'knocking away the props' and so on – as well as the context, and the truth is once again revealed. In March 1915, Henry James, 'sick beyond cure' that he had lived to see the war, gave an interview to the *New York Times*. 'One finds it in the midst of all this as hard to apply one's words as to endure one's thoughts,' James told the young journalist sent to interview him in London, Preston Lockwood, a Rhodes Scholar who would later serve with the French and then the US armies on the Western Front: 'The war has used up words; they have weakened, they have

* 'World War I: Western Front', in Gordon Martel (ed.), *Twentieth-Century Conflict: A Concise Encyclopaedia* (London, 2014). Woodward is the editor of Field Marshal Sir William Robertson's papers and of *Lloyd George and the Generals* (London, 2004).
† Allan Mallinson, *1914: Fight the Good Fight – Britain, the Army and the Coming of the First World War* (London, 2013).

deteriorated like motor car tires . . . and we are now confronted with a depreciation of all our terms, or, otherwise speaking, with a loss of expression through increase of limpness.'

When Clemenceau became president of the council of ministers in November 1917, one of France's darkest hours, he said simply: 'Je fais la guerre' – 'I [intend to] make war.' If he had then added by way of explanation: 'En raison de c'est une chose trop grave pour la confier à des militaires,' it would have been a criticism not only of the generals, whose stratagems to date had been both costly and unsuccessful, but also of the statesmen who had allowed the generals to dictate military policy – had surrendered to them, indeed, the whole gamut of strategy.*

In the fifth century BC the family of Greek words deriving from *strategos* (general) had a clear and basic military connection, *strategia* being the art of leading an army. But it was the practice of Athenian statesmen (*politikoi*) to take command of armies – Pericles being the signal example – and so the line between the civil and the military was not as clear as modern practice would suggest. Indeed, European kings and princes led their armies in the field until the eighteenth century (George II was the last British monarch to command in battle, in 1743 at Dettingen); it was the best way to be sure of the ultimate loyalty of subordinates. It was only with the writings of Clausewitz in the early nineteenth century that the distinction between the military and the civil in war became sharply defined.† The word 'strategy' in the sense of disposing military force had only recently come into use in Europe (the *Oxford English Dictionary* dates the first use in English to 1810‡),

* Clemenceau had purportedly used the phrase twenty years earlier in connection with the revanchist war minister General Georges Boulanger.

† Carl Philipp Gottfried von Clausewitz (1780–1831), Prussian general. His *Vom Kriege* (*On War*), from which the quotations here are taken, though unfinished at his death, remains a prime manual of military philosophy.

‡ Strategy (*Oxford English Dictionary*): 'The art of a commander-in-chief; the art of projecting and directing the larger military movements and operations of a campaign.' This level of military art – the campaign – is now referred to by professionals, rather ambiguously, as the 'operational' level, being that below strategic (sometimes 'military-strategic'), the highest level in military terms. Military strategy is

and Clausewitz's definition was still relatively narrow: 'Strategy is the use of engagements [battles] for the object of war' ('Die Strategie ist der Gebrauch des Gefechts zum Zweck des Krieges'). By the twentieth century, 'strategy' was understood more broadly as the art of distributing and applying military means to fulfil the ends of policy. Both understandings, however, gave pre-eminence to political over military goals. Indeed, Clausewitz was adamant: 'It is an inadmissible and even harmful distinction to leave a great military enterprise or its planning to a "purely military" judgment; more, it is absurd to consult professional soldiers on a plan for a war in order that they may judge from a "purely military" standpoint what cabinets are to do.'

Here, then, is the substance of what Clemenceau was talking about. The business of war is more than simply arranging and conducting battles. Political purpose must dominate all strategy, otherwise military 'necessity' may distort that purpose. The government states its policy – the desired outcome, or 'ends' – to the *militaires*, with appropriate guidance, sometimes called 'grand strategy' or 'war policy'. The *militaires* then determine the ways and means to secure the ends.

This sounds straightforward enough; but, as Clausewitz observed, war is a mix of instinct, art and reason (the so-called Clausewitzian trinity). It is first an affair of 'primordial violence, hatred and enmity . . . a blind, natural force'. The 'play of chance and probability, within which the creative spirit is free to roam', is an art not a science; while it is only as an instrument of policy that, theoretically, it is 'subject to pure reason'.

War, he wrote, is 'not merely a political act but also a real political instrument' – 'a continuation of political commerce, a carrying

---

determined by a government's principal military adviser within the government's 'grand strategy' (political, economic, information etc.). The operational level is the 'gearing' that turns pure strategy into a solid sequence of operations and battles, allocating resources in detail. In 1914–18 GHQ in France was an operational level headquarters. (Allied) strategy, in its present-day sense, was the business of London, Paris and Petrograd (as St Petersburg had become).

out of the same enterprise with other means' ('Der Krieg ist eine blosse Fortsetzung der Politik mit anderen Mitteln'). Unfortunately for the proper relationship of the political and the military in the First World War, the notion had gained purchase in some quarters that once war begins it becomes solely the business of soldiers. In Britain this was perhaps because the first full English text of *Vom Kriege* to be published renders *mit anderen Mitteln* not as 'with' but as 'by' other means, allowing the inference that the primary, non-military, means are at an end.* With his characteristic pithiness – 'La guerre! C'est une chose trop grave pour la confier à des militaires' – Clemenceau was in fact reclaiming Clausewitz's true original proposition.

Whereas 'tactics' is about knowing what to do to achieve a specific practical objective, strategy is about the overall objective(s) – beginning with recognizing the need to do anything at all. It is then about balancing overall objectives (or ends) with the ways and means of achieving them. And balancing is a business of give and take. The leaders of the state – politicians – set the policy, but before any attempt at implementation military officers must first apprise policy-makers of the extent to which those objectives are achievable with the ways and means available. If the necessary ways and means cannot be found, the objectives must be modified. This is a dynamic process – not least once battle begins – needing continual dialogue to ensure that ends, ways and means remain in balance. Without strategy, tactics fumble blindly, bloodily and with no assurance of success.

This dialogue, this understanding, was fundamentally lacking in most capitals before and during the First World War; and that lack was at the root of the strategic stalemate that occurred between 1915 and the middle of 1918, and of the consequential and unnecessary loss of life. Nowhere was it more evident than in London. Matters were very different in the Second World War after Winston Churchill became prime minister, for Churchill, uniquely, had

* *On War*, trans. Colonel James Graham (London, 1873).

seen the want of strategic dialogue in 1914–18 from the perspectives of both statesman and *militaire*. On taking office as prime minister in 1940 he at once made himself 'minister of defence' and thereby director of grand strategy, the art of which lay, he said, 'in foreseeing the outlines of the future and being prepared to deal with it' – a typically (and usefully) reductionist definition, cutting through the purism of Clausewitz and his posthumous disciple Moltke.* Indeed, it is probably the most realistic definition.

Yet before 1914 the British had thought themselves eminently superior in the constitutional arrangements for war-making. In *The English Constitution* (1867), Walter Bagehot, the foremost political essayist of the Victorian age, wrote of the great advantages of the British parliamentary system:

> At a sudden emergency, this people [the British] can choose a ruler for the occasion. It is quite possible and even likely that he would not be ruler before the occasion. The great qualities – the imperious will, the rapid energy, the eager nature fit for a great crisis – are not required, are impediments in common times . . . We often want, at the sudden occurrence of a grave tempest, to change the helmsman – to replace the pilot of the calm by the pilot of the storm. In England we have had so few catastrophes since our Constitution attained maturity, that we hardly appreciate this latent excellence . . .

He cited as his principal evidence the toppling of the government of Lord Aberdeen in the 1850s because of the early débâcles of the Crimean War, and Aberdeen's replacement by Lord Palmerston (he of the famous 'gunboat diplomacy'), saying: 'We turned out the Quaker, and put in the pugilist.'

And then he compared this with the US constitution:

> But under a Presidential government you can do nothing of the kind . . . You have got a Congress elected for one fixed period, going out perhaps by fixed instalments, which cannot be accelerated or

* On Moltke, see page 2 below.

> retarded – you have a President chosen for a fixed period, and immovable during that period . . . Come what may, you can quicken nothing, and can retard nothing. You have bespoken your Government in advance, and whether it suits you or not, whether it works well or works ill, whether it is what you want or not, by law you must keep it . . . The first and most critical years of every war would be managed by a peace Premier, and the first and most critical years of peace by a war Premier. In each case the period of transition would be irrevocably governed by a man selected not for what he was to introduce, but what he was to change – for the policy he was to abandon, not for the policy he was to administer.

But theory is one thing, events another. Bagehot was writing just after President Lincoln had been helmsman in the Civil War, and yet, curiously, he made no comment on this, though Lincoln had surely been the very model of a modern war leader in a democracy (as President Franklin D. Roosevelt would be in the Second World War, and, some would argue, Woodrow Wilson in 1917–18) – except that in the early years of the war Lincoln and his generals could come up with no strategy to defeat the Confederacy, leaving the Union army fighting battle after battle which led nowhere but to the grave for huge numbers of its men (Lincoln's ultimate triumph was to pick the right generals). Indeed, Bagehot, had he lived, would have had to add a substantial coda to extend his analysis to cover Britain up to December 1916. For the *six* years of the preceding peace, the prime minister, H. H. Asquith, had been not so much the 'pilot of the calm' as rather a helmsman capable only of letting the ship of state drift with the current. And then for two and a half critical years of war he stayed on as the 'pilot of the storm'. Yet not even Asquith's greatest supporter (probably his wife, Margot) could have claimed for him 'the imperious will, the rapid energy, the eager nature fit for a great crisis'. Indeed, in November 1916, as the Battle of the Somme – the nadir of generalship (until 1917) – gasped to a halt, one of his ministers would minute him on the inherent illogicality of a war for civilization in which civilization was itself being destroyed, a war of survival in fighting which the nation's strength does not survive: 'No one for a moment believes we are going to lose this war, but what is our chance of winning it in such a manner, and within such limits of time, as will enable us to beat our enemy to the ground and impose upon him the kind of terms which we so freely discuss?'*

For the military-strategic (as well as the tactical) record had not been a good one. In August 1914 the army's brightest and best had gone to France with the British Expeditionary Force (BEF), emptying the War Office of just about every trained, experienced and useful staff officer. Even the director of military operations (DMO), the man responsible for intelligence and operational planning, put on khaki and crossed the Channel.† Nor was the problem merely one of empty corridors. The few who remained proved frighteningly ineffective in the new scheme of things. The chief of the imperial general staff (CIGS) himself, Sir Charles Douglas, hastily appointed in April when Sir John French had resigned in the wake of the 'Curragh mutiny',‡ had never held a general staff appointment. Yet he was now to be the war cabinet's principal adviser on

* Lord Lansdowne, minister without portfolio, former foreign secretary in Balfour's (Conservative) government 1902–5. The minute attracted scathing criticism as expressing defeatism – cowardice indeed – from both colleagues and soldiers.

† Having practically devised the entire plan for the deployment of the BEF, Major-General Henry Wilson, DMO since 1910, joined the BEF as its sub-chief of staff.

‡ In April 1914 the secretary of state for war, Jack Seely, had somehow managed to give the GOC-in-C Ireland, Sir Arthur Paget (not the subtlest of officers), the impression that he was to seek the views of his command about the home rule bill. This Paget did by putting a hypothetical question to his commanding officers along the lines: 'Would they obey an order to take coercive measures against the Ulster unionists?' The great majority of officers of the 3rd Cavalry Brigade at the Curragh camp outside Dublin, several of whom (including their brigadier, Hubert Gough) were of the 'Anglo-Irish Ascendancy', wrote to Paget that they would resign rather than obey such an order. Confusion ensued over a vague promise to let officers with a personal interest take leave during such operations, which to London's eyes amounted to connivance at mutiny, and Gough was summoned to the War Office. There followed much petulance on the part of Gough and Seely, and an uncharacteristic lack of 'grip' by French. The King was drawn in and matters became very unedifying, ending in what appeared to be a climb-down by Seely, who ascribed the affair to a misunderstanding. It was not a true mutiny – no one had disobeyed a direct order – but the press said it was, and the name stuck.

military strategy, besides being in large measure its executive arm, as well as having the job of reconstituting the War Office staff. Poor man: he would die of the strain inside three months.

In any case, the War Office had been without an effective secretary of state since April, when Jack Seely, a man whose greatest admirer (probably his horse, the famous Warrior) could never have placed him in the first division, had felt obliged to resign alongside French.* Asquith had decided not to replace him, instead taking the portfolio himself. Yet industry was not Asquith's most notable attribute, and this addition to his workload made sense only in ensuring that he would not be troubled by an insistent voice at the War Office. In the latter days of the July crisis, as Europe stumbled into war, he asked the Lord Chancellor, Haldane,† the great reforming war minister of the Edwardian period, to keep an eye on his old department as well as his current one. And then the day after the declaration of war, 5 August, he appointed Field Marshal Earl Kitchener of Khartoum as secretary of state: a 'perilous experiment', as Asquith himself called it – a man in uniform in the cabinet, and one whose monocratic methods would be exacerbated by the weakness of his own War Office staff.

This was no way for a nation to wage any sort of war, let alone one as convulsive as that already raging from the North Sea coast to the Carpathian mountains, and soon to spread to the Near and Middle East, to the jungles, lakes and savannah the length of Africa – indeed to every ocean and continent. When something of its like, if not its intensity, had befallen the world in Napoleon's day, the British government had responded resolutely but subtly. Victory was long in coming – the Whigs complained of 'the

* Seely was a brave man. As a yeomanry officer in South Africa he had won a DSO, and he would serve almost the entire war in France, from 1915 as commander of the Canadian Cavalry Brigade. *My Horse Warrior* (London, 1934), a biography of his charger, is in effect a war memoir, somewhat shaky on fact and perspective, but nevertheless entertaining.

† Richard Burdon (Viscount) Haldane, Edinburgh- and Göttingen-educated philosopher, barrister and bachelor. Secretary of state for war, December 1905 to June 1912.

never-ending war' – but when it did come it was decisive and in no sense pyrrhic. The duke of Wellington's name is indelibly inscribed on that victory, but it had certainly not been a war left to the generals. Pitt and Castlereagh, whose astute economic strategy and international coalition-building did so much to defeat the 'Great Disturber', deserve equal if not greater laurels. The same can be said of the Second World War. To the former western allies, Eisenhower and Montgomery are names on a par with Wellington's; but the true architects of victory were Roosevelt and Churchill – superbly supported by their de facto military-strategic advisers, respectively Generals George Marshall and Alan Brooke (both graduates of the Western Front). Yet to whom should the laurels go for 1918; and why? Who indeed would wish to claim them when, as Clemenceau put it in another doleful remark, the war amounted to nothing but 'a series of catastrophes that results in a victory'?

The want of strategy and generalship, and its terrible price, that marked the war set the scene for the conference at Versailles in 1919, and the flawed peace treaties that followed. *Too Important for the Generals* is not, I think, without contemporary resonance in this respect – and in another. For strategy cannot flower without capable statesmen and skilled generals; but it positively wilts if there isn't trust between the two, and therefore continuous, productive discourse. That is perhaps the greatest lesson of the Great War – and it is the theme of this book. It was a lesson taken to heart in the Second World War in Britain and the United States, but one that in more recent times seems to have been quite forgotten.

Prologue

In the Beginning was the Plan

> War should be the only study of a prince. He should consider peace only as a breathing-time, which gives him leisure to contrive, and furnishes an ability to execute, military plans.
>
> Machiavelli

In 1905 *General der Kavallerie* Alfred Graf (Count) von Schlieffen was kicked by a horse. For fifteen years he had been chief of the German *Grosser Generalstab* (literally, 'great general staff'), and now, he wrote, 'nearly 75 years old, almost blind, half deaf . . . [I] have a broken leg'.

The general's misfortune became world news when his incapacity led to enforced retirement the following January, though not all the newspapers treated it with solemnity. Under the headline 'No fat men may apply for this job', the *Daily Sun* of St John, New Brunswick, Canada, explained that Schlieffen had been unable to attend the army manoeuvres that autumn: 'A rule of the general staff is that no one not physically sound may remain on the staff. Even fat men are excluded from the most honored department of the army.'

The *Sun* went on to report that the appointment of *Generalleutnant* Helmuth Graf von Moltke was expected shortly, and that he was a nephew of 'the great commander'.

The 'great commander' was Helmuth Karl Graf von Moltke ('the Elder Moltke'), born in 1800 and appointed chief of the Prussian *Generalstab* in 1857 – a post he retained for thirty years, until just three years before his death.* Prussia and then the Deutsches Kaiserreich prized continuity at the head of that 'most honored department of the army', the department which in an influential work of 1891 the British military commentator and subsequently the first Chichele Professor of Military History at Oxford, Spencer Wilkinson, dubbed the army's brain.† Without natural borders other than the Baltic and a little of the North Sea, Prussia – indeed the whole Deutscher Bund (the German Confederation created in the mid-nineteenth century) – relied absolutely on its army to guarantee its territorial integrity. The map of Prussia over the centuries, variously expanding and contracting, was a veritable atlas of the army's campaigns. Prussia, in the words of Voltaire, was 'an army with a country attached to it'.‡

The job of the *Grosser Generalstab* was to prepare for war. This indeed was the principal function of any nation's general staff – to make plans to deter attack, and then plans to fight should deterrence fail: 'Igitur qui desiderat pacem, praeparet bellum.'§ But the *Grosser Generalstab* prepared also to *wage* war for the consolidation, even expansion, of the *Reich*, as well as in what today would be called pre-emptive war. In other words, 'that most honored department of the army' was offensive-minded.

Preparation for war took many forms: calculations and arrangements for the annual draft; training of conscripts; allocating men

* The Prussian *Generalstab* formed the basis of the *Grosser Generalstab* after the unification of Germany in 1871.

† *The Brain of an Army* (London, 1891).

‡ Voltaire's words are rendered in various forms, including: 'Whereas some states possess an army, the Prussian army possesses a state,' and sometimes attributed to Count (Honoré) Mirabeau, vox populi of the French Revolution. Whatever the attribution, the phrase captures the essence of the Prussia of Frederick the Great (r. 1740–86), which the Kaiser was only too happy to emulate – without realizing the danger of the ultimate outcome, that he himself would lose control of state affairs to his generals.

§ 'Therefore, whoever wishes for peace, let him prepare for war.' Vegetius, *Epitoma rei militaris* (4th century).

to the various reserves at the end of their conscription; devising and promulgating military doctrine, including 'war games' (map exercises to test command and staff procedures) and the annual manoeuvres – and drawing up campaign plans for every contingency. In this last task, the 'honored department' – Schlieffen especially – kept its cards close to its chest. The Elder Moltke had been the military enabler of Bismarck's policy of unification, presiding over three short and highly successful wars,* and had a fine practical as well as theoretical grasp of campaign planning. Schlieffen, who took over indirectly from Moltke (the appointment was held briefly by Alfred von Waldersee, who fell out with the new, young Kaiser Wilhelm), did not have the same base of practical experience. This soon began to show in an increasingly theoretical consideration of the strategic problems Germany believed she faced. The *Generalstab*'s practice under Schlieffen of wargaming every idea and then deriving requirements, in particular troop numbers (which ultimately determined the size of the annual draft), from the exercise was admirably scientific but could have a perverse effect. For wargaming, even allowing for the element of 'friction', as Clausewitz called it, can by degrees, imperceptibly even, rationalize practical problems and downplay risks to such an extent that what in reality is an unrealistic course of action actually seems reasonable.†

This, in essence, was the problem with the celebrated 'Schlieffen Plan'. In the later years of the nineteenth century the Kaiser and

* These were the Prusso-Danish, 1864–5 (which led to the annexation of a large portion of Jutland), Austro-Prussian, 1866 (achieving the defeat and annexation of several of Austria's German allies), and Franco-Prussian, 1870–1 (which also brought the federation of the remaining German states under Berlin's hegemony).

† Clausewitzian 'friction' derives from the unpredictability of battle, during which combatants are subject to the physical and mental exertions and the life-threatening dangers of war; and from uncertainty, or the 'fog of war', arising from the imperfection of intelligence: 'Everything in war is simple, but the simplest thing is difficult. The difficulties accumulate and end by producing a kind of friction that is inconceivable unless one has experienced war . . . Countless minor incidents – the kind you can never really foresee – combine to lower the general level of performance, so that one always falls short of the intended goal' (*On War*).

his ministers began seeing war with Russia as somehow inevitable. The reasons were territorial in the sense that Voltaire (or Mirabeau) had described, fuelled by convictions of racial superiority and supercharged by paranoia. For centuries the Russian bear had been a rather lumbering presence in the various continental upheavals. Its ability to mobilize the vast manpower at the Tsar's command was notoriously poor, but in the 1890s the country began rapidly to modernize, with railways and telegraphy changing the game. Berlin would not be able to rely indefinitely on the greater agility of the German army if it came to war with Russia. And then when in 1893 St Petersburg completed a treaty of alliance with Paris, the *Grosser Generalstab* had to address the further problem of war on two fronts – for although the Franco-Russian Entente was purely defensive, at some point it might become aggressive.* Contingency planning was, after all, the meat and drink of a general staff.†

The first instincts of the *Grosser Generalstab* in the later years of the Elder Moltke's tenure had been realistic: war with both Russia and France would be unwinnable in the sense of the rapid and complete victories of the *deutschen Einigung*, German unification. The only way would be to stand on the defensive in the west, France being the stronger of the two powers in the short term, inflict crushing defeat on Russia, the lumbering bear, and then negotiate a favourable peace with the Franco-Russian Entente from

* While the details of the Franco-Russian military convention were of course secret, the *Grosser Generalstab* could perfectly well calculate its possibilities. Article 3 in fact ran: 'The available forces to be employed against Germany shall be, on the part of France, 1,300,000 men, on the part of Russia, 700,000 or 800,000 men. These forces shall engage to the full with such speed that Germany will have to fight simultaneously on the East and on the West.'

† The extent to which the Schlieffen Plan was a plan in the full sense – the basis for a definite course of action rather than merely a theoretical staff exercise for the purpose of determining resources – is occasionally called into question. In his *Inventing the Schlieffen Plan: German War Planning 1871–1914* (Oxford, 2002), Terence Zuber, a retired US infantry officer, goes so far as to claim: 'There never was a Schlieffen Plan.' But whatever it was called, in August 1914 the German army in the west was certainly marching to *some* plan, and one remarkably resembling that which for nearly a century historians have taken to be Schlieffen's basic concept.

a position of strength. This was also the military strategy advocated by Moltke's successor, Waldersee. However, it did not entirely fulfil the ends of policy: the Kaiser wanted the option of complete victory. When Waldersee proved not to be amenable in this, he was replaced by Schlieffen. What mattered now therefore was that the *Grosser Generalstab* should produce a plan that promised absolute victory; otherwise the Kaiser might be obliged to change its chief again. Schlieffen probably reckoned that as it was a plan unlikely to see action for some time (or indeed at all), the *theoretical* possibility of success would be enough to keep the Kaiser amused – for the time being at least. He certainly worked along those lines.

The premise of Moltke's and Waldersee's strategy had been that the French fortifications built along the new border after the humiliating defeat of 1870 and loss of Alsace-Lorraine to Germany were too strong to overcome rapidly, and that it would therefore be better to wait on the defensive for the attack which the French would be obliged to make under the terms of the alliance with Russia, and take the fight at once to the Russians. Schlieffen now challenged this logic by questioning the feasibility of an offensive against Russia alongside the Austrian army (Germany and Austria had signed a formal alliance in 1879, joined by Italy three years later – the 'Triple Alliance'). It would, he argued, be impossible to gain any conclusive victory over the Russian army – which would be only partially mobilized anyway, such was the incapacity even of the improved Russian railways – or prevent it from retiring out of reach. Besides, why should the undoubtedly formidable French fortifications on the border rule out an offensive in the west when there was the simple expedient of bypassing them by marching through Belgium?

The pre-eminent British military theorist of the mid-twentieth century, Captain Basil Liddell Hart, explained this change of thinking: '[Schlieffen's] conception of war was dominated by the theoretical absolutes of Clausewitzian doctrine. So when he came to the conclusion that such absolute victory was unattainable in the East, he came back to the idea of seeking it in the West.'* If it were necessary to invade Belgium, whose neutrality was guaranteed by a treaty of 1839 (signed by Britain, Prussia, Austria, France and Russia) then Clausewitzian absolutes not only justified but required it ('War is an act of force . . . [which knows] no logical limit').

The Kaiser agreed. The following year Schlieffen formally threw out Moltke's 'Russia first' plan and began working on a scheme to ignore Belgian neutrality. It was the German chancellor, Theodore von Bethmann Hollweg, who in August 1914 would call the 1839 treaty a 'scrap of paper', but in the secrecy of his office in the Königsplatz, hard by the new Reichstag building, Schlieffen had already in effect done so. His strategy would be 'France first (through Belgium)'; and it was again to be a business of weeks rather than months, just as in 1870, whereupon his victorious troops would be speeded east by the admirable *Reichs-Eisenbahnen* to deal with the lumbering bear.†

The plan he eventually came up with derived from his reading of classical history, in particular the battle of Cannae, of which he would write extensively in retirement. Cannae was a perfect battle – a simple concept, a complete victory, and an economical one. In 216 BC, near the present-day town of Barletta in southern Italy, the Carthaginian army of Hannibal defeated a Roman army twice its size by the bold gamble of presenting only a weak centre while sending cavalry and light infantry in a double envelopment deep into the Roman legions' rear. Sixty thousand legionary

* Foreword to Gerhard Ritter, *The Schlieffen Plan: Critique of a Myth* (New York, 1958). Basil Liddell Hart (1895–1970; knighted 1966) served on the Western Front briefly before suffering the effects of gas and being invalided to light duties. His theories of the 'indirect approach' much influenced the German army in the 1930s, which developed the doctrine of *Blitzkrieg*.

† There was always a contradiction in German thinking about the 'bear'. The plodding Russians, whose constitutional incompetence had been demonstrated only recently in the Russo-Japanese War of 1904–5, could be dealt with at some leisure, almost disdainfully; yet at the same time, the speed at which Russia was perceived to be modernizing convinced Berlin that in the not-too-distant future the 'bear' would have the unassailable advantage.

corpses attested to not just defeat but annihilation. Of Cannae and its modern relevance, Schlieffen wrote:

> A battle of annihilation can be carried out today according to the same plan devised by Hannibal in long forgotten times. The enemy front is not the goal of the principal attack. The mass of the troops and the reserves should not be concentrated against the enemy front; the essential is that the flanks be crushed. The wings should not be sought at the advanced points of the front but rather along the entire depth and extension of the enemy formation. The annihilation is completed through an attack against the enemy's rear . . . To bring about a decisive and annihilating victory requires an attack against the front and against one or both flanks.*

Schlieffen accordingly sought, on a much vaster scale, to replicate the shock of Cannae, although by a bold, deep, single envelopment rather than a double movement. While holding along the Franco-German border with relatively weak forces, he would put the greatest weight of troops progressively on the right, where the *Schwenkungsflügel* – the 'swinging' wing (the strongest and furthest right) – would wheel through Belgium to come upon the rear of the French armies trying to defend their borders (including those with Belgium and Luxembourg).

Schlieffen developed his plan annually by degrees. By 1905, to be sure of casting the net broadly enough, he intended the tip of his right wing to cross the Franco-Belgian border near Lille. But this in turn presented him with another problem: to avoid being delayed by the strong Belgian fortresses of Namur and Liège, he would have to outflank them by a march through the Maastricht corridor – violating Dutch territory. And in extending his right wing so, when it swung south he risked running into the strong defences of Paris, or, in turning south-east to avoid them, exposing his flank to a counter-stroke by its garrison (which is what, in the

* *Alfred von Schlieffen's Military Writings*, trans. and ed. Robert T. Foley (New York, 2003).

event, would happen in August 1914). So he decided to extend his wheeling movement wider still – *west* of Paris.

The Schlieffen Plan, even as modified by the Younger Moltke, who significantly weakened the *Schwenkungsflügel*, had elegance and daring; but, as Liddell Hart said despairingly: 'A swift victory over the main armies in the main theatre of war was the German General Staff's solution for all outside difficulties, and absolved them from thinking of war in its wider aspects.'* These wider aspects were, not least, Belgian neutrality and Britain's reaction to its infringement. As the German-born Professor Holger Herwig writes in a much-admired recent work, Schlieffen 'raised tactics [i.e. Cannae] to the level of operations, and subordinated statecraft to purely operational concepts.'† Hans von Seeckt, chief of staff of one of the corps on Schlieffen's right wing, and head of the army in the post-war *Reichswehr*, was even more categorical: 'Cannae: no slogan became so destructive for us as this one.'‡

But Schlieffen also ignored a good few military as well as political realities, not least among them the number of troops available, as well as 'time and space' and logistics. One of Hitler's best field marshals, Albert Kesselring, would make a telling remark about the *Grosser Generalstab*'s rarefied military intellectualism: of the instruction at the pre-1914 staff college he wrote that it was inadequate in too many practical fields, such as intelligence, logistics, air and naval warfare, applied science and 'anything to do with oil which soiled the fingers and hampered the tactician and strategist in the free flight of his ideas'.§ It is this otherwise apparently inexplicable gap between theorizing and military logic – inexplicable, given the professionalism of the Prussian general staff – that has

* Basil Liddell Hart, *The Real War (1914–1918)* (London, 1930), later republished as *A History of the World War (1914–1918)*.

† *The Marne 1914* (New York, 2009).

‡ See James S. Corum, *The Roots of Blitzkrieg: Hans von Seeckt and German Military Reform* (Lawrence, KS, 1992).

§ 'Training and Development of German General Staff Officers', unpublished paper, US Army Historical Division European Command, quoted in Kenneth Macksey, *From Triumph to Disaster* (London, 1996).

led some to the conclusion that the plan never existed in any form beyond a sort of military doodle. Yet events speak otherwise.

In fact the Elder Moltke, just before his death, spelled out the challenge of strategy. Replying to Spencer Wilkinson after receiving an advance copy of *The Brain of an Army*, he wrote:

> You touch on p. 112 upon the relation between the commander and the statesman. Neither of the two can set up for himself in advance a goal to be certainly reached. The plan of campaign modifies itself after the first great collision with the enemy. Success or failure in a battle occasions operations originally not intended. On the other hand the final claims of the statesman will be very different according as he has to reckon with defeats or with a series of un-interrupted victories. In the course of the campaign the balance between the military will and the considerations of diplomacy can be held only by the supreme authority.*

He made the point very clearly that strategy, like politics, isn't over when war begins. It is not 'the plan' alone, but includes managing the repercussions of the plan's implementation.

The French had their plans too, of course, notably 'Plan XVII', finally adopted in 1913. It was based on three primary considerations. First, the relative strengths of the armies: although Germany's population was two-thirds as much again that of France, only some 54 per cent of available imperial manpower was ever actually called up, compared with France's 80 per cent.† Budgetary constraints, an increasingly left-wing Reichstag, and reluctance within the army itself to recruit in the growing urban centres of population, which were perceived as politically unreliable, kept it at a peacetime strength in 1911 of 612,000, compared with France's 593,000. The law of unintended consequences also gave an advantage in reservists to

* Foreword to the second edition of *The Brain of an Army*, 1895. Moltke read and spoke English well, his wife being English.

† Germany in 1914 had a population of 68 million; France 41 million; Russia 160 million; Imperial Austria-Hungary 53 million; the United Kingdom 46 million (of which Ireland 4.5 million); Italy 36 million; Belgium 7.5 million.

France, where an intense mistrust of militarism kept compulsory military service at two years, compared with the Germans' three. So although French reservists were not as well trained as the German, the system produced a third more of them each year. As far as theoretical strengths went, then, there was not a great deal in it. And while in a 'France first' plan the Germans would have to keep troops in East Prussia to guard against a Russian spoiling attack (the *État-Major*, the French general staff, calculated twenty-two divisions, perhaps even twenty-seven), the French would also have to keep troops on the Italian border – at least nine divisions – to guard against a similar attack by the third member of the Triple Alliance.* However, the Germans would be able to choose the place at which they would concentrate their strength, while the French, uncertain where this would be, were obliged to spread their forces.

The second consideration of the architects of Plan XVII was really an assumption, namely that despite the heavy fortifications on the Franco-German border – and even if Berlin ignored Belgian neutrality – the main weight of any German offensive would fall in Alsace-Lorraine. For the Germans could not afford to leave this area weakly defended, thereby tempting a French offensive; in which case, reasoned the *État-Major*, if the bulk of the German army was to be in Alsace-Lorraine anyway, surely it would not simply sit on the defensive? So, they concluded, the German army would mount a strong offensive across the border, and in conjunction with that main effort would seek to turn the fortifications by a march through Luxembourg and the south-eastern corner of Belgium (the Ardennes). The *État-Major* saw no purpose in any greater German effort through Belgium – certainly not west of the River Meuse – because it would be too radically disconnected from the main offensive in Alsace-Lorraine; and in any case, they calculated,

* This seems a derisively small number of troops to contain the entire Italian army, but it was believed – with good reason – that in fact the Italians would operate alongside the Austrians on the Upper Rhine, or even in Galicia against the Russians. The Franco-Italian border was mountainous, and the narrow coastal plain easily defended.

the Germans would not have enough troops, given the need to keep over twenty divisions in East Prussia.

The third consideration was what is today known as the 'moral component of fighting power', i.e. the element beyond military hardware and numbers of troops – in particular, doctrine. The commander-in-chief, General Joseph Joffre, appointed in 1911, though an engineer officer with a reputation for plodding staff-work, had nevertheless embraced with a will the new doctrine of *offensive à outrance* – taking the offensive with the utmost hostility, to the limit, even to excess. This represented a semi-mystical belief in the superiority of the man advancing with the bayonet to the one waiting to meet the enemy with fire, and was more an atonement for the humiliation of 1870 than military doctrine as Clausewitz would have recognized it. For while Napoleon himself had pronounced that 'in war the moral to the material is as three is to one', it failed to recognize that in this ratio the material – even at 'one' – still had force, and that the ratio might well be variable depending on time and circumstance. The Russo-Japanese war of 1904–5 had shown how barbed wire and the machine gun could upset the calculation. Kipling, indeed, had made the case thirty years earlier in the opening lines of 'Arithmetic on the Frontier':

> A great and glorious thing it is
> To learn, for seven years or so,
> The Lord knows what of that and this,
> Ere reckoned fit to face the foe –
> The flying bullet down the Pass,
> That whistles clear: 'All flesh is grass.'*

Joffre had torn up the earlier Plan XVI, the epitome, it seemed to him, of defensive-mindedness, and with the help of the commandant of the staff college, Ferdinand Foch, the greatest apostle of

* Published in *Departmental Ditties and Other Verses*, 1886. 'All flesh is grass' is an allusion to Isa. 40: 6.

offensive à outrance, had begun work instead on a scheme more suited to the resurgent *esprit militaire* – the scheme that would become Plan XVII. And he would proclaim grandiloquently in the new field regulations: 'The French army, returning to its traditions, henceforth admits no law but the offensive.'

But an offensive where? Foch said into Alsace-Lorraine. That was where the enemy would be in the greatest number, and the effect on the German campaign plan would therefore be decisive. The French army would be recovering lost ground too, redeeming the humiliating defeats of 1870. And any Germans coming through Luxembourg and the Ardennes would be met with a counter-offensive into their flank: French troops would under no circumstances wait to receive an attack. Plan XVII therefore required four of the five French armies that formed on mobilization to assemble for offensive action, the main effort being into Lorraine towards Nancy and Saarbrücken, while the fifth army formed the reserve to deal with any hook through the Ardennes. This considerably reduced the overall length of the French line envisaged in Plan XVI: there would be no need to cover even half the Franco-Belgian border, for the Germans would not be crossing the Meuse in any appreciable strength. The *État-Major* were quite convinced of it.

They were wrong, of course. Schlieffen's dying words to the Younger Moltke are supposed to have been 'Only make the right wing strong!' The German main effort would come not in Alsace-Lorraine but through Belgium. Schlieffen's plan saw the 1st and 2nd German Armies, in all some 450,000 men, crossing the Meuse and pushing well to the west before turning south, enveloping Paris and eventually destroying the French armies – hammer and anvil – up against the Franco-German border.

'If ever a plan deserved victory it was the Schlieffen Plan,' wrote that singular soldier–scholar Field Marshal Lord Wavell three decades later; 'if ever one deserved defeat it was Plan XVII.'* Why? Because Schlieffen's was bold, following Moltke's advice to

* *Allenby: A Study in Greatness* (London, 1940).

'first reckon, then risk', while the *État-Major*'s was stubbornly doctrinaire.

But how, if the *État-Major*'s calculations were correct (which mathematically – in terms of the absolute numbers of men available – they were), did the Germans have enough troops in 1914 to risk all on Schlieffen's plan? The answer is that the Germans did something the French had not considered. First, they took a gamble in Alsace-Lorraine, as Hannibal had at Cannae in presenting only a weak centre, leaving just two armies, the 5th and 6th (Crown Prince Wilhelm's and Crown Prince Rupprecht of Bavaria's) to hold the fortified border. Secondly, instead of using the bulk of their older reservists as *ersatz Truppen* – replacements – they used them from the outset for subsidiary tasks that would otherwise have fallen to first-line troops, thereby almost doubling the fighting strength of each army. And thirdly, they took a further gamble: instead of leaving twenty and more divisions in East Prussia to guard against a Russian spoiling offensive, they left just nine.

If the Schlieffen Plan took too little notice of 'friction', Plan XVII broke a cardinal rule by taking even less notice of the enemy.

How to make the gods of war smile: tell them your plans. Schlieffen's and Plan XVII positively dovetailed with each other. Indeed, wrote Liddell Hart in *The Real War*, success in Plan XVII would actually increase the chance of success in Schlieffen's:

> The hazards of leaving only a small proportion to face a French frontal attack were not as big as they appeared. Moreover if the German defensive wing was pushed back, without breaking, that would tend to increase the effect of the offensive wing. It would operate like a revolving door—the harder the French pushed on one side [weakening their line elsewhere in order to do so] the more sharply would the other side swing round and strike their back.

In the event, this is indeed what would happen in August 1914. While the French pushed in Alsace-Lorraine, the Germans swung through Belgium and northern France practically unhindered, Joffre focusing on the apparent success of the French counter-offensive across the Franco-German border. And even when the door was abruptly arrested in its swing by a force cobbled together at the last minute (including the BEF), the damage had been done: upwards of a million Germans had been let into Flanders, Picardy and Champagne.

They had not achieved the rapid victory prescribed by Schlieffen, however: conquering German troops would not now be sent by train to the Eastern Front to complete the destruction of the Franco-Russian alliance. The short war that everyone had predicted might have been over, but no one had won.

Time and again, however, during the next three years, the French would come close to handing victory to the Germans in their increasingly frantic attempts to eject them from French soil. And the tragedy is that some saw it coming – as they had seen, indeed, the débâcle of the 'battle of the frontiers'. Towards the end of 1914, the first lord of the Admiralty, Winston Churchill, wrote to the prime minister: 'I think it is quite possible that neither side will have the strength to penetrate the other's line in the Western theatre [of war] . . . My impression is that the position of both armies is not likely to undergo any decisive change – although no doubt several hundred thousand men will be spent to satisfy the military mind on the point.'

Several hundred thousand: if only it had been so few.

PART ONE

1914:

'Over by Christmas'

You will be home before the leaves have fallen from the trees.

Attributed to Kaiser Wilhelm, addressing
troops in the first week of August 1914

Chapter One

THE CONTEMPTIBLE LITTLE ARMY

After the war, reflecting on the army's rapid expansion during its course, the chief of the imperial general staff, Field Marshal Sir Henry Wilson, declared: 'There are a great many advantages in a voluntary army; there are a great many disadvantages. But whatever the advantages, and whatever the disadvantages, there is this constant factor in a voluntary army: it solves no military problem alone – none . . . in 1914, if we take that year, there was not one single campaign that the wit of man could imagine where the right answer was: "Six Regular divisions and fourteen Territorials."'*

Yet in 1914 the then Major-General Wilson, as director of military operations (DMO), had been content to send just four of the BEF's divisions plus the cavalry division to fight along the Belgian border on the left wing of the French, whose army consisted of some *ninety* divisions – had argued, indeed, that it was not just the best but the only strategic option, one on whose details he had

* Lecture at the Royal United Services Institution, December 1920 (*RUSI Journal*, January 1921). The reference was to the six regular (infantry) divisions plus the cavalry division ('six plus') that would comprise the expeditionary force, whether bound for the continent, South Africa, India or the Suez Canal, and the fourteen divisions of the Territorial Force (TF – after the war renamed Territorial Army), designated for home defence.

been working since 1910.* Either his own eyes had been opened by four years of needless losses, or he was attempting to pull the wool over those of any in his audience who might question his earlier judgement. Unfortunately there is no record of the subsequent discussion.

There had been no treaty binding the BEF to action alongside the French. Indeed, on the morning of Sunday, 2 August, when the first shots were exchanged prematurely after German troops had roamed across the French border near Belfort the day before Germany declared war on France, Paris was looking to London increasingly anxiously: would 'John Bull' stand by 'Marianne', his partner in the Entente Cordiale, or would he stand her up?† The cabinet had met at eleven o'clock and come to no decision – or rather, in the words of one minister of an earlier meeting, 'It had decided not to decide.' Asquith, as prime minister, summarized the discussion thus:

1. We have no obligations of any kind either to France or Russia to give them naval or military help.
2. The despatch of the Expeditionary Force to help France at this moment is out of the question & wd serve no object.
3. We mustn't forget the ties created by our long-standing & intimate friendship with France.

* Wilson would of course have preferred to send all six divisions (plus the cavalry division – 'six plus'), and urged the cabinet to do so, but he was desperate to get BEF boots on the ground in France – even just four divisions' worth. (The designation *British* Expeditionary Force – earlier called the 'Striking Force' – did not come into use until the force left for France several weeks later. Here, however, it will be referred to throughout as the 'BEF'.)

† The Entente Cordiale, signed on 8 April 1904, resolved a number of longstanding colonial disputes and established a diplomatic understanding between Britain and France, but did not commit either to any military undertaking in support of the other. This and the Anglo-Russian Convention of August 1907, which firmed up boundaries (and therefore respective control) in Afghanistan as well as in Persia and Tibet, together with the Franco-Russian military alliance of 1894, opened the way to the 'Triple Entente', an informal understanding among Great Britain, France and Russia. This could not, however, be equated with the Triple Alliance, referred to loosely as the Central Powers – which specified military action by each party.

4. It is against British interests that France shd. be wiped out as a great power.
5. We cannot allow Germany to use the Channel as a hostile base.
6. We have obligations to Belgium to prevent her being utilized and absorbed by Germany.*

It is extraordinary that ten years after the signing of the Entente (and, indeed, seventy-five after the Treaty of London guaranteeing Belgian neutrality) there should have been any doubt on these fundamental issues. The threat of a split in the cabinet was real, however; hence the hesitation even at this late hour. Yet Germany and Russia were already at war, Russia and Austria too; France and Germany must follow at any moment. Corporal Jules Peugeot, killed in the premature skirmish near Belfort, would be the first of the French Empire's 1,385,000 war dead. What was Britain to do?

The foreign secretary, Sir Edward Grey, one of the gentlest men ever to hold that office, was adamant. He had told the cabinet he would resign if Britain stood aside. That afternoon he received the French ambassador, Paul Cambon, who had been wondering aloud 'if the word "honour" is to be expunged from the English dictionary'. Grey assured him that if the German fleet came into the Channel or through the North Sea with hostile intent, 'the British fleet would give all the protection in its power'. He then went on to say that in any event Britain would not be sending the BEF to France at once 'as it would entail the maximum of risk . . . and produce the minimum of effect'.†

This late flowering of strategic common sense was undermined

* *H. H. Asquith: Letters to Venetia Stanley*, ed. Michael and Eleanor Brock (London, 1982).

† G. M. Trevelyan, *Grey of Fallodon* (London, 1937). The Anglo-French naval agreement of 1912 was not a treaty of mutual assistance if attacked, but an operational understanding that if it came to war with the Triple Alliance, France would take care of the Mediterranean while Britain would rule the waves in the North Sea and the Atlantic. This allowed both navies to concentrate their battleships, in response to the pre-war 'dreadnought race', the attempt by Germany to outbuild them.

by the fact that no other option had been studied, and doing nothing immediately with the BEF – the path of cool calculation – somehow seemed impossible. The 'maximum of risk' was a reference not just to the security of India and the Suez Canal but to the threat of invasion to a Britain denuded of regular troops – perhaps also, even intuitively, a reversion to that old default setting of British strategy: no continental engagement until it could no longer be resisted. Instead the Royal Navy – the old 'wooden walls' – would guard these islands and wage economic warfare.*

Yet there was, as Asquith recognized, an existential threat. If the Channel coast on the other side of the water became a haven to the German navy (and if the French fleet, and perhaps even the Russian, fell into German hands), Britain's naval supremacy, the whole basis of her national security and prosperity, would be at an end. It was clear that action on land was going to be necessary to avert such a catastrophe. With exquisite irony, therefore, to protect the Royal Navy, to guarantee naval supremacy, Britain would have to send an army to France – but in the Kaiser's words, supposedly, it could be only a 'contemptible little army'.

Just what was it, Grey enquired, that Cambon expected the BEF to do?

His reply emphasized the 'moral effect': even if just two of the six divisions were sent, the French army would know they were not alone. And undoubtedly, though he did not say so, the two divisions would be the harbingers of more – *many* more? In January 1910 the arch-Francophile Henry Wilson – at that time Brigadier-General Wilson and still commandant of the staff college – had visited Ferdinand Foch, his opposite number at the French war college, St Cyr. 'What would you say was the smallest British military

* This had, after all, been the successful strategy on which Britain had based her defiance of Napoleon: the Royal Navy blockaded the Continent and ranged the world taking French colonies and gold, which was used to subsidize the coalition allies – notably Russia, Prussia and Austria. It was only after 1808, in Spain and Portugal, that Britain began seriously to commit troops to the continental fight; and even then, the Peninsula was hardly the heartland of Europe.

force that would be of practical assistance to you in the event of a contest such as we have been considering?' he asked.

'One single private soldier,' Foch replied; 'and we would take good care that he was killed.' For if one British soldier were to arrive, more would surely follow, especially once blood had been shed. Foch's response showed that for all his professional belief in the short war, he was entertaining the possibility that it might in fact be a long one – one in which Britain's potential military strength, and that of her empire, would be decisive.

A BEF at 'six plus' – some hundred and fifty thousand men, all regulars or mobilized regular reservists (former regulars recalled to the colours), embodying the equivalent fighting power of one of the smaller French armies – would be a significant augmentation to the left flank of the French line in any counter-move into Belgium and beyond. By 1914 the War Office was in no doubt of it; indeed Wilson, as DMO, had been working for four years on every detail of a plan to send the BEF at 'six plus' to Maubeuge, just short of the Belgian border on the left of the French line. It was not an endorsed plan in the sense that it carried any commitment to implementation; rather it was the product of the airiest of political nods (by Grey as early as 1906 and by Asquith again in 1911, along the lines of 'by all means talk to the French, but nothing is to be decided until the day'). It was equally the product of Wilson's Francophilia – *Francomania* indeed, for he and Foch, the brain behind Plan XVII, had become almost joined at the hip. Wilson had talked to the French so much (in fluent French), and in such detail – down to the last train into Maubeuge – that the *État-Major* and the French war ministry had come to think of his scheme as a done deal.

And so on 3 August, with German troop-trains arriving by the quarter-hour at the frontiers to disgorge their field-grey passengers, and still no decision in Whitehall to mobilize, Wilson was beside himself. All his planning had been based on the assumption that Britain would mobilize simultaneously with the French, and the president of France had signed the order for mobilization the day before – and authorized precautionary measures even earlier, which was why some reservists, like Corporal Peugeot, were already at their posts. Three days before, Wilson had told the French military attaché, Colonel le Vicomte de la Panouse, to 'get Cambon to go to Grey tonight and say that, if we did not join, he would break off relations and go to Paris'.*

In saying this, of course, Wilson was crossing the line between strategy and policy. He had been making the strongest representations through the CIGS and Haldane for mobilization at once, which was perfectly constitutional – his duty, indeed, to warn of the consequences of delay in reaching a decision; but an attempt to force a decision by diplomatic intimidation was not only unconstitutional, it was in fact treasonable.

But Wilson had been pursuing his own policy of Anglo-French military cooperation ever since becoming DMO in 1910, at which point he had found himself with virtually a clean sheet of paper. Then, there had been in theory two options for a continental deployment in the event that Germany violated Belgian neutrality: one to Belgium, the other to France. The Belgian option was the logical consequence of the 1839 Treaty of London; the French option was the consequence of the assumption that Belgian resistance might collapse before the BEF could deploy. Having vaguely authorized the secret talks between the British and French staffs, Grey had taken no interest in the discussions, and nor had the cabinet, not least because they were not formally made aware of them – and indeed, under Wilson's predecessor, Spencer Ewart, the talks themselves had proceeded only very half-heartedly. As the Belgian option had seemed to Wilson to be no option at all – there would be no time to get the BEF forward to the Belgian fortress line on the Meuse, and reinforcing the national redoubt at Antwerp was fraught with problems over the mouth of the Scheldt, Dutch territorial waters – he had simply shelved it. (The Belgians

* Major-General Sir C. E. Callwell, *Field Marshal Sir Henry Wilson: His Life and Diaries* (London, 1927).

themselves were not keen to discuss anything, believing that it would compromise their neutrality and perhaps forgetting that circumstances change rapidly, as they did in August 1914 and would again in May 1940.) Instead Wilson had thrown all his energies into what he perceived was the only option – one which also suited his own sympathies.

But the BEF was not going anywhere unless the huge question of mobilization – bringing the army onto a war footing – was properly addressed, for the BEF relied heavily on reservists to reach its proper war strength; an average infantry battalion would draw some 60 per cent of its 'war establishment' from former regulars recalled to the colours.* In 1910 Wilson single-mindedly set out to put mobilization on a proper footing, in which he brilliantly succeeded; but in doing so he failed to make the distinction between mobilization and deployment, seeing the two processes as peas in the same pod. Rather than make broad *plans*, giving ministers options when the time came to decide, he had produced and systematically finessed a single *plan*; and in August 1914 the cabinet would be given Hobson's choice – to go to Maubeuge, or nothing.

The prime minister could have felt aggrieved that the War Office had failed in one of its primary functions, for the ideal general staff identifies and examines *all* possible alternatives to provide policy-makers with genuine choices, ruling out nothing where the material facts – in this case, the Germans' intentions – are

* The first requirement of the army in Britain was to keep the overseas garrisons up to strength. Each regiment of infantry therefore comprised, usually, two regular battalions (some had four), and the one stationed at home sent drafts periodically to the other overseas, which meant the home battalion was invariably under strength. When mobilized for war, the home battalion relied on the recall of regular reservists, men who had completed their service 'with the colours' and who remained liable to recall for seven years after discharge. In August 1914 these reservists would be mobilized in a masterly programme that was completed in three days. Their fitness, efficiency and enthusiasm were variable, as might be imagined, though on the whole they performed well. When the BEF of August 1914 is referred to as all-regular, this is technically correct, but a good many of them had not put on uniform for nearly seven years.

unknowable. In the end decisions have to be made, but the job of the staff is first to keep asking 'What if . . .?'

Asquith had only himself to blame, however, for three years earlier Wilson had given him an exceptionally clear briefing about what he was doing. On 23 August 1911, during one of the periodic crises that, at least in retrospect, showed just how combustible was the general situation in Europe, the prime minister had called a meeting of the Committee of Imperial Defence (CID) to hear the respective Admiralty and War Office appreciations of the situation, in particular what assistance might be given the French if it came to war.

The CID was a rather under-horsed organization set up in 1904 to consider the strategic implications of policy and to advise the cabinet and government departments accordingly. The prime minister, its only permanent member, chaired the meetings, inviting others to attend on an ad hoc basis, including, as appropriate, chief ministers of the dominions. It was served by a small secretariat which in 1916 would become the war cabinet secretariat, introducing to cabinet meetings for the first time the practice of writing minutes.*

Among those attending the August 1911 meeting was Winston Churchill. As home secretary he would have certain responsibilities during any transition to war, but on this occasion he had been invited because, as an indefatigable activist on military matters, he had himself pressed for the meeting. Besides, he was the only member of the inner cabinet with direct experience of war.

Churchill sent Asquith a preparatory memorandum, entitled 'Military Aspects of the Continental Problem',† in which he predicted a massive German offensive through Belgium. The issue, he argued, was not the relative strength of the opposing armies on the

* There were four standing sub-committees of the CID: Colonial (later Oversea) Defence; Home Ports (later Home) Defence; Co-ordination of Departmental Action; and Air. The CID's permanent secretary, in 1912, was Lieutenant-Colonel Maurice Hankey – later Lord Hankey – a Royal Marines officer who had earlier been its assistant naval secretary. He would in turn become secretary of the war cabinet and then, in 1919, the first permanent cabinet secretary.

† PRO CAB 38/19/50.

borders (Franco-German or Franco-Belgian) but what was to happen *after* the Germans had invaded; for, having the initiative and therefore being able to concentrate their forces, they would certainly penetrate the defences at one point or another: 'France will not be able to end the war successfully by any action on the frontiers. She will not be strong enough to invade Germany. Her only chance is to conquer Germany *in* France' (emphasis added). The French must accept invasion, he argued – even the investment of Paris.

It was, of course, a view entirely at odds with that of the *État-Major* (and therefore of Henry Wilson) which in its Plan XVII did indeed envisage invading Germany – a strong offensive into Elsass-Lothringen (Alsace-Lorraine), as required by the doctrine of *offensive à outrance*. The *État-Major* had calculated very carefully the number of troops the Germans would be able to field: the enemy's main effort would be on the Franco-German border, and the French counter-offensive would dislocate it.

Churchill demurred. Why would the Germans attack where the French defences were strongest? Why not, if they were prepared to violate a corner of Belgium – with all the political risk that involved – as the *État-Major* thought they probably would, make Belgium the site of their main effort, thereby outflanking the entire French army, not merely the border fortifications? Better for Britain, therefore, he argued, not to be drawn into battles on the frontiers but to wait until the fortieth day of mobilization:

> Germany should be extended at full strain both internally and on her war fronts, and this strain will become daily more severe and ultimately overwhelming, unless it is relieved by decisive victories in France. If the French army has not been squandered by precipitate or desperate action, the balance of forces should be favourable after the fortieth day [and improving] . . . Opportunities for the decisive trial of strength might then occur.

It could easily be supposed that this memorandum had been written in August 1914 rather than 1911, for the fortieth day of

German mobilization would be 9 September, the day the BEF crossed the Marne in the great allied counter-offensive which followed a fortnight's bloody retreat.*

Instead of sending the BEF at once to Maubeuge, as Wilson planned, Churchill advocated sending four divisions plus the cavalry division to Tours, more or less equidistant between St Nazaire and Paris, for 'moral effect'; these were to be joined by the two remaining divisions 'as soon as the naval blockade is effectively established' and the threat of invasion thereby ended.† As soon as the colonial forces in South Africa could be mobilized to take its place, the 7th Division could be recalled and sent to join the forces in France. To these would be added fifteen thousand Yeomanry and cyclist volunteers of the TF. And – perhaps the greatest gamble (though in fact it was exactly what would happen in 1914) – six out of the nine divisions of the Indian army could be brought back to the BEF, 'as long as two native regiments were moved out of India for every British regiment', to add a further hundred thousand troops, 'brought into France via Marseilles by the fortieth day'.

In total, by 14 September this would have furnished a BEF of some 290,000, which the actual arrival of the 7th Division (and soon afterwards the 8th) and the Indian Corps before the battles of Ypres in October shows was perfectly possible. And, although Churchill did not mention it in his memorandum, there would also have been time to assemble additional heavy artillery, of which the

* And much of the French army had indeed been squandered. By the end of August, in less than two weeks' actual fighting, it had suffered just over 210,000 casualties, including 4,778 officers – 10% of the entire French officer corps.

† The primary object of the blockade was to neutralize the German navy and prevent its forming a blockade of the United Kingdom. Fast cruisers and destroyers would patrol from the south-western tip of Norway to the middle of the North Sea, and then south to the Dutch coast, while the Grand Fleet would be stationed at Scapa Flow in Orkney ready to intercept the *Hochseeflotte* (High Seas Fleet). This plan would be revised in July 1914 to close the two entrances into the North Sea (between the Dover Straits and northern France, and between Norway and Scotland), the war plan stipulating that the movement of HM ships would be 'frequent enough and sufficiently advanced to impress upon the enemy that he cannot at any time venture far from his home ports without such serious risk of encountering an overwhelming force'.

BEF was to prove critically short. In all this, Churchill was being entirely consistent with his long-stated view of strategy. As early as 1903, in a parliamentary debate on army organization, he had said:

> There were two kinds of success – initial and ultimate. Both were very desirable, and should occupy the attention of those who had the care of public affairs; but what he would most earnestly press on the notice of our statesmen was, that they should not risk the certainty of ultimate success in order to gain triumphs at the beginning. The certainty of ultimate success required the power of finally mobilising and bringing into the field the whole of the immense resources of the State.*

So much for the view that in his early years Churchill was a liability.

At the August 1911 CID meeting the young home secretary cross-questioned Wilson and the CIGS (Field Marshal Sir William Nicholson) on the *État-Major*'s estimate of German strength and intentions, but the DMO was in no mood to give the 36-year-old Yeomanry major's ideas anything other than the politest brush-off: 'Winston had put in a ridiculous and fantastic paper on a war on the French and German frontier, which I was able to demolish,' he wrote in his diary.†

The navy's appreciation of the situation, presented in person by its professional head, the first sea lord (1SL), Admiral Sir Arthur Wilson VC – the meeting would become known as the 'battle of the two Wilsons' – was badly received. What little 1SL was prepared to vouchsafe of his intentions for the Grand Fleet in the event of war was sound enough – neutralizing the German High Seas Fleet and preventing a blockade – but he strayed into the purlieus of the War Office by proposing diversionary landings in

* Hansard (Commons), 24 February 1903.

† Callwell, *Field Marshal Sir Henry Wilson*. Wilson's diary is held by the Imperial War Museum.

Churchill commanded a squadron of the Oxfordshire Hussars, a Yeomanry regiment, part of the TF. He wore uniform on his regular visits to observe the German army manoeuvres, at which he would meet the Kaiser.

the Baltic once the German fleet had been overcome, a strategy that looked as expensive and irrelevant as the Elder Pitt's habit in the eighteenth century of mounting 'tip and run' raids on the French coast – what his critics called 'breaking windows with guineas'. The navy's strategic objective, sea control, was shared by Churchill: 'He did not defend unpreparedness, but, with a supreme Navy, unpreparedness could be redeemed; without it, all preparation, however careful, painstaking, or ingenious, could not be of any avail.'* Unlike the Admiralty's, however, Churchill's thinking always went ashore, for that was where the contest was usually decided.

The meeting ended with Asquith's saying he would reflect on matters (including the Admiralty's alternative proposal for a principally naval war). Unfortunately he did so without expert advice, or even that of the CID, and, in the words of Field Marshal Lord ('Dwin') Bramall, one of the twentieth century's most experienced and intellectually engaged chiefs of defence staff, a golden opportunity 'of developing a Defence Policy Staff to undertake the essential task of evaluating strategic options on an impartial national basis was lost'.† Its lack would be felt throughout the war. All that Asquith would do was appoint Churchill to be first lord of the Admiralty to shake up that institution.

British strategy in the run-up to war was decided on little more than a beauty contest between a brilliant but partisan display by an Irish showman and an apparently superficial and unquestionably badly presented plan by a salty hero of a bygone age – judged solely by a man who was constitutionally indisposed towards making any decision. 'Wait and see' was a favourite phrase of Asquith's; or, as he put it more elegantly in the context of the 23 August meeting, 'the expediency of sending a military force abroad or of relying on naval means alone is a matter of policy which can

* Hansard (Commons), 24 February 1903.

† Bill Jackson and Dwin Bramall, *The Chiefs: The Story of the United Kingdom Chiefs of Staff* (London, 1992).

only be determined when the occasion arises by the Government of the day'.*

Wilson's plan would become strategic policy by default.†

Had there been a proper strategic evaluation, it is difficult to see how it could not have concluded that incorporating the BEF into the French order of battle was fundamentally unsound. Which is why, only days before the Germans invaded Belgium, Grey told the French ambassador that sending the BEF to France immediately would incur the maximum of risk with the minimum of effect. Certainly Churchill remained unconvinced. At the 'council of war' on 5 August 1914, the first full day of hostilities, he argued again that the BEF should not go to Maubeuge but concentrate instead at Tours as a 'strategic reserve'.‡

Perhaps when questioned at his RUSI lecture in 1920, in defence of urging the despatch of the BEF even at 'four plus', Henry Wilson said that his preferred solution would have been to send every soldier in the United Kingdom – regular *and* territorial – to France at once, for he himself had believed there was no realistic threat of invasion and the Franco-German military scales were so finely balanced that the British contribution would be decisive. And he might have been right; but he would have been trying to fashion a coat from cloth that was simply not available – or rather, was available but beyond his pocket. The TF's *raison d'être* was home (hence 'territorial') defence. There was nothing to stop a territorial

* PRO CAB 38/19/50.

† Letter from Asquith to Haldane, 31 August: 'Sir A. Wilson's "plan" can only be described as puerile, and I have dismissed it at once as wholly impracticable . . . in principle, the General Staff scheme is the only alternative.'

‡ Sir Douglas Haig thought the same. A day or so before, he had written to Haldane, the lord chancellor and suddenly – on Asquith's realizing his predicament – acting war minister: 'I venture to hope that our only bolt (and that not a very big one) may not suddenly be shot on a project of which the success seems to me to be quite doubtful – I mean the checking of the advance into France. Would it not be better to begin at once to enlarge our Exped[itionar]y Force by amalgamating less regular forces with it? In three months time we should have quite a considerable army.' *Douglas Haig: War Diaries and Letters 1914–18*, ed. Gary Sheffield and John Bourne (London, 2005). Where not otherwise attributed, all subsequent quotations of Haig are from this source.

volunteering for service overseas, but he could not be compelled. That was the deal. Why were there fourteen divisions of territorials? On the one hand because fourteen was the maximum that could be raised from the money voted by Parliament, and on the other because it was the minimum the county TF associations would accept when in 1907 Haldane had reformed and reorganized all the volunteer forces, some of which were almost private armies. The associations formed a powerful lobby with no wish to see their power reduced.

In any case, Wilson could send only four of the six home-based regular divisions to France because in 1912 the CID had recommended that, despite the fourteen TF divisions and the might of the Royal Navy, two regular divisions should remain in the British Isles until the threat of invasion was reduced. In the event, therefore, it would be just four infantry divisions and the cavalry division – around eighty thousand combatants – who would find themselves facing several times that number of Germans in their first encounter of the war, at Mons on 23 August. A fifth division, sent out hurriedly, would be caught on the hop a few days later as it detrained at Le Cateau in the middle of the BEF's fighting retreat; a sixth would join during the counter-attack on the Marne in early September and be cut up in the battle to take the heights on the River Aisne; a seventh – a scratch division made up of regular troops pulled back from various overseas garrisons – would join a few weeks later, and an eighth in November as the fighting intensified around Ypres. At intervals thereafter three more divisions from overseas garrisons would arrive (as well as hastily formed divisions of the Indian army) until there were no more regular troops to send. All of these divisions were committed to battle piecemeal instead of en masse, breaking Clausewitz's first principle of war: 'The first rule is therefore to enter the field with an army as strong as possible.'

By the end of November the old regular army was a shadow of its former self. Or, as A. E. Housman wrote, with reference to the Kaiser's other sneer – that Britain's was an army of mercenaries:

These, in the day when heaven was falling,
The hour when earth's foundations fled,
Followed their mercenary calling
And took their wages and are dead.

Their shoulders held the sky suspended;
They stood, and earth's foundations stay;
What God abandoned, these defended,
And saved the sum of things for pay.*

The Kaiser can be forgiven for reputedly calling the BEF, as well as an army of mercenaries, a contemptible little army.† In fact he protested after the war that he hadn't, but that he might have said *contemptibly* little – an indisputable description of a tiny, if highly trained, army seeking to influence a war between two nations with universal adult male conscription. Why had Britain not followed suit with compulsory enlistment?

There had indeed been voices in Britain calling for it. The National Service League, founded in February 1902 in the latter stages of the Boer War (that great shock to the army's prestige), argued for compulsory military training for men aged between eighteen and thirty for the purpose of home defence. In 1910, under the presidency of the former commander-in-chief, Lord Roberts, membership of the league had reached sixty thousand. Churchill, as home secretary, expressed some private, if guarded, support, as did the chancellor of the exchequer, Lloyd George, though he preferred a militia system on the Swiss model, which he saw as implying

* 'Epitaph on an Army of Mercenaries', first published in *The Times*, 31 October 1917, with a commemorative article on the BEF at Ypres.

† The jibe is specious, supposedly made in an order of 19 August 1914, the only solid reference to which is Charles Horne (ed.), *Source Records of the Great War*, vol. II (London, 1923): 'It is my Royal and Imperial command that you concentrate your energies, for the immediate present, upon one single purpose, and that is that you address all your skill and all the valour of my soldiers to exterminate first the treacherous English and walk over General French's contemptible little army.' The 'contemptible' remark is hardly out of character for the Kaiser, but the evidence is just not solid enough.

a less aggressive stance than full-blown conscription (in truth the differences were very small); but anti-conscription sentiment in the Liberal party, which formed the government, was too strong, and the nettle was never grasped. Haldane, in his army reforms, did however manage to turn the old militia – in which service could still in theory be compulsory through the 'militia ballot', though in practice it had not been enforced for a century – into an all-volunteer force to provide battle-casualty replacements for the regulars, renamed the Special Reserve (SR). In August 1914 this would work well, especially in providing replacement officers, who had joined the SR through the school and university officer training corps.

But this was all small beer in a clash of continental titans. Fortunately, on the first full day of the war, there was one man at least who was capable of, in Churchill's definition of strategy, 'foreseeing the outlines of the future and being prepared to deal with it' – Kitchener. This would be a long war, he reasoned, needing a far larger army than the BEF and the fourteen divisions of the TF could constitute, even if legislation were enacted to compel the territorials to serve overseas. He intended in addition therefore to raise in stages a new citizen-volunteer army, which by 1917 would number some eight hundred thousand. In the meantime France would have to take the strain in the west, but in 1917 Britain would be strong enough to take decisive action.

The problem was that there were not enough experienced men to train and lead them. Nor indeed the materiel to equip them. The photographs of men in civilian clothes drilling with old weapons, and even broom handles, were meant to convey the nation's patriotic response to Kitchener's call to arms – 'Your Country Needs You!' – but soon they would suggest rank amateurishness, all the more poignantly when these same men began falling in droves on the Western Front.

Losses among the regulars in 1914, and then among the territorials who were sent to France to reinforce or replace them, and then among the partially trained Kitchener volunteers sent to the Western Front prematurely to replace the losses in regulars and territorials, led in 1916 to the introduction of conscription and, at last, the proper regulation of manpower. For Britain was having to fashion a new army from scratch while at the same time fighting the enemy, unlike the continental powers, who could mobilize huge numbers of reservists while continuing to prepare those coming of conscript age in a well-oiled system; and unlike, indeed, the United States, whose army at the beginning of 1917 numbered (at most) a hundred and fifty thousand, but who eighteen months later, after her entry into the war, would put two million men into Europe. This could be done because the task of the hundred and fifty thousand regulars was first to build an army, and only then to fight. The British army, on the other hand, was knocked off balance in the first month of fighting and thereafter could only play 'catch-up' until the summer of 1918, when conscription and hard-won experience had at last fashioned a strong instrument.

What a terrible indictment of strategic thinking in the pre-war years.

If only conscription – universal military training or whatever it might be called – had been introduced in 1911, when the Second Moroccan Crisis showed how real was the possibility of war between Germany and France, and how strong were Britain's perceived obligations to the French. Or, failing that, if only Henry Wilson had cut the BEF's military coat according to its cloth – and to keep out the worst of the weather that it *could* face rather than that which the French were forecasting. These and the Foreign Office's failure to think through the ultimate implications of the Entente Cordiale – 'the great question', as Grey called it – are the indictments against Asquith's pre-war administrations.

After the war, Haldane reflected on all this:

> No doubt it would have been a great advantage if . . . we could have produced, at the outbreak of the war, 2,000,000 men, so trained as to be the equals in this respect of German troops, and properly fashioned into the great divisions that were necessary, with full equipment and auxiliary services. But to train the recruits, and to command such an

army when fashioned, would have required a very great corps of professional officers of high military education, many times as large as we had actually raised. How were these to have been got?*

Now Haldane was a man of the highest intellect and integrity. No war minister in peacetime, with perhaps the exception of Leslie Hore-Belisha in the late 1930s, gave so much to his job. And yet the assertion 'How were these to have been got?' is quite extraordinary, even disingenuous – for in 1917 the Americans had shown how.

What in fact lay at the root of British thinking – wishful thinking – was that if the war were to be brought to a swift conclusion by superior manoeuvre, as both Schlieffen and Plan XVII envisaged, not least because neither the French nor the Germans had the ready resources for a long war, why did Britain need a large standing army? And if the combined forces of France and Russia were not enough to deter Germany from making war in the first place, what difference would a large British army make if the country were not committed in any formal alliance, as Britain's unstated policy of 'splendid isolation' required? Perhaps it might have made Schlieffen and the Younger Moltke think again about violating Belgian neutrality; perhaps it might have forced a reversion to the strategy of 'Russia first'; but such was the confidence in rapid victory that not even the threat of war with the Royal Navy – which Tirpitz, the navy minister, knew in his heart he could not win – could keep the German army out of Belgium (and would Britain really go to war over a 'scrap of paper'?).

No, the Kaiser and his chancellor would place their faith in the *Grosser Generalstab*, as earlier monarchs (and Bismarck) had done to their satisfaction. The *Grosser Generalstab* promised that war with France would be over quickly, just as it had been in 1870 – because it *had* to be; there was Russia to deal with next.

Paris thought along the same lines. There were just not the resources for a long war – and besides, the army's newly reclaimed

* R. B. Haldane, *Before the War* (London, 1920).

offensive spirit would see it to a rapid success: 'The French army, returning to its traditions, henceforth admits no law but the offensive.'*

So while the Schlieffen Plan promised *Paris vor Weihnachten*, Plan XVII believed it would be *Berlin avant Noël*.

How indeed to make the gods of war smile.

* The words are those with which Colonel Louis de Grandmaison, chief of the *3me Bureau* (operations) *L'Etat-Major*, began the French Service Regulations (*Règlement*) of 1913.

Chapter Two

MIRACLES

The Germans may have had *Gott Mit Uns* (on their helmets and belt buckles), but God – or rather, one or more of his angels – was with the British at Mons, holding back the Hun to allow the greatly outnumbered BEF to slip away to fight another day.

That at least was one of the more picturesque accounts of the fighting; harder heads identified the saviour as General Sir Horace Smith-Dorrien, commanding II Corps – and the fifteen rounds a minute of his infantrymen. Smith-Dorrien's feat was all the more remarkable for the fact that he had arrived only hours before, summoned from his headquarters on Salisbury Plain to take the place of Lieutenant-General Sir James Grierson, who had died of a heart attack in the train on the way to Maubeuge.*

* The myth of 'the Angel of Mons' did not originate on the Western Front. On 29 September 1914, inspired by accounts of the fighting at Mons, and his fertile Celtic imagination, the Welsh author Arthur Machen published a short story entitled 'The Bowmen' in the London *Evening News* describing a phantom company of archers summoned from Agincourt by a soldier calling on St George, who duly destroyed a German host. The *Evening News*, not unreasonably, did not consider it necessary to label the story as fiction, and Machen had a number of requests to provide evidence for his sources. Machen then received requests from the editors of parish magazines to reprint the story. In his introduction to *The Bowmen and Other Legends of the War* (1915) Machen relates that the editor of one of these magazines, a priest, asked if he would write a short preface to a pamphlet reprinting the

And then there would be the 'miracle' on the River Marne, General Joseph Joffre turning defeat into victory by hurling back the Germans from the very gates of Paris (the government having already decamped to Bordeaux) with troops conjured seemingly from nowhere and sent into battle in taxicabs. This, at any rate, was how some of the popular press portrayed the events of August and September 1914. It is hardly surprising that divine intervention was mooted, for why otherwise should the allies have been spared the consequences of their absurd doctrine and miscalculations? *

On 22 August, a Saturday, the advance elements of the BEF had reached the line of the Mons–Condé Canal just over the border into Belgium, where they halted, Sir John French having received reports from the Royal Flying Corps (RFC) and the cavalry that there were Germans directly in front of him, and from Lieutenant

---

story, giving his sources. Machen replied that he was welcome to reprint but that he could give no sources since he had none. The priest replied that Machen must be mistaken, that the 'facts' of the story must be true, and that Machen had just elaborated on a true account. As Machen later said: 'The snowball of rumour that was then set rolling has been rolling ever since, growing bigger and bigger, till it is now swollen to a monstrous size.' On 24 April 1915, an account was published in the *British Spiritualist Magazine* of visions of a supernatural force that had held back the Germans, and stories of angelic intervention followed. These were spiritualist times, however. Three years later came the story of the 'Cottingley Fairies', taken up with enthusiasm by Sir Arthur Conan Doyle.

* On 8 September, the Feast of the Nativity of Mary, as prayers were being said throughout France for deliverance from the Germans, the bishop of Meaux (whose diocese encompassed the department of Seine-et-Marne) made a vow that if Paris were spared he would build a monument to divine intervention. The same day, stories of an apparition of the Virgin Mary began to circulate. There was a supposed letter addressed to the Carmel of Pontoise recounting that 'On 3 January 1915, a German priest, wounded and taken prisoner during the Battle of the Marne, died in a French ambulance where he was cared for by some nuns. He said to them: "As a soldier I should keep silent, but as a priest, I must say what I have seen. During the Battle of the Marne, we were surprised to be pushed into retreat, because our numbers were legion compared to the French, and we expected very soon to arrive in Paris. But we saw the Virgin Mary, dressed all in white, with a blue belt, leaning her head toward Paris. She turned her back to us, and with her right hand seemed to push us away . . . I saw her myself and a good number of my companions also."' Tired men in action sometimes see, hear and recall strange things – or rather, perceive normal things differently – especially when comparing notes with others.

Louis Edward Spears, the liaison officer at General Charles Lanrezac's 5th Army headquarters, that the 5th to their right were in severe trouble around Charleroi. Their offensive, on which Joffre had insisted, had run into very much harder opposition than *Le Grand Quartier Général* (*GQG*: Joffre's headquarters) had told Lanrezac to expect.

But what had been the rush to hurl the 5th Army at the Germans? The great advantage that Joffre enjoyed from the outset was that the Schlieffen Plan unfolded at walking pace, on exterior lines, and reported almost in real time, while the strategic movement of French troops, on interior lines, could be conducted at the speed of the railway engine. In other words, Joffre could afford to wait to see what the Germans were really doing and then move his reserve and uncommitted troops to deal with them. The Elder Moltke had said as much to Bismarck: 'Build railways, not forts.' Never before had a commander-in-chief had so much time in which to make his critical decisions – nor has any since. But *offensive à outrance* did not permit of 'wait and see'; and so the 5th Army had got a very bloody nose, and was reeling from the blow.

Yet reports from *GQG* were still painting a picture of all going to plan – Plan XVII: the offensive in Alsace-Lorraine was making progress, the Germans in Belgium were relatively few and, although admittedly perhaps rather more than the French had hoped, still largely cavalry. Quite what the Germans were doing flinging themselves with such ferocity at the great Belgian fortress of Liège, on the Meuse, does not seem to have troubled *GQG* (and what a surprise their hard fight was; neither the Germans nor the allies had expected the Belgians to put up much of a contest) – yet why would they need to take the fortress if they didn't intend crossing the Meuse in strength? It was a case of what would later be called 'cognitive dissonance'.

Whatever the optimism of *GQG* and the curious lack of information coming from Lanrezac himself – Spears was acting on his own, and very junior, initiative in driving to GHQ – Sir John French decided that to advance further would risk being cut off, and so ordered his two corps commanders (Haig and Smith-Dorrien) to take up defensive positions along the canal, with Haig's corps echeloned back on the right to protect the flank. Next morning, Sunday 23 August, the advance guards of *Generaloberst* Alexander von Kluck's 1st Army clashed with Smith-Dorrien's II Corps (3rd and 5th Divisions) while Haig's I Corps (1st and 2nd Divisions) were still not fully in position, with *Generaloberst* Karl von Bülow's 2nd Army, which had also crossed the Meuse, forcing Lanrezac's men back in some disarray. One of the reasons for the 5th Army's difficulties was that the magnificent *soixante-quinze*, the quick-firing French 75 mm field gun, which with the bayonet was the very symbol of *offensive à outrance*, did not have the weight of shell to halt the advance. In 1914 'Notre Glorieux 75', like the Royal Artillery's 13- and 18-pounders, fired shrapnel not high explosive (HE): ideal against troops in the open and to support an attack, but of limited effect where the country was wooded or built up, and where the Germans did not oblige the gunners by appearing in the open en masse (which in truth they kept doing to an astonishing degree).

That night, after heavy fighting all day along the canal, and on learning that Lanrezac's 5th Army was withdrawing, Sir John French issued orders for the BEF to do likewise. Next day L Battery Royal Horse Artillery (RHA), supporting the 1st Cavalry Brigade, fired more rounds than it had during the whole of the Boer War. Indeed, not only was the lack of heavy artillery a real deficiency on the allied side, ammunition supplies too were proving woefully inadequate, though in London this took a while to sink in. Sir John French was soon writing to the War Office saying that his expenditure of artillery rounds was high and that he needed more – especially HE – but received a cool response. At the end of September he wrote again calling urgently for more shells. The master-general of the ordnance (MGO), Major-General Sir Stanley von Donop, a Royal Artillery officer who had steadfastly refused to Anglicize his name (his family had come to England when Bonaparte had invaded Lippe-Detmold), replied: 'With reference to your letter of 28 September I am commanded by the Army Council to point out that they have provided in the first instance, and have also sent out, replenishments in almost every case fully up to the quantities of gun ammunition which were laid down before the war.'

And to a subsequent request likewise discouraged, Kitchener added: 'You will of course see that economy is practised.'

This is easy to write off as the proverbial parsimony of the storekeeper, but the War Office was in fact faced with a serious problem: where was it to find the shells? The ordnance factories did not have significant spare capacity, and building more or outsourcing to industry was not an overnight affair. Donop was accused of being bureaucratic about both shell and gun production, but he was primarily concerned with quality control, not least for safety in both production and use. In September the French General St Claire Deville, co-designer of the *soixante-quinze*, came to London with a new design for an HE shell that could be manufactured quickly from readily available components. Everyone was impressed except Donop. After the conference Kitchener asked why he had been so 'stuffy' about the design. Donop said simply: 'Because in my opinion it is unsafe.'

Four months later, perhaps as many as eight hundred French guns were to experience 'barrel burst' – rounds exploding while still in the barrel – deranging Joffre's planned offensive in Artois and Champagne. Kitchener told Asquith that had it not been for the restraining hand of Donop they would have been 'hanged on the gallows of public opinion'.*

* Sir George Arthur, *Life of Lord Kitchener*, vol. III (London, 1920). (Unless otherwise attributed, all subsequent quotations of Kitchener are taken from this source.) On 2 April 1916 there was a devastating explosion in a factory at Faversham, Kent, killing over a hundred workers. Windows were broken as far away as Southend across the Thames estuary, and the tremor was felt in Norwich. The crater made by the explosion was 40 yards across and 20 feet deep. There was no direct attribution to inexperience or faulty techniques, but the pressures following the 'shell scandal' (see p. 131) were seen as a contributory factor in the factory's haphazard safety measures.

On 19 October Donop sent a trial batch of 18-pounder HE ammunition to France, and three weeks later GHQ confirmed that it wished the future scaling to be 50 per cent HE and 50 per cent shrapnel for both the 18- and the 13-pounder, though a few more weeks later, after intense fighting around Ypres, mainly above ground, the desired proportion of HE was reduced to 25 per cent.

If Kitchener seemed slow to acknowledge the requirement for more field artillery ammunition, he was certain about the need for more HE and more heavy guns. Indeed, the trial batch of 18-pounder HE was the result of the War Office suggesting that it might be useful, not the other way round. The chief gunner at GHQ, Major-General W. F. L. Lindsay, remained doubtful: 'Consensus of opinion among gunners seems so far to be that high explosive from the German field-guns is terrible in its moral effect, but that the actual result is not very great . . . if you really have safe explosive for field-guns, by all means proceed to manufacture . . . I suppose money is but little object.'*

The fact is that the self-sacrificing courage of the gunners in the first weeks of the war was not matched in the rigour of their pre-war thinking, which put virtually all the eggs in the basket of shrapnel. It was without question the right weapon against troops in the open, but not in hard cover. Nor was it very effective reaching into places unseen, such as assembly areas. It also tended to draw the guns onto the forward slope of a defensive position to get a direct line of sight to the target instead of firing indirectly from cover. Three days after Mons, at Le Cateau, gunners and their

* Arthur, *Life of Lord Kitchener*, vol. III. Money was indeed but little object. As soon as the war began, Lloyd George told the War Office that it need no longer follow the tendering process, nor did it need prior approval to exceed the Treasury's delegated spending authority. All he asked was to be kept informed of what they were spending. This, however, at least initially, had rather the opposite effect of that intended: the War Office's new-found spending freedom acted as a sort of inhibitor, propriety and value for money no longer something checked by process and external scrutiny.

In November 1914 Kitchener formed a new branch of the War Office procurement department for HE alone, bringing in to run it John Fletcher (Baron) Moulton, a lord of appeal and scientist.

horses would be cut down in pitiful numbers as they tried to withdraw in full view of the Germans. It would take a long time for the Royal Artillery fully to embrace HE, not least because they believed shrapnel cut barbed wire better. In any case, in 1914 – and indeed, throughout 1915 – GHQ, like *GQG*, believed that the war of movement would soon be restored.

II Corps were dog-tired. The march up to Mons, the battle the following day along the canal, the fighting withdrawal over the next two days in the stifling August heat – it was the rudest of reverses. And they had not been able to break clean, the Germans harrying them every inch of the way with artillery, and frequently the rifle. The cavalry division had given up their cherished role as information-gatherers and were instead trying to cover the infantry as they plodded wearily back towards the line on which – surely? – they would make a stand, exactly as the Earl of Uxbridge's cavalry had done so skilfully on the retreat to Corunna a century earlier.* A decade's dispute on the role and equipment of cavalry – the so-called *arme blanche* (sword and lance) debate – was settled in just forty-eight hours. Yes, once or twice a squadron went at the Germans with the point; but it was dismounted action with the 'SMLE' (Rifle, Short, Magazine, Lee–Enfield), the same weapon the infantry carried, that determined things. A pre-war headline on the annual army manoeuvres, which ranged over East Anglia to test the theories of war, had put it bluntly: 'Futility of Manoeuvres. Bullet the Only Real Umpire'.

After three days of fighting, and rearward marching, from Mons, Smith-Dorrien was anxious for the cohesion of his corps. On the evening of 25 August, now supported by the 4th Division, which the war cabinet had belatedly agreed to send to France, and which had reached Le Cateau some 30 miles south-west of Mons only the day before, Smith-Dorrien decided to stand and fight. He intended giving the Germans what he called a 'smashing blow' so that his

* Uxbridge (later Marquess of Anglesey) famously lost a leg at Waterloo.

troops could properly break clean and put some distance between them and their pursuers.

Sir John French, who during those three days had made no personal visit to Smith-Dorrien's headquarters (indeed, he seems to have had a knack of being in the most inconsequential of places throughout), neither approved nor forbade the stand, instead sending a half-hearted message that Smith-Dorrien must judge things for himself.

Morale picked up at the news they would stand and fight, exactly as it had at Corunna after weeks of being harried in retreat. Private Frank Richards, a reservist with the Royal Welsh Fusiliers, would write: 'At dawn we marched out of Le Cateau with fixed bayonets. Duffy ['a time-serving soldier with six years service'] said: "we'll have a bang at the bastards today." We all hoped the same.'*

After a rainy night the 26th dawned even hotter, and the battle got off to a bad start on the extreme left flank where the 4th Division, who had been covering II Corps' withdrawal, were hastily taking up positions. They had had little rest in the cattle trucks bringing them up from Calais; they had then marched north to relieve the 5th Division as rearguard and fought their way back again all through the night, so that by first light they needed rest as badly as Smith-Dorrien's own divisions. Confusion began to mount.

With the 4th Division was the 1st Battalion the King's Own, commanded by Lieutenant-Colonel Alfred Dykes, who had won the Distinguished Service Order (DSO) as adjutant of the 2nd Battalion in South Africa. Believing they were now to the rear of the firing line and covered by cavalry and French territorials, he ordered his companies to pile arms, remove equipment and rest, despite being on a forward slope. At about six o'clock a party of horsemen appeared from the trees a thousand yards to their front, but Dykes took no notice, assuming them to be French. Soon after, a horse-drawn vehicle came out of the woods and moments later a

* Frank Richards, *Old Soldiers Never Die* (London, 1933).

machine gun opened up in long, raking bursts which killed 83 men, including Dykes himself, and wounded two hundred. Artillery accounted for another hundred in the scrambling minutes that followed, and those King's Own who emerged unscathed were extricated only by the spirited support of the 1st Royal Warwicks, one of whose platoon commanders was Lieutenant Bernard Law Montgomery, the future field marshal.

Nothing could have demonstrated better the new reality of war than this killing burst against one of the most experienced regiments in the army. If the Germans had had a rude shock at Mons on first encountering the BEF's fifteen rounds a minute, the British were now having theirs at Le Cateau.

Fighting intensified throughout the morning, though the Germans paid a heavy price for their gains: Smith-Dorrien had chosen a position obliging them to advance down a long forward slope which gave his marksmen and gunners full opportunity to show their skill. But although II Corps were able to repel the frontal attacks, the flanks were, as the phrase is, 'in the air'. To the left (west) the French territorials were a distinctly unknown quantity, and General Sordet's cavalry corps were worn out and unable to hold ground. On Smith-Dorrien's right, where Haig's I Corps should have been, there was no one, for Haig had fallen behind, pushed further east by the Forêt de Mormal and the River Sambre.

Soon after midday, the pressure on Smith-Dorrien's right flank became too much. By now, however, he was confident that he had given the Germans enough of a smashing blow to be able to order his divisions to start slipping away. And indeed by nightfall he had been able to disengage, although the rearguard paid heavily, as did the artillery, for the guns had almost all fought forward with the infantry, exactly as they had at Waterloo, and when the horse teams came up to haul them out of action they were shot down in their hundreds. The Royal Artillery lost thirty-eight guns that day, more than in any action of the army's 250-year history to that date, or in any since, excepting only at Dunkirk, Singapore and the evacuation of Burma.

The losses throughout the BEF had indeed been heavy in those first days of fighting, though it is difficult to establish with any certainty just how many of these were suffered in the stand at Le Cateau. Some 7,812 men were accounted killed, wounded or taken prisoner on 26 August, most of them from II Corps, though the initial figures were much higher, for there were men everywhere trying to get back to their units – the only place where they could be included in a head count. Sir John French's intense dislike of Smith-Dorrien, stemming from personal and professional differences stretching back ten years, now began to tell.* Although he wrote in his despatches of Smith-Dorrien's 'rare and unusual coolness, intrepidity and determination', privately he blamed him for disobeying orders, and believed the battle to have been both unnecessary and at the same time more costly than in fact it was. From now on Smith-Dorrien was a marked man, and in May 1915 he would be sent home. It is difficult to escape the conclusion that the real reason was that French knew he was the better soldier, and feared for his own position.

Meanwhile the retreat continued. But the French commander-in-chief, the massive, imperturbable Joffre, had at last realized what was happening – that the German main effort was coming through Belgium, not in Alsace-Lorraine – and, by withdrawing divisions from his armies there and in the centre, with the aid of the extensive and efficient French railway network, managed to cobble together a new army (the 6th) to cover Paris. His days were spent speeding from one headquarters to another, driven by Georges Boillot, the Peugeot racing team's lead driver.

Indeed, the petrol as well as the steam engine now came to his rescue. For some days the RFC had been reporting a change of

* The root causes of the dislike almost certainly included jealousy (although French was Smith-Dorrien's senior, the latter had seen more action), but ostensibly it was professional – a profound disagreement over the role of cavalry, Smith-Dorrien being a proponent of the 'mounted infantry' school. After Grierson's death on the way to Amiens, French had wanted Sir Herbert Plumer to replace him as commander of II Corps; Kitchener sent him Smith-Dorrien instead.

direction south-east by Kluck's 1st Army, and then on 2 September a pilot from the Paris garrison brought the news that there were no Germans marching westward of the city. Rather than envelop the city, as Schlieffen had originally envisaged, the right wing of the great wheeling movement – the 1st and 2nd Armies – was going to present a flank to the Paris garrison, which had now been heavily reinforced. The allies could at last attack a significant and vulnerable objective.*

At once the military governor of Paris, the wiry veteran General Joseph Gallieni, rounded up every omnibus and taxicab he could find and sent the garrison forward to the Marne in comfort and the high spirits that go with clever improvisation and the prospect of turning the tables, while Joffre tried to persuade the BEF, who had been pushed back to the eastern suburbs of Paris, to join in. Sir John French was still smarting (not unreasonably) at how Lanrezac had 'left him in the lurch' at Mons by withdrawing without telling him. Joffre had subsequently sacked Lanrezac, in part to appease his ally but principally because Lanrezac had made the same mistake as Smith-Dorrien – being right. He had not been persuaded by *GQG*'s assessment that the German offensive in Belgium was a small-scale affair, and before the BEF had begun arriving had asked Joffre to keep them clear of Maubeuge as he would need the manoeuvre space to his rear. This – implying a fighting withdrawal rather than a counter-offensive – was not what Joffre had wanted to hear. Lanrezac remained in command for just days before Joffre replaced him with one of the 5th Army's more thrusting corps commanders, Lieutenant-General Louis Franchet d'Espèrey – or, as he would be known to the BEF, 'Desperate Frankie'.

Franchet was certainly more to Sir John French's liking, but even so, on 2 September, as *GQG* first mooted the idea of a counter-offensive, the commander-in-chief of the BEF was not convinced

* On 1 September papers had reportedly been found on a dead German staff officer indicating that Kluck was so alarmed by the gap opening up between his army and Bülow's that he saw no option but to close with him and give up the Schlieffen idea of a western envelopment of Paris.

that the situation was propitious. Only the day before, Kitchener had had to come to France in person to dissuade him from withdrawing south of the Seine so that the BEF could lick its wounds in peace. On 5 September Joffre himself came to GHQ, now housed in a villa at Melun on the banks of the Seine, to beg – literally – that the BEF join the counter-offensive: 'Monsieur le maréchal, c'est la France qui vous supplie.'

Sir John French, reduced to tears, tried to reply but language failed him. Turning to his interpreter he said: 'Dammit, I can't explain. Tell him all that men can do, our fellows will do.'

A massive, mustachioed *général d'armée* wringing his hands, begging on behalf of La France, and a British field marshal with tears rolling down his cheeks – 'Marianne' imploring 'John Bull': one day it 'would probably furnish the theme of a great historical picture', wrote Spears (though it never has).

In any case the BEF had had enough of retreating. They had twice done what the British army had done so well in Wellington's day – occupy a position and defy the enemy to evict them – but it was now time to do what the army had also done well for even longer, since Churchill's ancestor the first duke of Marlborough's day, in fact: go to it with the bayonet.

The counter-attack began next morning, the main weight of it in the valley of the Marne. For the French it was very much the moment, 'En avant!' the order of the day. The BEF's advance, however – the cavalry, much reduced, leading – was at first hesitant, for Sir John French's head had not quite caught up with his heart. Although the Germans soon began to give way before the wholly unexpected onslaught of three French armies – and in some alarm (they too were dog-tired, with as much as 90 per cent of their mechanical transport broken down) – Smith-Dorrien's and Haig's corps were too slow in following up and allowed the Germans to retreat in reasonable order. The French were undoubtedly more aggressive but were never quite able to turn harassing pursuit into war-winning rout. By 13 September the whole of *Generaloberst* von

Kluck's 1st Army had fallen back to the River Aisne – and then the swelteringly hot weather broke at last, torrential rain swelling the rivers and streams which lay between them and the allies snapping at their heels.

The Germans now dug in on the high ground north of the Aisne, and the BEF's sappers and infantry won many a gallantry medal as they threw assault bridges across the swollen river and attacked the heights. But to no avail: the Germans had seized the best ground, and the counter-offensive was running out of steam.* Indeed, the whole nature of the battle in north-west France was now changing, as Sir John French noted in a letter to the King: 'The spade will be as great a necessity as the rifle, and the heaviest types and calibres of artillery will be brought up on either side.' (It was as well that the War Office – or rather, Kitchener and the MGO's staff – had been thinking ahead about the type of gun needed, as well as HE.)

At the *Oberste Heeresleitung*, the German army's high command, Moltke, in a state of nervous collapse, reportedly told the Kaiser: 'Your Majesty, we have lost the war.'

He was replaced by the former Prussian war minister, General Erich von Falkenhayn.

Neither side was ready quite yet to concede that the war of manoeuvre was finished. There remained the open flank – the gap between General Michel-Joseph Manoury's improvised 6th Army on the BEF's left, and the sea – and both the allies and the Germans would now begin two months of increasingly desperate scrabbling to turn each other's flank.

But with tactical mobility still determined by the marching pace of the infantry, the race for the flank succeeded only in extending the defensive lines – at this stage merely scrapes, shallow trenches and sandbagged strongpoints – north across the uplands of the

* The BEF lost 561 officers and 12,980 men killed, missing or wounded during the Marne counter-offensive, mainly on the Aisne – a small enough 'butcher's bill' by later standards, but the loss of 'quality' would have its multiplier effect on the expansion of the army.

Somme, on in front of the ancient city of Arras, then down into the polder and sandy lowlands of Flanders – and eventually to the dunes at Nieuport in Belgium (thereby preserving a symbolically important piece of sovereign territory after the Belgian army quit Antwerp in October and marched to join with the allies in Flanders). On the way, the BEF would have the worst of its fighting so far, in a battle that would all but extinguish the old pre-war regular army, the men who had sailed for France only two months before.

Reinforcement had been continual since those heady days in August. Regulars redeployed from both home defence and overseas garrisons, volunteer units of the TF, and British and Indian troops from the subcontinent swelled the BEF to five corps – four of infantry, including the Indian Corps, and one of cavalry. By the middle of October Sir John French had some 250,000 men at his disposal, a match at last for Kluck's army opposite him. And it looked as if he had at last found the German flank – at Ypres. Urged on by General Ferdinand Foch, whom Joffre had sent north to re-energize the fighting, French put the BEF onto the offensive along the Menin Road on 21 October.

They soon ran into trouble, for Falkenhayn had reinforced his right flank by bringing Prince Rupprecht of Bavaria's 6th Army from Alsace-Lorraine, and Rupprecht at once attacked.

A month's hard fighting followed in which the BEF lost some 58,000 officers and men in what would become known as the First Battle of Ypres. Most of the casualties were the irreplaceable regulars who could march all day, use cover cunningly and fire fifteen aimed rounds a minute. By Christmas in many battalions there would be no more than a few dozen soldiers and a single officer left who had been at Mons.

The battles of late summer and autumn 1914 were the breaking of the 'Old Contemptibles', as well as of many French units. But whereas the French had a replacement system that kept the status quo in being – rather as a river remains the same river even though the water is constantly changing – the British army would have to be remade by Kitchener's men. And until 1917, when by Kitchener's calculations Britain's full military potential could be reached, the fort would have to be held by territorials, by 'New Army' battalions as soon as they could pass muster, and by troops cobbled together from every corner of the Empire.

The 'fort' would be the trenches. From the North Sea to the Swiss border the armies on both sides were digging, wiring and sandbagging, sometimes within a hundred yards of each other. A continuous line of trenches and breastworks – continuous *lines*, indeed, as the defences developed depth with fire trench, support trench, reserve trench, and linking communication trenches – soon lay across the French countryside like giant railway tracks. For the most part, the Germans held the best of the ground – higher, for good observation, and drier, so that they could build their shelters deep. When Kitchener's New Armies were ready to go to France, they would have to face the problem of how to get across the ground between the lines – 'no-man's-land' – before the Germans could come out of their holes with machine guns; and then how to break through the deep defensive belt into the open country beyond before the Germans could seal the breach with troops brought up from reserve. Many hundreds of thousands of them would die trying to find the answers.

The question remains, then: did the British have any alternative but to sacrifice the BEF (and thereby many hundreds of thousands of 'New Army' men and others afterwards) in those early months? Would, for example, Churchill's alternative proposal to send the BEF not to Maubeuge but to Tours (or perhaps Amiens, as the council of war decided initially on 5 August, before Kitchener changed his mind at Henry Wilson's urging) have produced a more favourable outcome? What if Joffre, recognizing his unique strategic advantage of having so much time in which to discover where the true danger lay and make his critical decisions, had been prepared to surrender ground, at far less cost to his troops and to civilians – as the Tsar had done during Bonaparte's invasion in 1812 – and then deploy his fresh and eager forces, including the BEF, accordingly?

If the BEF had assembled at Amiens or Tours as a strategic reserve, building up its strength to some three hundred thousand during August and September, what, for instance, might Joffre have done about the gap that would have opened up in the French line of battle, on the extreme left flank? What if the BEF hadn't gone to Mons?

The answer lay in the nine French divisions – two corps – earmarked for the army of observation on the Italian border. These could have been put at notice to move as soon as Italy declared its neutrality on 3 August (a decision confirmed at the council of war by Sir Edward Grey on 6 August), and the move begun as soon as French intelligence confirmed that the Italian army, although recalling some reservists to the colours, was not moving to a war footing. In case such a redeployment sounds too hypothetical, it is worth noting that in the event it is exactly what happened: the French Army of the Alps was stood down on 17 August (at which time much of the BEF was still encamped near its ports of landing), and its divisions then spread across the entire French line.

Had these dispositions been made, the situation at the end of September would have been the same as actually transpired, with French forces mounting a successful counter-attack on the Marne, and then stalling on the Aisne. Having the BEF in the line may well have boosted French morale (and it certainly 'punched above its weight'), but it is unreasonable to suggest that the French would not have been able to manage things on their own. Indeed, there would have been considerably more cohesion.

Joffre improvised brilliantly and delivered a blow on the Marne that sent the flower of Brandenburg reeling; but it was not enough. He had executed the first two of the four requirements of victory – 'find' and 'fix': he had found the weak point, the flank of the great hook through Belgium by the armies of Generals Kluck and Bülow, and he had fixed them – temporarily – on the Aisne. What he needed to do now was 'strike' and then 'exploit' (cf. Churchill's 'Her only chance is to conquer Germany in France'). However, he had not been able to create a further striking force. A BEF concentrated at Amiens or Tours – a fresh, strong, virtually all-regular army, by then numbering nearly three hundred thousand – would have been made for the job.

The job, however, was not simply to attack on the Aisne, to apply more brute force where brute force had already exhausted itself. What was needed was overwhelming force applied not as a sledgehammer but as a lever. The German flank was not just open in a localized way after the retreat to the Aisne; the entire *Schwenkungsflügel* of the vaunted Schlieffen Plan was extended in an east–west line through mid-Champagne and southern Picardy, and it was already beginning to bow back on the right. With each successive encounter on the extremity of that flank (what became known as the 'race for the sea' – a misnomer, for the sea wasn't the objective, and in truth it was less a race and more a crawl), even as the Germans brought up new troops, their line backed further north rather than projecting further west.

In the third week of September, therefore, with the Belgians still holding out at Antwerp, a three-hundred-thousand-strong BEF, fully equipped, its reservists fighting fit, and with a confident RFC to direct its advance, could have launched a counter-stroke from Abbeville east between Arras and Albert (or even more boldly, further north between Arras and Lille), on a 30-mile front. It could have clouted rather than dribbled. And with simultaneous pressure by the French along the Aisne – indeed, across the whole front (and the Belgians making another sortie from Antwerp) – to fix the Germans in place so that they could not further reinforce their right, all that Falkenhayn's armies in western France would have been able to do to avoid being enveloped would have been to turn through 90 degrees to face west. And they would have had to pivot somewhere that did not form too sharp an angle and therefore a dangerous salient – Rheims, or even Verdun. In the best case for the allies, with the Germans unable to find a natural line on which to try to halt the BEF, and a renewed offensive by the French and

Belgians, the German 1st, 2nd and 4th Armies would have had to pull back to the Meuse.*

Supposing all this, then – even if at that point the Germans had been able to check further allied progress east – the situation on the Western Front would have seen a strategic sea change. The allies, to exploit their position, could now have used the growing Russian strength on the Eastern Front to advantage: the Germans would have been truly caught between two giant hammers. With so catastrophic an end to Schlieffen, the possibilities are intriguing. The allies would have been in a vastly superior strategic position to that in which they actually found themselves in 1915. The possession of most of Belgium would have been significant in terms of the extra men and materiel available. And the failure of Germany to achieve victory would not have been lost on the neutrals. It was almost certainly impossible that Britain could have avoided war with Turkey, but if it were possible in May 1915 to persuade Italy to enter the war on the allies' side it should also have been possible to persuade the Dutch and the Danes to consider their positions, especially once the Germans had been removed from the southern Dutch border.

At the very least the BEF counter-stroke, forcing the Germans back into Belgium, perhaps as far as the Meuse, would have given the allies far better ground on which to fight – along with a strong Belgian army and a much shorter front, and therefore more reserves. At the very best, an offensive by British, French and Belgian armies on the Meuse in the spring of 1915, with Dutch–Danish action directed against the Kiel Canal and the submarine base at Heligoland, might have ended the war that summer.

This is all supposition, of course; but not to allow it is to concede

* Lloyd George's memoirs hardly have the authority of scripture, but they are worth quoting on this point: 'I have heard it said, at the battle of Ypres, the troops on both sides were so tired out by the end that the irruption of one fresh division on either side would have achieved victory for the army lucky enough to secure so timely a reinforcement.' *War Memoirs of David Lloyd George*, new edn (London, 1934).

a sort of inevitability in war, which is fatal. The Dutch historian Johan Huizinga put it thus: 'The historian must always maintain towards his subject an indeterminist point of view. He must constantly put himself at a point in the past at which the known factors still seem to permit different outcomes.'*

Asquith had missed the greatest opportunity in 1911 – after the CID meeting – to form an authoritative naval–military strategic staff to analyse these matters and to deal then at the highest level with the French. In an exchange of memoranda with Sir Edward Grey at the end of November 1916, after the Somme, the CIGS, General (later Field Marshal) Sir William Robertson – 'Wully', who had risen from the ranks – nailed the essential truth very plainly: 'Our military preparations were out of step with our diplomacy . . . the pre-war policy, which *I* think we could not have avoided, practically committed us to assist France in defeating Germany, but the bulk of our officers held the opinion that our military preparations were inadequate to carry out that policy.'† He could not apportion blame – 'I do not know what advice the military advisers gave the Government before the war' – though he implies criticism of both the government and the War Office: 'I have papers in this office which I myself wrote some 15 years ago, when here, calling serious attention to the danger of Germany. I was not then military adviser to the Government, but in my subordinate capacity it was my duty to call attention to what was going on and I did so.' This is hardly a statement of confidence in his pre-war predecessors as CIGS, or in Henry Wilson.

If the capacity or will for rigorous strategic thinking, in the War Office especially, was not available in 1911, it most certainly was not in late 1914. On mobilization the corridors had been filled with officers gaily leaving their desks to join the BEF – even the DMO, the man responsible for strategic considerations in connection

* 'The Idea of History', in Fritz Stern (ed.), *The Varieties of History* (New York, 1956).
† PRO FO 800/102, Grey MSS, cited in *The Military Correspondence of Field Marshal Sir William Robertson*, ed. David Woodward (London, 1989).

with the military operations, the CIGS's principal adviser and thereby the cabinet's. Now the corridors would be filled with 'dug-outs', men brought out of retirement or the reserve, on their way to those very desks. The army's intellectual centre of gravity would be in north-west France, not Whitehall, and this would have the most perverse consequences.

As Robertson later put it to Grey: 'We had a very bad start.'

Chapter Three

THE STUMBLING BEAR

Without the Dual (Franco-Russian) Alliance of 1894, the French general staff would not have been able to develop Plan XVII with any confidence.* For whatever the supposed moral superiority of the offensive, unless large numbers of German troops were tied down in East Prussia and on the Polish border, the Kaiser's army would be too strong for the French in Alsace-Lorraine. And the Germans were not going to be tied down by a ponderously mobilizing Russian army that could not attack for several months. Only an immediate offensive into East Prussia, Posen or Silesia would trouble the *Grosser Generalstab.* Article 2 of the treaty therefore required that 'in case the forces of the Triple Alliance or of any one of the Powers belonging to it, should be mobilized, France and Russia, at the first news of this event and without previous agreement being necessary, shall mobilize immediately and simultaneously the whole of their forces, and shall transport them as far as possible to their frontiers'. Article 3 further specified that 'the available forces to be employed against Germany shall be, on the part of

* Article 1: 'If France is attacked by Germany, or by Italy supported by Germany, Russia shall employ all her available forces to attack Germany. If Russia is attacked by Germany, or by Austria supported by Germany, France shall employ all her available forces to attack Germany.'

France, 1,300,000 men, on the part of Russia, 700,000 or 800,000 men', with the additional stipulation that 'these forces shall engage to the full with such speed that Germany will have to fight simultaneously on the East and on the West'.*

In the subsequent staff discussions, however, it was agreed that Russia would be able to choose her own operational priorities – an offensive against *either* Austria *or* Germany – although in his novel *August 1914* Alexander Solzhenitsyn describes a third option: 'At this point Sukhomlinov [in 1909 chief of staff of the Imperial Russian Army], with the irresponsible ignorance so easily mistaken for decisiveness, had come to the General Staff and "reconciled" the contending factions. "We shall", he declared, "advance on Germany and Austria simultaneously." Of the available alternatives he made the worst possible choice: to attack both at once.'†

The following year, when Vladimir Sukhomlinov became war minister, Yakov Zhilinsky took his place at the head of the general staff. Zhilinsky, like Henry Wilson, was a strong Francophile, and now directed planning towards a major attack on Germany even before mobilization was complete. This, however, demanded another decision: should that attack be into East Prussia or towards Berlin?

Zhilinsky's nerve deserted him; the answer was to be further strategic bifurcation. 'And now [in August 1914] Russia was in honour bound not to disappoint her allies,' continued Solzhenitsyn. 'But the Russian mind hates being faced with an "either-or" situation such as whether to attack [East] Prussia or Berlin, so what easier solution than to do both at once?'

* The remaining articles were: 4. 'The General Staffs of the Armies of the two countries shall cooperate with each other at all times in the preparation and facilitation of the execution of the measures mentioned above. They shall communicate with each other, while there is still peace, all information relative to the armies of the Triple Alliance which is already in their possession or shall come into their possession. Ways and means of corresponding in time of war shall be studied and worked out in advance.' 5. 'France and Russia shall not conclude peace separately.' 6. 'The present Convention shall have the same duration as the Triple Alliance.' 7. 'All the clauses enumerated above shall be kept absolutely secret.'

† *August 1914*, trans. Michael Glenny (London, 1972).

Accordingly, in August 1914, while the 10th Army was being cobbled together (a good deal of it on paper) to march on Berlin, the 1st and 2nd Armies, again only partially mobilized, at once marched into East Prussia. They were only partially mobilized because, wrote Solzhenitsyn, General Zhilinsky in his meetings with Joffre the year before had 'brought forward the date of such an attack so generously at Russia's expense: totally unprepared as they were, the Russians had been committed to moving forward on the *fifteenth* day after mobilization instead of the sixtieth'.

This *attaque brusqué* would unnerve Moltke. In accordance with one of his illustrious uncle's precepts, to 'first reckon, then risk', he had indeed reckoned – that the Russians would not be ready for sixty days – and then risked leaving only nine divisions in the east rather than the twenty-two or more that the French general staff had calculated were necessary.

And things began well for the Russians, Zhilinsky himself taking command of the North-West Front ('front' being the Russian term for a group of armies, or 'army group'). On 20 August, General Paul von Rennenkampf's 1st Army defeated General Friedrich von Prittwitz's numerically weaker 8th Army at Gumbinnen, while Alexandr Samsonov's 2nd Army (though deprived of the Guards Corps to give body to the 10th) moved quickly to cut the 8th Army's line of communications. Prittwitz panicked and announced he was withdrawing to the Vistula river, which would have meant abandoning most of East Prussia including the fortress-capital, Königsberg.

He was at once replaced by General Paul von Hindenburg who, with his chief of staff Erich Ludendorff – names that would later become synonymous with total war and military control – immediately launched a counter-offensive.

An attack such as Zhilinsky's, by two armies only partially mobilized and thinned out to provide troops for the 10th Army, was really a bluff, and against hard-headed professionals like Hindenburg and Ludendorff was sooner or later going to be exposed as such. By 27 August they had surrounded Samsonov in a double envelopment at Tannenberg, and after three days his entire command had disintegrated, the Germans taking 92,000 prisoners. Samsonov committed suicide.

A fortnight later at the Battle of the Masurian Lakes, Rennenkampf's 1st Army lost another hundred thousand – the size of the BEF that had marched up to Mons the month before. Zhilinsky was relieved of command and sent to Paris as military representative. He must have cut an awkward figure in the boulevards (French generals relieved of command were sent to Limoges under virtual house arrest) – but at least he had fulfilled his pledge to attack.

And it was not all bad news from St Petersburg – or Petrograd as the Tsar, wishing to eradicate any Germanic note, had renamed it. In Galicia, in the south of Poland, Imperial territory, the Russians had got the better of the Austro-Hungarians who, having been preoccupied with Serbia, had only lately launched their promised offensive. Waiting for them were four fully mobilized and well-supplied armies under Generals Nikolai Ivanov and Aleksei Brusilov. On 30 August these mounted a counter-offensive which, by the end of September, had forced the Austrians out of Galicia and inflicted 130,000 casualties.

Even the precipitate Russian invasion of East Prussia at a date brought forward, as Solzhenitsyn put it, 'so generously at Russia's expense', proved not without its upside, for in order to prevent another Gumbinnen and exploit the success at Tannenberg, Moltke had switched two army corps to the east from France and Belgium, to the great advantage of the allied counter-attack on the Marne. In its chaotic way, the Franco-Russian strategy had in fact worked: France had not fallen, and neither had her eastern ally, who still had ample reserves to call on.

But the Russian bear had undoubtedly stumbled, and Moltke's successor, Falkenhayn, believed this presented the opportunity to send troops west – more than just those that Moltke had switched – to force a decision in France. Paradoxically, however, Joffre was keen to do all he could to take the pressure off his ally by *keeping* Germans on the Western Front, for if Berlin diverted troops east to finish off the stumbling bear, there would in turn be far more available to send west.

That was the strategic-level conundrum. Meanwhile at the theatre level, Hindenburg and Ludendorff saw opportunity too. Having checked the immediate threat to East Prussia, and thereby in all probability to Posen and Silesia, they argued for switching troops to Galicia instead to reinforce the Austro-Hungarians. However, Russian mobilization had continued apace, and sheer numbers began to tell: Austro-German gains in Poland would prove to be negligible. Had the troops been switched to the Western Front instead, they might just have been able to turn the allied flank as it 'raced' for the sea. Such are the opportunity costs in strategy.

There was another factor: Serbia, all too often the 'forgotten ally' of the Entente. The Austrians were making no better progress against them than they had against the Russians. The tough and experienced Serbian General Radomir Putnik had brought their first invasion to a rapid end on the Cer Mountain and at Šabac (before the first shots were fired at Mons) and in early September mounted his counter-offensive on the Sava river, in the north. Although this had to be broken off when the Austrians began a second offensive, against the Serbs' western front on the Drina river, weeks of deadlock followed, which tied down many Austrian troops on whom the Germans had been counting for operations in Poland.

Then, on 29 October, the war took a critical turn for the Triple Entente with the entry of the Ottoman Empire on the side of the Central Powers. A secret Turco-German treaty had been signed on 2 August, but Constantinople had at first been reluctant to act. Berlin therefore decided to force its hand. The battle-cruiser *Goeben* and light cruiser *Breslau* of Admiral Wilhelm Souchon's Mediterranean squadron had managed to give the Royal Navy the slip and reach the Bosporus, and Souchon now took these under Ottoman colours together with a Turkish squadron into the Black Sea to shell Odessa and Sevastopol. With the western allies' subsequent declaration of war on the Empire, fighting would now spread to the

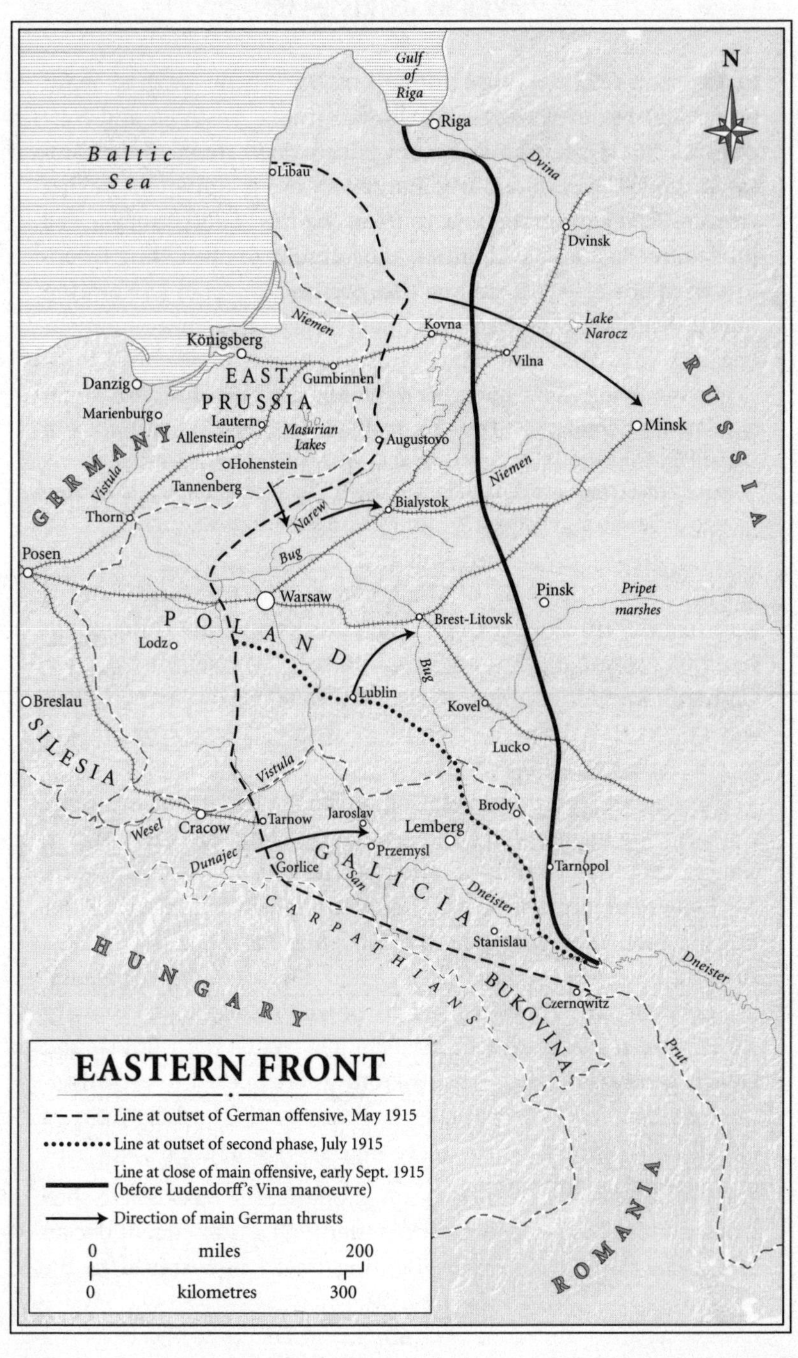

EASTERN FRONT

Line at outset of German offensive, May 1915

Line at outset of second phase, July 1915

Line at close of main offensive, early Sept. 1915 (before Ludendorff's Vina manoeuvre)

Direction of main German thrusts

0 miles 200

0 kilometres 300

Middle East, at huge opportunity cost in British imperial manpower and resources, not least those of India, Australia and New Zealand. But the Russians also now faced a new front, in the Caucasus, while the closure of the Dardanelles to shipping meant that armaments could not be sent to them via the Mediterranean. The road to the Russian Revolution was beginning to open up.

It need not have. As early as 1 September Churchill had written (privately) to the CIGS:

> I arranged with Lord Kitchener yesterday that two officers from the Admiralty should meet two officers from the D.M.O.'s Department of the War Office today to examine and work out a plan for the seizure, by means of a Greek army of adequate strength, of the Gallipoli Peninsula, with a view to admitting a British Fleet to the Sea of Marmora.

His ancestor, the duke of Marlborough, who had fought all his wars in awkward alliances, had said it plainly and often enough: in coalition warfare the first object was to keep the coalition together. Churchill knew it and now strove hard to do so; too many British generals, if they knew it, seemed incapable of accepting what it meant. Russia was simply 'noises off'.*

Throughout November, fighting on the Eastern Front remained fluid. Having managed to defeat the Austro-Hungarian offensive in Galicia and the combined attempts to take Warsaw, in early November the Russians began a counter-offensive into Silesia. After heavy losses, they withdrew the following month to a new and stronger line closer to the Polish capital. But soon, under pressure in the Caucasus, Petrograd would be calling for a diversionary effort to be made against Constantinople. While both British and French generals on the Western Front were opposed to any diversion of resources, Paris was keen to heed the call for help from its old ally, and in London too there were sympathetic ears, not least of course at the Admiralty.

* See chapter 4.

Churchill was confident that from its main anchorage at Scapa Flow and smaller stations along the east coast the Royal Navy could maintain its blockade of Germany (primarily to prevent German exports, not so much to prevent imports) and keep the German High Seas Fleet penned up in its anchorage at Wilhelmshaven. And having already eliminated the threat to the trade routes – sending every armoured cruiser to the bottom or to skulk in some East African creek – he believed that the Admiralty could now spare a few obsolescent warships to force the Dardanelles straits. Not only would this open up communications with the Russians in the Black Sea, it would, he argued, encourage Italy, Greece, Romania and Bulgaria, who were still sitting on the fence, to come in on the allied side.

The strategic advantage would be enormous. It would be the classic exercise of sea power, Britain's traditional forte. But it would need wholehearted support and execution.

Chapter Four

THE EMPTY CORRIDORS OF POWER

Writing at the end of the war, Major-General Sir Frederick Maurice, DMO from January 1916 to his dismissal in May 1918, extolled the achievements of the British – the raising of the new armies, the control of the oceans, the management of food supply and, not least, the innovation in war materiel, of which the tank was only the most spectacular example: 'The enemy has produced no weapon or device applicable to modern war which we have not at least equalled, and in most cases surpassed.' However, all this could so easily have come to naught, and the superiority was certainly not exploited to the full, because: 'The one respect in which we have failed has been the organization of our Higher Command.'

By this Maurice meant not merely, or even primarily, the arrangements for command of naval and land forces, 'but rather the machinery for the coordination of policy with naval and military strategy, machinery which I may call, in short, the government of the war'.*

The problem began with the pre-1914 expectation of what war in Europe would be like, and what would be the nation's part in it – a rapid clash of arms and a quick decision, in which Britain would have

* Major-General Sir F. Maurice, *Forty Days in 1914* (London, 1919).

but a limited liability. For on that principle of limited liability, believing there would be no further requirement for military policy-making, in August 1914 the General Staff at the War Office, led by the DMO, crossed to France, leaving the CIGS without the necessary continuity and experience in the intelligence and operations branches. It was as if a notice had been put up: 'Closed for the duration.'*

This was unfortunate because the CIGS, General Sir Charles Douglas, had never served on the General Staff before being thrust into the appointment in April 1914 when Sir John French resigned over the Curragh 'mutiny'. All his staff experience was in adjutancy – discipline and administration – culminating in his appointment as adjutant-general (AG) between 1904 and 1909, after which he was made inspector-general of home forces. When French stood down, amid some sympathy for the difficult position he had been placed in by Seely and one or two hotheads in uniform, he was found another billet by the expedient of a job-swap with Douglas. Douglas himself was in no doubt about his own unsuitability for the appointment (though in truth, he was no more unqualified than French, who also had not attended the staff college or held a General Staff post), telling General Sir Ian Hamilton, C-in-C Mediterranean forces, an old regimental friend, that he had only accepted the job 'because discipline had broken down under mismanagement, and because he had been assured that the

* The Germans faced similar problems, but had anticipated them. On mobilization, most of the *Grosser Generalstab* were reassigned to the headquarters of the armies and corps. Those remaining became the 'General Staff of the Field Army', part of the *Oberste Heeresleitung* (Supreme Army Command). Under the chief of the general staff – now commander-in-chief – Moltke, and his chief of staff (*Generalquartiermeister*) Hermann von Stein, this streamlined staff was now divided into three departments: operations, intelligence and political affairs. Superior staff work at division, corps and army level throughout the war contributed to Germany's remarkable run of successes. However, attrition led to premature deployment of *Kriegsakademie* students to army and corps general staffs, some of them after just a year at the war college. Later the *Kriegsakademie* was closed altogether and qualifying officers served staff apprenticeships instead. This was far from the Prussian ideal of the *Generalstab* officer, carefully selected, instructed and examined over an extensive period, but it was far less haphazard than what the British were forced to do.

Army at large would welcome his taking up the reins'.* But while admirable in its way, it was the answer of a C-in-C, not a CIGS. Discipline was not the responsibility of the chief of the intelligence, policy and operations staff. When, therefore, the hastily convened 'council of war' of 5 August 1914 discussed what it supposed were the strategic options for the employment of the BEF, Douglas would have nothing to say but what his DMO, Henry Wilson, told him. It is the greatest pity that despite his relative youth (fifty-two) and lack of seniority (being at this point a mere *lieutenant*-general), Sir Douglas Haig was not translated from Aldershot Command to the post instead, for there was no one with more experience of that side of the War Office.†

It was doubly unfortunate because on 25 October Sir Charles Douglas would die of overwork and the strain of the impossible task he had taken on, not least of reconstituting a General Staff. Whence were the officers to be found? Even the staff college had closed, its staff and students too joining the BEF. The answer could only be from among the ranks of those retired, whether early or after long service.

The first priority was to find a new director of military operations (and intelligence). Colonel Charles Callwell, a Royal Artillery officer and notable writer on military affairs, had been deputy DMO ten years before, having previously worked in intelligence, but had resigned in 1909 on being passed over for promotion. At the age of fifty-five, by no means advanced years for a senior officer of that time, he was recalled in the temporary rank of major-general to take the place of Henry Wilson (himself only five years younger). Other empty desks were filled in the same way, the military secretary's staff being inundated with requests from retired officers to be 'dug out'.

It was not ideal. But a faltering CIGS and a scratch General Staff

* Sir Ian Hamilton, *The Soul and Body of an Army* (London, 1921).

† In December 1937 Lieutenant-General the Lord Gort would be made CIGS at the age of fifty-one.

was not the end of the problem. There was also Asquith's 'perilous experiment' – Lord Kitchener. His instinctive grasp of the nature of the conflict from the moment of the first council of war, that it would be a long war requiring the mobilization of national resources, was the first glimpse of strategy at the War Office. It was a winning card; correctly played, it would bring ultimate victory, and in such a way as to give Britain a strong voice when it came to the peace treaties. But while on the one hand it is obvious why Asquith chose to experiment so perilously in making Kitchener secretary of state for war, the chain of events leading to the appointment is nevertheless unedifying. 'K' himself had wanted to be viceroy of India, and in July 1914 happened to be in London in part to lobby for the post, but others (such as *The Times*'s influential war correspondent Colonel Charles à Court Repington) had been advocating publicly that Kitchener go to the War Office. Who else was there indeed? Haldane looked compromised. His mission to Germany in 1912 on Asquith's behalf to end the naval arms race had been unproductive, inviting charges that his heart wasn't in it. Having studied philosophy at Göttingen he was 'clearly a Germanophile', and after an increasingly nasty whispering campaign would be forced from his government position of lord chancellor in May 1915. Churchill had his hands full at the Admiralty, Lloyd George was putting the Treasury onto a war footing, and there was no other obvious man of standing whom Asquith could recommend to the public as someone with comparable knowledge of war and the army.

And so began the unprecedented experiment of having a serving soldier, albeit a field marshal hitherto filling the role of 'viceroy' in Egypt, and a man of Olympian stature in pre-war England, as war minister – unprecedented, that is, in Britain; in Prussia it was the norm. It was an experiment made all the more unstable by Kitchener's taciturn, almost secretive, nature, his authoritarianism and his innate mistrust of politicians. 'How can I speak on matters with men [cabinet ministers] when we have not been introduced?' he is said to have asked in exasperation. And then there was the problem of his relationship as a man in uniform with the C-in-Cs, and indeed the War Office staff. Would he be a minister or a sort of 'super C-in-C'? Who was to be the cabinet's principal military adviser – 'K' or the CIGS?

At least Asquith chose the soldier in whom the country had the greatest confidence – leaving aside Lord Roberts, who at eighty-one, though still able to ask searching questions at the council of war of 5 August, was unquestionably past his best (and would in fact die of pneumonia three months later while visiting the front). Kitchener had won all his battles and all his wars. Unfortunately, almost all of his service had been spent in the far-flung spaces of the Empire. He was not familiar with cabinet government, and had not seen the General Staff at work, for it had been formed in the aftermath of the Boer War, since when he had been in India and latterly Egypt.

Although he made no declaration, 'K' saw his appointment as twofold. First, he was to be not merely the minister but in every respect head of the War Office's administration, whose efforts were to be directed primarily towards raising the army to the rank of a first-rate military power. Why should he *not* make himself head, for he was a field marshal (and a lord)? Secondly, he saw it as his right and duty to be the supreme military adviser to the government on the conduct of the war. Why should he *not* be, for he was a field marshal and de facto the nation's senior military officer? It was, besides anything else, an enormous burden to take on, but then, he had been raised in the old 'stove pipe' system of the commander-in-chief, in which staff officers were merely executives, rather than a general staff system in which the CIGS made decisions on the basis of staff advice; he would use the old top-down methods.

Unfortunately, by the time he realized that this approach could not serve, it had broken down, and in the most catastrophic way – in Gallipoli and the Dardanelles the following year. And the Dardanelles Commission, set up to investigate the failure, concluded: 'We are of the opinion that Lord Kitchener did not sufficiently avail himself of the services of his General Staff, with the result that more work was undertaken by him than was possible for one man to do, and that confusion and want of efficiency resulted.'*

The new DMO, Callwell, though an admirer of Kitchener (who could not but admire one of the great figures of the Empire?), was even less restrained: 'The fact is that – to put the matter quite bluntly – when he took up his burden the Chief did not know what the duties of his subordinates were supposed to be, and he took little trouble to find out.'†

Callwell's words are doubly revealing. The General Staff saw 'K' as 'the Chief' and themselves as his subordinates. This was not however the constitutional position. The officers of the General Staff were the subordinates of the CIGS, the minister's adviser on operational policy (just as the staff of the adjutant-general, quartermaster-general and master-general of the ordnance – AG, QMG and MGO – were subordinates of their respective members of the Army Council). To a man in a hurry, as Kitchener very properly was, this could all seem like tiresome bureaucracy. Callwell recalls how one day the new minister sent for him (rather than sending for the CIGS, as courtesy – and indeed good practice – would have required) and 'directed me to carry out a certain measure in connection with a subject that was not my business at all, and I was so ill-advised as to say "It's a matter for the Adjutant-General's Department, sir, but I'll let them know about it."'

Neither Haldane nor even Seely would have snapped back: 'I told you to do it yourself!'

Callwell says he soon sorted out the matter pragmatically, but the short-circuiting of staffwork could only be sorted out if the error – or, worse, omission – came to light in time. The case of Antwerp was one such piece of short-circuitry that almost didn't. In early October 1914, at Sir Edward Grey's instigation, Churchill was despatched to the Belgian national redoubt to assess the army's

* Dardanelles Commission, First Report, 1917 (after Kitchener's death at sea, in 1916).
† Major-General Sir C. E. Callwell, *Experiences of a Dug-Out, 1914–1918* (London, 1920).

sticking power. As a result the decision was taken, inter alia, to despatch the 7th Division and the newly formed 2nd Cavalry Division to Antwerp to stiffen the Belgians (rather than to the by now hard-pressed BEF). It is not clear that the CIGS had been informed, let alone given the chance to express his view, for even a CIGS as inexperienced in General Staff matters as Sir Charles Douglas could hardly have thought it unnecessary to tell the DMO:

> The Director of Military Operations did not on this particular occasion hear about the Seventh Division and the cavalry being diverted to the Belgian coast until after instructions for the move had been issued and the troops were preparing to proceed to the port of embarkation . . . Sometime later after I had learnt what was going forward – it was next day, I think – the idea occurred to me to find out what steps had been, or were being, taken to provide the necessary organization for a base and line of communications for this force which was about to be projected suddenly across the narrow seas. Enquiries elicited the startling information that nothing whatever had been done in the matter; some of those most concerned in such questions in Whitehall had not even heard that the force was preparing to start. The problem, such as it was, was promptly solved as soon as it was grappled with. The Directors dealing with such subjects met in my room, and in a few minutes the requisite staff had been selected, arrangements had been decided upon, and orders had been despatched – it was as easy as falling downstairs once machinery had been set in motion.*

But perhaps Douglas, who a fortnight later would be dead, was already failing. What then possessed Kitchener to choose as his successor General Sir James Wolfe Murray, a man whose curriculum vitae was no more fitted for the appointment than the unfortunate Douglas's? It is difficult to say – except that Wolfe Murray had been QMG in India when 'K' had been commander-in-chief. He would therefore be a capable and compliant administrator who would run the army while he, 'K', decided everything for himself. That was

* Callwell, *Experiences of a Dug-Out.*

Kaiser Wilhelm and (*behind*) Count Helmuth von Moltke, chief of the *Grosser Generalstab*. The Kaiser had willed an aggressive plan to fight France and Russia simultaneously, Schlieffen had invented it, and Moltke would put it into practice – badly.

Tsar Nicholas (*left*) and his commander-in-chief, his cousin the Grand Duke Nicholas. Neither man was a master of strategy, but at least the Grand Duke was not a bad judge of men, and retained something of the common touch. When the Tsar dismissed him in September 1915 and took personal command of his armies, the Revolution was all but assured.

The French commander-in-chief, Joseph Joffre (*centre*), with Noël de Castelnau (*left*) and Paul Pau, the two army commanders whose immediate offensive in Alsace-Lorraine in August 1914 was meant to be the decisive move of 'Plan XVII'. Unfortunately the offensive took no account of where the actual German main effort turned out to be – through Belgium.

A step ahead of the military? The chancellor, David Lloyd George (*left*), soon to be minister for munitions, then war minister and ultimately prime minister, and the first lord of the Admiralty, Winston Churchill, in early 1915. Both were opposed to offensives on the Western Front, favouring instead a traditionally British maritime and indirect strategy.

Henry Wilson, from 1910 to 1914 the War Office's director of military operations, responsible for the plans to despatch the British Expeditionary Force to France. Though he was uniquely mistrusted by both politicians and fellow soldiers, and a failure as a corps commander, in February 1918 Lloyd George would appoint him chief of the imperial general staff.

Field Marshal Lord Kitchener, secretary of state for war (Asquith's 'perilous experiment'), leaving the War Office in 1916 not long before his death at sea. Behind him is the CIGS, Sir William Robertson – 'Wully' – who had risen from the ranks. Robertson had done much to hold the BEF together during 1914 and 1915, first as quartermaster-general, and then as chief of staff, but as CIGS saw himself essentially as Haig's man in Whitehall.

German troops bringing a siege gun into action at Liège in August 1914. If the French Plan XVII took too little note of the enemy, the Schlieffen Plan underestimated the physical and logistical problems of marching long distances through Belgium – and the resistance that the Belgian army would offer.

It was only a matter of time, however, before the hopelessly outnumbered Belgian army buckled, the great national redoubt of Antwerp surrendering on 10 October. The Belgian army would remain in the field nevertheless, under the personal command of their splendid young King Albert, holding on to a few square miles of sovereign territory on the coast on the extreme left of the eventual allied line.

Left: Things got off to a bad start for the Germans on the Eastern Front in August 1914 when a Russian spoiling attack sent General von Prittwitz's 8th Army reeling. Moltke replaced Prittwitz with Paul von Hindenburg, who rapidly turned the tables on the Russians at Tannenberg, taking 92,000 prisoners by the end of the month.

Above: The BEF in retreat after Mons. Except for the deliberate stand at Le Cateau on 26 August, the retreat would continue for a week and some 200 miles – to the outskirts of Paris.

Above: 'Notre glorieux soixante-quinzes' – the quick-firing French 75 mm field gun, one of the emblems of *offensive à outrance*.

Above: Field Marshal Sir John French, C-in-C of the BEF, with his personal staff in France, 1914.

Right: Erich von Falkenhayn, who replaced Moltke in September 1914 after the failure to gain rapid victory in France.

Left: Infantry of the BEF resting during the fighting at Ypres, October 1914. Though the BEF was technically all regular, up to 60 per cent of the men in some units had served their time with the colours and, having a reserve liability, were recalled from their civilian occupations.

Right: Franz Conrad von Hötzendorf, the Austrian chief of staff, visiting troops at the front in Galicia, 1914. Conrad allowed himself to be manipulated by Berlin in the run-up to war, and thereafter found himself fighting desperately, with a less than cohesive army, on three fronts (and for a while, until the collapse of Romania, four).

Below: The forgotten ally. After a year of fighting the Austrians unaided, the remnants of the Serbian army would be evacuated from the Adriatic coast by allied ships and taken to the new front in Salonika. King Peter of Serbia, in bullock cart, on the march to the sea through the mountains of Albania before the combined Austro-German–Bulgarian offensive of October 1915.

Left: Austrian trenches in Galicia (now southern Poland), 1914. Although both sides dug trenches on the Eastern Front, these never became the defining feature as on the Western. Because of the huge untrodden spaces of Galicia, Poland and East Prussia, the fighting remained more fluid throughout.

Right: 'Are there not other alternatives than sending our armies to chew barbed wire in Flanders?' asked Churchill. Britain's strength had always lain in her ability to use naval power as an indirect lever. Instead the main effort would be put into the campaign on the Western Front – as here at Ypres in March 1915 by Canadians, who would face one of the first attacks by poison gas.

Above: The men who would try, but fail, to turn the flank of the war in Europe – at Gallipoli: Admiral Robeck (*second from left*); on his right his chief of staff, Roger Keyes; and General Hamilton, with (*on his left*) his chief of staff, Walter Braithwaite.

Above: 'Anzacs': some of the men trying to turn the flank at Gallipoli who found themselves instead in an entrenched stalemate as bad as, if not worse than, on the Western Front.

Right: Seeing for himself: Kitchener with Lieutenant-General Birdwood, commanding the Australian and New Zealand Army Corps – 'Anzac' – in November 1915 before deciding on evacuation.

Below: Troops of the Mesopotamian Expeditionary Force – largely from the army of India – crossing the Tigris in the painfully slow advance from Basra to Baghdad. It was a badly managed campaign, but one that tied down increasing numbers of Ottoman troops nevertheless.

Above: Turkish (Ottoman) prisoners taken just before the MEF's repulse almost within sight of Baghdad in November 1915, the subsequent withdrawal to Kut and the surrender of General Townshend and 12,000 of his men in April the following year.

Right: 'The gardeners of Salonika', Clemenceau called the allied force on the Macedonian front: instead of attacking (the Austrians and Bulgarians), 'all they do is dig'.

Below: 'The white war.' Although the main Italian offensives were on the plain of the Isonzo in the northeast, towards Trieste, much of the border with Austria lay in the Alps, the most physically demanding conditions of any theatre of the war.

Above: German troops attacking at Verdun in February 1916, and French reinforcements arriving along the 'Voie Sacrée' (*right*). Falkenhayn's ploy to 'bleed the French army white' in defence of the fortress-town would cost the German army dearly and lead to his own dismissal.

Right: 'All quiet on the Western Front.' A classic trench scene in the British sector: a sentry keeps watch while others rest, work to strengthen the defences or bring up ammunition and defence stores along communication trenches. In some stretches of the line there were 20 miles of auxiliary trenches for each mile of fire trench.

Left: Haig in his office with his private secretary, Philip Sassoon. Paperwork was not unknown in the duke of Wellington's day, but the sheer size of the BEF – at its peak some two million – made the position of C-in-C increasingly that of a board chairman or chief executive.

the old C-in-C way. It had worked for Wellington; 'it beat the French', as the duke was wont to say in later life when any change was proposed.

If this was indeed the reason for Wolfe Murray's appointment then 'K' got what he wanted; so supine in councils of war did the new CIGS prove that Churchill dubbed him 'Sheep Murray'. Critically, he would be head of the General Staff during the planning for the Dardanelles and Gallipoli, the campaign that did so much to weaken Kitchener's standing with the war cabinet. With its failure, Wolfe Murray would be replaced by his deputy, Lieutenant-General Sir Archibald Murray – formerly the BEF's chief of staff until 'kicked upstairs' in January 1915 by Sir John French, who could no longer bear his repeated physical and nervous collapses.

The penny – that without a first-rate CIGS there would be third-rate staffwork – was taking an extraordinarily long time to drop.

As for the Antwerp episode, it reflected a lack not just of internal staffwork but of discussion between the War Office and GHQ (or indeed the *Ministère de la guerre*). The BEF were steadily (though as yet they did not know it) making for Ypres in the 'race for the sea'. The situation of the Belgian army, the bulk of which had withdrawn into the fortified city at the mouth of the Scheldt, looked grim. With the prime minister in Wales, in the early hours of 3 October, Grey and Kitchener had asked Churchill to go and assess the Belgians' holding power. 'I don't know how fluent he [Churchill] is in French,' wrote Asquith to his confidante Venetia Stanley when he got back to London, 'but if he was able to do himself justice in a foreign tongue, the Belgians will be listening to a discourse the like of which they have never heard before. I cannot but think that he will stiffen them up to the sticking point.'*

He did indeed stiffen them up. The Belgian prime minister agreed to continue the defence of Antwerp if the remainder of the army's withdrawal routes into the fortress could be protected by allied troops. Churchill promised British reinforcements and telegraphed

* *Asquith: Letters to Venetia Stanley.*

London that the two naval brigades formed from surplus sailors for home defence should be sent at once, along with the Royal Marine Brigade from Dunkirk (all of which would be agreed). Then came a Churchillian rush of martial blood: 'If it is thought by HM government that I can be of service here, I am willing to resign my office and undertake command of relieving and defensive forces assigned to Antwerp in conjunction with Belgian army, provided that I am given necessary military rank and authority and full powers of a commander of a detached force in the field.'

This proposal was received in cabinet with much laughter. But Kitchener didn't laugh. Indeed he said he was willing to give Churchill the rank of lieutenant-general. Common sense prevailed, however: there were others who could be sent to Antwerp, but few who could be sent to the Admiralty. Lieutenant-General Sir Henry Rawlinson was despatched to take command instead, but he would not arrive for forty-eight hours, so during that time Churchill simply conducted himself as if he were indeed a lieutenant-general.

The line between *politikos* and *strategos* was becoming very blurred – just as in ancient Greece. And the experience of a few days' de facto generalcy cannot but have made a profound impression on Churchill, again bearing its full fruit in 1940.

But did it make sense for the Belgian army to withdraw into Antwerp? Temporarily, perhaps; the defences would afford them some respite. The Germans would soon be able to invest the city, however, and as it was flanked by sovereign Dutch territory, with, behind it, the Scheldt closed by international treaty to all but merchant ships, there was no chance of either escape or resupply. 'The commander of a retiring army who throws himself into a fortress acts like one who, when the ship is foundering, lays hold of the anchor,' wrote Sir Edward Hamley in his influential *The Operations of War* (1867). No one in the War Office appears to have read, or remembered, this in the desire to keep the Belgians from giving up the fight, nor does GHQ appear to have grasped what was the most valuable role the Belgian field army could yet play – covering the gap between Ypres and the coast, a gap which, if forced, would mean the capture of the Channel ports. The object was still to find the German flank and turn it.

Liaison in such a matter between GHQ and the War Office, and thence the council of war, the supreme if still ad hoc policy-making body, was the business of the DMO, who was quite evidently in the dark (as indeed was Sir John French). Little wonder there was, to put it mildly, a lack of clarity. Fortunately, Albert, king of the Belgians, in personal command of the field army, possessed a cool head. Despite the arrival of the Royal Naval Division, on 8 October he quit the city (legend has it that he fired the last, parting, shot with his pistol), to lead the army west and south along the coast until they could take up a line of defence on the River Yser.*

A week later the BEF crossed into Belgium for the second time, to Ypres, 70 miles north-west of Mons, to attack east along the Menin Road. As they did so, the duke (Albrecht) of Württemberg's 4th Army, which had been brought by rail from the upper Aisne and reinforced by fresh troops from Germany and Antwerp after its surrender, attacked the Belgians on the Yser. They were stopped only when the king ordered the sea-locks at Nieuport to be opened, flooding the surrounding country. The Belgians had again saved the day (their stand at Liège had bought the BEF at least forty-eight hours to assemble in good order at Maubeuge), but it was no thanks to coherent thinking in London, or at GHQ and *GQG* in France. George Bernard Shaw's wit was ever at others' expense, but his famous quip in *The Devil's Disciple* (1897), a play set in the only war the British army had lost – the American Revolution – seems perfectly to sum up 1914: 'The British soldier can stand up to anything except the British War Office.'

Yet things could have been worse. Though the CIGS was ailing, and his able deputy (the director of military training), Major-General

* Some of the marines and sailors of the Naval Division were able to escape only by crossing into Dutch territory south of the Scheldt, whereupon they were interned. The 'neutrality' of the Scheldt itself was never, in the end, put to the test, since the only British vessel to enter Antwerp was a hospital ship to evacuate the wounded, which was allowed passage specifically after Dutch permission was sought.

'Wully' Robertson, had been sent to France as the BEF's QMG, the second military member of the Army Council was a safe pair of hands. This was Lieutenant-General Sir Henry Sclater, who as AG was responsible for recruiting, recruit training, discipline and all the requirements of a soldier as an individual ('personal services'). He had only recently come into the post, and most of his staff had gone to France; but he too had worked with Kitchener before, and was evidently unperturbed by the whirlwind created by the war minister's throwing open the doors of the recruiting offices and pointing his finger at the public. The man of the match, so to speak, was however Lieutenant-General Sir John Cowans, the army's QMG, responsible for feeding, clothing, moving and quartering the troops – *logistics*, a phenomenal task in an army expanding with an impetus of its own. Though Cowans' department too had lost staff to the BEF and lines of communication, Sir Charles Harris, assistant financial secretary at the War Office, would write:

> I do not think I ever saw him really rattled . . . When Kitchener came to the War Office in August 1914, and began to give everybody impossible orders about everybody else's business, Cowans (who had the advantage of having served under him in India) said to me, 'That's his way; we must give him what he wants if we possibly can, but don't take any notice if he gives wrong orders about the things he doesn't understand.'*

Asquith called him 'the best quartermaster since Moses'. He had been appointed in 1912, and would remain in post until the end of hostilities, the only member of the army hierarchy to begin and end the war in the same appointment. Significantly perhaps, in John Singer Sargent's triumphal group portrait *Some General Officers of the Great War* (1922), commissioned by the South African diamond-mining magnate Sir Abe Bailey and presented to the nation,

* Cited in Major Desmond Rutter and Major Owen Chapman-Huston, *General Sir John Cowans GCB, GCMG: The Quartermaster-General of the Great War* (London, 1924).

Cowans stands in the absolute centre, behind the senior 'players' of the Western Front, as if to underline his essential role in their support; the only purely 'London' staff officer to be so honoured.

The effect of 'Closed for the duration' lasted for longer than the time it took to find replacements, and it was twofold. First, it allowed Kitchener to establish at once his perverse working practice ('Thus, in a few days, was the higher organization of the British Army destroyed,' wrote Ian Hamilton*); and secondly, it allowed GHQ – the men running the BEF – to assume a larger role in the direction of the war than was healthy, quite simply because virtually the entire thinking capacity of the British army – its experience, knowledge, reputation and authority – had gone with it to France. The destruction of the army's higher organization and the rustication, alienation even, of its analytical capacity created a perverse rather than a virtuous circle. It was cumulative, and it carried on revolving to the very end.

Curiously, Sir Ian Hamilton, who in *The Soul and Body of an Army* expounded with such pungency on the chaos in the War Office, was so keen to acknowledge Kitchener's stature as a great man that he suggested: 'A smaller S. of S. for War would at once have recalled Sir Douglas Haig from France to the War Office to help him. K. would not do that.'

Yet that is precisely what the War Office – the war effort – needed: a man who knew the General Staff system thoroughly and had the stature to stand up to 'the Chief'. Haig would have served the secretary of state, the army and the nation immeasurably better than by commanding I Corps, and later the BEF.

Hamilton was, of course, keen to extol Kitchener's strategic wisdom in perceiving at once, on the very first day, the war's true nature and what the only response could be: national mobilization (if at first on a voluntary system). He had said at the time of the Agadir Crisis (1911) that victory in a continental conflict would come only with the 'last million' men that Britain could throw

* Hamilton, *The Soul and Body of an Army*.

into the scale, and, as his first biographer wrote, 'On August 6, 1914, the day he entered the War Office, Kitchener made up his mind that England could and should put 70 divisions of Infantry into the field.' Even more remarkably, in January 1916 'he was able to say that 67 were afoot and 3 were in the making'.*

Although he thought that conscription would come, he believed that in August 1914 the time was not propitious and compulsion was not necessary. Even as late as July 1915, when the National Registration Act was passed as a means of compiling an inventory of national resources, a necessary preliminary to introducing national service, he believed conscription would be – his word – 'harmful'. The voluntary system had in under a year produced two million recruits, and was still producing twenty thousand a week. This much another man might have been able to calculate, though few had been the voices calling for it in 1914 (one notable exception was Haig); what was singular was Kitchener's vision as to how these divisions were to be formed. Callwell wrote:

> I do not believe there was one single military authority of any standing within the War Office, except himself, who would not have preferred that the cream of the personnel, men who had served in the regulars [but who no longer had a reserve liability], who flocked into the ranks in response to his trumpet call to the nation, should have been devoted in the first instance to filling the yawning gaps that existed in the Territorial Forces, and to providing those forces with trained reservists to fill war wastage. Such a disposition of this very valuable material seemed preferable to absorbing it at the outset in brand-new formations, which in any case would be unable to take the field for many months to come.

This determination certainly antagonized many in the War

* K's calculation and preference were for 100 divisions, comparable with what the French were fielding, but he recognized the concomitant calls on manpower for the Royal Navy, and for the expansion of the armaments and munitions industries in particular.

Office, but as Callwell conceded, 'we were thinking of the early future; he [Kitchener], as was his wont, was looking far ahead'.

On one point, as Callwell noted, there was apparently universal agreement: 'None of us in Whitehall . . . wished the New Armies to be set up under the auspices of the Territorial Associations; that was a different matter altogether.' They were instead to be enlisted 'for the duration' and trained by the regular army. No matter that the regular army hadn't the resources to lead and train more than the first hundred thousand adequately; needs must. But in its opposition to diverting some of its officers and NCOs to train and command the new units, the BEF, in effect the regular army, revealed, said Callwell, a 'lack of sense of proportion'. At the council of war of 5 August (prior to which, at a preliminary meeting in the War Office that morning, Henry Wilson had insisted there could not be a long war because no nation had the resources to sustain it) there was a deal of wrangling, Sir John French finally conceding three officers per battalion for the task – hardly the core of an army of any substance. In fairness, the council of war had concluded that only four divisions (and the cavalry division) could be spared, rather than the six that had been presumed, so he was being asked to weaken an already weakened force. This was extemporizing verging on – becoming, even – recklessness.

There was, however, one promising part of the machinery (perhaps significantly, outside the War Office) that, although under-horsed, was still working well – the CID. As the only body left with any practised capability of thinking, it began producing papers on the strategic aspects of the war that had hitherto either been taken for granted or simply not considered. And no paper was more significant than that of 28 December 1914: 'The Apparent Deadlock on the Western Front and Possible Redeployment of Forces'.*

* PRO CAB 37/122/194.

PART TWO

1915:
Deadlock

Those who had come to manhood under the discipline of the old tradition had suddenly to face the demands of a new age. Indeed, the war was as much an awakening to these demands as it was a military event. And one of the clearest demands after that 'monstrous August' was that the war must correspond with the essential character of civilization which was becoming increasingly industrialized.

Sir Herbert Read MC, Green Howards 1914–19,
in *Promise of Greatness* (London, 1968)

Chapter Five

THE PROBLEM OF THE WESTERN FRONT

In November 1914, in place of his ad hoc councils of war, Asquith formed the 'war council', a slimmed-down cabinet attended by 1SL and the CIGS, to consider the general conduct of the war – in other words, strategy. It was advised and assisted by the permanent secretariat of the CID, which kept detailed minutes and issued memoranda; and because the council met infrequently the CID – especially its secretary, Lieutenant-Colonel Maurice Hankey – gained steadily in influence by the sheer flow of papers from its various sub-committees and from Hankey's own commanding pen. In particular his appreciation of the situation in France and Flanders – 'apparent deadlock' – and of where the alternative application of 'the great forces of which we shall be able to dispose in a few months' time' might pay greater dividends, spoke powerfully to the various concerns of the individual members of the council, though it was received with far less enthusiasm at GHQ, with its suggestion that France was not the right place for Britain to make its main effort.

Hankey and the CID identified the coming fork in the road of British strategy, one to which the nation had come in the past – in the Revolutionary and Napoleonic Wars, and in the dynastic wars of the eighteenth century. The destination, the end, was clear enough: the ejection of the German army from France and Flanders. But down one road the fingerpost pointed to the nation's traditional strengths – its island status and command of the oceans – while down the other was something not seen since the days of Marlborough, a great continental commitment. Was it to be Kitchener's 'last million men' across the Channel, or was it to be the course that both Pitts had preferred, 'blue water', economic, militarily tangential – Britain the 'Great Amphibian'? Or might there be some combination of both that did not lead to loss of direction?

Hankey's paper began with a hard-headed look at fighting conditions on the Western Front:

> The experience of the offensive movements of the allies in this theatre within the last few weeks seems to indicate that any advance must be both costly and slow. Days are required to capture a single line of trenches, the losses are very heavy, and as often as not the enemy recaptures his lost ground on the following day, or is able to render the captured ground untenable. When viewed on a map the total gains (except possibly in Alsace-Lorraine) are almost negligible, and apparently incommensurate with the effort and loss of life. Moreover, the advance is so slow that the enemy has time to prepare fresh lines of defence in rear of his many existing lines to compensate for the trenches lost. The defensive power of modern weapons is so great that these attacks do not draw into the front trenches any large proportion of the enemy's armies, so that they do not seriously affect the *moral* of the mass of his forces, which are at any given moment outside the fighting line.

He therefore drew the inescapable conclusion that there was 'no reason to suppose that the enemy's successive positions can be captured merely by weight of numbers', citing as further evidence the deadly experience of the Germans in trying to break through 'thinly held, hastily constructed, and incomplete positions occupied by the widely extended British army after our advance to Armentières and Ypres'.

WESTERN FRONT
Approximate line at end of 1914
Line at end of Hindenburg Retreat, Feb. 1917
Line on 11 Nov. 1918
0 miles 100
0 kilometres 100
ENGLAND
Dover
Folkestone
English Channel
Ostend
Zeebrugge
Dunkirk
Calais
Boulogne
St Omer
Ypres
Passchendaele
Hooge
Gheluvalt
Menin
Hazebrouck
Lillers
Lille
St Pol
Lens
Douai
Arras
Doullens
Abbeville
Somme
Albert
Amiens
Cambrai
Le Cateau
Maubeuge
Mons
Peronne
Jul 1916
St Quentin
Ham
Montdidier
Guise
Oise
Lassigny
Noyon
La Fère
Beauvais
Compiègne
Laon
Oise
Chantilly
Senlis
Soissons
Apr 1917
Ourcq
Seine
Paris
Chateau Thierry
Riems
Marne
Epernay
Py Morin
Gd Morin
Chalons
ARTOIS
PICARDY
FLANDERS
HOLLAND
Waal
Maas
Antwerp
Ghent
Scheldt
Dyle
BELGIUM
Brussels
Gette
Charleroi
Namur
Meuse
Huy
Liège
Aix la Chapelle
Sambre
Givet
ARDENNES
Mézières
Sedan
Neufchâteau
GERMANY
Virton
Trier
Luxembourg
Longuyon
Saarburg
CHAMPAGNE
Aisne
Feb 1916
Verdun
Briey
Thionville
Saar
Moselle
LORRAINE
Metz
St Mihiel
Ornain
Bar le Duc
Morhange
FRANCE
Meuse
Marne
Nancy
Toul
Moselle
Meurthe
Charmes
Epinal
VOSGES
N
Yser
Jul 1917
Jun 1917
Lys
Messines
Bailicul
Armentières
Scheldt
Mar 1915
Aubers
Neuve Chapelle
Bethune
La Bassée
Sep 1915
Loos
Vimy Ridge
Valenciennes
Escaut
Apr 1917
Bapaume
Nov 1917
Somme
0 miles 20
0 kilometres 30

Indeed, if the deadlock on the British side were complete, it must be no less complete for the Germans. And on this latter point, *GQG*'s assessment concurred: there was now no possibility of a German breakthrough unless very significantly reinforced.

Hankey then pointed out that such deadlocks were not unprecedented, and that 'two methods have usually been employed for circumventing an *impasse* of the kind. Either a special material has been provided for overcoming it, or an attack has been delivered elsewhere, which has compelled the enemy so to weaken his forces that an advance becomes possible.'

In listing the variations of 'special material' that 'modern science' might provide he previewed – albeit in shadowy outline – what would become the tank:

> Numbers of large heavy rollers, themselves bullet proof, propelled from behind by motor engines, geared very low, the driving wheels fitted with 'caterpillar' driving gear to grip the ground, the driver's seat armoured, and with a Maxim gun fitted. The object of this device would be to roll down the barbed wire by sheer weight, to give some cover to men creeping up behind, and to support the advance with machine gun fire.

It would receive no acclamation at GHQ, however, which was still thinking of a breakthrough in the spring of 1915 – far too soon for such a device to be available. And so it would be left to Churchill to develop the idea. In February he formed the Admiralty Landships Committee.*

Hankey then turned to the area in which British seapower had in

* When the news of the first use of tanks (in September 1916) emerged, Lloyd George commented: 'Well, we must not expect too much from them but so far they have done very well, and don't you think that they reflect some credit on those responsible for them? It is really to Mr Winston Churchill that the credit is due more than to anyone else. He took up with enthusiasm the idea of making them a long time ago, and he met with many difficulties. He converted me, and at the Ministry of Munitions he went ahead and made them.' Statement to the press, quoted in *Daily Sketch*, 19 September 1916.

the past served so well: economic warfare – blockade – 'the greatest asset we have in the war'. The close blockade had been established at a stroke when the Grand Fleet had sailed for Orkney at the end of July, and the distant blockade had followed not long after when the Royal Navy had swept the oceans clear of the *Kaiserliche Marine*'s cruisers. However, German trade with Holland and Denmark was offsetting their effects, 'and at the best', Hankey acknowledged, '[economic pressure] is a weapon slow in operation', although 'in the meantime there is every reason for using our sea power and our growing military strength to attack Germany and her allies in other quarters'. German colonies in Africa would, he argued, make strong bargaining counters when it came to peace (it is interesting that such a peace was still contemplated at this stage, rather than the unconditional surrender that would in effect be embodied in the Armistice of 1918). But then Hankey addressed the more speculative question of strategic diversion, that is, forcing the enemy to withdraw troops from one theatre to reinforce another that was under threat. And here he spoke to the flaw in pre-war assumptions about Russian military potential: 'Up to the present time the great Russian diversion has not proved sufficiently powerful to cause the enemy to denude his forces on the western frontier to a dangerous extent.' It had always been a tenet of French strategic thinking that the Russian bear, albeit slow to gather its strength, would eventually bring overwhelming weight to the fight, and that all France needed to do was to stay in that fight and tie down as many German troops as possible so that the bear could establish its full power as quickly as possible – in months rather than years. Hankey was sceptical.

> Recent events give no ground to suppose that the eastern diversion will be sufficiently powerful in the near future to enable the allies to crush the German armies opposed to them in the western theatre of war. The Servian diversion, though extraordinarily powerful in weakening the Austrians, is probably too small to be in any way decisive unless supported from elsewhere.

He dismissed the other possibility – Schleswig-Holstein – because it was accessible only through neutral Holland or Denmark, and therefore clearly not an option (though it might have been had events in Belgium developed as Churchill had wished).*

One of the reasons the bear was proving slow in approaching full strength was shortage of arms and munitions, exacerbated by the much higher than expected rates of expenditure, and within days of the Hankey memorandum, the Tsar, now with a third enemy on his borders – the Ottoman Turks mounting an offensive in the Caucasus – was calling for a diversionary effort to be made against Constantinople. The call for help dovetailed nicely with Hankey's strategic analysis, for not only was this an area in which British sea power might be used to effect, there was the possibility of forging a Balkan alliance that would be a serious threat to both Constantinople and Vienna. Bulgaria and Romania were neutrals still, as was Greece (her government pro-allies, her king pro-German), with much to gain territorially; but, left to themselves, their mutual distrust heightened by the recent Balkan wars, they would be 'unable to realize their overwhelming opportunity'. Therefore, he argued, if 'Britain, France and Russia, instead of merely inciting these races to attack Turkey and Austria, were themselves to participate actively in the campaign', Bulgaria in particular (whose independence from the Ottomans the Russians had in large part won for them) would be reassured: 'It is presumed that in a few months' time we could, without endangering the position in France, devote three army corps, including one original first line army corps, to a campaign in Turkey . . . This force, in conjunction with Greece and Bulgaria, ought to be sufficient to capture Constantinople.'

* Hankey makes no mention of Italy, and although Italy would declare war on Austria in May there was clearly little potential seen in developing operations from the Adriatic, though the logistical problems in supporting an offensive towards Trieste, for example, would have been far fewer than those encountered in the Eastern Mediterranean. As yet the Macedonian Front was not even considered as a theoretical possibility.

Hankey concluded his strategic *tour d'horizon* by suggesting that if Russia were to hold the Germans along an entrenched line – as the western allies would do in France and Flanders – and 'simultaneously combine with Servia and Romania in an advance into Hungary, the complete downfall of Austria-Hungary could simultaneously be secured'.

Here, then, was a complete strategy for fighting (and perhaps even winning) the war indirectly while developing the technical means of victory on the Western Front in case the indirect levers failed to eject the million German troops from France and Belgium. Implicitly it took a longer view of the war than that which had hitherto prevailed, for not only was economic pressure 'a weapon slow in operation', the defeat of the Germans' allies *first* – a process which would crudely and unhelpfully become known as 'knocking away the props' – appeared to GHQ and its supporters as merely postponing the inevitable fight against the Germans in France, the only means by which they could be made to quit the ground.

Churchill himself had for some time been thinking along these indirect lines, and at the end of December, in a prose typically more vivid than Hankey's restrained professionalism, wrote to Asquith:

> I think it is quite possible that neither side will have the strength to penetrate the other's line in the Western theatre . . . My impression is that the position of both armies is not likely to undergo any decisive change – although no doubt several hundred thousand men will be spent to satisfy the military mind on the point . . . On the assumption that these views are correct, the question arises, how ought we to apply our growing military power. Are there not other alternatives than sending our armies to chew barbed wire in Flanders?*

As for the 'growing military power' to which Churchill confidently referred, in the short term this meant those few regular troops still in overseas garrisons, together with territorials volunteering for

* Quoted in Martin Gilbert (ed.), *Winston Churchill: Companion Volume III* (Boston, 1973).

overseas service and 'colonial' troops, principally Indian, Canadian and Australian (the 1st Canadian Division, assembling in England, would cross to France in early February). In the longer term, the additional strength would lie in Kitchener's 'New Armies', formed in successive tranches of a hundred thousand, known unofficially as K1, K2 etc., each to mirror the original BEF. K1 would not be ready to take to the field for at least six months, however, and K2 and K3 not for a year, given the absence of both the equipment and the instructors to train them any more quickly. Kitchener certainly liked the Dardanelles idea, and thought a hundred thousand men, with the navy, would do the job. Unfortunately he had no troops to offer, for he would not risk weakening the BEF.

Lloyd George, who Asquith's 'Liberal imperialists' had once feared might be a dove but who had thrown himself into the war with some passion – even managing to rally Nonconformist Wales to the cause – was as suspicious as Churchill of the collective military mind, and had also been thinking 'indirectly', if for a different reason. The New Armies would, he argued, be

> a force of a totally different character from any which has hitherto left these shores . . . drawn almost exclusively from the better class of artisan, the upper and the lower middle classes. In intelligence, education and character it is vastly superior to any army ever raised in this country, and it has been drawn not from the ranks of those who have generally cut themselves off from home . . . So that if this superb army is thrown away upon futile enterprises, such as those we have witnessed during the last few weeks, the country will be uncontrollably indignant at the lack of provision and intelligence shown in our plans.*

His fear that they *would* be thrown away would prove only too well founded. Yet it is remarkable that neither the country nor indeed the army (uniquely among the belligerents) ever did become 'uncontrollably indignant'. It had great cause to be.

* *War Memoirs*, new edn.

There were, however, two problems with Hankey's appreciation, one acknowledged, the other not. First was the French. Hankey had made an assumption that they would, at least in part, share his analysis: 'If, therefore, the new armies are thrown into France, all that can be done is extend our lines and set free more French troops for an attack in some more promising quarter. But is it certain that a more promising quarter exists, or that the French want more troops?'

The answer to whether a more promising quarter existed was, in truth, 'no', but the French *believed* there was – and therefore they most certainly did want more troops. For what Hankey – or for that matter anyone else, it seems – had not yet appreciated was that the French were still viscerally committed to the doctrine of *offensive à outrance*. To *GQG* a 'promising quarter' meant simply anywhere there were Germans: 'For the attack, only two things are necessary; to know where the enemy is and to decide what to do. What the enemy intends to do is of no consequence.'*

Deciding what to do – tactics – had also been simplified. The object and method of all attacks, said the *Règlement*, was 'to charge the enemy with the bayonet in order to destroy him'. In fairness, the French were not alone in their view of the miraculous properties of *la baïonnette*, although the British army's famous 'bull ring' at the base depot at Étaples was as much to do with inculcating offensive spirit in men joining or rejoining their units as with true doctrine. In fact the sentiment remained in its manuals until 1924, if in less fundamentalist terms than the French doctrine, which actually required the infantryman to unload his rifle before the attack, thereby forcing him to rely on the steel that topped it.

This simplification of operational and tactical doctrine, coupled with the fervent desire to recover without delay territory over-run by the Germans – whether out of patriotism (women had jeered

* The words are those of Colonel Louis de Grandmaison, author of the *Règlement* of 1913, which began: 'The French army, returning to its traditions, henceforth admits no law but the offensive.'

French troops during their August retreat) or practicality (40 per cent of France's coal deposits and 90 per cent of her iron ore now lay in German hands) – made for strategic impatience at *GQG*, narrowing the compass of thought and dominating war policy.

Although Clausewitz was German, no army had embraced 'the apostle of violence' quite so completely as the French in this regard, perhaps even without their realizing it. Grandmaison had written of 'the French army, *returning to its traditions*': they merely followed the precepts of Napoleon, did they not – whom Clausewitz had of course studied. And Napoleon had said that there were only two forces in the world, the sword and the spirit, and 'in the long run the sword will always be conquered by the spirit'.

Foch, in overall control of the western group of armies, had declared that 'the fate of Europe has always been decided in Belgium', and so it must be that a strong attack would decide matters now: 'I remain faithful to pure theory – that which asserts that the destruction of the enemy's military force will settle everything.' He himself was there; therefore it must be the point of decision.

But this certainty ignored one inconvenient truth: the allies did not possess the technical means to destroy the enemy's military force. All they could do was what the textbooks told them: concentrate superior force, which the French saw as the maximum number of *baïonnettes* and artillery pieces, at the decisive point. This in turn disregarded another inconvenient truth, the corollary – that concentrating force meant bringing it away from other parts of the line, which in turn allowed the Germans to bring away theirs to meet the attack without prejudice to the security of the line as a whole. And since the Germans would always have notice of the French (and later allied) intentions – because it was next to impossible to concentrate so many troops unseen, and the intensity of preparatory fire would also signal the time and place of the attack – they could react in a perfectly timely fashion.

The creed of the apostle Foch and those of his school, 'faithful to pure theory', was the same as that of which Kesselring would complain in the pre-1914 German staff college – the unwillingness to let practicalities hamper 'the tactician and strategist in the free flight of his ideas'.

The second problem with Hankey's appreciation was the viewpoint of GHQ. It too was afflicted by strong convictions. The BEF was also led by generals of prominence and ambition believing that here therefore must be the point of decision. On 1 January, Kitchener, having told the cabinet that the Germans were transferring troops to the Eastern Front and that there was 'nothing in front of them [the BEF] but men and boys', wrote to Sir John French:

> I suppose we must now recognize that the French Army cannot make a sufficient break through the German lines of defence . . . [to] bring about the retreat of German forces from Northern France. If that is so, then the German lines in France may be looked upon as a fortress that cannot be carried by assault, and also cannot be completely invested – with the result that the lines can only be held by an investing force, while operations proceed elsewhere . . . The feeling here is gaining ground that, although it is essential to defend the line we now hold, troops over and above what is necessary for that service could better be employed elsewhere. The question of *where* anything effective could be accomplished opens a large field, and requires a good deal of study. What are the views of your staff?

Was this question – one of overall strategy – a legitimate one to put to the C-in-C of a deployed force? In part, yes, for a C-in-C works within the overall strategy, and the War Office needed to understand the effect of any redeployment of troops. This, however, should have been a matter for the CIGS and DMO, whose concern the overall strategy was, to determine with Sir John French; in writing direct to French, Kitchener had invited him to debate the larger strategy, which was neither constitutional nor prudent. The bigger picture was always to be seen from London and Paris, not St Omer (GHQ) and Chantilly (*GQG*). But in the absence of military advice he could rely on at the War Office, it is not surprising that 'K' continued to act as if he himself were its professional head and GHQ his staff in the field – which of course gave them unwarranted sway.

And Sir John French was alarmed. He and Joffre estimated that although the Germans had suffered one and a half million casualties on the western and eastern fronts together, they had a further eight hundred thousand men in training. By March or April, he wrote, they would be able to 'wipe out their existing inferiority and even once again make themselves superior to us . . . It seems, therefore, of the utmost importance that we should take the offensive and strike at the earliest possible moment with all our available strength.'*

Besides, he explained, while Joffre did not believe a catastrophic Russian collapse was in prospect, the French C-in-C did think there was a chance of German troops coming back from the Eastern Front, and therefore there was a need to build up reserves to cover Paris. French himself was far less sanguine about the Russians; he thought their collapse a distinct possibility, in which case every available man would be needed in France to preserve the necessary 'margin of safety' for defence of the Channel ports. Of the alternative theatres, he rejected a descent on Gallipoli as being likely to draw off only two or three Ottoman corps from the Caucasus – 'a result wholly incommensurate with the effort involved'. Indeed, he believed that an attack towards Constantinople would simply serve the German strategy of trying to divert allied troops from the decisive point – France. If there *were* to be an allied diversionary effort, he thought the best prospects would be with Serbia through Salonika.

It is tempting to think of this as a show of willingness to undertake an operation confident in the belief that it would be judged too difficult – a not unheard-of tactic, even today.

In any case, the C-in-C rejected the premise that the German lines could not be pierced. The thing was feasible enough, he argued,

* Memorandum by Sir John French, 3 January 1915, PRO CAB 37/123/9.

with an adequate supply of guns and HE shells. And he had in view a very 'promising quarter', one which offered distinct operational advantages and exploited the navy's command of the Channel – a joint (land–sea) operation to recapture Ostend and Zeebrugge. For this he would need a reinforcement of some fifty-five TF or New Army battalions plus copious artillery, especially heavy guns, in addition to the already promised Canadian Division and the last two regular divisions, the 28th and 29th. He had discussed the scheme with Churchill as early as November, and the first lord had been keen, for it would remove the enemy from the immediate flank of the cross-channel sea lanes, and his warships could provide 'absolutely devastating support' during the operation (Churchill was not alone in thinking the effect of naval bombardment would be far greater than it would prove*).

Such an operation would, of course, preclude the diversion of troops elsewhere, especially to the Dardanelles.

'K' was much taken with Sir John French's proposal, writing at once to the British ambassador in Paris, Sir Francis Bertie, urging him to press Joffre and the French government to switch the BEF to the extreme left flank, with control of Dunkirk, in preparation (though with GHQ he reserved his position until the details had been worked out). The French reaction was not enthusiastic. Joffre was now concerned that the Germans would next mount an offensive south of the Somme towards Amiens, thence threatening Paris; not only would an operation on the sea flank be difficult in itself, in diverting troops to the north it would be perilous for the Western Front as a whole.

The war council, the first lord especially, were also initially attracted by Sir John's scheme and the prospect it offered of clearing the submarine nests from the Belgian dunes – but December's

* The problem lay in the trajectory of the guns – they were not howitzers, capable of high-angle fire and therefore greater crest clearance, sending shells plunging to the target with greater chance of striking it, or coming very close – and the inexperience of the crews with HE rather than armour-piercing ammunition, as they would discover in the Gallipoli landings.

infantry losses, on both sides, had demonstrated all too clearly the price and outcome of frontal attacks. After receiving France's response, Kitchener told the war council on 7 January that: 'An advance could only be made by means of developing a tremendous volume of artillery fire, and the ammunition for this is simply not available.' Two days later the war council vetoed the plan.

Kitchener wrote a lengthy explanation to Sir John French assuring him that he would still send the reinforcements already agreed to, including the 28th Division, though he needed to consult further on the best way to make use of the New Army battalions; the war council had

> [come] to the conclusion that, certainly for the present, the main theatre of operations for British forces should be alongside the French army, and that this should continue as long as France was liable to successful invasion and required armed support . . . [and] that should the offensive operations subsequently drive the Germans out of France and back into Germany, British troops should assist in such operations.*

However, he stressed the concern that the Western Front might have developed into a deadlock (it could be argued that this had been recognized at ground level in the 'Christmas truce'), and that the council therefore sought 'some other theatre where such obstructions to advance would be less pronounced, and from where operations against the enemy might lead to more decisive results'.

This truly alarmed Sir John French, who at once sent his chief of staff (at this time, but only for a fortnight more, Archie Murray), and sub-chief, Henry Wilson, to London to whip up support for his approach.

Two men less likely to receive a favourable reception at that moment it is difficult to imagine – Wilson, the arch-schemer, and Murray, whose dismal performance to date was an open secret. Not surprisingly, on 12 January French himself felt it necessary to come

* Arthur, *Life of Lord Kitchener*, vol. III.

to London to press his case with the war council. He was confident, he told them: he was stockpiling ammunition and he expected 'only' between seven and eight thousand casualties. The Germans were running out of copper for the driving bands of their shells, he said (this intelligence had not come from the Secret Service Bureau; and surprisingly, GHQ had not yet learned that *GQG*'s intelligence was unreliable*). They were also near to exhaustion of reserve manpower. By October or November they would reach the end of their resources.

Therefore, he argued, if the weather improved, Joffre's own planned offensive at Rheims and Arras in the spring had a good chance of breaking through, and his own offensive towards Ostend and Zeebrugge might well clear the coast as far as the Dutch frontier (the enclave south of the Scheldt estuary). In the final analysis, however (and quite contrary to his earlier argument that their eastern ally was about to collapse), he did not think that a decision could be reached on the Western Front: he 'relied on the Russians to finish the business'.†

French's confidence impressed the war council enough for Kitchener to speak in his favour; but it also strengthened the argument for doing all that could be done to support the Russians – by forcing a way through the Dardanelles to the Black Sea, a campaign of which Churchill now spoke persuasively. The admiral in the

* The foreign section of the new Secret Service Bureau (later the Secret Intelligence Service, SIS) had been established in 1909 on the recommendation of the CID, but inevitably establishing its organization, procedures and focus took time, especially as funding was tight. It was only when the war landscape settled into the familiar pattern of the Western Front that the section really began to count. Most of the intelligence establishing the German order of battle and dispositions in 1917 and 1918 – of key importance to GHQ in coping with the massive German offensive of spring 1918, and then the counter-offensive preceding the Armistice ('the Hundred Days') – was the work of SIS, whose agents were supplying a stream of information especially through neutral Holland, not least through close observation of train transports (Keith Jeffery, *MI6: The History of the Secret Intelligence Service 1909–1949*, London, 2010; Michael Smith, *SIX: A History of Britain's Secret Intelligence Service*, London, 2010; correspondence with Sir John Scarlett, former director-general of SIS).

† Lord Hankey, *The Supreme Command 1914–18* (London, 1961).

Eastern Mediterranean, Sir Sackville Carden, had been told in November to prepare plans to force the straits, and had indeed done so, proposing a methodical advance reducing the shore batteries as he proceeded. But since then, at the instigation of Churchill and Admiral Lord (Jacky) Fisher, 1SL, a bolder concept had emerged to make use of the surplus of pre-dreadnought warships, expendable because the seas worldwide had been swept clear of German cruisers and the Grand Fleet was confining the *Hochseeflotte*'s dreadnoughts to the North Sea.* The council was persuaded that this new Dardanelles scheme was worth a try – which it most certainly was, for the potential gains were enormous.

It was also persuaded that Sir John French's scheme was worthy. He was therefore promised two territorial divisions by the middle of February, and a decision to approve the offensive or otherwise within a fortnight. Meanwhile the CID was to consider alternative theatres of war for the New Armies in case the Western Front did indeed develop into a deadlock.

Something for everyone, indeed.

And there was the rub: the war council had failed to concentrate the effort, thereby contravening one of the principles of war.† If forcing the Dardanelles was to be truly a strategic *coup de main*, it deserved more than a bold but risky experiment with obsolescent warships. It needed a full-blown joint operation. If the naval bombardment of the shore batteries were not immediately

* On 2 December 1906, with the launching of HMS *Dreadnought*, every battleship afloat was made obsolescent. For one man at least had taken note of the lessons of the Russo-Japanese war. The decisive battle of Tsushima had convinced the new first sea lord, the then Sir Jacky Fisher, that above all what counted was long-range gunnery *as well as* heavy armour. *Dreadnought* – which became the generic name for the new class of capital ships built on this principle – was designed, laid down and built in record time. Every existing battleship was decisively outclassed by her all-big-gun (12-inch) battery and the speed she could develop with her revolutionary steam turbines – 21 knots (24 mph; 39 km/h).

† Curiously, *Field Service Regulations 1909*, the superb two-manual compendium of the British army's doctrine for war, had not specified these principles, perhaps because to do so was considered too doctrinaire and therefore restrictive; but they were well known and generally accepted from the works of Clausewitz and, more recently, Foch.

successful – for whatever reason – there had to be landings in strength, not just a few ships' companies of marines, to do the job, otherwise the scheme would lose momentum, giving the Turks time to reinforce and consolidate.

Unfortunately the CID had neither the capacity nor the authority to produce an appreciation of the forcing of the Dardanelles; if they had, the true extent of the problem might have been identified and a robust campaign plan produced. Instead the proposal was picked over in a thorough but plodding way by Admiral Lord Fisher's inexperienced naval staff until, at the end of January, Fisher himself began to have serious doubts, principally because he feared weakening the Grand Fleet.

There is no credible evidence that, as is sometimes claimed (not least in the Australian official history), Churchill pressed for the naval operation to go ahead in the face of Fisher's professional advice. The record shows only that in the absence of any new information he was keen to hold the members of the war council (of whom Fisher was one) to their decision of 13 January. And his sudden cooling towards the Ostend–Zeebrugge operation after Joffre decried it was merely the view of the naval war staff (or, at least, Fisher – again fearful of taking any ships from the 'fleet in being' at Scapa Flow), though it did give added impetus to his enthusiasm for the Dardanelles gambit. There can be little doubt, however, that his preference had for a month and more been for decisive action somewhere other than the western theatre of operations – 'chewing barbed wire in France'.

'A single, prolonged conference, between the allied chiefs, civil and martial, in January, 1915, might have saved us from inestimable misfortune,' he would later write* – with hindsight, yes, but entirely consistently with what he had argued at the time. It is easy to see whence came his appetite for such conferences in the Second World War.

Churchill's emphasis on a '*prolonged* conference' is significant. In

* *The World Crisis* (London, 1923).

his history of the Irish Guards, written in homage to his son, Jack, killed serving with the 1st Battalion later that year, Rudyard Kipling sums up the perennial problem of tactics *vis-à-vis* strategy – the question of seeing the bigger picture: 'a battalion's field is bounded by its own vision'.* In January 1915 the chief allied military players – on both Eastern and Western Fronts – had just fought a four-month battle of immediate survival. It was not surprising that their field was bounded by their vision – Sir John French's in particular. It takes time to appreciate the whole. Yet in fact the whole was not that difficult to comprehend. 'The essence of the war problem was not changed by its enormous scale,' wrote Churchill in *The World Crisis*:

> The line held by the Central Powers, from the North Sea to the Aegean – and, loosely, even to the Suez Canal – was in principle no different from a line held across a peninsula or isthmus by a small force whose flanks rested on water. As long as France was treated as a self-contained theatre, a complete deadlock existed, and the front of the German invader could neither be pierced nor turned.

This required a fundamental change of vision, for 'once the view was extended to the whole scene of the war, and that vast war conceived as if it were a single battle, and once the sea power of Britain was brought into play, turning movements of a most far-reaching character were open to the allies'.

Commanders whose field was limited by the vision of those four months, and by where they stood that January, would need time to be persuaded of the truth of this. Sir John French thought of the war in terms of holding Ypres (the city he would take as part of his title – Earl of Ypres – on being ennobled later that year) and securing the Channel ports. Joffre thought of recovering French territory. Few were thinking about the grand object in *strategic* terms – the defeat of Germany. 'At the very moment when the French High

* Rudyard Kipling, *The Irish Guards in the Great War* (London, 1923).

Command was complaining that there were no flanks to turn,' Churchill declared,

> the Teutonic Empires were in fact vulnerable in an extreme degree on either flank. Thus the three salient facts of the war situation at the beginning of 1915 were: first, the deadlock in France, the main and central theatre; secondly, the urgent need of relieving that deadlock before Russia was overwhelmed; and thirdly, the possibility of relieving it by great amphibious and political-strategic operations on either flank.

But few allied commanders perceived this, even later, committing themselves instead to driving at the enemy where he was strongest. 'Battles are won by slaughter and manoeuvre,' Churchill asserted. 'The greater the general, the more he contributes in manoeuvre, the less he demands in slaughter.' It was a maxim taught in every military academy in Europe; and yet it would be set aside by the products of those academies, on both sides, and replaced by the abysmal notion of, as Joffre called it, *guerre d'usure* – war by 'wearing down', war of attrition.

'Je les grignote,' he declared: 'I will nibble [at] them'.

'Wully' Robertson would come to the same conclusion. In June 1915 he urged 'slow attrition, by a slow and gradual advance on our part, each step being prepared by a predominant artillery fire and great expenditure of ammunition'. It was better, certainly, than going to it with a mystical belief in the bayonet. But *generalship*?

Maurice, the DMO, added that such attacks were best carried out in places where the Germans were, for political or strategic reasons, reluctant to retreat so were bound to take heavy losses – in other words, *biting* rather than nibbling.* In battering against a brick wall, therefore (a phrase Robertson himself used), it appeared that

* This same logic of forcing an attritional battle by choosing a place that the enemy would feel morally – as opposed to tactically – bound to defend would inspire Falkenhayn to mount his offensive at Verdun the following year (see chapter 11). Poor generalship was by no means confined to the allies.

it was better to go for the thickest part, for in doing so more bricks could be destroyed. The logic was irrefutable, but the premise begged the question whether the bricks could actually *be* destroyed. Hankey would later describe the outcome as 'sheer slogging in its crudest form'.

So the art of generalship was to be reduced to the 'strategy' of attrition, the wearing down of the enemy in bloody offensives that would prove just as costly to the allies as to their opponents – the remorseless process of simply trading lives and taking tally at the end.

This was not generalship; this was military accountancy.

Chapter Six

THE GREAT AMPHIBIAN

By mid-March 1915 the naval operation to force the Dardanelles had stalled. Not because the massive, fortified shore batteries outgunned the allied warships, including the newly launched super-dreadnought *Queen Elizabeth*, the first of a new class armed with 15-inch guns, oil-burning and extra fast – but because of mines and timidity. The minesweepers – for the most part auxiliaries with non-naval crews – were barely up to the task, and their work was harassed by fire from mobile howitzers on both shores, which the covering warships found extraordinarily difficult to locate and destroy.

The war council now sanctioned the operation to take the batteries on the Gallipoli peninsula from landwards, Kitchener accepting that he would just have to conjure the troops from somewhere.

The body of troops formed for this task was the Mediterranean Expeditionary Force (MEF), and the officer appointed to command it was General Sir Ian Hamilton, clever, brave, but diffident and, said many, lacking the essential ruthlessness in dealing with both subordinates and superiors. The force would comprise Britain's sole remaining regular division, the 29th, consisting of battalions brought from the further reaches of empire; the Royal

Naval Division, comprising Royal Marines and surplus naval ratings, who had seen action at Antwerp but were ill-equipped and ill-trained; the Australian and New Zealand Army Corps ('Anzac'), consisting of one Australian and one mixed Australian and New Zealand division, under the command of the outstanding 49-year-old Indian Army Lieutenant-General William Birdwood, currently training in Egypt in the expectation of moving to France; and a weak division of the French Corps Expéditionnaire d'Orient, colonial troops, also largely untried. Hamilton had hoped for the all-regular 28th Division too, but Kitchener had promised it to Sir John French for one more offensive in Flanders. Indeed, even assigning the 29th had proved painful, for Joffre seemed to regard it as a token of Britain's commitment to the Western Front. Fortunately Paris had been persuaded that an effort to do something to bring the Balkans into the allies' camp was necessary, and accepted the logic of the Gallipoli landings, though the French cabinet had lately come to believe that direct aid to Serbia through Salonika would be more effective. And of course there was the clinching issue of opening up new lines of communication with Russia and helping take Turkish pressure off the Caucasus.

Kitchener told Hamilton that in the coming months he could expect 'New Army' divisions – men who had flocked to the recruiting offices in August and September – and perhaps some territorials and Indian Army men; but the 'New Army' units would consist of raw troops, to begin with fit only for defensive tasks and labouring.

Hamilton had little time to prepare for what would be the first amphibious assault in history mounted against on-shore opponents armed with machine guns. Critically, he had little up-to-date intelligence. Nor had much preliminary planning been carried out at the War Office, for the new DMO's staff had not yet found their feet or gained Kitchener's confidence. Hamilton's first problem was that the MEF was scattered around the eastern Mediterranean and its equipment and supplies embarked haphazardly, and he saw no alternative but to delay further by recalling them to Egypt to reorganize and regroup before sailing for the advance base on the Greek island of Lemnos.*

The Turks were by now, not surprisingly, thoroughly on the alert. In January they had had two weak divisions at most on the peninsula; by the end of March, the transfer of troops from the Caucasus had increased the number to four, with another two on the Asiatic shore (this had, at least, served one of the allies' strategic objects, taking pressure off the Russians). The war minister, Enver Pasha, appointed Lieutenant-General Otto Liman von Sanders, head of the German military mission to Constantinople, to command them. Sanders was supremely confident of his ability to repel invasion, 'if the English will only leave me alone for eight days'.

'The English' would in fact leave him alone for a whole month.

Not only was Hamilton now deprived of strategic surprise, his room for manoeuvre was limited. To the problem of inexperienced troops (even the 29th Division had been so hastily cobbled together that it had had little time for divisional training) was added that of landing places. The Gallipoli peninsula is about 45 miles long and only 10 miles across at the widest point. Cape Helles lies at the southernmost tip overlooked by the heights of Achi Baba (709 feet), with Sari Bair ridge (971 feet) some 12 miles north overlooking both sides of the straits at the narrowest point, 5 miles across. At Cape Helles there were a number of small sandy beaches on the western side, but none on the eastern, which in any case was covered by fire from across the straits on the Asiatic shore. There were no towns, just a few settlements, of which Krithia in the south and Bulair in the north were the most important. The roads were unmade tracks.

Hamilton's first priority, therefore – besides reordering his force – was to achieve some tactical surprise by deceiving the Turks as to where the main effort was being made. Had he known that

* Despite the strong wish of their prime minister to join the Entente, the Greeks were still officially neutral; they merely acceded to the occupation of Lemnos as a sort of *fait accompli*.

Liman von Sanders expected it to be in the Gulf of Xeros (Saros) he could have played to that,* but in the absence of that information he very reasonably concluded that the more distant from each other the landings the more confusion would be sown. So while he assigned the 29th Division to the main landings at Cape Helles to capture the forts at Kilid Bahr, the 'Anzacs' would come ashore some 15 miles up the west coast at Gaba Tepe to advance across the peninsula at its narrowest point (over the formidable heights of Sari Bair) to cut off any Turkish retreat and/or prevent reinforcement, with the French making a diversionary landing on the Asiatic shore and the Royal Naval Division a demonstration in the Gulf of Xeros.

The plan was sound if perhaps rather pedestrian, covering all bases as it were, but with so much dispersal as to increase the likelihood of something going wrong, and left nothing by way of ready reserves. In the event the Anzacs did gain tactical surprise by landing before dawn on 25 April without preliminary bombardment, though with a deal of confusion over exactly where the boats had beached, and some intermingling of units, which led to a loss of momentum. While they then made some progress inland, casualties and the inexperience of commanders began to tell, and soon, in crude terms, their luck simply ran out, not least in finding themselves opposed by the Turkish 19th Division commanded by the brilliant 34-year-old Mustafa Kemal Bey ('Atatürk'), one of the original 'Young Turks' of the reformist movement. Their counter-attacks were so intense and the cohesion of the Anzacs now so precarious, despite on paper a significant superiority in numbers, that for a time Birdwood considered evacuation.

* The Gulf of Xeros would have been the right place to make the main effort if the object had been to take the peninsula; but the MEF's task was to help the navy through the Dardanelles by destroying or neutralizing the guns; what happened subsequently on Gallipoli was therefore not relevant to the strategy. Yet it is difficult to see how warships alone could have reduced Constantinople and toppled the Ottoman government; at the very least there would have had to be landings to consolidate the navy's coup, though if at that point the navy commanded the Dardanelles the landings would have been largely unopposed.

The matter was settled by Hamilton's order from his headquarters on Lemnos: 'Dig, dig, dig, until you are safe.'

At Cape Helles the 29th Division, under Major-General Aylmer Hunter-Weston, a sapper (Royal Engineers) officer who though unimaginatively fearless – he had been at the forefront of the attacks on the Aisne – had limited experience of handling infantry, impaled themselves on the cliffs and machine guns in broad daylight after a preliminary naval bombardment that left the defenders in no doubt what was happening. Despite suicidal gallantry on the part of his regulars – the Lancashire Fusiliers famously winning six VCs 'before breakfast' – only very limited beachheads could be gained. A curious lack of impulsion and initiative then beset the division, spread as it was over five beaches around the point of the peninsula, 7 miles from one end to the other. Even where the landings were relatively lightly opposed, there was confusion over how to exploit gains and provide mutual support.

Notwithstanding this hesitancy, it is still puzzling that Hamilton did not put the more experienced 29th Division ashore at Gaba Tepe – what would become known as 'Anzac Cove' – instead of Birdwood's. Cutting across the peninsula was undoubtedly the more difficult task, and it would unquestionably have been the winning move. And such a move needed troops practised in fire and manoeuvre – regulars – and a divisional commander with recent experience of the offensive, as Hunter-Weston was. On the other hand, what Cape Helles needed primarily was guts, which the 'Anzacs' proved themselves to have in spades. The desire to maintain the Australians and New Zealanders as a corps clearly trumped purely operational thinking, although there is no reason why they should not have landed at Cape Helles as a corps but in successive waves.

As it was, at no stage of the campaign, anywhere, could Hamilton's forces drive further than a few miles inland, and the Turks remained in possession of the commanding ground. Planning had concentrated almost exclusively on the landings, which were seen as the decisive act – hardly surprising, given that some in London believed landings to be impossible – with insufficient thought about what would happen subsequently. Reserves, battle-casualty replacements, enough shells (the lion's share of the still inadequate supply was still going to the Western Front): all these questions never left the 'too difficult' tray. Naval gunfire also proved far less effective than expected, limited by both the nature of the explosive shells and the difficulty of achieving plunging fire.

By 5 May the 29th Division had lost half its initial strength, including two-thirds of its officers.

The Gallipoli peninsula would indeed become a salient every bit as lethal as Ypres, with the added complications of supply across open beaches, water shortage, intense heat and insanitary conditions. As on the Western Front, barbed wire, machine guns and artillery put paid to tactical manoeuvre. The only alternatives were head-on attacks or evacuation. Attacks were tried, but at increasing cost as the Turks brought up reserves and more artillery, and the British could do neither. Evacuation would have been at calamitous cost to national prestige. The troops dug in deeper and prepared to sweat out the summer.

Meanwhile the navy could make no headway up the straits. Fisher, fearing for the *Queen Elizabeth*, ordered her recall. Admiral John de Robeck, who had taken command when Carden became ill, was seemingly unable to accept that there were ready replacements for his pre-dreadnoughts, and failed to show any of the 'Nelson touch' that would have seen him pressing on regardless, much to the exasperation of his chief of staff, Roger Keyes, who would himself display plenty of it in 1918 during the raids on Ostend and Zeebrugge.

The Dardanelles squadron was now supporting the army ashore, the two forces' intended roles wholly reversed.

London became anxious. The war council was redesignated 'the Dardanelles Committee',* reflecting the depth and breadth of

* In September it would be renamed again as 'the war committee'. The Dardanelles Commission, set up in 1916 as a committee of inquiry into the failed campaign, was unconnected.

the anxiety, but two months passed before it could be persuaded, principally by Churchill, to make a significant reinforcement – an increase to twelve divisions (by which time the Turks would have fifteen; but again, this meant a significant drawing off of Ottoman troops from the Caucasus and, indeed, the Middle East). Both *GQG* and GHQ continued to object to any diversion of troops who might reinforce the Western Front, especially after the German offensive at Ypres in April. Despite for the first time using poison gas,* however, the Germans had not broken through. The real reason why Joffre and Sir John French were insisting on keeping every man in France, and calling for more, was their own planned offensives. Joffre was quite sure he could defeat the Germans by Christmas.

Yet besides the question of who was running Britain's grand strategy – the war council, or GHQ and 1SL – what strategic factors had materially changed since January when the war council made its decision to turn the flank where once 'the topless towers' had stood? None. The High Seas Fleet remained in its lair at Wilhelmshaven, the Grand Fleet waiting at Scapa Flow to destroy it should its new and notably cautious commander-in-chief Admiral Hugo von Pohl be so *in*cautious as to sortie in strength. On 2 February the German chancellor had agreed to the request of the navy minister, Grand Admiral Alfred von Tirpitz, to launch unrestricted submarine warfare against all ships, including neutrals, bringing food or supplies to the Entente powers, but this was a desperate measure, a sign of weakness. The campaign on land, the Schlieffen Plan, had failed, and in truth the German high command saw no immediate prospect of decisive success on either the Western or the Eastern Front. Why, therefore, did the allied generals? Joffre was an engineer, and his mind was that of the engineer: there was a practical problem; how was it to be solved? His thinking was not narrow, but characteristically linear: 4 per cent of France (not including Alsace-Lorraine, which he, like most, believed *was*

* See p. 133 below.

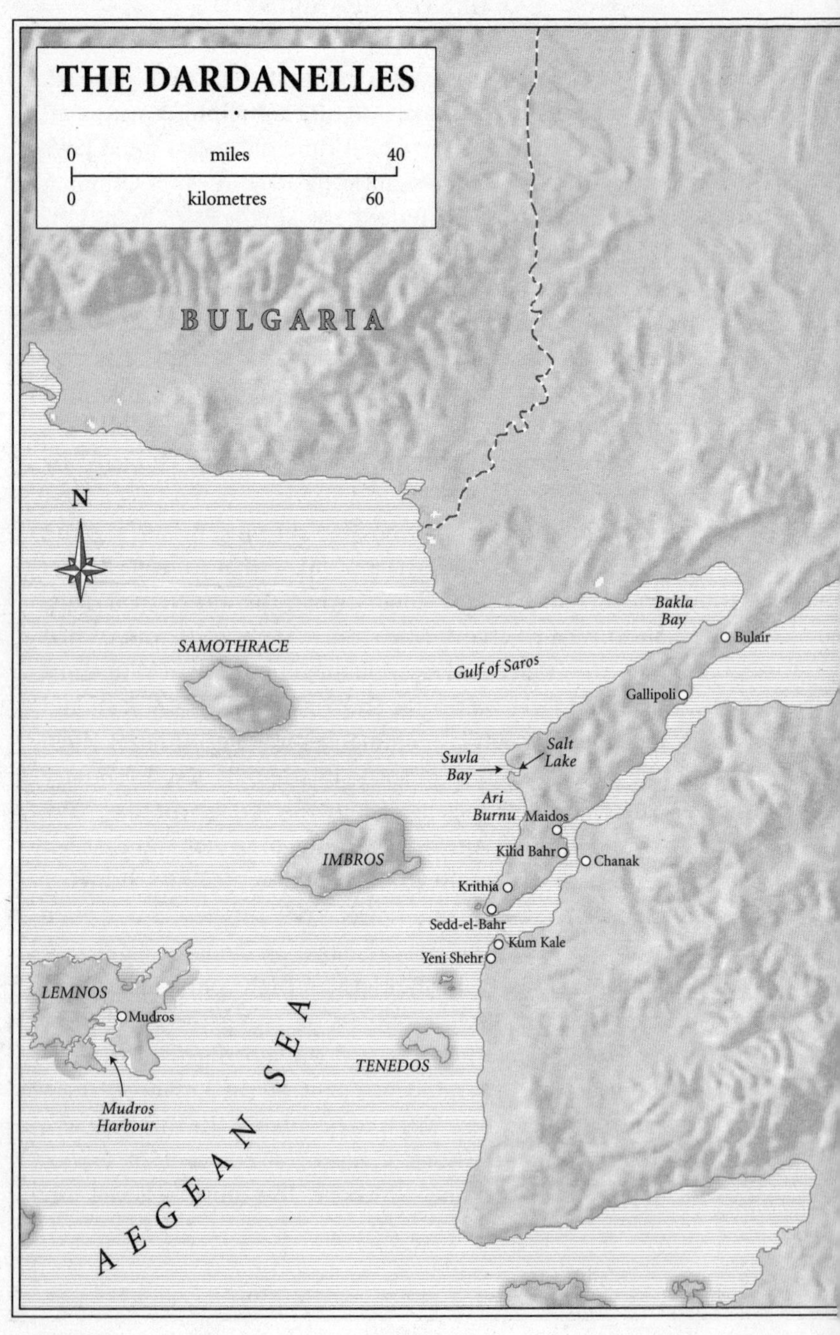

THE DARDANELLES
0
miles
40
0
kilometres
60
N
BULGARIA
SAMOTHRACE
Gulf of Saros
Bakla Bay
Bulair
Gallipoli
Salt Lake
Suvla Bay
Ari Burnu
Maidos
Kilid Bahr
Chanak
IMBROS
Krithia
Sedd-el-Bahr
Kum Kale
Yeni Shehr
LEMNOS
Mudros
Mudros Harbour
TENEDOS
AEGEAN SEA

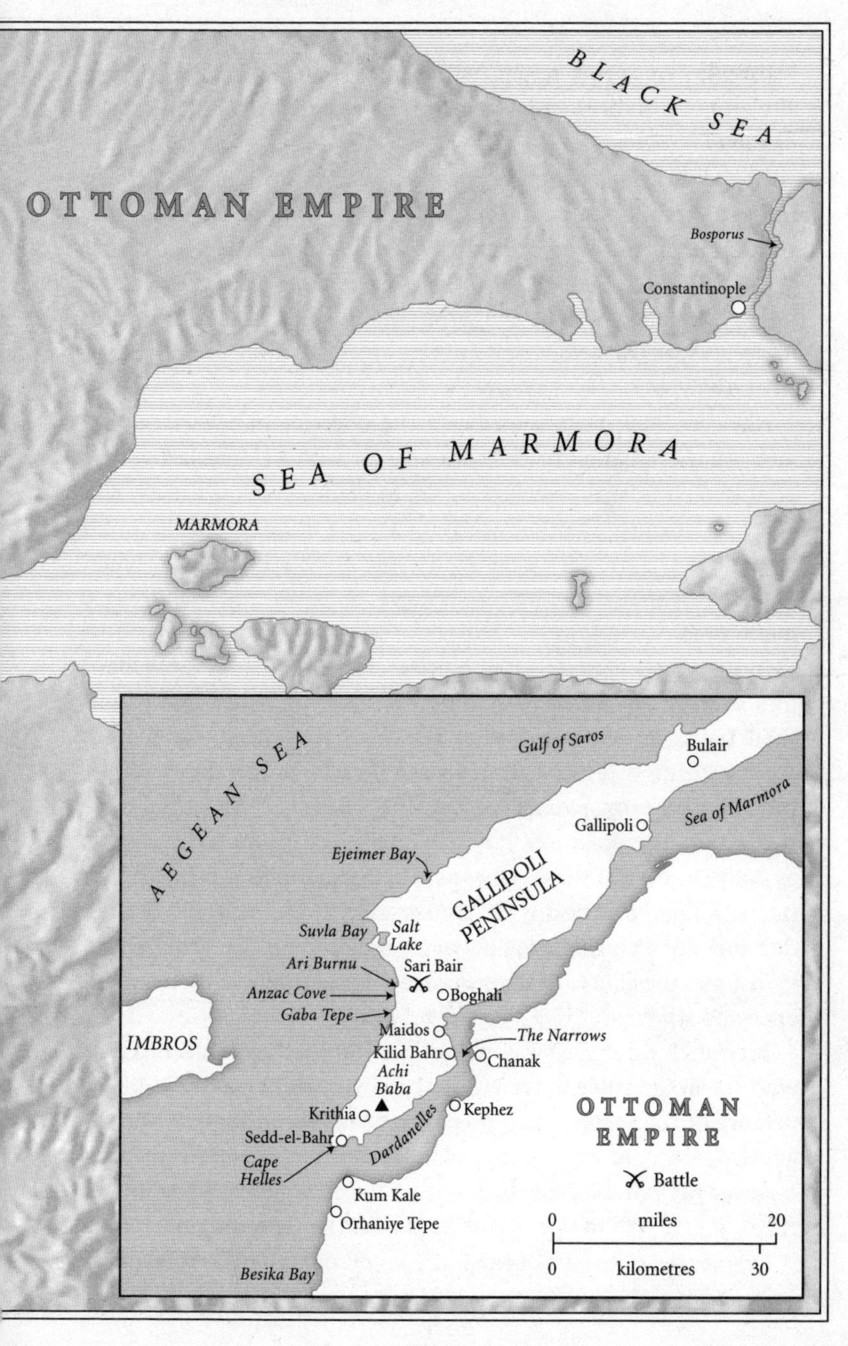

BLACK SEA
OTTOMAN EMPIRE
Bosporus
Constantinople
SEA OF MARMORA
MARMORA
AEGEAN SEA
Gulf of Saros
Bulair
Sea of Marmora
Gallipoli
Ejeimer Bay
GALLIPOLI PENINSULA
Suvla Bay
Salt Lake
Ari Burnu
Sari Bair
Anzac Cove
Boghali
Gaba Tepe
Maidos
The Narrows
IMBROS
Kilid Bahr
Chanak
Achi Baba
Krithia
Kephez
OTTOMAN EMPIRE
Sedd-el-Bahr
Dardanelles
Cape Helles
Battle
Kum Kale
Orhaniye Tepe
0
miles
20
0
kilometres
30
Besika Bay

France) lay in enemy hands, with almost half her coal and virtually all her iron ores – how was it to be wrested back as quickly as possible?

Sir John French, the cavalryman who from the saddle had relieved Kimberley, was the embodiment of *l'arme blanche*; and the sword and lance were not defensive weapons. Besides, *Field Service Regulations* (*FSR*) were clear on the matter: 'Decisive success in battle can be gained only by a vigorous offensive,' and the chief factor in success was 'a firmer determination in all ranks to conquer at any cost'.

However, *FSR* did not advocate the doctrine of *offensive à outrance*: 'If the situation be unfavourable for such a course [a vigorous offensive], it is wiser, when possible, to manoeuvre for a more suitable opportunity.' In other words, when the situation was that of 'a fortress that cannot be carried by assault' it was wiser not to assault, especially when there was a shortage of shells and well-trained manpower.

In any case, *FSR* spoke of battles, not campaigns. Campaigns link strategy and battles, deciding *which* battles, when and where, shall be undertaken and what resources they need. Campaigns are the business of the C-in-C in the theatre of operations. While the offensive principle holds good at this level too, it requires more subtlety in interpretation. It may be that a campaign is designed so as not to lose a war while a means is being found to win it, if necessary in another theatre or dimension. There was no written doctrine for campaigning; it was somehow an art acquired by C-in-Cs in the course of their service, the aggregate of their experience and study.

Yet one thing at least was certain, for *FSR* said so: it was the CIGS who was responsible for advising the government on 'the military defence of the Empire', and preparing plans accordingly, while the government, 'on approving a plan, accept responsibility in principle for the provision of the requisite forces', and 'modification, or revision of a plan of operations rests with the Government'.

Despite the decisions of the war council in January and February to make the Dardanelles operation a priority, decisions emanating in part from Lloyd George's particular demand that the New Armies be used in a way that befitted the class of man from which they were drawn (in essence, not on the Western Front), between May and September no fewer than sixteen (largely) New Army divisions would be sent to France, but only five to Gallipoli.

Hamilton was not yet beaten, however. He determined now, in the summer of 1915, to break the stalemate, applying the same principle that had brought forth the Dardanelles campaign in the first place – turning the flank by amphibious means. Suvla Bay, 8 miles north of 'Anzac Cove', was tricky to approach on account of the shoals, but there was plenty of room to land boats and there was a plateau beyond, even if a good deal of it was salt marsh, so that the initial beachhead would not be as confined as at Anzac Cove or Cape Helles. His aircraft told him it was not defended in any strength – no more than a regiment's worth of infantry, around a thousand men, lightly armed, keeping watch. The plan would be to reinforce Birdwood's corps in a renewed offensive to tie down the Turks around Sari Bair, while landing (initially) two divisions at Suvla. The Suvla divisions would thrust across the peninsula, taking the high ground dominating the 'Narrows' so that the naval operation could begin anew. In doing so, Hamilton reckoned, they would throw the Turks off balance, allowing the Anzacs to break out of their confinement, and in turn releasing the troops around Krithia and Cape Helles.

Having seen earlier that fighting spirit availed little without the strongest leadership at brigade and divisional level, he asked London for some younger generals fresh from the fight in France, not least for command of IX Corps – comprising two K1 divisions, the 10th (Irish) and 11th (Northern) – which was to land at Suvla. The request was both reasonable and realistic: the first six months of the war had seen the rapid promotion of talent, and Hamilton asked specifically for Lieutenant-Generals Julian Byng or Henry Rawlinson. But the worst reversionary instincts for seniority suddenly took hold at the War Office; both these officers were junior to GOC 10th (Irish) Division on the peacetime gradation list, so Sir Frederick Stopford was appointed instead.

Stopford, though sixty-one, had seen little actual fighting, and had never commanded men in battle. In 1915 he was Lieutenant of the Tower of London. It was by any measure a risky appointment at best, at worst a reckless one.

Hamilton's original intention was to open the offensive on 6 August with a diversion at Helles, then launch the offensive from Anzac Cove in early evening, with the landing at Suvla beginning in darkness at 10 p.m., an hour after the two assaulting columns were to break out of Anzac Cove towards the Sari Bair heights. The IX Corps plan was to put 32nd Brigade of the 11th (Northern) Division ashore during the night just south of Suvla Bay, as the shoals made it unsafe to land in the dark within the bay itself, with the 30th and 31st Brigades and the 10th (Irish) Division landing within the bay the following morning, followed later by the 53rd (Welsh) Division.

The immediate objective was to seize the ring of hills overlooking the Suvla plain. When Stopford was first shown the plan in late July he thought it 'a good plan. I am sure it will succeed and I congratulate whoever has been responsible for framing it.' This confidence was then undermined by the most perverse of counsels: his chief of staff, the newly promoted Brigadier-General Hamilton Lyster Reed, thought otherwise. Reed was a gunner who had won the VC in South Africa and, fresh from the Western Front, believed not unreasonably that no assault on entrenched positions could be made without considerable – indeed overwhelming – artillery support: 'The whole teaching of the campaign in France proves that troops cannot be expected to attack an organized system of trenches without the assistance of a large number of howitzers.'*

However, at Suvla aerial reconnaissance had established that

* Brigadier-General J. E. Edmonds, *History of the Great War Based on Official Documents* [hereafter *Official History*], 29 vols (London, 1923–49), vol. 1.

there were no entrenched positions. Prudence demanded some thinking along the lines of 'What if the intelligence were faulty?', especially if the Turks got wind of the landings in time to reinforce, but the intelligence was verifiable right up to the last minute. *What if?* should not have dominated the planning.

And yet it did. Compton Mackenzie, later the author of *Whiskey Galore* and *The Monarch of the Glen*, was a counter-espionage officer with the Secret Service Bureau in the Eastern Mediterranean. He recalled meeting Stopford and Reed at Imbros during the planning:

> Next to me was Sir Frederick Stopford, a man of great kindliness and personal charm, whose conversation at lunch left me at the end of the meal completely without hope of victory at Suvla. The reason for this apprehension was his inability to squash the new General opposite . . . This Brigadier was holding forth almost truculently about the folly of the plan of operations drawn up by the General Staff, while Sir Frederick Stopford appeared to be trying to reassure him in a fatherly way. I looked along the table to where Aspinall and Dawnay [junior staff officers] were sitting near General Braithwaite [Hamilton's chief of staff]; but they were out of earshot, and the dogmatic Brigadier continued unchallenged to enumerate the various military axioms which were being ignored by the Suvla plan of operations. For one thing, he vowed, most certainly he was not going to advance a single yard until all the Divisional Artillery was ashore. I longed for Sir Frederick to rebuke his disagreeable and discouraging junior; but he was deprecating, courteous, fatherly, anything except the Commander of an Army Corps which had been entrusted with a major operation that might change the whole course of the war in twenty-four hours.*

Slowly but surely Stopford began limiting the objectives of the landing, a process which, inexplicably, Hamilton failed to reverse. The final IX Corps orders, and in consequence those of GOC 11th Division, were imprecise, requiring only that the high ground be taken 'if possible' – and yet this was the essential task if the object

* C. Mackenzie, *Gallipoli Memories* (London, 1929).

of the landings was to be achieved; was indeed the whole purpose of the August offensive.

Stopford's 'if possible' was, of course, gratuitous: if it were *not* possible to take the high ground then it would not be taken. Worse, such a rider puts in the mind of those who are to execute the orders a doubt as to how important the objective really is, especially in terms of urgency and casualties.

In the event, the offensive miscarried. At Anzac Cove the assaulting troops took the Turks by surprise towards last light, but then ran out of steam, the commanders over-cautious, the troops overburdened. At Suvla the steam was never got up. Twenty thousand men were put ashore safely enough, albeit in the pitch dark mixed up in some places, and with some sharp fighting in others, and for thirty-six hours there was nothing barring their way across the peninsula but a tenth their number of Turks at most, with no machine guns, very little artillery, and no reserves within 30 miles.

And some hard climbs.

Stopford was extraordinarily supine, and the divisional commanders – even the previously thrusting Bryan Mahon of the 10th Division – showed no more address, their concern being to consolidate rather than push on. When Hamilton at last realized what was happening, he found that the naval arrangements had broken down and he couldn't leave Imbros.

In the growing confusion that comes with hesitation, casualties began to mount – seventeen hundred in the first twenty-four hours, more than all the Turks at Suvla. The German officer with them reported to Liman von Sanders on the evening of the 7th: 'No energetic attacks on the enemy's part have taken place. On the contrary, the enemy is advancing timidly.'

Liman von Sanders rushed reinforcements to Suvla, sacking the local Turkish general for failing to act quickly enough and replacing him with Mustafa Kemal. When Stopford, at Hamilton's less ruthless urging, at last pressed his attack, on the ninth, the odds had almost evened. The casualties now really began to multiply, and the offensive began to stall.

It was soon all too clear that nothing had been gained bar another tenuous bridgehead. Stopford was replaced in temporary command by Beauvoir de Lisle (commanding 29th Division, Hunter-Weston having earlier been promoted to command of VIII Corps, formed at Helles with the arrival of the New Army divisions, but subsequently relieved of command, 'exhausted') while Byng hurried from France to take the reins. Two of the divisional commanders were also sacked (Bryan Mahon just survived, though piqued at de Lisle, his junior, being promoted over his head). London began thinking of withdrawing altogether from Gallipoli, though some, including Churchill, still believed the object both worthwhile and achievable – and even Kitchener was not yet persuaded otherwise. Hamilton's staff came up with the eye-watering figure of up to fifty thousand casualties as the cost of withdrawal, which London found bearable only by comparison with the thought of greater casualties if they stayed.*

In October Hamilton himself was relieved of command. In his place came General Sir Charles Monro, from 3rd Army in France, with instructions from Kitchener to assess the situation. Evidently he had assessed it already and come equipped with the Western Front solution: give up the whole scheme altogether and withdraw from Gallipoli as quickly as possible. So rapidly did he reach his conclusion – in a single morning (prompting Churchill to jibe: 'He

* 'From General Sir Ian Hamilton to Earl Kitchener: Our losses would depend on such uncertain factors, enemy's action or inaction, weather, question whether we could rely on all troops covering embarkation to fight to the last, that impossible to give you straight answer especially until I have permission to consult Admiral. Once discussing this very problem with General Gouraud, we came to the conclusion that at Cape Helles we must sacrifice two divisions out of total of six divisions and Cape Helles easiest of three places to get away from. My opinion now is that it would not be wise to reckon on getting out of Gallipoli with less loss than that of half the total force as well as guns, which must be used to the last, stores, railway plant and horses. Moral[e] of those who got off would fall very low. One quarter would probably get off quite easily, then the trouble would begin. We might be very lucky and lose considerably less than I have estimated. On the other hand, with all these raw troops at Suvla and all these Senegalese at Cape Helles, we might have a veritable catastrophe': General Sir Ian Hamilton, *Gallipoli Diary* (London, 1922).

came, he saw, he capitulated') – that Kitchener refused at first to accept it, and rushed out to judge for himself.

Again, this was 'irregular'. Monro had been asked for his military judgement. If the CIGS had gone to see for himself it would have been pardonable – even reasonable; for the secretary of state to question military judgement by repeating the same exercise was neither, for he thereby combined both military and political counsel in cabinet. Unfortunately, the man who had replaced Wolfe Murray as CIGS, his deputy, Lieutenant-General Sir Archibald Murray, whom Sir John French had sacked in January, was no more likely to challenge the secretary of state, a field marshal, than he was to question Monro, a full general. Little wonder the cabinet was wary of what hat Kitchener wore in his counsels.

In any event, the war committee had wearied of the Dardanelles adventure – as had other influential opinion – and 'K' reluctantly conceded. The prospect of fifty thousand casualties, most of them falling into Turkish hands, was a strategic nightmare, but in fact the withdrawal from Suvla Bay and Anzac Cove would be completed on the night of 18 December practically without loss, and from Cape Helles on 8 January equally without loss at the hands of the enemy. Paradoxically, the evacuation showed what remarkable feats could be pulled off with boldness, ingenuity and thorough preparation – to wit: time, and meticulous staffwork.

If only this level of adroitness had accompanied the initial landings in April, or at Suvla in August. If only, somehow, it could be applied to offensive operations elsewhere – notably on the Western Front.

'Thus ended a sound and farsighted venture which had been wrecked by a chain of errors hardly to be rivalled even in British history,' wrote Liddell Hart, with not a jot of over-statement.* Hamilton deserved better luck in his subordinates, and he deserved better support from the war council; but the war council deserved a more single-minded commander-in-chief. And both deserved a functional general staff at the War Office.

* *World War I in Outline* (London, 1936).

'That the effort failed is not against it,' wrote John Masefield in 1916, within a few months of the evacuation; 'many great things and noble men have failed.'*

Erich von Falkenhayn, chief of the *Grosser Generalstab* throughout the Dardanelles campaign, would testify to the value of the strategic prize had it been won:

> If the Straits between the Mediterranean and the Black Sea were not permanently closed to Entente traffic, all hopes of a successful course of the war would be very considerably diminished. Russia would have been freed from her significant isolation. It was just this isolation, however, which offered a safer guarantee than military successes were able to do, that sooner or later a crippling of the forces of this Titan must take place, to a certain extent automatically.†

Falkenhayn's opinion might be dismissed as a piece of self-justification, as any war memoir tends to be, especially those of the vanquished, but General Max von Hoffmann, guiding brain of the *Grosser Generalstab* in the campaigns against Russia, had held firmly to the same view, writing in his diary in August 1915: 'We cannot hope to wear the Russians down in the course of the winter unless we keep the Dardanelles firmly closed.'‡

When therefore the allies failed to prise that door open, the fate of Russia was sealed – four million casualties by the end of 1915, and revolution practically assured. For every hundred Russian soldiers who fell in battle in the course of the war, three hundred surrendered.§

So much for the strategic wisdom of the enterprise; was there *any*

* John Masefield, *Gallipoli* (London, 1916).
† *General Headquarters 1914–1916 and its Critical Decisions* (London, 1919). When war began, essential imports to Russia dried up and her export trade (largely grain from southern Russia), blockaded at the Dardanelles, declined by 70%. Domestic production could not fill the gap. The Russian armies, as others, rapidly ran out of ammunition, guns and small arms.
‡ Major-General Max von Hoffmann, *War Diaries*, trans. Eric Sutton (London, 1929).
§ Compared with only twenty-six Germans, twenty-four French and twenty British: Richard Pipes, *The Russian Revolution 1899–1919* (London, 1990).

return on the investment? In pointing to the benefits of miscarriage and disaster there is always a risk of dissimulation: saying valuable lessons were learned from the sinking of the *Titanic* was no comfort to the families of the passengers. Nevertheless, the Gallipoli campaign was not without its benefits to the Western Front. Falkenhayn had seen the threat that would be posed to Vienna if the rest of the Balkans (and Italy) were raised to the allied cause. Austria-Hungary was already creaking under pressure from Serbia and Russia, and he concluded that the German army must push the Russians back a safe distance in order for Austria to knock out the Serbs before the allies could (belatedly) reinforce them. The Western Front did not therefore suffer the predicted German onslaught in anything like the strength that might have been applied. This, of course, was something of a perverse benefit, for it would allow Joffre and French to pursue their pipe dream of decisive victory that year; and many a *poilu* and Lloyd George's 'better class of artisan, the upper and the lower middle classes' would die in the autumn of 1915 in that pursuit.

But perhaps worst of all was the passing, like a shooting star, of imaginative strategic thinking, and in its place the exaltation of the Western Front as the incontestable theatre of decision – though as yet without the means of forcing such a decision except, in Churchill's words, 'the breasts of brave men'. The war committee had decided against reinforcing failure, only to reinforce deadlock instead.

The Dardanelles campaign was the first and last attempt by the 'Great Amphibian' to use admiralcy as a decisive weapon in land operations. Other than maintaining the 'fleet in being' and countering the nascent submarine threat, blockade was now the Royal Navy's principal objective. Machiavelli had said it: 'It is better to defeat the enemy by hunger than with steel; in such victory fortune counts more than *virtù*.'*

* *Dell'arte della guerra* (translated as *The Art of War*), 1521. *Virtù* was a Machiavellian concept of the martial spirit and ability of a people or leader, encompassing a

But starving a nation – or rather, its armed forces – is not a business of mere months, though in fact it would prove a powerful factor in final victory on the Western Front; indeed, arguably *the* factor in the overall defeat of Germany.

For the time being at least, notwithstanding the recall of Ian Hamilton, the Dardanelles–Gallipoli campaign was seen as primarily a politicians' failure, and so on 25 May 1916 Asquith would be forced to acquiesce in coalition government, an administration in which the Tories would be wed very firmly to the Western Front strategy and the unflagging support of Haig. Churchill would lose the admiralty, and Kitchener his mantle of infallibility.

'That the effort failed' was very much against *them*.

---

number of factors necessary for the maintenance of the state and 'the accomplishment of great things'.

Chapter Seven

SLAUGHTER WITHOUT MANOEUVRE

On 2 June 1915 Asquith had been visiting Sir John French at his headquarters in St Omer. At dinner that evening, seated on French's right, with the BEF's sub-chief of staff, Henry Wilson, a few places to the C-in-C's left, he said absently: 'It is a curious thing, Field Marshal, that this war has produced no great generals.'

Wilson could not contain himself. 'No, Prime Minister,' he snapped, before French could reply; 'nor has it produced a statesman.'*

Both men had a point; but Asquith had the greater one. The Germans had been thrown back at the Marne, yes; Paris had been saved. But in truth the generals' plans had miscarried, and the blame could not be laid at the feet of the statesmen. The Gallipoli landings had got nowhere, at mounting cost, and the BEF's offensive at Neuve Chapelle in March had ended no more successfully than those before Christmas, and every bit as bloodily. It was true that the BEF had held on to the Ypres salient throughout May – the Germans had attacked three days before the Gallipoli landings, on 22 April – and had had some success in counter-attacks, notably by the Canadian Division at St Julien; but the prospect of ending the war in 1915, as Joffre kept suggesting, looked increasingly remote.

* Quoted in Callwell, *Field-Marshal Sir Henry Wilson*.

Wilson's truculence in response to Asquith's insensitivity was not without justification, however. The political generation of 1914 on both sides of the Channel, though towering over their immediate predecessors and those who succeeded them, was in the words of John Terraine, that most assiduous and generous historian of 1914–18, 'unable to grasp the broad structure of the War, and guide its courses firmly'.* Churchill deserves exemption from Terraine's strictures, for he did indeed 'grasp the broad structure of the war', though he was not in a strong enough position to guide its courses – and after the formation of the coalition government in May 1915 was effectively excluded from the councils of war. But Churchill didn't seek victory at all costs on the Western Front; and Terraine was the staunchest supporter of the Western Front strategy (and of Haig).

Also worthy of at least partial exemption, though grasping the mechanics of the war at times imperfectly, and in 1915 lacking either the position or the skill to guide its courses at all, let alone firmly, was Lloyd George. It was a tragedy that by the time the one man save Churchill (out of the political picture since November 1915†) able to grasp and guide did become Britain's war leader, in December 1916, mutual confidence between the 'brass hats' and the 'frocks' had fallen to such a low that he was able to do little but be carried along by events on the Western Front.

Meanwhile, Wilson's less-than-great statesmen, and Asquith's less-than-great generals, would carry on with no common understanding of what was needed to win the war, and therefore with no strategic synergy. Worse, indeed – mutual incomprehension, even distrust, would undermine the efforts of both. The War Office could not even see eye to eye with the Admiralty. The politicians (as in all the belligerent nations) had neither the capacity nor, critically, the

* *The Western Front 1914–1918* (London, 1964).

† He was in effect ejected from the Admiralty as a price of the Conservatives' joining the coalition, and given instead a cabinet post without true portfolio; this he resigned towards the end of 1915, after the decision to withdraw from Gallipoli, to join the army in France.

machinery to formulate strategy on the scale required by the expanding world conflict. There was no Pitt, no Castlereagh – nor indeed any Metternich, Nesselrode or Hardenberg – no figure commensurate with the architects of victory in the Napoleonic wars to foresee the outlines of the future and prepare to deal with it. For Britain especially, 'the Great Amphibian', this was doubly tragic, for in having to improvise a mass army while fighting desperately in France she incurred needlessly high losses, while never fully bringing to bear her natural strength – command of the sea.

The statesmen's failure lay in the absence of any allied grand strategy worthy of the name. Strategy, such as it was (and at times it was little more than higher tactics), was effectively in the hands of the generals. Not even the Admiralty could make its weight truly felt against the voice of GHQ and its second, the War Office. And Robertson, in this second year of the war the BEF's chief of staff, seemed heartily to approve of the position. In a paper of 30 June 1915 entitled 'Notes on the Machinery of the Government for the Conduct of the War' he contended that strategy should be in the hands of the CIGS alone, arguing in pseudo-Clausewitzian terms that the government should simply state its war aims (in this case the liberation of Belgium and the destruction of German 'militarism') and then leave their pursuit to the professionals.

In fact, Clausewitz himself had always said this approach was folly: 'It is an inadmissible and even harmful distinction to leave a great military enterprise or its planning to a "purely military" judgment; more, it is absurd to consult professional soldiers on a plan for a war in order that they may judge from a "purely military" stand-point what cabinets are to do.' Clemenceau was merely restating this pithily in his 'trop grave pour la confier à des militaires' remark, which he is supposed to have used again in despair on learning of the 'strategy' of attrition. With weary cynicism, after the Armistice in 1918 he would sum it all up with: 'La guerre est une série de catastrophes qui se terminent par une victoire.'*

* 'War is a series of catastrophes that ends through a victory.'

When Asquith sat down to dinner at GHQ that June evening he could scarcely have imagined how great the catastrophes would be, or how many (let alone that one of them would rob him of a son) – Gallipoli, Verdun, the Somme, Passchendaele, to name but the better-known misfortunes.

Without knowing how to achieve it, he could not even be certain that victory would be theirs; or, crucially, what sort of victory it would be. For the price of victory shapes a peace, as Churchill's judgement of 1918 portended: 'No splendid harmony was to crown the wonderful achievements. No prize was to reward the sacrifices of the combatants. Victory was to be bought so dear as to be almost indistinguishable from defeat.'*

'Victory bought so dear' is a terrible indictment of strategy, and of generalship. If war is indeed to be *une série de catastrophes*, then the general's art amounts to little more than the management of a process (of catastrophes) until victory emerges – or is stumbled upon – and the statesman's little more than the choosing of generals.

For the actual combatants this is a bleak formula: 'As flies to wanton boys are we to th' gods, / They kill us for their sport.'† War certainly has its own dynamic, a flood tide in the affairs of man, in which without steering the participants are simply taken by the current. Strategy seeks somehow to regulate that current and provide the means to steer. Tactics is the actual steering. The two – strategy and tactics – are inseparable. If the sixth-century BC Chinese military philosopher and author of *The Art of War*, Sun Tzu, really did exist – and there is a doubt, in which case there is a genius to fame and fortune unknown – then his encapsulation of the relationship between strategy and tactics has been hallowed by the experience of two and a half millennia: 'Strategy without tactics is the slowest route to victory. Tactics without strategy is the noise before defeat.'

* *The World Crisis*.
† *King Lear*, IV: i.

But if war were really a matter of such formulae, there should not have been the problem of the Western Front. In October 1914, with the symptoms of deadlock already becoming evident, Lloyd George called on General Noël de Castelnau, commander of the French 2nd Army. How many troops did he command? asked the chancellor of the exchequer. Nine army corps was the answer. Lloyd George replied that that was more than Napoleon had ever commanded in a single battle (it is noteworthy that 'LG' knew this).

'Ah, Napoleon, Napoleon,' said Castelnau, with a sigh; 'If he were here now, he'd have thought of the "something else".'

So a French general had said it before Asquith: where *were* the great generals?

John Terraine quoted this exchange in a seminal essay, 'The Napoleonic Legacy'.* Castelnau's remarks, he said, had a profound effect on Lloyd George, 'which time did not diminish'. Indeed, in his memoirs 'LG' wrote of the situation in which he found himself on becoming prime minister at the end of 1916, after the blood-letting on the Somme, and with 1917 looking as if it would be nothing but a re-run of things past. 'It had become a war of endurance. The strategy on both sides was unimaginative and commonplace. There was no military genius *on either side* [emphasis added] to devise, execute and exploit a stroke that transformed the course of the War and determined the result. Castelnau's penetrating observation about Napoleon still held good.'

In other words, they could do only what they knew.

Terraine then went on to demolish this myth of Napoleonic genius: the 'Great Disturber' went to St Helena not as a tourist but as a prisoner of war, the consequence of his defeat. 'Nor is it simply a matter of Napoleon being defeated *in the end*; he was frequently defeated all through his career, and mostly by the play of the very elements which brought about his final fall.' Indeed, St Helena always *was* his destination.

* Originally published in *History Today*, June 1962; reprinted in *The Western Front 1914–1918*.

Terraine's case is, on the face of it, compelling. So too is his argument that staff colleges throughout Europe had dangerously bought into the myth, embracing Napoleon's 'strange series of aphorisms' (not least 'the moral is to the material as three is to one'), so that early in the war 'attempts to emulate his performance, to follow his "instructions", had had the almost universal effect of increasing the damage'.

Certainly in 1914 the belief in the superiority of the 'moral component' – the fundamental tenet of the doctrine of *offensive à outrance* – sent many *poilus* to their deaths in *pantalons rouges* to the cry of *à la baïonnette.* It scarcely seems credible, but when in 1911 the Chamber of Deputies had debated replacing the *poilu*'s red trousers with something more suitable for the modern battlefield, a grey-green uniform known as *la tenue reseda* (or *bleu d'horizon*) there was furious opposition, on the grounds that it was ugly, too similar to German *feldgrau* (field grey) and not at all in keeping with the way the French made war. Alexandre Millerand, who would become war minister the following year, declared: 'Le pantalon rouge, c'est la France!' So in August 1914 the French army would march to war clad in *le pantalon rouge* – as well as the red *képi* (hat). As Lieutenant Spears observed, many officers 'thought it chic to die in white gloves'.

The rapid change of uniform to *bleu d'horizon* in 1915, and the concession that infantry would charge with loaded rifles rather than just fixed bayonets, made no difference to the fundamental belief in the power of the offensive. To the collegium of French generals the whole business of war, as elaborated by Napoleon, boiled down to two things: attacking the enemy immediately and attacking him in full strength. And it was this unshakeable conviction that continued to pile up the dead on both sides even in the face of experience. For what else was a general to do when things went badly but follow the teaching of the greatest general who had ever lived, hoping that at some point – miraculously – 'luck', in which Napoleon professed his profound belief, would go with him?

As Clausewitz had concluded, 'every fault and exaggeration of [a] theory is instantly exposed in war'.

Terraine also pointed to the terrible militarism – the belief that in matters of war the military knew best – that had taken hold across continental Europe in the late nineteenth century. Politicians were 'hopeful that the generals would display such ['Napoleonic'] talents, so that the ultimate cost of policies might not be fully exacted'. Militarism, he argued, allowed the Napoleonic myth to endure long after it was exposed: 'It was a dream; there was no other way.'

Yet in one of his largely overlooked dicta Napoleon in fact displayed a profounder view of war: 'The whole art of war consists in a well-reasoned and circumspect defensive, followed by rapid and audacious attack.'

A disciple might ask: 'And how long must the "well-reasoned and circumspect defensive" last?' To which there could be only one answer: for as long as necessary.

It did not suit Napoleon, of course, to display too freely this sort of declaratory caution, but he knew its truth and embraced it when he had to, for, as Terraine pointed out in a memorable phrase, 'he had the advantage of not having to graduate in Napoleonic studies'.

But if it is true that much of Napoleon's reputation is essentially built on myth, it does not follow that the concept of genius is flawed, only that the defining qualities are rather different from those learned by the French generals of 1914–18 and by many of their German and Russian counterparts – and even some British, for in places *Field Service Regulations* would not have been unrecognizable to the Great Disturber. 'The transcendent capacity for taking trouble' has become the utilitarian definition of genius. Foch, appointed Allied *generalissimo* in April 1918, the darkest month of the war, said in a newspaper interview in London before the victory parade the following year:

> The stroke of genius that turns the fate of a battle? I don't believe in it. A battle is a complicated operation, that you prepare laboriously . . . You think out every possible development and decide on the way to deal with the situation created. One of these developments occurs; you put

> in operation your pre-arranged plan, and everyone says, 'What genius to have thought of that at the critical moment!' whereas the credit is really due to the labour of preparation done beforehand.*

This is certainly the repudiation of a purist Napoleonic concept – and it is instructive that Foch should effectively downgrade *L'Empereur* to the status of *un bon général ordinaire*, a commander with merely an infinite capacity for taking pains (although Napoleon himself would have endorsed the notion of thorough preparation as an element in victory). But in the realm of generalship there is *command* – which boils down to understanding the question and deciding the course of action – and there is *staffwork*, which identifies the courses available if the commander has not already decided, and then puts the decision into action. Foch was talking essentially about staffwork. Military genius is the intuitive perception, the instant, incisive comprehension – what was once called the *coup d'œil* – that, combined with innate originality and audacity, can see the question and the answer, the object and the way, and then seize the moment.

It is curious that the British high command did not have its own version of the Napoleonic necromancy that obsessed the French, for its obvious magus might have been Napoleon's nemesis, the duke of Wellington. Lord Raglan, commander-in-chief in the Crimean War, was wont to ask himself whenever a problem of administration or tactics arose: 'What would the duke have done?' Sadly it proved no more winning a way than the French generals' communing with the lonely ghost of St Helena. 'What would a genius do?' is a doubtful methodology. But there are things to be learned from studying the genius's central intellectual position, for it is this from which – in part at least – intuition, comprehension, originality and boldness surely derive.

And in 1915 Wellington would have been an eminently suitable case for study. One of his maxims was that a good general knows

* *Daily Mail*, 19 April 1919.

when to retreat and has the courage to do so. It was, indeed, the basis of his success in the Peninsula – earning him the sobriquet the 'fabian general'. Not that strategic retreats of Peninsular War dimensions were an option in 1915; the French were never going to surrender a yard more of ground without a fight (though Napoleon would have). Though ground, unlike the lives of men, could always be recovered, the lives of their *poilus* were ultimately nothing compared with the sacred soil of *La Patrie*. Nor could the BEF give much ground in Flanders if the Channel ports were not to be put in even greater jeopardy. However, local, tactical withdrawals *were* an option, and where this would have placed the defenders in a safer position – the Ypres salient being an obvious case in point – or given them the better ground (which might then have been held with fewer troops) it would have been the sounder military course. In other cases, just not to attack, rather than actually to withdraw, would have been prudent. The duke never believed that he had to go onto the offensive merely to keep his troops' fighting edge (a view shared by Montgomery in the Second World War).

It was, of course, the extensive withdrawals in the face of the great German offensive of spring 1918 that created the opportunity for the decisive allied counter-offensive. These were not willing withdrawals, however; in some cases they were chaotic retreats, and for these General Sir Hubert Gough, whose 5th Army had 'broken', was relieved of his command. It is ironic that if 5th Army had held, the counter-offensive might have failed.

Wellington would have endorsed Napoleon's assertion that 'the whole art of war consists in a well-reasoned and circumspect defensive, followed by rapid and audacious attack'. He would in fact have taken it as axiomatic, self-evident. Rapid and at times audacious attack – 'the Hundred Days' (not Napoleon's but Foch's and Haig's) – did indeed end the war in 1918; but the defensive that had preceded it for three and a half years was neither well-reasoned nor circumspect.

The BEF's first offensive of 1915, at Neuve Chapelle, would set the pattern for GHQ's mental approach to the problem of the

Western Front. In early spring, as the situation of the Russians on the Eastern Front (and in the Caucasus) eased a little, Sir John French suddenly began thinking strategically. Notwithstanding his earlier disdain of the object of the Dardanelles project – support of Russia – he now advanced this very cause in favour of his planned offensive in Artois. He cited 'particularly the marked success of the Russian Army in repelling the violent onslaughts of Marshal von Hindenburg, the apparent weakening of the enemy in my front, and the necessity for assisting our Russian Allies to the utmost by holding as many hostile troops as possible in the Western Theatre'.*

It was not primarily French's business to think in this way; his was command of the BEF. The strategic purpose of the BEF was the business of London. However, a commander-in-chief must have a clear understanding of how his theatre of operations fits into grand strategy, and French's proposal accorded with the overall aim of keeping the Russians in the fight. London could only welcome therefore the help that the BEF might give – though, of course, there would be the little matter of supplying shells, reinforcements and casualty replacements.

In fact the strategic was not the prime consideration for French. In the words of his later despatch, again, there was 'perhaps the most weighty consideration of all, the need of fostering the offensive spirit in the troops under my command after the trying and possibly enervating experiences which they had gone through of a severe winter in the trenches'.

And the need of demonstrating that spirit to the French. Certainly the Indian Corps, not long formed and consisting of the Lahore and Meerut Divisions, wanted to prove themselves. The courage displayed by the newly arrived sepoys in the fighting at Ypres in October and November could not be doubted – but the tactical skill of their commanders had been wanting.

Joffre certainly approved, as long as the offensive was not towards the Belgian coast, and while the French C-in-C had no

* Quoted in *The Despatches of Lord French* (London, 1917).

official authority over the BEF he carried the moral authority of the stronger ally. His own intention was to reduce the great German-occupied bulge in north-western France made in the first months' fighting of 1914 by attacking its extreme points in Artois and Champagne. If the lateral railways in the plain of Douai could be recaptured, he reasoned, the Germans, deprived of the means of supply and rapid reinforcement, would have to withdraw. And there was always the chance of breakthrough and the restoration of mobile warfare, the holy grail of the allied command. Without breakthrough there could be no decision.

By March 1915, although still but a fraction of the size of the French forces holding the 400-mile line of trenches from the Belgian coast to the Swiss border, the BEF had grown to such a strength that it had been reorganized into two armies: 1st Army, commanded by the newly promoted General Sir Douglas Haig, and 2nd Army under Sir Horace Smith-Dorrien. French delegated the planning of the British part in the Artois offensive – the attack at the village of Neuve Chapelle – to Haig and 1st Army, which consisted of IV Corps and the Indian Corps, while the exploitation was to be the business of Smith-Dorrien and 2nd Army. Logic would have suggested the roles be reversed – Smith-Dorrien, the infantryman, planning the set-piece attack, and Haig, the cavalryman, ready to exploit – but besides the actual positions of the armies, which suggested 1st Army undertake the initial attack, Haig's stock stood particularly high after holding the line at Ypres in November, whereas Smith-Dorrien's decision to stand and fight at Le Cateau in August had become such a bone of contention with Sir John French that this peppery infantry general was increasingly sidelined.

Neuve Chapelle lay on the road between Bethune and Armentières, the ground flat and cut by drainage ditches. A mile beyond the British lines lay Aubers Ridge, which though barely 20 feet higher than the surrounding country gave a significant advantage in artillery observation, while some 15 miles to the south lay the far greater heights of Vimy Ridge. In consequence, perhaps, the

German lines were relatively lightly held, the defenders being able to place greater reliance on their artillery to defeat any attack.

The French assault was to be at Vimy Ridge to threaten the road, rail and canal junctions at La Bassée from the south, while the British attack would menace them from the north. However, the attack on Vimy Ridge was cancelled when Sir John French said he was not able to relieve the French IX Corps in the line north of Ypres to release them for the assault. So instead of IX Corps in support of the BEF, Joffre promised them heavy artillery.

Haig's preparation was thorough. Despite poor weather in late February the RFC had carried out much aerial photography. The Royal Engineers Survey Branch was therefore able to map the area over which the attack was to take place to a depth of nearly a mile, each corps receiving fifteen hundred copies of 1:5,000-scale (1 cm to 50 metres) sheets. Neuve Chapelle was the first deliberately planned British offensive, and would provide something of a template for the BEF's future attacks on the Western Front: a scheduled artillery bombardment followed by infantry advancing at a fixed time, conforming as best they could to the fire plan, while the cavalry waited for the word to 'gallop through the "G" in "Gap"', as the wags had it, thereby restoring mobility.

Haig was able to concentrate 340 guns – as many as the BEF had taken to France the previous August – against the German salient at Neuve Chapelle, a ratio of one gun to every 6 yards of front attacked. But guns were one thing, ammunition another – and here the shell shortage (shell *scandal*) wrought its effect, restricting the artillery preparation to thirty minutes. Even so, initially it seemed to prove effective enough. Though the night before the attack (9 March) was wet and snowy, turning to damp mist in the morning, the shock of the hurricane bombardment – what the Germans afterwards described as 'the first true drum-fire [*Trommelfeuer*] yet heard' – kept the defenders' heads down just long enough for the assaulting infantry to gain their first objectives. In Artois the water table was so high that the German trenches were dug relatively shallow and built up with earthworks, making them more susceptible to HE and the troops in them more vulnerable to shrapnel. However, after the first set-piece attack the tempo faltered, command impaired by poor communications and the gunners' consequent inability to respond quickly to the infantry's needs owing to shellfire cutting the field-telephone cables (there was no tactical radio – now or at any time during the war).

It did not help that Haig was excessively keen to keep things 'tidy', allowing checks on both flanks to hold up the centre while he brought up reserves to deal with them. Meanwhile, as the *Official History* records picturesquely, some '10,000 men . . . lay, sat or stood uselessly in the mud, packed like salmon in the bridge pool at Galway, waiting patiently to go forward'.

Not until after five o'clock was the advance resumed, and it then petered out in the dusk.

The next day Haig sought to renew the advance by attacking where the original assault had failed, repeating the detailed preparation of the first day and thereby expending precious time. The casualties mounted. A German divisional counter-attack early on 12 March was beaten back but at heavy cost, and soon afterwards Haig cancelled further attacks and ordered the gains to be consolidated prior to mounting a new attack further north, which he said was to be pressed 'regardless of loss'.

Loss was the only result. The shell shortage was now so acute that this new attack was soon abandoned but for a local effort by the 7th Division, which also failed, again with high casualties.

Indeed the losses in many battalions were catastrophic. Of the 750 men of the 2nd Scottish Rifles (2nd Battalion the Cameronians) who went into battle on 10 March, many of the officers with swords drawn, only 143 came out three days later, led by the surviving officer, a second lieutenant, and the regimental sergeant-major. Their dead, wounded and missing included 29 sergeants, a devastating loss of experienced NCOs.*

* Their story is told in one of the finest studies of men in battle, *Morale* (London, 1967), by the late Sir John Baynes, himself a former Cameronian.

In all, out of the forty thousand who took part, the fighting cost some seven thousand British and 4,200 Indian casualties, and the Germans almost as many. Heroism was common currency, with ten Victoria Crosses awarded. Among the posthumous recipients was Rifleman (Private) Gabar Singh Negi of the Gharwal Rifles, a brigade whose tenacity in the attack had been particularly marked. His citation read: 'During our attack on the German position he was one of a bayonet party with bombs who entered their main trench, and was the first man to go round each traverse, driving back the enemy until they were eventually forced to surrender.'

If the battle showed no appreciable gain, the French at least were to become cautiously optimistic that the BEF might be reliable in offensive operations. Given their obsession with the offensive, however, this would prove a distinctly mixed blessing. In Champagne in February and March they had lost fifty thousand men, 'nibbling' just 500 yards. In April they would lose sixty thousand in a disastrous attack to eliminate the salient at St-Mihiel. But before Joffre could launch his grand offensive in Artois in late spring it would be the turn of the Germans to attack – at Ypres.

For weeks prisoners taken by the French had been telling their interrogating officers that the Germans were preparing to discharge poison gas from cylinders brought into the fire trenches (on 13 April a deserter even brought a primitive gas mask with him). The warnings were ignored. On the evening of the twenty-second a strange mist drifted across no-man's-land from the German trenches towards the left (north-west) of the Ypres salient – trenches occupied by the French (mainly North African troops). It was chlorine gas: 168 tons of it, released across a 3½-mile front. Those troops who could, fled; those who could not, suffocated. A 4-mile-wide gap was opened, into which the Germans advanced – but none too quickly. Fortunately for the allies, the German high command had had as little confidence in the new weapon as the French had had belief in its existence. There were simply not enough reserves to exploit the break in the line. The magnificent

Canadian Division, on their first time in action proper, held their ground on the French right, allowing British (English) and Indian reinforcements to be brought up, thereby saving the situation. Two days later the Germans released a further 15 tons of chlorine near St Julien which struck the Canadian 8th Brigade, drawing in the rest of the Canadian Division with only the most primitive of gas masks – towelling or handkerchiefs soaked in urine. In heavy fighting the Canadians lost seventeen hundred dead, nearly two thousand wounded and almost as many as prisoners. And for all their ardour and courage, the 50th (Northumbrian) Division, Territorial Force, the first 'terriers' to see heavy fighting, showed how much greater would be the price when relatively raw troops were engaged: one of its brigades took two-thirds casualties.

The gas attack at Ypres was another milestone in German 'frightfulness', which did not go unnoticed in America. First the atrocities in Belgium (civilians deliberately killed, including women, children and priests), then the shelling of seaside towns (Scarborough, Whitby and Hartlepool in December), lately the torpedoing of unarmed liners and merchantmen (*Lusitania* would be sunk the following month) – and now poison gas. The Germans were sowing the wind. They would eventually reap the whirlwind – America's entry on the allied side – though the harvest would be agonizingly late.

Meanwhile they had nothing tactically – let alone strategically – to show for their innovative frightfulness.

The increasing evidence of just how bitterly this war would be fought was certainly not lost on Kitchener, who now wrote to French:

> The use of asphyxiating gases is, as you are aware, contrary to the rules and usages of war. Before, therefore, we fall to the level of the degraded Germans [by retaliating in kind] I must submit the matter to the Government . . . These methods show to what depth of infamy our enemies will go in order to supplement their want of courage in facing our troops.

Notwithstanding this hesitation, the British would soon become far more proficient than the Germans in the use of gas.*

Meanwhile the conventional logic of defence insisted that if ground is worth holding in the first place, it is worth counter-attacking to regain once lost. Foch, in actual command of French troops in the north-west, and moral command of the BEF, ordered just this – a whole series of costly attacks ('Second Ypres', which would continue until late May).

The alternative, to acknowledge that the Ypres salient was worth hanging on to only if it came without a price – which with a restive German opponent was never likely to be the case – seemed out of the question. When Smith-Dorrien, who had not been laggard in the fight to restore the situation on the left at Ypres, protested at the counter-attacks and suggested straightening the line by withdrawing from the now even more constricted projection in the line, Sir John French took the opportunity he had been looking for since Le Cateau and dismissed him on 6 May, appointing Sir Herbert Plumer, V Corps, in his place.

It was not as if Smith-Dorrien was in any sense a passive sort of general. Le Cateau alone had shown that, as had his pre-Christmas directives on offensive action to overcome the iniquities of trench life close to the enemy. Indeed, with his sacking the BEF lost its best potential commander-in-chief – as French well knew; or rather, he knew that Smith-Dorrien, as it were, waited in the wings. Smith-*Doreen*, as his detractors (including Haig) couldn't help but call him, knew his business and had the strength of character to prevail. He was a year younger than Plumer, six years younger than French and only three years older than Haig. When James Grierson suffered his heart attack in the train to Maubeuge, French had

* Poison gas had been used on the Eastern Front but the western allies had no provisions to counter it other than the urine-soaked handkerchief expedient hastily advised by the regimental medical officers. Some 7,000 gas (chlorine) casualties, including many temporarily or permanently blinded, were treated by the field ambulances, with 350 British deaths recorded. The BEF would release gas from cylinders at Loos in September, but quickly appreciated the limitations – not least the reliance on wind – and instead developed gas-filled shells.

telegrammed the War Office and asked for Plumer to be sent out in his place. Kitchener – exceeding his authority as secretary of state (appointments subordinate to a commander-in-chief were the business of the CIGS) – sent Smith-Dorrien instead. Plumer was more than capable, and four-star generals, of which Smith-Dorrien had been one for a full two years, were few; there was no reason to appoint one to a three-star command without particular cause – in this instance, almost certainly to 'understudy' the C-in-C.

Smith-Dorrien's weakness, besides an explosive temper (if that *is* a weakness), was his failure to perceive the vulnerability of his own position and the insincerity of his chief.*

Had Kitchener seen him as the man to take over from French, 'as and when'? There is no firm evidence. However, in her diary of 19 May, Margot Asquith recorded a conversation with 'K' at dinner in which she asked his opinion of French. He told her that in terms of intuition and courage he was 'the greatest soldier living in the field', that 'If you say "Mass your men up there", or "Take this or that position", he will carry out your orders better than anyone'; but, he added, 'he is the worst organizer, and a stupid man. He can't make a plan of any kind; he is bad at staff work, and has a bad staff.'†

There could be no more complete a statement of the hopelessness in which the BEF found itself.

Nor could there be a much more contrary statement, and on the face of it something must be awry. Margot Asquith took particular pains with her diary, however, and 'stupid' is not a word easily misheard. That the secretary of state thought this an apt epithet for

* Haig's diary entry of 30 April is illuminating: 'Sir John also told me Smith-Dorrien had caused him much trouble. "He was quite unfit (he said) to hold the Command of an Army" so Sir J. had withdrawn all troops from his control except the II Corps. Yet Smith-D. stayed on! He would not resign! French is to ask Lord Kitchener to find him something to do at home. . . . He also alluded to Smith-Dorrien's conduct on the retreat, and said he ought to have tried him by Court Martial, because (on the day of Le Cateau) he "had ordered him to retire at 8 am and he did not attempt to do so but insisted on fighting in spite of his orders to retire".'

† *Margot Asquith's Great War Diary 1914–1916*, ed. Michael and Eleanor Brock (London, 2014). All subsequent references are to this edition.

the commander-in-chief of the largest British army in the field is troubling, to say the least. But his remarks shed even more light on his reservations about GHQ: 'He has a bad staff.' He certainly had had a bad staff with Archibald Murray at its head and Henry Wilson meddling, but by this time 'Wully' Robertson had replaced Murray (thereby clipping Wilson's wings somewhat). Kitchener's opinion of the BEF's new chief of staff did not augur well, for in December Robertson would become CIGS. In fact, 'K' would appoint him, which suggests a troubling case of *faute de mieux*.

And then Margot, possibly mindful of the persistent rumours that 'K' himself wanted to be commander-in-chief (even Generalissimo) when the time came for the final victorious advance, asked: 'If you moved French tomorrow, who would you put there?'

The secretary of state appeared to accept that imminent removal was a possibility: '(shrugging, and looking like a Tom-cat quite straight in my face) [he said] I don't know! – perhaps Haig.'

'I don't fancy he would do any better,' Margot suggested, to which the unusually loquacious 'K' replied: 'Well, I can only say the muddle at the front is something <u>awful</u>,' adding that French had changed since South Africa, that 'All of you have spoilt him', that he 'won't take orders now' and 'does things on his own' – and that 'He has just Stellenbosched Smith-Dorrien.'*

This was almost a full two weeks after the 'Stellenbosching', which indicates a certain decency in the handling of the matter in London if Kitchener could presume that Margot did not know of it. Indeed, on his return to England Smith-Dorrien was honoured by being advanced to Knight Grand Cross of the Order of St Michael and St George, and then a month later was appointed GOC-in-C 1st (Home) Army. So, in answering Margot's question who would take over from French, 'K' had no real option but to suggest Haig, for to have recalled French and replaced him with the man he had

* Reference to the army base at Stellenbosch in the Boer War, to which officers found wanting were consigned. Joffre sent the generals he relieved of command to Limoges, which likewise coined a verb – to be *Limogé*.

just sacked would have been a humiliation of the greatest order, and counter-productive at least in the short term. As it was, when French was eventually recalled, in December, it could be 'spun' as a perfectly regular relief after sixteen months in command – and a perfectly reasonable appointment to replace him with the BEF's senior army commander, Haig. Smith-Dorrien would by this time be sailing to take up the appointment of GOC-in-C East Africa in a troublesome campaign against German regulars and levies (though he would never get to his new command, contracting pneumonia on the journey south and returning home unfit for further active duty).

Kitchener was anyway dismayed with French over the 'shell scandal', as Margot knew full well, for her husband had told her before dinner: 'Don't mention munitions, Darling, as naturally K. is very sore over the Repington article.'

The war council's refusal to impose its will on GHQ on the question of priorities – Gallipoli or France – had come back to haunt it; indeed, to plague it. *The Times*'s war correspondent Charles à Court Repington, who had originally lobbied for 'K' to be appointed secretary of state, had on 14 May – at French's prompting – written a coruscating piece on the shell shortage (French had also sent two of his personal staff to London to brief a number of politicians, including Lloyd George and Arthur Balfour, in what Kitchener's biographer calls a 'minor coup d'état'). It had been an accident waiting to happen, for French had been determined to open his own offensive in support of Joffre's ('Second Artois'), and Kitchener had let him, despite what must certainly have been his better judgement:

> Sir John, undeterred by the drain on his resources during his recent struggle [the German attack at Ypres on 22 April and the BEF's counter-attacks], was determined to adhere, on its broad lines, to his main plan. 'The ammunition will be all right,' he had told Kitchener on May 2; he knew his men to be in as high fettle as ever.*

* Arthur, *Life of Lord Kitchener*, vol. III. The effects of the shell shortage were not confined to major offensive operations; the routine of trench warfare required local offensive action, which needed artillery support. An officer of the 7th

And so in the early morning of 9 May the BEF had attacked at Festubert towards Aubers Ridge, while Foch's armies attacked at La Bassée–Artois towards Vimy Ridge, where they were to have attacked in March. Joffre said it was 'the beginning of the end': the war would be over in three weeks. For General Foch, in direct command of the offensive, was employing a new tactic: prolonged and heavy bombardment instead of surprise – six days' hard pounding by 1,250 guns, against four German divisions along a 12-mile front, which eighteen French divisions would then assault.

The attack soon broke down, however, except in the centre, where the corps commanded by General Philippe Pétain, later the hero of Verdun (and later still, in the Second World War, the 'arch-collaborator', president of Vichy France), advanced to a depth of 2 miles; but the Germans managed to close the gap before the French could bring up reserves to exploit the success – a story that would be repeated many times in the coming *série de catastrophes*.

Nor had there been progress in the British sector. As Kitchener's biographer put it, with a solemn respect verging on the sardonic: 'It was quickly and unhappily evident that Sir John would be unable to make good the substantial support he had so manfully intended to lend. He could do little but to employ and destroy a considerable number of Germans, and capture – at sad cost to himself – some not very important trenches.' He added that the

---

Suffolks, a K1 battalion, and one of the first to go into the line, at Ypres, wrote of an action in August to destroy a redoubt being built 100 yards in front of their trenches. 'As those were the days when shells were scarce, we couldn't ask the gunners to blow it up.' Instead a bombing party was assembled under 20-year-old Lieutenant Charles Sorley, a Marlborough schoolboy only eighteen months before. They crawled out at night to do the job, but the raid miscarried when one of the bombers dropped his grenade having pulled the pin. The Germans opened fire, but Sorley, though himself wounded slightly, got the casualties back, including the unfortunate bomber, who died of his wounds the following day. Three rounds of 18-pounder shrapnel would have done the job admirably. Sorley would be killed by a sniper on 13 October at Loos – in the opinion of Robert Graves, 'one of the three poets of importance killed during the war' (*Goodbye To All That*, London, 1929), and in that of John Masefield, Poet Laureate, the greatest loss of all.

French had fared no better: 'Foch was balked of his ardent desire to rush the Vimy Ridge, and his movements were as costly and as devoid of immediate material advantage.'*

Costly indeed: 102,000 casualties.

In fact, for the BEF the cost was proportionately even worse: there had been over eleven thousand casualties on 9 May alone, the great majority within yards of their own front-line trenches – portent of things to come (again and again). Mile for mile, division for division, this was one of the highest rates of loss during the entire war.

But Sir John French knew where the blame lay. When he returned to his headquarters on the ninth, in despondent mood having watched the attack from atop a church tower, he found a telegram from Kitchener asking him to 'hold in readiness for despatch to the Dardanelles via Marseilles by quickest route 20,000 rounds 18-pounder ammunition and 2,000 rounds 4.5-inch howitzer ammunition'.

He at once replied: 'This morning I commenced an important attack, and the battle is likely to last several days. I am warding off a heavy attack East of Ypres at the same time. In these circumstances I cannot possibly accept the responsibility of reducing the stock of ammunition unless it be immediately replaced from home.'

Kitchener reassured him that he would 'see that it is replaced', but insisted that the 'state of affairs in the Dardanelles renders it absolutely essential that the ammunition which has been ordered should be sent off at once'.

The Dardanelles consignment was indeed replaced within twenty-four hours of being despatched, and the temporary depletion of the reserve in no way interfered with French's offensive plans. Yet he briefed Repington as if it had. Why?

To excuse the failure of his attack is the obvious reason, but there was another – to increase the pressure on London to send him the New Army divisions that were ready and otherwise

* Arthur, *Life of Lord Kitchener*, vol. III.

earmarked for Gallipoli, so that he could maintain his offensives throughout the summer. This ploy nearly miscarried when Kitchener pointed out that if French believed he did not have enough ammunition it was unwise to send any more troops, but in the end – indeed on 18 May – 'K' sent him the 14th Division, and others quickly followed, so that by early June the BEF was able to form another army: the 3rd, under command of General Sir Charles Monro (who five months later would replace Hamilton at the Dardanelles).

Thus fortified, Sir John French now felt ready once more to lend full support to Joffre's plans for a grand offensive to finish the war. On 11 June he wrote a long letter to Kitchener, concluding:

> I would urge most strongly that it is very inadvisable that the rôle of the British Army in the field should be one of passive defence. Such a course can only have a disastrous effect upon the moral[e] and offensive spirit of our troops. The prestige of the British Army must suffer if we remain inactive and watch our French comrades attacking day after day. I would also point out that if I denude myself of reserves and pass to the defensive, I cannot undertake to defend the Channel ports should the need arise . . . The only course which in my judgement is compatible both with the requirements of the military situation and the honour of British Arms is that I should co-operate in the proposed French offensive in July with all the resources which His Majesty's Government can place at my disposal.

The honour of British arms. Sir John did not explain why a third BEF offensive that year stood any greater chance of success than the previous two, suggesting only, in a subsequent letter, that 'I never like to anticipate anything in this war, but I am not without hope that before the end of the month affairs may wear a different aspect here.'*

They would not.

Except in the vital case of French morale, which was now on

* Arthur, *Life of Lord Kitchener*, vol. III.

a distinctly downward path. One corps commander (François Anthoine) wrote that his troops had 'lapsed into a gloomy sort of resignation' – his letter was read out in the Chamber of Deputies – while another (Pierre Dubois, who would command 6th Army with great resolution at Verdun), begged President Poincaré when he visited the Arras sector in July 'to put a stop to these local offensives; the instrument of victory is being broken in our hands'.*

Nearly a million French casualties in 1914, and a million and a half in 1915: little wonder that Clemenceau, from the other side of the chamber, was warning Poincaré of incipient mutiny.

In fact the only allied success of any note in 1915 would be diplomatic: on 23 May, Italy declared war on Austria.

* Quoted in Basil Liddell Hart, *Foch: The Man of Orleans* (London, 1931).

Chapter Eight

THE HONOUR OF BRITISH ARMS

Three days after Italy joined the war, Asquith's new coalition cabinet met for the first time. The change of government had come about not through any vote of no confidence but from a general sense of drift that made the Unionist opposition restless.* The stalling of the Dardanelles campaign, the consequent resignation of Admiral Fisher, the 'shell scandal' – Asquith judged he had no option but to shore up his premiership by bringing the Tories into government. In the event it would buy him only eighteen months.

By what secret, black and midnight process the portfolios were distributed is uncertain (Margot Asquith's diary testifies to the murk), but Arthur Balfour, the last Conservative prime minister (1902–5), went to the Admiralty, and Churchill was made chancellor of the duchy of Lancaster, a sinecure which carried a seat in cabinet, from which he would continue to argue for the Dardanelles campaign – until November when, with its abandonment, he would put on uniform and go to France. Lloyd George left the Treasury to take charge of the new Ministry of Munitions. It was ostensibly a

* The Liberal Unionist Party had been formed in 1886 by a breakaway faction of the Liberals opposed to Irish home rule. With the Conservatives they had formed the coalition Unionist government of 1895–1905 until formal merger in 1912 as the Conservative and Unionist Party. The Ulster unionists took the Tory whip.

step down, but at that moment it placed him at the key point of the war effort, and represented an implied criticism of Kitchener.

Save, however, for the improvement in munitions supply that Lloyd George achieved, and the eventual introduction of conscription (or, at least, the mechanism for it), the new cabinet would prove no more effectual in determining grand strategy than its predecessor.

On the Western Front it was business as usual. Despite the views of the French corps commanders who had taken part in the Artois offensive that further attacks would be fruitless, and that of General Castelnau (who had so impressed Lloyd George in October 1914) that the French army should stand on the defensive until there was a genuine chance of decisive action, as well as that of Foch, even, who now thought the situation unpropitious, Joffre and his staff at Chantilly were of the contrary opinion. Chantilly, a pretty town on the northern outskirts of Paris, was geometrically perfect for the headquarters of a C-in-C whose eyes (and staff car) necessarily ranged the length of the line of trenches running from the Belgian sand dunes to the Swiss border in visiting his subordinate headquarters, which were themselves suitably 'triangulated'. Importantly, it was out of German artillery range; indeed, when the weather conditions were favourable, it was even out of *earshot*. That it was so far back from the front line cannot but have been a factor in his dismissal of the opinions of subordinates.

President Poincaré knew of the generals' almost universally pessimistic views but was evidently not minded, or not able, to relieve Joffre. After all, in August 1914 the government had bolted from Paris, and Joffre had been its saviour – or so it appeared. The generals too seemed helpless to act on their own opinions. Even Castelnau – Noël Édouard Marie Joseph, Vicomte de Curières de Castelnau – though there was none more honourable, put aside his doubts on being made commander of the central group of armies. And so plans for an autumn offensive went ahead, 'so strong is the binding power of the chain of command', as Liddell Hart put it.*

* *World War I in Outline.*

After the Boulogne conference of 19–20 June – a British gathering with French observers, called principally to discuss munitions and chaired by Lloyd George – the War Office and GHQ staff conducted a new study of the relative artillery strengths on the Western Front. They concluded that the proportion of German heavy artillery to field guns was twice that of the allies, and that their daily shell production was double the allied output. The *Official History* says that the British military authorities then concluded that for any allied offensive to have a reasonable chance of success it would have to be made on a continuous front of 25 miles, by a force of no fewer than thirty-six divisions supported by 1,150 heavy guns and howitzers *and* the normal quantity of field artillery. But as this quantity of guns and the associated ammunition could not be provided before the spring of 1916 it was 'preferable, whatever the general situation, to remain on the active defensive in the western theatre of war'.*

In his memoirs, Lloyd George says that he cannot recall Kitchener ever communicating this analysis to the cabinet or the war council, though he recalls that 'K' did tell the cabinet that he was opposed to Joffre's autumn offensive, in which the BEF was expected to play a significant part, and yet felt obliged to go along with it for the sake of allied relations. 'In consequence of this weak decision [by the cabinet as a whole] the great autumn offensive was undertaken.'†

Nevertheless, on the eve of the offensive the cabinet did send Kitchener to France to try once more to persuade Joffre to call it off. The effort failed. The offensive was essential, Joffre insisted, on both political and military grounds: the situation on the Eastern

* *Official History*, vol. I.

† Kitchener's opinion was perhaps more Delphic on this matter than any other. Churchill recalled seeing him at the War Office in the third week of August: 'He told me that he had agreed with the French to a great offensive in France. I said at once that there was no chance of success. He said that the scale would restore everything, including of course the Dardanelles. He had an air of suppressed excitement like a man who has taken a great decision of terrible uncertainty, and is about to put it into execution.' Churchill, *The World Crisis*.

Front was once again perilous. Sir John French agreed. Significantly, however, Haig, whose 1st Army would have to carry out the attack, had objected when first seeing the proposal (in June) because the supply of heavy guns and shells was still inadequate, and the ground was unfavourable – though Joffre thought it 'particularly favourable'. By September he too had come round, in part because of the visceral instinct that standing on the defensive was the prelude to defeat. Indeed, when in July Joffre gathered his army group commanders together and discussed Kitchener's arguments for waiting until British manpower and munitions had reached full flow, they agreed that it was 'heresy'. Besides, leaving all military judgement aside, 'Kitchener [could] pronounce at his ease, having no invaded provinces to liberate.'*

Thus allied strategy was to be subordinated to patriotic sentiment.

And far more would be sacrificed to that sentiment than just the immediate loss of life. In its haste to liberate the invaded territories, the Entente had forfeited, and would continue to forfeit, one chance after another to improve its overall strategic situation through its obsession with the quasi-Clausewitzian ideal of not merely defeating but *destroying* the main army of the main enemy. Joffre and his adherents in GHQ, who in turn dominated their respective national perspectives, would see Bulgaria join the Central Powers, let their ally Serbia be over-run, let slip the chance of fatally weakening Austria, let Russia drift away from the fight, and cause significant numbers of British forces to be pinned down in the Near and Middle East for the rest of the war. For four years they would pursue an ideal without seriously asking: 'Do the conditions make it practicable?'

And in the end, as the crowning irony, victory against the main army of the main enemy would come from an unanticipated

* Quoted in Liddell Hart, *Foch*. The *Official History* remarks that Kitchener may have expected that in the great breakthrough and decisive advance he would be invited to take overall command, and was therefore not inclined to be too obstructive (cf. Margot Asquith's dinner party conversation *re* a successor to Sir John French). It is a dispiriting possibility, perhaps, but the evidence is practically non-existent.

change of conditions: an over-reaching German offensive in 1918 that broke the stalemate of the four-year siege that was the Western Front – but an offensive by a German army much weakened by indirect action and by another (in a sense even greater) siege, the Royal Navy's economic blockade, which lethally undermined both civil and military capacity to fight.

The great autumn offensive of 1915, with its simultaneous attacks in Champagne (Castelnau) and Arras (Foch, with the BEF in a supporting attack on his left at Loos) began on 25 September. It had, said Joffre at his final conference before the battle, 'a certain guarantee of success'; he was 'confident of a great and possibly complete victory'. The cavalry were to move up ready to pour through the breaches and 'make a relentless pursuit without waiting for the infantry, and with the frontier as their objective'. A four-day bombardment would suppress or destroy the defences.

Falkenhayn would be taken by surprise. He disbelieved the indications of an offensive – the activity identified by aerial reconnaissance, the increased signal traffic, the talk in the streets of Paris and London of a 'big push', even the bombardment itself – for the *Grosser Generalstab*'s assessment was that the French were simply not in a condition to attack. This was not unreasonable, since it was the view of the French corps commanders too. Accordingly, Falkenhayn refused to reinforce either sector. When the shelling began, the local commanders pulled back their forward troops to secondary positions to avoid its worst effects, and when the French attacked in Champagne, where Joffre had located the main effort, allocating thirty-four divisions (giving them a superiority of five to one, as opposed to three to one in Foch's sector), they quickly overran the first line. But then they ran into serious opposition. For three days Castelnau's army group battered away at the Germans' second line, giving Falkenhayn time to rush in reserves, until Pétain, now commanding 2nd Army, called off his attack in defiance of orders.

Not only had Castelnau's attack failed; its early success had had the perverse effect of hastening the failure of Foch's, and therefore Haig's. Foch's subordinate commanders, after a year on the receiving end of his vacuously aggressive precepts and vehement orders, were already taking the *outrance* out of *offensive* by what Liddell Hart called 'gentle evasion'; now, seeing Castelnau's spectacular progress on the first day, with its delusive promise of breakthrough and the victory that he had been predicting, Joffre decided to put all his weight behind Castelnau and told Foch to halt his attacks temporarily, though he must 'take care to avoid giving the British the impression that we are leaving them to attack alone'.

For the British attack at Loos appeared to be going quite well. It was the biggest the BEF had yet carried out – six divisions and one of cavalry (more than had gone to France in August 1914) – with the Indian Corps of two divisions in support, and three more in reserve under the control of GHQ. But of these nine (British) infantry divisions, only five were regular; three were 'New Army', of which two had not yet been in the trenches, and one a territorial. Although this did not mean any deficit in courage and eagerness for the fight – these men had been the first to answer Kitchener's call for volunteers* – in terms of battle skill there would certainly be shortcomings. A year is no time in which to train an individual soldier, let alone battalions, brigades and divisions.

The Loos battlefield, uniformly flat and dominated by slagheaps, lay immediately north and west of the mining town of Lens. Joffre was right: it was 'particularly favourable' – but for the defence. Haig's earlier misgivings had been to some extent allayed by resort to a new and secret weapon – gas. The cabinet had approved its use after the German chlorine attacks at Ypres in April (French would probably have resigned had they not done so, on the grounds that it would have been impossible to maintain morale and discipline without dealing like for like), but he 'reminded Gough [GOC I

* Though there would be strong criticism of some of the territorials, notably by Cavan, commanding the Guards Division.

Corps] that we shall win "Not by might nor by power, but by *My spirit*, saith the Lord of Hosts".'

It might have been more apt to seek the intercession of St Barbara, patron saint of artillerymen – or the direct help of the god of the west wind, for Haig's high hopes for his gas attack were to be cruelly dashed. Gas shells had yet to be developed, so the chlorine had to be released from cylinders, needing a breeze strong enough to carry it to the enemy's trenches but not so strong as to disperse it.

On 25 September, Colonel John Charteris, Haig's intelligence officer (or 'Haig's evil counsellor', as he would become known when he moved with his chief to GHQ in December), noted:

> There was not a breath of wind until 5 a.m., but before that Gold's* reports had become pretty confident that the wind would be favourable. I went to D[ouglas].H[aig]. at 2 a.m., when we had just received a report from a distant station that made Gold reasonably hopeful. Our own report from the line was that it was dead still. At 3, when the decision had to be made, I took Gold . . . to D.H. Gold was then more confident and D.H. ordered zero hour for 5.50 [in present-day terms, 'H Hour' – the time at which the leading troops cross the start line. Haig's diary says 5.30] . . . At 5 he came to our office with Fletcher [ADC]. There was quite a faint breath of wind then, and Fletcher's cigarette smoke moved quite perceptibly towards the Germans. But it died away again in a few minutes, and a little later D.H. sent down a message from the tower to 1st Corps to enquire if the attack could still be held up. Gough replied that it was too late to change. I was with D.H. when the reply was brought in. He was very upset.†

With strongly hierarchical communications – the landline principally – these things were bound to happen; what is more

* (Temporary) Captain (later Lieutenant-Colonel) Ernest Gold, formerly Reader in Dynamical Meteorology at Cambridge, and the Meteorological Office's superintendent of statistics. His employment as Haig's meteorological officer was an example of the army's sometimes willing embrace of civilian expert opinion. At other times, notably in the development of the tank, it was not so far-sighted.

† Brigadier-General John Charteris, *At G.H.Q.* (London, 1931). There are significant discrepancies between this account and that presented in Haig's diary, the latter making no mention of the attempt to delay the attack.

difficult to understand is the decision of GOC 2nd Division, Major-General Henry (later General Lord) Horne, to ignore the advice of his gas officer not to release the cloud because of insufficient breeze. As a result of his insistence that 'the programme must be carried out whatever the conditions', his own division, with their rudimentary gas hoods, suffered over two thousand gas casualties, though mercifully only a handful of these were fatal.

In all, 140 tons of chlorine were released from five thousand containers. Some of it did indeed serve its purpose. On the extreme right, where the 15th (Scottish) Division attacked, the gas carried well into the German lines, and the Scots nearly broke through, causing considerable consternation in the German command. The 47th (London) Division, the territorials, despite heavy casualties also made good progress, in one case with unconventional and unauthorized tactics. Disobeying orders, just before zero hour Rifleman Frank Edwards, one of the London Irish Rifles' football team, pulled a leather football from his knapsack and started to inflate it. 'Just imagine, as I did,' he later recalled, 'a party of London Irishmen, with our war cry of "Hurroo" charging across No Man's Land passing the ball forward to finish up the mad rush by leaping into their trench with the rifle and bayonet.'* The ball got stuck in wire, but enough of the riflemen didn't, though Edwards himself was wounded.

Haig had no reserves to exploit these partial successes, however, having put all his divisions into the attack, trusting instead to the early release of the GHQ reserves; and these had been kept, at Sir John French's insistence, 16 miles to the rear, which now meant a forced approach march. The delay was exacerbated by French's own perambulation: during the morning he and some of his staff moved unexpectedly to Chateau Philomel, 3 miles south of Lillers, the original concentration area for XI Corps (the reserve). (French had a habit of moving around unpredictably like this; he had

* Michael MacDonagh, *The Irish at the Front* (London, 1916).

frequently been out of communication during the retreat from Mons – and, indeed, during the battle itself.) From here he could communicate only by public telephone, and it was not until early afternoon that Haig learned that XI Corps was now under his command – though not, of course, to hand. Nor did it help that Haig, understandably, wanted to make up for lost time; and a commander receiving new troops invariably imagines that on arrival they are already watered, fed and rested and therefore ready for immediate use. The divisions pushed on across country in the dark. By dawn the men were already tired, with several miles still to go to the German front line. Congestion on the roads further slowed their progress. As the *Official History* put it: 'It was like trying to push the Lord Mayor's procession through the streets of London without clearing the route and holding up the traffic.' And two-thirds of the 'procession' (the New Army divisions) had never been in the 'streets of London' before – or, indeed, in a procession of any kind. When they eventually reached the front, in heavy rain again, tired and hungry – and, worse, confused – they would make their attacks with inadequate artillery support against defences which the Germans had worked all night to strengthen. In the words of Liddell Hart: 'The attack broke down and the survivors broke back.'*

John Buchan, author of *The Thirty-Nine Steps*, visited the battlefields only days later:

> Let me describe it. Looking from the high road, the skyline is about a thousand yards distant, and beyond it rise the strange twin towers of Loos, like the rigging of a ship seen far off at sea. The place is not very 'healthy' – no hinterland is – but, though the shelling was continuous, the trenches were fairly safe.
>
> Beyond the old British front trench you pass through the debris of our wire defences and cross the hundred yards of No Man's Land over which, for so many months, our men looked at the enemy. Then you

* *World War I in Outline.*

reach the German entanglements, wonderfully cut to pieces by our shell-fire [the wire was not as deep and thick as that of 1916, and it had been cut in large measure by the troops following up in support]. There our own dead are lying very thick. Presently you are in the German front trenches. Here, in some parts, are masses of German dead, and some of our own. This is the famous Loos Road Redoubt, a work about five hundred yards in diameter. It is an amazing network, ramified beyond belief, but now a monument to the power of our artillery. It is all ploughed up and mangled like a sand castle which a child has demolished in a fit of temper. Fragments of shell, old machine-gun belts, rifle cartridges, biscuit tins, dirty pads of cotton wool are everywhere, and a horrible number of unburied bodies.

But the chief interest of the Redoubt is the view. The whole battlefield of our recent advance is plain to the eye. Below, in the hollow, lie the ruins of Loos around the gaunt tower. Beyond is the slope of Hill 70, with the houses of Lens showing to the south-east. North, one can see St Elie and Haisnes, hidden in a cloud of high explosives, and west of them the Hohenzollern Redoubt and the ill-omened slagheap, Fosse 8. It is that sight rare in this present war, an old-fashioned battlefield, all quite open and bare and baked. The tactical elements can be grasped in a minute or two.

And, to complete the picture, the dead are everywhere around one, high explosives and shrapnel boom overhead, the thresh of an airplane's propeller comes faint from the high heavens, and up towards Fosse 8 is a never-ending mutter of machineguns. Only living soldiers seem to be absent, for, though battle is joined two miles off, scarcely a human being is visible in the landscape.*

Joffre, French and now Haig were determined to continue; so many lives lost already could not become a worthless sacrifice – and the enemy must surely be suffering too? (In fact the German dead at Loos were around half the number of British lives lost.) But German counter-attacks and heavy rain delayed the renewal of the offensive in all three sectors, with the British the last to return to

* *The Times*, 6 October 1915.

the fray on 13 October. Fighting continued officially until 18 October. In the opinion of the official historian, the renewed attacks 'had not improved the general situation in any way and had brought nothing but useless slaughter of infantry'.

The Battle of Loos was one of the British army's bloodiest defeats ever – fifty thousand casualties, of which at least eight thousand were killed in action or died of wounds. One of them was 2nd Lieutenant John ('Jack') Kipling of the Irish Guards, Rudyard Kipling's only son, who was just eighteen and had been in France just a month. The Commonwealth War Graves Commission only identified his remains in 1992. Another was Captain the Honourable Fergus Bowes-Lyon of the 8th Black Watch, the late Queen Mother's brother, who has no precisely known grave. Another casualty, who might well have died but for the devotion of his own guardsmen, was the future Conservative prime minister Harold Macmillan.

Three divisional commanders (major-generals) were killed, along with three brigade commanders and a staggering twenty-nine – one in four – commanding officers. Not surprisingly, the great majority of the commanding officers were of New Army battalions: the less experienced the unit, the more visible the leadership had to be. These losses could be made up relatively easily – there is always a man ready and waiting for promotion – but the losses in junior leadership, the company officers, could not. The weakening of the battalions in the numerical sense was a temporary setback; battle-casualty replacements had been earmarked and in many cases were already in France at the base depots. But the loss of junior officers weakened the battalions far more in the longer term. The typical 'bayonet' (attacking) strength of a battalion at this time was 650–750 men and 30–35 officers. In thirty-two battalions the loss of officers was over 50 per cent. The 8th Seaforth Highlanders and 12th Highland Light Infantry lost twenty-three officers each, and the 8th Royal West Kents and 8th Royal East Kents (The Buffs) twenty-four each. Six battalions lost over six hundred men, two of them almost seven hundred. So appalled – or grimly satisfied – were the

Germans with their machine guns that they called the battle *Der Leichenfeld von Loos*, 'The Field of Corpses of Loos'.

And the great majority of the corpses were from Lloyd George's 'better class of artisan, the upper and the lower middle classes' – exactly as he'd feared.

This was not a disaster that could be easily explained away. Yes, the war council had failed to heed its own conclusions about priorities – Western Front versus Gallipoli – and it had given way over the date of the offensive – this year rather than next, meaning that raw troops were brought to France too quickly (as well as to Gallipoli); but it surely could expect some more competent performance from the high command?

The press were certainly beginning to think so. On 15 October, following the foreign secretary's statement on policy in the Balkans, *The Times* thundered:

> The House of Commons was muzzled yesterday by the Prime Minister's procedure, and was constrained to listen in silence to a singularly jejune statement from Sir Edward Grey. But the House of Lords, which is less susceptible to Ministerial management, not for the first time refused to be gagged, and in a short and spirited debate gave expression to some of the doubts which haunt the nation. The country has treated this Government and its predecessor with a confidence no former Government ever ventured to ask of it; but, in spite of all the ill-judged efforts to withhold from it information it has a right to possess and the concealment of which can serve no purpose, it has learnt too much not to feel that confidence sorely shaken. When the amplest allowance has been made for the delicacy of the European situation, it is impossible not to describe the statement of the Foreign Secretary as utterly disappointing.
>
> The Government are under a dangerous delusion if they suppose that criticism has been exaggerated by the Press. Dissatisfaction is expressed in all quarters, and the reflection it finds in the newspapers is pale. It extends to the diplomacy, the strategy, and the general conduct of the war. The want of cohesion and direction in the Government is felt everywhere. The true story of the Dardanelles expedition is becoming a matter of common knowledge, and it is not a story that

redounds to the credit of those responsible for the scheme. It is not possible to stifle the truth in a matter of this kind. The letters which are weekly reaching thousands of homes all over the country speak for themselves. The wounded who are returning tell the tale of blunders and mismanagement they have witnessed, and from which they have suffered.

Lord Lansdowne confined himself to the usual assertions that, while Ministers were eager for debate, duty forbade them to take part in it at the present moment. There may be force in these contentions, but they have been repeated too often. They recur whenever it has been desired to submit any of the blunders of the Government to examination. It is never the time, in their opinion, for even the most discriminating discussion. The situation is always delicate for them, and that inevitably deepens the misgivings of the public.

Haig was only too aware of how the questions about Loos would be formed, and on 29 September had written to Kitchener:

You will doubtless recollect how earnestly I pressed you to ensure an adequate Reserve being close in rear of my attacking Divisions, and under my orders. It may interest you to know what has happened. No Reserve was placed under me. My attack, as has been reported, was a complete success. The enemy had no troops in his second line, which some of my plucky fellows reached and entered without opposition. Prisoners state the enemy was so hard put to it for troops to stem our advance that the officers' servants, fatigue-men, etc., in Lens were pushed forward to hold their second line east of Loos and Hill 70. The two Reserve Divisions (under C-in-C's orders) were directed to join me as soon as the success of First Army was known at GHQ. They . . . crossed our old trench line . . . at 6pm. We had captured Loos 12 hours previously. We were in a position to make this the turning point in the war . . . but naturally I feel very annoyed at the lost opportunity.

A turning point of the war? Hardly; not with an exploitation force of one division of cavalry and three of infantry, two of which were hearing their first shots fired in anger; but they might at least have been able to hang on to the initial gains, which would have been some consolation bearing in mind the casualties, and would also, as the only success of the allied offensive, have given Sir John French more leverage in his future dealings with Joffre.

Besides his letter to Kitchener – irregular to say the least – Haig was also in constant and close touch throughout October with the King and with Haldane (Lady Haig had been one of Queen Alexandra's ladies-in-waiting, and Haig had been one of Haldane's men at the War Office during his great reforms), and through these channels was encouraged to express his views of Sir John French – which he was quite ready to do.

French's own PR operation, predictably leaden, was also under way. His official despatch was published in *The Times* on 2 November, not only with many (perhaps understandable) minor errors of detail, which undermined its authority, but also containing misstatements of fact about the transfer of the GHQ reserve to 1st Army command. French also primed Repington – this had, after all, worked to his short-term advantage over the shell shortage – who wrote a supporting article suggesting things might have gone better had French rather than Haig been in command of the battle. Haig at once wrote to French asking for the despatch to be publicly corrected, which French refused to do.

Kitchener was at this point at Gallipoli, where he had gone to assess the situation for himself in light of Monro's recommendation to evacuate, and in his absence the cabinet decided to take action. 'On Kitchener's return from the Dardanelles [30 November] he found that the government had decided to relieve Sir John French of his command in the field,' wrote his biographer somewhat blithely. There were 'other important duties' awaiting Sir John at home, and now 'the Government sought a soldier who would add to Sir John's fine military qualities an even temper, a cool judgement, a broad outlook – and an aloofness from politics'.*

* Arthur, *Life of Lord Kitchener*, vol. III. Sir George Arthur (1860–1946) had served with the Life Guards in Kitchener's Egyptian Campaign in 1882, on the Nile

In other words, suggested Arthur, Sir John French may have had some fine military qualities, but he was of uneven temper, hot-headed, narrow-minded and meddlesome.

Fortunately, such a man as they sought 'was to their hand in the person of Sir Douglas Haig'.

De mortuis nil nisi bonum – unless by way of praise for his successor.

On 3 December Kitchener told Haig that he would approach the prime minister to recommend that he succeed French. Seven days later he sent Haig a telegram saying that Sir John French had indeed resigned, and that he was therefore appointed commander-in-chief subject to the formality of the King's assent.

He would take command of the BEF at midday on 19 December.

In addition Haig learned that Sir William Robertson, 'Wully', was to be appointed CIGS.

Box and Cox.

The die was now cast for 1916.

Expedition of 1884–5 and with the Yeomanry in South Africa. He was Kitchener's personal private secretary between 1914 and 1916, rejoining the army and fighting in France after his principal's death in 1916.

PART THREE

1916: Attrition

The world bloodily-minded,
The Church dead or polluted,
The blind leading the blinded,
And the deaf dragging the muted.

Israel Zangwill, '1916'

Chapter Nine

THE GATE OF THE YEAR

'The situation which the War Secretary and the Chief of the Staff [*sic*] had to consider at the close of 1915 was none too rosy,' wrote Kitchener's biographer, with masterly understatement.

It was certainly a very different one from that which few but Kitchener had foreseen when the impromptu council of war had gathered in the Cabinet Room on 5 August 1914, the day after Britain formally declared war on Germany. France had entered the war with ninety-seven active infantry divisions and the equivalent of thirty-seven territorial divisions; and it was expected that Russia would muster 128. On the other hand, Britain had been able to count just eleven regular divisions – of which five were not fully formed, with only the constituent battalions, lacking the infrastructure of command and control, combat support and logistics, and scattered all over the world – and fourteen territorial divisions. The war council's immediate decision had simply been whether and where to send the five or six divisions that constituted the British army's striking force, or 'Expeditionary Force' as it had lately become known. Now, in January 1916, the army had more than quadrupled in size, as Kitchener had willed it to (in June the BEF, including the Indian and Dominion forces, would have a million men), giving Britain a stronger voice in military strategy – not least because it promised more to follow. The BEF had managed to keep its regular units topped up throughout the first winter by recalling reservists to the colours, and between August 1914 and January 1916 through voluntary enlistment alone nearly two and a half million men had passed through the recruiting offices into the 'New Army' units.

France, on the other hand, having borne the brunt of the fighting on the Western Front, was nearing the bottom of her immediate casualty replacement barrel. Italy's entry into the war offered some relief, but although she now had 36 divisions in the line, they were critically short of heavy artillery, and though she had an ample reserve of manpower her losses in a series of artless attacks astride the Isonzo river had mounted to sixty thousand dead and more than a hundred and fifty thousand wounded, a quarter of her mobilized forces. The only new divisions likely to be available to the allies in 1916 would therefore be British – Kitchener's New Armies, and a few more territorials, once they completed their training.

These, however, would be greener than any troops yet to enter the field. 'I have not got an Army in France really,' Haig would write in his diary at the end of March, 'but a collection of divisions untrained for the field.' He did not think they would be ready for battle until, at the earliest, the middle of summer.

In January, after the evacuation of Gallipoli, Asquith's war committee, as it was now called, took stock. The British army, including imperial (dominion and Indian) troops in Europe and Egypt, now totalled fifty-nine first-line divisions and thirteen of second-line (home service) territorials. GHQ considered that a minimum of twenty-eight divisions was needed to maintain a purely defensive front in France and Flanders. Thirteen divisions were needed in England and Ireland (in England for defence against invasion and in Ireland to keep the peace) and eight divisions for the defence of the Suez Canal; five had been despatched to Salonika. This left a surplus of eighteen divisions, which if employed in France could generate a force of between forty-two and (theoretically) fifty-nine

British divisions for an offensive, the committee calculating that the Germans would not risk landings in England while under attack on the Western Front, and that therefore the home-defence divisions could be transferred thither (though legislation would be required to compel the second-line territorials). On the other hand, an offensive in Salonika would release no divisions from home defence. The calculation was further complicated, however, when in late January the CID concluded that no fewer than ten German divisions – some 160,000 men – could be secretly embarked and then put ashore on the east coast of England without the navy being certain of intercepting them.

To meet this threat, Viscount French of Ypres and of High Lake in the County of Roscommon, as the new C-in-C home forces was now styled, demanded nine divisions, plus seventeen mounted and ten independent (Yeomanry and TF) brigades – a field force of 230,000 men – in addition to the garrisons for defended posts and vulnerable points which separately amounted to 220,000 men (indeed, with the 'Easter Rising' of 1916 – the IRA offensive in Dublin – the number of troops in Britain and Ireland would rise to half a million).

And still there was no conscription.

As the war committee struggled with what must have looked like a giant board-game called *Strategy*, they were still unable to see all the counters on the table, and the dice seemed strangely loaded. Despite the continuing blandishments of Joffre, there was no prospect of a decisive breakthrough on the Western Front. The Gallipoli campaign had come to an ignominious end, redeemed somewhat by the skilful withdrawal and evacuation, though as Churchill would say of the even more famous 'miracle of deliverance' from Dunkirk twenty-five years later, wars are not won by evacuations. The Middle East, where things had begun well enough, was not looking nearly as promising as it had at the beginning of the year. A half-hearted Ottoman attack on the Suez Canal had been repulsed, but Sinai was still in enemy hands, prompting the taunt in the BEF and the London clubs: 'Is the army of Egypt protecting the Suez Canal, or is the Suez Canal protecting the army of Egypt?' In Mesopotamia (modern Iraq) the force that had quickly secured the oil fields around Basra in 1914 had begun advancing upriver the following May, almost reaching the gates of Baghdad, but then after an indecisive battle at Ctesiphon had withdrawn to Kut-al-Amara, to which in December the Turks had laid siege, and which in April would surrender in humiliation.*

Above all, the situation on the east European fronts was verging on the catastrophic, even if neither Paris nor London had yet realized. Serbia, the forgotten ally, had fallen. Indeed, leaving Serbia to fend for herself in 1915 remains one of the more mystifying blind spots of allied grand strategy. After all, this outpost in the Balkans had been both pivotal and promising. The Serbs were a hardy nation, and the country was tough going at the best of times. In the winter it was deadly, as the Austrians had soon found out. Serbia's situation had been not unlike that of Spain in 1808, when Britain had poured troops into the Peninsula under the command of Sir Arthur Wellesley, duke of Wellington, in the belief that here at last was somewhere that a small but capable army could make a difference, and where sea power could be brought to bear on the campaign. The 'Spanish ulcer', Bonaparte had called it. There was no reason why in 1915 there should not have been a 'Serbian ulcer', except that Joffre, who blew hot and cold on the subject, and Sir John French, seeing things only in terms of mass, could not see how enough troops could be spared to exploit it.

Yet the Serbian army had not been small – some 450,000 men when fully mobilized. What it lacked was equipment and certain expertise (heavy artillery and aircraft would have been particularly useful in that terrain). For the first half of 1915, however, Paris and London (reflecting the opinion of *GQG* and GHQ) regarded the options as all or nothing; and, being unable or unwilling to provide the former, opted for the latter. By the summer of 1915 Berlin

* Although the Mesopotamia campaign was run by the government of British India, there were inevitably implications for London.

had become anxious to close the account with Belgrade both for reasons of prestige and to secure rail communications with Turkey. And in this, Bulgarian muscle would be desirable, if not essential. For months Sofia had been sitting on the fence trying to see which way the winds of war were blowing, and after the Suvla Bay débâcle it was clear that they were not blowing the Entente any good. In August, Berlin had begun sending reinforcements to Austria's southern front, and on 6 September the Central Powers concluded a secret treaty with Bulgaria, offering her territory to be taken from Serbia. On 6 October an Austro-German force under General August von Mackensen, who had commanded a corps at Tannenberg with great skill and tenacity, crossed the Danube, while on 11 October Bulgarian troops, undeterred by a Russian ultimatum, struck at eastern Serbia and a few days later at Serbian Macedonia.

After months of Byzantine negotiations, therefore, 'one of the most important chapters in the history of diplomacy' was closed, wrote Asquith – and most unsatisfactorily, for which he blamed Russia and, most of all, Serbia and her 'obstinacy and cupidity'.* Bulgaria's entry into the war had made the allies' position on Gallipoli increasingly perilous, introducing a major new source of men and materiel as well as a hostile power on the Black Sea even if there had been a naval breakthrough. In many respects it had sealed the fate of the campaign. When 'Wully' Robertson minuted Sir Edward Grey in the New Year lamenting that diplomacy had not had much success of late in the war (forgetting, rather, the Italian coup), Grey replied not unreasonably that diplomacy in war depended on military success – and there had been precious little of that.†

And now there was another counter on the *Strategy* board – a half-hearted expeditionary landing in the southern Balkans, for when Paris and London had learned of the October offensive on

* Asquith to the King, PRO CAB 37/135.

† It was, of course, a variation on what Frederick the Great had said: 'Diplomacy without arms is like music without instruments.'

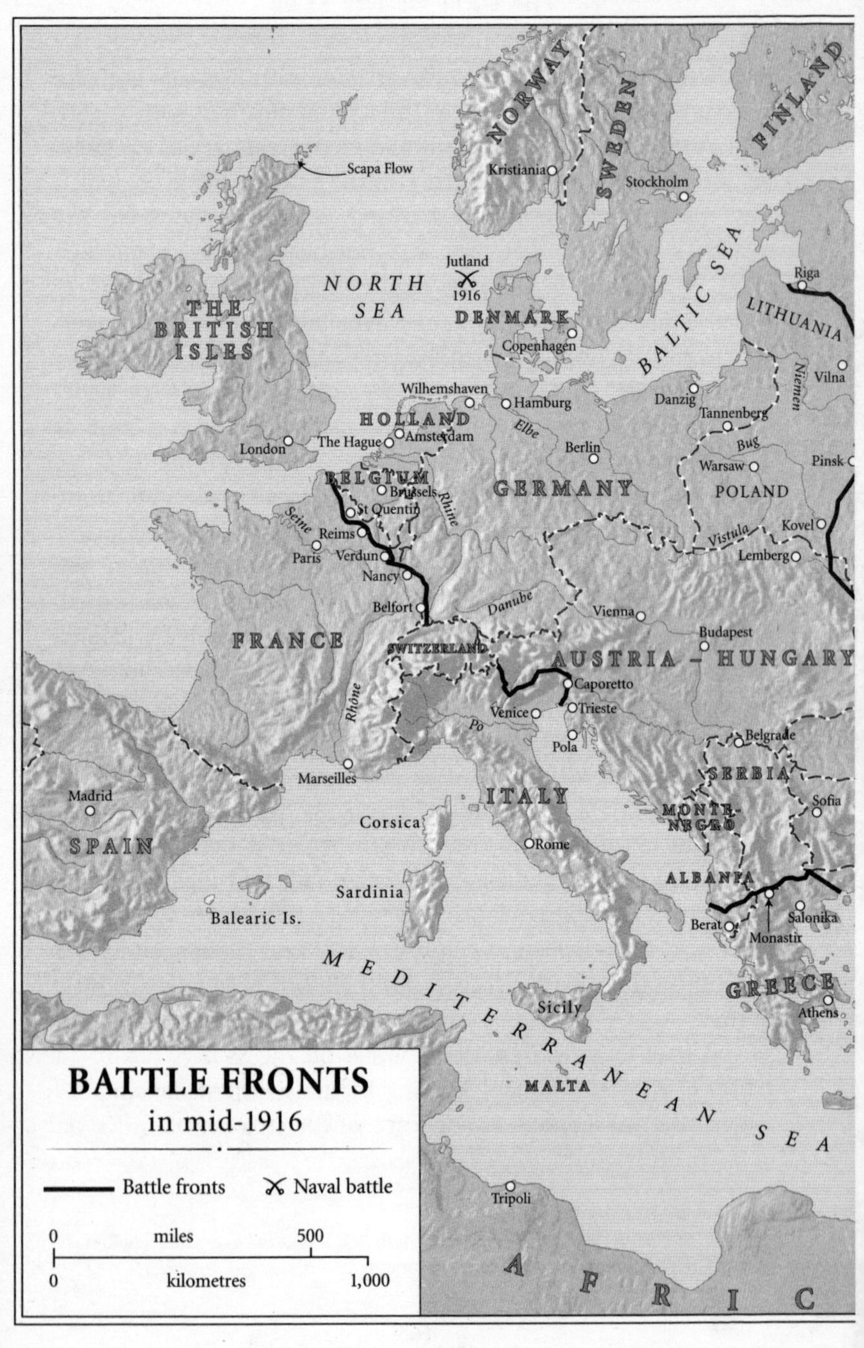

NORWAY
SWEDEN
FINLAND
Scapa Flow
Kristiania
Stockholm
Jutland
1916
NORTH SEA
BALTIC SEA
Riga
LITHUANIA
THE BRITISH ISLES
DENMARK
Copenhagen
Vilna
Niemen
Wilhemshaven
Hamburg
Danzig
HOLLAND
Tannenberg
Elbe
London
The Hague
Amsterdam
Berlin
Bug
Pinsk
BELGIUM
Brussels
Warsaw
GERMANY
POLAND
Seine
St Quentin
Rhine
Reims
Vistula
Kovel
Paris
Verdun
Lemberg
Nancy
Belfort
Danube
Vienna
Budapest
FRANCE
SWITZERLAND
AUSTRIA – HUNGARY
Caporetto
Rhône
Trieste
Venice
Po
Pola
Belgrade
Marseilles
SERBIA
Madrid
ITALY
Sofia
MONTE-NEGRO
Corsica
SPAIN
Rome
ALBANIA
Sardinia
Berat
Salonika
Balearic Is.
Monastir
MEDITERRANEAN SEA
GREECE
Sicily
Athens
MALTA
Tripoli
AFRIC
BATTLE FRONTS
in mid-1916
Battle fronts
Naval battle
0
miles
500
0
kilometres
1,000

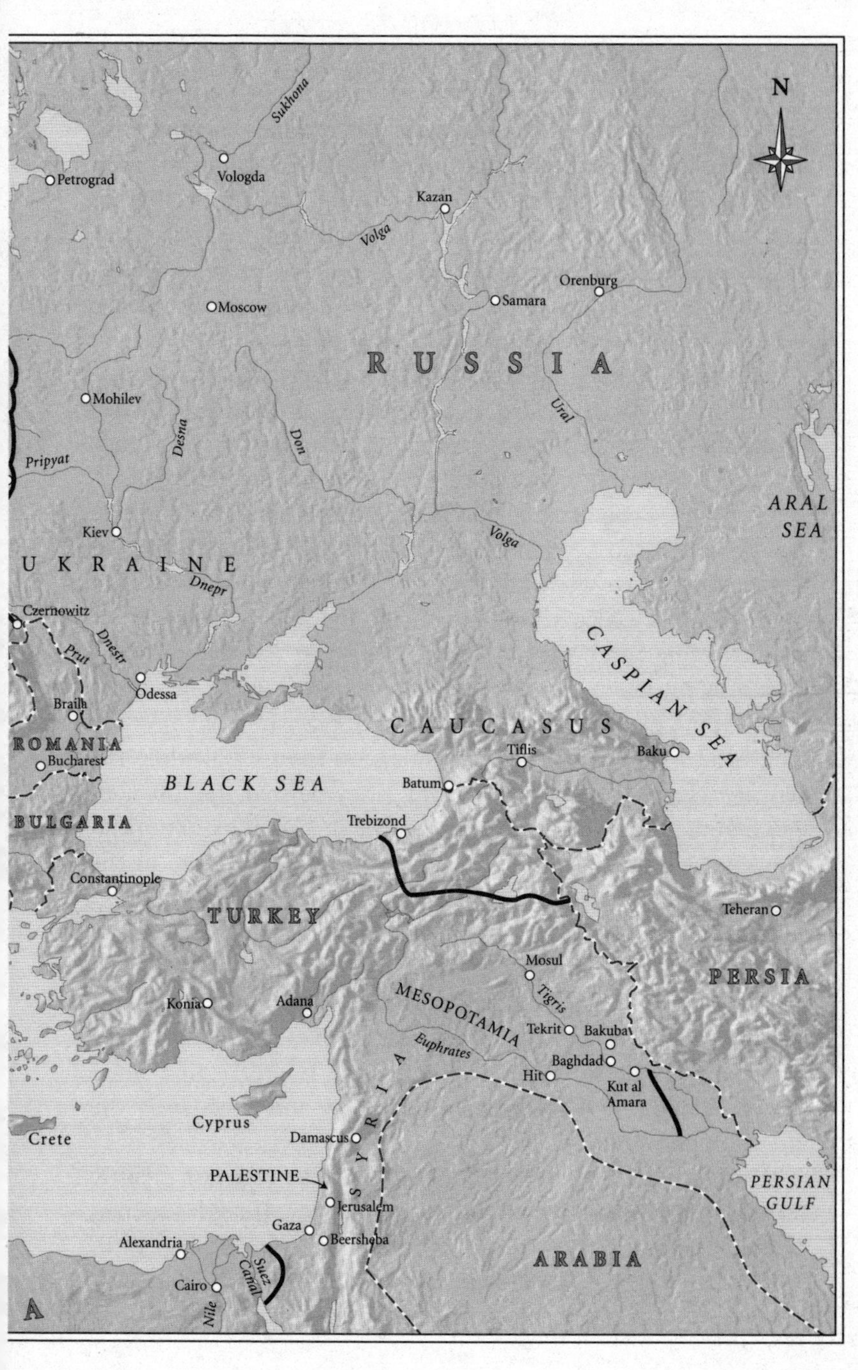
N
Sukhona
Petrograd
Vologda
Kazan
Volga
Orenburg
Moscow
Samara
RUSSIA
Mohilev
Ural
Desna
Don
Pripyat
ARAL SEA
Kiev
Volga
UKRAINE
Dnepr
Czernowitz
Dnestr
Prut
CASPIAN SEA
Odessa
Braila
CAUCASUS
ROMANIA
Bucharest
Tiflis
Baku
BLACK SEA
Batum
BULGARIA
Trebizond
Constantinople
Teheran
TURKEY
Mosul
PERSIA
Tigris
MESOPOTAMIA
Konia
Adana
Tekrit
Bakuba
Euphrates
Baghdad
Hit
Kut al Amara
SYRIA
Cyprus
Crete
Damascus
PALESTINE
PERSIAN GULF
Jerusalem
Gaza
Beersheba
Alexandria
ARABIA
Suez Canal
Cairo
Nile
A

Serbia they had hastily despatched help through the port of Salonika (now Thessalonika). Greece was still officially neutral, and while her king tended towards the Central Powers, her prime minister, Eleuthérios Venizélos, was pro-Entente. Indeed, in 1914 he had suggested taking Gallipoli from the landward side with Greek troops alone – much to the dismay of the Russians, who wanted Constantinople renamed in Cyrillic, not Greek, script. In the event, however, troops had moved in the opposite direction – to Greece *from* Gallipoli – under the French general Maurice Sarrail. The advance parties landed at Salonika on 5 October, the day before the Austro-German offensive; but that same day Venizélos fell from power, and their welcome was suddenly muted.

Nevertheless this scratch allied force pushed northwards up the Vardar valley into Serbian Macedonia to make contact with the Serbian army. The westward thrust of the Bulgars, however, had nicely driven a wedge between them and the Serbs, who were now fast retreating south-west. All the allies could do was withdraw back over the Greek frontier into Salonika. By mid-December the British contingent had swelled to five divisions who were now digging in to halt the expected Bulgarian invasion. Meanwhile the Serbian army was having to run for safety beyond the Albanian mountains, whence they would be rescued in a Dunkirk-like operation by the Italian navy and taken to Corfu. From there in the spring, reorganized and re-equipped, they would join the allies in Salonika, the 'Macedonian Front', and be joined in their turn by Italian and even Russian troops in what Berlin would soon be calling derisively 'our biggest internment camp'. Eventually some half a million allied troops would dig for themselves what Liddell Hart called a 'strategic sump pit' – although in late 1918 that sump would suddenly and spectacularly overflow and wash away the Bulgarian props.

At the beginning of 1916, however, Salonika was just a costly point of disagreement between the western allies. Almost as soon as he was appointed CIGS, 'Wully' Robertson began advocating withdrawal, arguing that in the light of the failed Gallipoli campaign, all resources not needed for the Middle East should be concentrated on the Western Front. In a remarkable strategic somersault, however, Joffre was now insisting on their remaining in Salonika – even reinforcing them.*

Joffre's insistence on this point had much to do with his perception of the need to reassure Russia; and at the beginning of 1916 it was the situation of Russia that gave the greatest cause for anxiety. The summer offensives by the German and Austro-Hungarian armies had pushed the Russians back to a line from Riga on the Baltic to Czernowitz on the Romanian border, which besides aught else had done nothing to encourage the Romanians, who were still sitting on the fence, to declare for the Entente. In this 'Great Retreat', which though well conducted had been a severe blow to morale, the Russians surrendered practically the whole of Poland (Warsaw had fallen on 5 August) and the Germans took three-quarters of a million prisoners. Indeed, by the close of the year, the Russian army since August 1914 had lost in all some four million men, with another million in that baleful category 'missing'. All thoughts in Paris and London of the 'Russian steamroller' slowly but surely destroying the German army on the Eastern Front were now gone. Joffre himself continued to see no likelihood of actual Russian collapse, but he did see a need to draw off German troops from the east by mounting offensives in the west. After the failure of the Dardanelles campaign to open warm-water communications, supporting Russia ought certainly to have been the guiding strategic concern.†

* In February 1916 Robertson wrote a paper proposing that the allies either offer a separate peace to Turkey or offer Turkish territory to Bulgaria to encourage her to break with the Central Powers, so that effort could be concentrated on the Western Front. Grey replied that Britain needed her continental allies more than they needed her, and that in view of her imperial interests Britain could not incur the risk (by, for example, reneging on the promise that Russia was to have control of the Turkish straits) that they might choose to make a separate peace with Turkey.

† On 4 September 1914 the Triple Entente powers had signed a pact: 'The British, French, and Russian Governments mutually engage not to conclude peace separately during the present war. The three Governments agree that when terms of peace come to be discussed, no one of the Allies will demand conditions of peace

Drawing off German troops from the east was sound enough theoretically, except that the Germans understood the game and were not prepared to play it. Throughout 1915, because none of the offensives had had the remotest chance of breakthrough given the Germans' agility in switching local reserves to seal any breaches in the line, only two divisions had been transferred from the Eastern Front to the Western. Why should the offensives of 1916 be any more successful?

And yet there were voices in Vienna arguing that Russia, for all her setbacks, was simply too powerful to overcome. In January 1916 the Austrian chief of staff, Franz Conrad von Hötzendorf, confided to the Hungarian prime minister, Count István Tisza, that 'there can be no question of destroying the Russian war machine; England cannot be defeated; peace must be made in not too long a space, or we shall be fatally weakened, if not destroyed'.*

Indeed, the German and Austro-Hungarian armies had suffered a million casualties on the Russian front in 1915, and despite the Austrians' recent success – finally – in over-running Serbia, the increasing alienation between the German and Austrian high commands was feeding an increasing cynicism in Berlin, some German officers complaining: 'We are shackled to a corpse.'

Conrad had appreciated, however, that the problem for the Russians was not, in fact, the absolute number of Austrian and German troops facing them – there were huge reserves, still, of Russian manpower – but the lack of arms and munitions with which to fight. This, as Conrad perceived, was not a problem beyond solution.

For a year it had seemed so, nevertheless. As early as December 1914 the chief of the *Stavka*, the Russian high command, Nikolai

---

without the previous agreement of each of the other Allies.' But this could not bind a future government, especially a Marxist one, such as would take power in 1917. Haig himself was certainly alive to the possibility of a Russian collapse, writing in his diary on 18 January: 'But to wear the Enemy and cause him to use up his reserves all the Allies must start at once. But Russia may not be ready till later, say July. In that case Germany may turn on her and defeat her – she (Russia) may then make peace!'

* Quoted in Martin Gilbert, *The First World War* (London, 1994).

Yanushkevich, had written to the war minister, General Vladimir Sukhomlinov, that the shortage of ammunition was 'a nightmare', as was that of war materiel in general. 'Why should we perish of hunger and cold, without boots?' his men were asking; 'the artillery is silent, and we are killed like partridges.'

On average the Russian army had one surgeon for every ten thousand men, and with medical staff stretched thinly across a 500-mile front, many soldiers were dying from wounds that would have been successfully treated on the Western Front. In June 1915 Yanushkevich wrote that because of the lack of shells 'the enemy can inflict loss unpunished' and that the fighting was 'pure murder'.

But if the western allies couldn't or wouldn't help Russia directly, neither could she help herself. The closure of the Dardanelles had been calamitous – essential imports dried up, and her exports, largely grain from southern Russia and Ukraine, declined by over two-thirds – but it was not a calamity beyond the wit of a resourceful bureaucracy to cope with. Alas, the Russian bureaucracy was made for another age, if for any age at all, and court intrigue was pernicious. In September the clique which dominated the Winter Palace persuaded the Tsar to dismiss his cousin, the Grand Duke Nicholas, and to take command of the armies himself. This was unfortunate, on three counts. First, although the grand duke was no strategist, his judgement of men was on the whole quite sound, which was not a capacity that his cousin the Tsar could claim. Secondly, the Tsar's absence in the field left the Tsarina and her reactionary coterie free to block all attempts at reform. Thirdly, as the cabinet, which had unanimously opposed the change, pointed out, any further reversals would inevitably be blamed on the Tsar himself.

Tsar Nicholas took no notice. (He never did.)

Social and industrial unrest then spread quickly throughout the country, with food even in the capital becoming scarce. By the end of 1915 Russia had become virtually ungovernable. The country desperately needed some military success to put heart into both the army and the civil population. Fortunately – in the short term at least, for it would in fact highlight the hopelessness of the *ancien régime* and feed the appetite for revolution – the self-help system of *zemstva*, the semi-official local councils which sorted out all manner of affairs in pragmatic fashion, began to make the running. By the spring of 1916 they would bring about a significant improvement in the supply of armaments and munitions, and their welfare work began to raise military morale.

In truth, Joffre had been calling for better coordination between the allies – France, Russia, Britain, Belgium, Serbia and now Italy – since the middle of 1915. He had managed to hold an inter-allied military conference at Chantilly that July, and in December he convened another to try to concert a common strategy for 1916 across the multiple fronts. It was not a job for Joffre, chief of staff and commander-in-chief, but it seemed that only he could do it – and in this sense Henry Wilson had been right when he said that the war had not produced a great statesman. As the man who had worked the 'miracle of the Marne', Joffre was almost as irresistible in grand strategy as he was in tactical detail on the Western Front. Only days before the December inter-allied conference, at an Anglo-French conference in Calais, Kitchener had persuaded the French prime minister, Aristide Briand, to abandon the Salonika campaign. Yet Joffre swiftly persuaded Briand to reverse the decision. But then Joffre, who might have been expected to welcome the Calais decision – after all, he had opposed the Gallipoli reinforcements on the grounds that they were diverting resources from the Western Front – needed to placate the Russians, whose representative, Zhilinsky, argued forcefully for a diversion in support of their planned summer offensive.

British resources would be further stretched, and therefore spread ever more thinly.

At the December conference at Chantilly, Joffre had carried out a thorough review of the strategic situation. But, while impressive in its scope, the *État-Major*'s appreciation was lacking in imagination and realism. Assessing Germany's war aims (Austria was regarded merely as Berlin's creature), it concluded that after the failure to defeat the Entente quickly, the *Grosser Generalstab* would wish to slow the process of attrition in order to husband men and resources for a long war. This would mean making full use of existing allies, finding new ones, and diverting Entente forces to secondary theatres by threats at vulnerable points. At the same time, Germany would pursue its policy of *Drang nach Osten* to increase its prestige in the world, raise the morale of its own people, and acquire so strong a position in the east that, whatever the outcome of the struggle, Berlin could not be forced to surrender it.*

To defeat Germany's war aims and frustrate the *Grosser Generalstab*'s intentions, argued the *État-Major*, the allies (the appreciation used the word 'coalition', redolent of Pitt's day) would have to maintain their principal objective, that is, to destroy the German and Austrian armies and at the same time 'foil Germany's attempt at imperial domination in the East'. Therefore:

> There must be no indecision regarding the means by which the first of these objectives is to be achieved.
>
> The Allied armies ought to resume the general offensive on the Franco-British, Italian and Russian fronts as soon as they are in a state to do so.
>
> All the efforts of the Coalition must be exerted in the preparation and execution of this decisive action, which will only produce its full effect as a co-ordination of offensives.
>
> It must be borne in mind that an offensive by our troops in France would now be a very considerable undertaking, owing to the large forces of the enemy opposed to us. This operation would be facilitated if a Russian attack in force caused the Germans to move troops from the Western Front.
>
> Conversely, if Franco-British demonstrations, judiciously carried out,

* *Drang nach Osten*, a term from Bismarck's Prussia, translates variously as a yearning or desire to push east, or simply the thrust or drive eastward, i.e. German expansion into Slavic lands. Cf. Voltaire's/Mirabeau's 'Prussia . . . an army with a country attached to it'.

> succeed in pinning to their ground the whole of the forces opposed to us, the field will be clear for the reorganized Russian Armies.*

The delegates agreed unanimously that whenever one ally came under clear threat, the others would immediately launch diversionary offensives. And herein lay the seed of some of the worst blood-letting of the war, for each of the allies was already contemplating an offensive in 1916 – Joffre was intending to attack on the Somme, with British support – and so the most expeditious way of mounting a diversion would simply be to bring forward the start date. As the Germans were bound to attack somewhere in 1916, there was a good chance that they would do so first, in which case the allied counter-offensives would to varying degrees be premature, and therefore less well prepared and therefore less likely to succeed.

Joffre's plans were in fact bankrupt of any unifying notion but more men, more guns, more shells. It was the equivalent of taking a bigger hammer to drive in the screw that the smaller hammer had failed to sink. The great general – the Napoleon of Lloyd George's conversation with Castelnau – or even just a thoughtful one would have recognized the need of a screwdriver.

But then the *État-Major* saw all these offensives in terms of *grignoter*, 'nibbling', wearing down – attrition:

> From what we know of the conditions of the Allied Armies, they are not ready now to undertake the co-ordinated action which we judge necessary in order to bring about a decision.
>
> It is therefore necessary for each of the Powers to combine their means and increase their resources, pursuing meanwhile an energetic policy of wearing down the opposing forces.
>
> In conclusion, so far as the principal theatres of war are concerned, the Allies must adopt the following policy until such time as it is possible to launch the combined offensive.
>
> Great Britain, Italy and Russia should use every endeavour to wear

* French memorandum to the second inter-allied conference at Chantilly, 6 December 1915, quoted in *Official History*.

> down their opponents. France will co-operate so far as her resources in man power permit.
>
> France, Great Britain and Italy should complete their organization and equipment and also supply Russia with the material she lacks, so that the Russian Armies may be raised to their full offensive value as soon as possible.*

Given the failure to provide the Gallipoli campaign with the necessary resources, this last – keeping Russia supplied and in the fight – looked like a case of slamming the stable door when the horse had bolted. Russia needed a million rifles alone to replace those lost and equip her new troops.

In January 1916 the Germans, who were of course not without their own difficulties, had to answer the same question that Paris and London were asking: east or west? In Berlin there was now very little pretence at civil control of strategy: the Kaiser was increasingly a creature of the *Grosser Generalstab.* Perhaps he always had been; certainly from summer 1916 he was unquestionably so. The chancellor, Theodore von Bethmann Hollweg, had been made honorary colonel of a regiment, entitling him to wear uniform, but he and his ministers found themselves with no voice in the counsels of war. After August 1916, when Hindenburg replaced Falkenhayn, Bethmann would lose all remaining influence with the Kaiser (who had little enough say in the running of the war anyway) and eventually resigned, to be replaced by a nonentity, thus completing the military coup towards which Hindenburg and his presiding brain Ludendorff had long been working. They had indeed almost claimed Falkenhayn's scalp early in 1915 when he refused to assign the newly created 10th Army to the Eastern Front, urging the Kaiser to dismiss him, but the Imperial war leader had temporized: he kept Falkenhayn but gave the 10th Army to Hindenburg.

It had been the worst of compromises. A commander-in-chief,

* French memorandum, 6 December 1915, quoted in *Official History.*

which was in effect Falkenhayn's position, has two principal functions – to advise the war council (whatever it is called) on military strategy, and to allocate resources. Although technically the Kaiser was C-in-C, in practice Falkenhayn had usurped both of these functions. His days were therefore numbered unless he could pull off a spectacular military success on the Western Front – this, and not the Eastern Front, being in his view the decisive theatre – or at least could demonstrate that there was such potential for success there that resources would be reallocated from East to West. He had no 'wish to slow the process of attrition in order to husband men and resources for a long war', as Joffre had calculated. On the contrary.

Thus in the disaffected mind of the chief of the *Grosser Generalstab* would be conceived the *Blutpumpe* ('blood pump') that was Verdun.

Meanwhile at St Omer in the frosty first days of an Artesian January, General Sir Douglas Haig had decisions of his own to make.* Some – appointments – he had had to make as soon as he'd taken over from Sir John French – *For I am a man under authority, having soldiers under me: and I say to this man, Go, and he goeth; and to another, Come, and he cometh.*

But to whom should he say 'come' and to whom might he say 'go'?

On 12 December, before sending for his military secretary (the staff officer responsible for appointments), he had had a conversation with 'Wully' Robertson, who was just about to leave for London to take up his appointment as CIGS. They discussed 'the difficulty of finding a place for General Henry Wilson', he wrote in his diary. As sub-chief of the BEF's general staff and a substantive major-general (and, indeed, a knight since the summer), Wilson might reasonably have expected to take Robertson's place, just as he had expected that he, rather than Robertson, would take Murray's

* One of which would be to move GHQ from St Omer to Montreuil (in March), better to reflect the changed dispositions of the BEF on the Western Front.

place at the beginning of the year. But Wilson had the unique distinction of being distrusted by both politicians and soldiers. 'Wully' despised what he regarded as his lack of professional capability. In early 1914, as director of military training at the War Office, Robertson had overseen an exercise for GHQ in the gymnasium at Sandhurst in which Wilson had acted as chief of staff and, he reckoned, displayed marked ignorance of procedures: 'If you go to war with that operations staff,' he told French, 'you are as good as beaten.'* Wilson's performance during the retreat from Mons had not brought about any change in that opinion. Haig himself mistrusted his Francophilia – *Francomania* indeed – and his intriguing, as did the politicians, above all Asquith, who harboured deep resentment over Wilson's role in the Curragh 'mutiny'. Haig wondered what to do with him. He couldn't possibly trust him to continue in the role invented for him by Sir John French – principal liaison officer to the French (in the rank of local lieutenant-general) – but, he noted in his diary, 'Robertson thought he would do less harm in France than in England!' French had offered him a corps in August, which he turned down, and although Haig was not averse to the appointment he believed Wilson ought first to command a division (he had not yet commanded even a proper battalion, let alone a brigade). In the event he would be given command of IV Corps, which was not a success.

As his chief of staff Haig wanted Major-General Richard Butler, who had filled that role in 1st Army, Haig's former command. Butler had risen rapidly on the outbreak of war: a lieutenant-colonel in August 1914, by the following June he had been promoted three ranks. Haig thought that no one had greater practical staff experience in the field, or had done so well. Robertson rated Butler's staff ability highly too, but vetoed the appointment on the grounds that he was too junior. Instead Launcelot Kiggell,

* Quoted in Brian Bond, *The Victorian Army and the Staff College 1854–1914* (London, 1972).

Robertson's successor as commandant of the Staff College and lately director home defence at the War Office, would become chief of staff, and Butler his deputy. This decision too would not prove to be a good one.

The larger question, on the face of it, was who should take Haig's own command, 1st Army. The field was not a large one, and both Haig and Robertson agreed that Henry Rawlinson, commanding IV Corps, was the best choice: 'Though not a sincere man,' Haig wrote in his diary, 'he has brains and experience.'

Not a sincere man – not 'free from pretence or deceit', not 'proceeding from genuine feelings', as the dictionary would have it. Indeed, Rawlinson's nickname was 'the cad'. And he had shown that side earlier that year when he tried to blame a subordinate for a fault that was entirely his own. It was not auspicious.

On 1 January, however, after visiting Joffre, Haig had further thoughts. *GQG* now believed a German attack to be likely – indeed imminent – on the axis Roye–Mondidier in the *département* of the Somme, and also south of Arras, threatening Paris. He concluded therefore that it was imperative to form a GHQ reserve, or 4th Army, and wrote to Kitchener saying that as the campaign in Gallipoli was ending, Monro should command 1st Army, and that he would recommend Rawlinson for command of the new 4th Army 'and hope you will concur'. It was not the business of the secretary of state to concur, or otherwise, in anything below the appointment of a commander-in-chief; it was the business of the CIGS, but 'Wully' was not yet firmly in the chair, and Haig was clearly hedging his bets. As it was, 4th Army would be formed on 5 February, with Rawlinson in command.

Having said 'Come' to Monro and Rawlinson, in mid-February Haig considered saying 'Go' to the commander of 2nd Army, Plumer. He had not been pleased with the state of defences in 2nd Army's sector, and Plumer had said 'he was quite ready to go if [Haig] thought it desirable'. But then, once again, Haig had second thoughts: 'Altogether he [Plumer] behaved in such a straightforward way, and is such a thorough gentleman' that he would think it over, for sacking an army commander was 'a matter of no small importance' – a remark of no little pomposity as well as a statement of the obvious. He might have added that with one army commander lacking in sincerity, it would be useful to have one with excess of it. Plumer wrote to him again, saying he would take matters in hand with his corps commanders. Indeed, it is difficult to see quite how such a meticulous infantryman had presided over inadequate defences, but he had the sense not to argue. Haig decided to keep him on. It was as well, for 'Plum' would prove the most methodical and effective of the army commanders. Perhaps Haig had just thought that sacking him would have been like shooting a pheasant on the ground. It is noteworthy, for example, that he would not sack Rawlinson after the Somme, which was 4th Army's battle and a demonstrable disaster, unlike the state of 2nd Army's defences, which was a question of opinion.

As for the question of judging Haig, he is a perennially elusive commander to assess. Dedicated and professional he was, but his experience of actual command, especially of infantry, was in fact limited. His whole outlook in many respects was quite remarkably narrow. Although unlike most of his contemporaries he had been at Oxford, his pre-war diaries reveal no interest in affairs of the world, or the arts or literature, yet they detail innumerable rounds of golf and games of polo. They record only one visit to the theatre, and that to see a play on a military subject. When John Masefield came to GHQ in October with a view to writing something similar to his apologia *Gallipoli*, published earlier in the year, Haig wrote in his diary: 'Mr John Masefield came to lunch. He is a poet but . . .' Now Masefield was certainly not as prominent as Kipling, but his success was well established (he would be poet laureate from 1930 to 1967); in 1916 it should not have been necessary to state his profession.* And the rider is interesting: '. . . but I am told that he

* Masefield had served on the Western Front as a medical orderly before going to the Dardanelles to write propaganda for the Foreign Office. *Gallipoli*, a work of great lyrical beauty (in it he had written: 'On the body of a dead Turk officer was a letter written the night before to his wife, a tender letter, filled mostly with

has written the best account of the landing in Gallipoli.' Perhaps a general might reasonably have been sceptical of a poet's qualification to write an account of battle, but it is curious that a commander-in-chief had not heard of *Gallipoli*, even if he had not read it, for it was after all a major initiative by the Foreign Office to counter German propaganda in the United States. It would be perilous to read too much into this single instance of insularity – and absence of evidence is not evidence of absence – but many a historian has commented on Haig's lack not so much of 'culture' as of interest in any matters beyond the purely military, and, indeed, his own part of it. Margot Asquith – unreliable, certainly, but not without discernment – wrote of Haig and Lady Haig coming to lunch in November 1915: 'He is handsome and Scotch, and though a very fine soldier a remarkably stupid man to talk to.'

Does this matter in a senior commander? Is it inevitable that narrow interests will mean lack of imaginative breadth, an inability to think beyond established doctrine – in modern parlance, 'outside the box'? Kipling's assertion that 'a battalion's field is bounded by its own vision' is easy to comprehend. And a battalion bounded by its own vision is at most a minor tactical problem (if indeed it is a problem). But what if the words applied to GHQ too – *bounded by its C-in-C's vision*?

Haig did not have a closed mind; there is plenty of evidence of his accepting new ideas, such as the tank (of which he knew nothing until taking command of the BEF).* He was not the men-

---

personal matters. In it was the phrase, "These British are the finest fighters in the world. We have chosen the wrong friends"'), apparently so raised the public spirits in lauding what there was to be proud of in an otherwise inglorious episode that he was sent to France in October 1916 with a brief to do the same for the Somme.

*On Christmas Day 1915, Haig read a memorandum in the papers left by Sir John French referring to armoured 'machine-gun destroyers' on 'caterpillars', which had apparently been the pet project of the then first lord of the Admiralty, Churchill.

'Is anything known about the caterpillar referred to in Para 4, page 3?' he wrote in the margin.

A sapper officer on the staff of GHQ, Major Hugh Elles, like Haig an Old Cliftonian, was sent to England to find out. He would return with encouraging news of a tracked device that could crush barbed wire, cross trenches and bring fire tal tram portrayed by some writers; but his thinking was always rooted in conventional military norms. He was more the mental trolley-bus.

And so as he approached the 'campaigning season' of 1916 Haig was thinking not of a wholesale change in the military policy of his predecessor but simply of doing things better. It was the approach of a first-rate staff officer, or a good tactical commander, but not that of a great general. It might have served, had there been a surer hand on the tiller of allied strategy, but for now that

---

to bear on the enemy from behind steel protection. Churchill's 'Admiralty Landships Committee', set up in February 1915, had finally borne fruit through the engineering skill of William Foster and Co. Ltd of Lincoln, specialists in agricultural machinery. A first design, little more than an armoured box on American tractor tracks, had been tested in September, but it could not cross a gap of 5 feet – the average trench width – which GHQ had prescribed, the tracks being prone to shedding. Known as 'Little Willie', either after Foster's chief engineer and managing director, William Tritton, or else (following the derisive sobriquet conferred by the British press) the Kaiser's son, Crown Prince Wilhelm, commander of the German 5th Army, it nevertheless gave Fosters the solution to the problem of the caterpillar tracks. A few weeks later Tritton would send a telegram in veiled speech to the Admiralty: 'New arrival by tritton out of pressed plate STOP. Light in weight but very strong STOP. All doing well Thank you STOP. Proud parents END.'

With Lieutenant Walter Wilson of the Royal Naval Armoured Car Division, Tritton had produced a completely new design with bigger tracks wrapped round a hull with forward-sloping 'prows' projecting beyond the crew compartment, a rhomboid giving the machine huge reach. Weighing 28 tons and variously known as 'Centipede', 'Mother' or 'Big Willie', the prototype was ready just three months later. It was armed with either machine guns or quick-firing 6-pounders mounted on sponsons either side, had a crew of eight and moved at walking pace. On the night of 19 January 1916, sheathed in tarpaulins and referred to as a 'tank', a deliberately vague term alluding to its boxy shape, it was taken to Burton Park outside Lincoln and put through its paces the following day, crossing a trench 8 feet wide, climbing a 5-foot parapet and crushing barbed wire entanglements.

A week later the 'tank' was on its way by rail to Hatfield Park in Hertfordshire, seat of the Marquess of Salisbury, whose cousin, Arthur Balfour, had succeeded Churchill at the Admiralty, for a series of demonstrations to the War Office out of public view. On seeing the tank going through its paces Kitchener was doubtful, calling it 'a pretty mechanical toy but without serious military value'. Fortunately, General Butler (an infantryman), Haig's deputy chief of staff, whom Elles had primed beforehand, asked simply: 'How soon can we have them?' (The answer was eventually 'September'.)

Major (later Lieutenant-General Sir) Hugh Elles would become the first commander of the Tank Corps when it was established as a separate entity the following year.

strategy was simply to wear down the Germans on the Western Front.

However, the gods of war – or Falkenhayn at least – had other ideas: Verdun.

And if the *Kaiserliche Marine* could gain mastery of the North Sea . . .

Chapter Ten

WINNING THE WAR IN AN AFTERNOON?

'We shall dig the rats out of their holes.' It was Churchill at his most combative, if not his most eloquent. Indeed, he came to regret the remark that if the 'rats' of the German High Seas Fleet (*Hochseeflotte*) didn't come out and fight, the Royal Navy would come and prise them out. In September 1914 it 'had slipped from my tongue in a weary speech at Liverpool'.* Not only did the King himself consider Churchill's language unworthy, within days of the speech *Hochseeflotte* warships had sunk three obsolescent cruisers of what was known with black humour in the Royal Navy as 'the live bait squadron'. Churchill himself was blamed for this by apparently tempting fate, although the professionals knew it was an operational matter. But at the beginning of 1916 the *Hochseeflotte* had still not obliged Admiral Jellicoe's Grand Fleet by presenting themselves for battle in the North Sea.

For Grand Admiral Alfred von Tirpitz, the German navy minister, the war at sea had taken a frustrating turn. Having lost all his cruisers, except those with the *Hochseeflotte,* to the guns of the Royal Navy (with a little help from the Royal Australian Navy), commerce-raiding on any scale was out of the question, to be left

* *The World Crisis,* vol. I.

to auxiliaries – and communication with the one remaining German colony, Deutsche Ostafrika, was virtually impossible.* British sea supremacy, guaranteed by the Grand Fleet in its lonely anchorage at Scapa Flow, underpinned the entire national – indeed, allied – grand strategy. Tirpitz knew that the *Hochseeflotte*, based at Wilhelmshaven, had no chance of victory in a straight fight with the Grand Fleet, and so his strategy had from the outset been to wear down the Royal Navy's dreadnought numbers in the North Sea by mines, torpedoes, opportunity skirmishes and deliberate ambushes into which the British were to be drawn by deceit or provocation – not least by raids on coastal towns, of which Scarborough in December 1914 had been the first and most infamous target. On the whole the Royal Navy had not been drawn, however; Jellicoe, well aware of the German intention, was usually alerted to the ruses through the superb signal intercept capability at the Admiralty ('Room 40').

Tirpitz had always wanted to use submarines as his prime strategic weapon. Pre-war calculations – based, as it turned out, on false premises – showed that Britain would be brought to her knees in months, perhaps only weeks, if her food imports were intercepted. A good deal of imported food was carried by neutral shipping, however, and while surface ships of the Royal Navy could intercept neutrals taking similar cargoes to Germany, the *Kaiserliche Marine* could not reciprocate. Only its submarines could get into the trade approaches. By pre-war convention, the so-called 'cruiser rules', before sinking a merchantman the submarine was meant to surface, issue a warning and allow the crew to take to the lifeboats. This had obvious dangers, and Tirpitz for one was a keen advocate of unrestricted submarine warfare – sinking without warning. The Kaiser had initially sanctioned this in early 1915, but the international outcry, not least after the sinking of the Cunard passenger

* Germany's colonies in the Pacific and China had been taken in 1914 by Australian, New Zealand or Japanese troops, while in Africa, Kamerun and Togoland quickly fell to Anglo-French forces, and German South-West Africa (now Namibia) finally capitulated to South African troops in July 1915.

liner *Lusitania* in May with the loss of 1,191 lives, including 128 American citizens, forced him to rescind the order in September 1915 (President Woodrow Wilson, initially slow to vent his anger, gave him what amounted to an ultimatum). In March 1916, frustrated by the Kaiser's reluctance to reauthorize unrestricted warfare, Tirpitz resigned.

Three months earlier, Reinhard Scheer had replaced Hugo von Pohl, a notably cautious admiral who had become too ill to continue, as commander-in-chief of the *Hochseeflotte*. Scheer was determined to pursue a more aggressive stance to whittle down the Grand Fleet's superiority. Taking the fleet north from Wilhelmshaven into the German Bight on 31 May he hoped to tempt Vice-Admiral David Beatty's battle-cruisers (and perhaps even some dreadnoughts), charged with ranging the North Sea, into a fight with his own battle-cruisers under Franz von Hipper, in which they would in turn be drawn onto the guns of his battleships, thereby reducing the odds in the subsequent expected encounter with Jellicoe's main battle squadrons. The relative strengths were certainly not propitious for Scheer. His fleet comprised sixteen dreadnoughts (to the twenty-eight Jellicoe and Beatty would send out), six pre-dreadnoughts, six light cruisers and 31 torpedo boats, together with Hipper's five battle-cruisers (against Jellicoe and Beatty's nine), supporting cruisers and torpedo boats. Jellicoe and Beatty had no fewer than seventy-eight destroyers.

In one sense, however, Scheer had a psychological advantage, for he had nothing to lose. By maintaining his 'fleet in being' at Wilhelmshaven he was undoubtedly fixing the capital ships of the Grand Fleet in their anchorage at Scapa Flow, and its battle-cruisers and cruisers in their North Sea ports, but even if the Royal Navy were to have complete freedom of movement it would not change the strategic situation: the economic blockade was already so complete that Germany was beginning to famish. On the other hand, in Churchill's memorable words, Jellicoe was the only man on either side who could lose the war in an afternoon. Loss of sea supremacy, allowing the German surface fleet to range wide against merchant shipping and to challenge the British blockade, interrupting communications with India and the dominions – even threatening the Channel – would be catastrophic for the longer game of building military strength on the Western Front and starving Germany, now the only keys to victory. Indeed, loss of sea supremacy would mean national defeat.

Consequently Jellicoe's task was to maintain that supremacy, not to destroy the German fleet. While Scheer therefore could be bold, Jellicoe *had* to be cautious.

And while Jellicoe could take calculated risks based on what he could see and reasonably anticipate were the actions of Scheer's surface ships, he could have no certain knowledge of where and in what strength lay his submarines. Gunnery did not trouble him, although Scheer's would prove unnervingly good, the Royal Navy's less so (vitiated by unsafe ammunition handling in particular); the torpedo did.

Room 40 had as usual intercepted and decrypted German radio traffic giving plans of the operation. Jellicoe left Scapa Flow and Invergordon, and Beatty the Firth of Forth, at last light, 10.30 p.m., on 30 May, intending to cut off and destroy as much of the *Hochseeflotte* as possible, but with the imperative of retaining sea supremacy come what may. High winds made the use of airships impracticable for both sides, so both were relatively 'blind'.

At four in the afternoon of the thirty-first, after a sweep to the south, Beatty's battle-cruisers, with the 5th Battle Squadron of dreadnoughts, ran into Hipper's force, beginning a running fight as Hipper turned south to draw Beatty on to Scheer's battle fleet. For his part, having once made contact with the *Hochseeflotte*, Beatty turned back north to try to lure Scheer towards Jellicoe's rapidly approaching battle squadrons. The leading ships of the *Hochseeflotte* now began engaging Beatty's 'Queen Elizabeth class' battleships (known in the fleet as 'Barhams', after the fourth ship of the class – the fastest, most heavily armed of the dreadnoughts, or 'super-dreadnoughts'), which convinced Scheer that he had indeed caught an isolated portion of the Grand Fleet, and therefore that he had his long-looked-for opportunity for attrition. At six-thirty, however, his hopes were shattered when Jellicoe's ships, in one of which, HMS *Collingwood* of the 1st Battle Squadron, the twenty-year-old Prince Albert, the future King George VI, was serving as a sub-lieutenant, steamed into view in a position to 'cross the T' from the north-east.

'Crossing the T' had been a favourite tactic since Nelson's day, allowing the ships doing the crossing to bring a full broadside to bear (or, in the case of the dreadnoughts, all the main armament, for the turrets could rotate onto either beam), while those steaming in line ahead could not. To extricate himself from what looked like certain death, Scheer ordered a turn to the south-west. Twenty minutes later, however, he decided to turn back to attack Jellicoe's main force. This manoeuvre again put Scheer in a dangerous position, for Jellicoe had turned the Grand Fleet south and was again threatening to 'cross the T'. And so Scheer made a third 16-point turn to break off contact, covered by Hipper's mauled battle-cruisers, which boldly charged the British line to cover the retreat.*

He then ordered the fleet to adopt night cruising formation, a tighter deployment which allowed securer signalling and precaution against torpedo attack, which he managed to complete just

* During the early stages of the fight the light cruiser *Chester*, scouting ahead of Rear-Admiral Horace Hood's 3rd Battle-cruiser Squadron, came under intense fire from four of Hipper's light cruisers. The crew of the forward 5.5-inch gun, which was shielded rather than turreted, were at once killed or mortally wounded. The sole remaining member standing, 16-year-old Jack Cornwell, though himself severely wounded, remained at his post until, with only one main gun still working, *Chester* retired from the action and was ordered to Immingham. Three months later her captain wrote to the Admiralty commending 'the instance of devotion to duty by Boy (1st Class) John Travers Cornwell who was mortally wounded early in the action, but nevertheless remained standing alone at a most exposed post, quietly awaiting orders till the end of the action, with the gun's crew dead and wounded around him. He was under 16½ years old. I regret that he has since died, but I recommend his case for special recognition in justice to his memory and as an acknowledgement of the high example set by him.' On 15 September Cornwell was posthumously awarded the VC, the youngest recipient since 1860. The gun is on permanent display at the Imperial War Museum, as is the medal.

before midnight. Meanwhile Jellicoe's destroyers were keeping up a ferocious, if unequal, fight with his battleships, though Scheer eventually managed to punch his way through the destroyer screen and make for Horns Reef – the shallows 10 miles off the westernmost point of Denmark (now one of Europe's biggest offshore wind farms). Jellicoe, sensing danger in following up to inflict any more damage – particularly from a concerted torpedo attack by submarines – broke off the pursuit and turned for home.

The *Hochseeflotte* reached Wilhelmshaven in the early afternoon. They had sunk more British ships (but no dreadnoughts) than the Grand Fleet had sunk German, and at once claimed victory, while Jellicoe was slower to return to Scapa and slower still to make capital of the fact that the Germans had been forced back to their anchorages and that the Royal Navy still ruled the waves. To untutored eyes it looked as if he had lacked the 'Nelson touch', failing to win the complete victory that was in his grasp while incurring over six thousand casualties killed.

Yet Scheer's leading battleships had taken a terrible hammering, and it was only in the coming weeks that the foreign section of the Secret Service Bureau (in time, the Secret Intelligence Service, MI6) was able to gather details of the extent to which the Grand Fleet's gunnery had disabled the *Hochseeflotte*. Several capital ships and most of the battle-cruisers were in dry dock for extensive repairs for at least two months. The day after the Battle of Jutland, the British had twenty-four capital ships in fighting condition, compared to only ten German.* Moreover, though the world did not know it, the Germans had a very good idea that British shipbuilding capacity was much greater than theirs, and therefore that as the months passed the relative strengths would only diverge in British favour. Yes, the Grand Fleet – in the words of the *Official History* – 'could only put to sea with an escort of nearly one hundred destroyers, no capital ship could leave its base without an escort of small craft, and the German U-boats had hampered our

* For a full list of vessels lost on either side, and casualty numbers, see annex A.

squadrons to an extent which the most experienced and far-sighted naval officer had never foreseen'; and less than three months after Jutland the *Hochseeflotte* sortied again and almost reached the English coast without being brought to battle (and did so again, more tentatively, in October); but the fact was that at Jutland the *Hochseeflotte* had been stopped in its tracks.*

The Battle of Jutland, like almost every battle of the First World War, has been debated for a century – and not just because it was the first, and last, dreadnought fleet action in history; for it was also, uniquely, a grand-strategic battle – existential. The debate centres on Jellicoe's failure to achieve a numerical, tactical victory, the usual measure by which a naval engagement was gauged. Although the brilliant but tricky 45-year-old Beatty had succeeded in leading the *Hochseeflotte* onto the guns of the Grand Fleet, the 'over-cautious' Jellicoe is argued to have then let them escape. He was and is criticized for failing to pursue Scheer when the German admiral turned away in daylight, and for his posture at night, which was entirely defensive. However, this was exactly as agreed beforehand with the Admiralty, the permutations of a fleet action having been exhaustively discussed. Engaging the enemy in any circumstances where other factors might destroy Britain's priceless advantage of 'the fleet in being' would have been contrary to the theories of sea power expounded by the British naval historian and geo-strategist Sir Julian Corbett, whose *Some Principles of Maritime Strategy* (1911) was the handbook of the naval staff, and by the American Admiral Alfred Thayer Mahan, whose *The Influence of Sea Power upon History* (1890) the Kaiser had made every one of his captains read. In fact, Jutland was one of the few battles of the First World War that was fought to a cogent strategy as previously agreed. Jellicoe could not *win* the war in an afternoon, which is the blunt fact that some commentators ignore in criticizing his failure

* Though, of course, the threat of invasion had not been removed, and it would be many months before the war committee felt able to send abroad troops hitherto reserved for home defence.

to send more German ships to the bottom; Churchill said only that he could *lose* it in an afternoon – and he did not.

Indeed, by not losing – by assuring the continuance of sea supremacy, albeit having to retain destroyers (which would have been of greater use elsewhere) to accompany the dreadnoughts – Jellicoe helped shorten the war by tightening the noose of blockade and by forcing Berlin to make a catastrophic decision which within months would bring the United States into the war. For Tirpitz's successor, Admiral Eduard von Capelle (who had hitherto been opposed to unrestricted submarine warfare) now drew the inevitable conclusion that the only way to break out of the North Sea was below surface, and that for the submarine to have the necessary strategic impact it must be allowed to sink without warning any ship bound for British waters. On 4 July Scheer himself wrote to the Kaiser:

> The disadvantages of our geographical situation – and the enemy's vast material superiority – cannot be coped with to such a degree as to make us masters of the blockade inflicted on us . . . A victorious end to the war at not too distant a date can only be looked for by the crushing of English economic life through U-boat action against English commerce.*

There would be a price to pay for this, of course, and not just in terms of international opprobrium. Because the Germans did not have enough submarines to wage economic warfare *and* protect the fleet, the latter would have to confine itself to harbour. Conversely the Royal Navy did not have enough destroyers both to protect the Grand Fleet *and* her merchant shipping. In the words of the *Official History* again, 'A deadlock had thus been reached, and it seemed that for the future the two great battle-fleets could but lie inactive, watching one another across a kind of "no-man's sea", where attack and defence were concerned only with transport and commerce.'

* Reinhard Scheer, *Germany's High Seas Fleet in the World War* (London, 1920).

The German naval leaders lobbied hard, encouraged by the success of their U-boats in the Channel: in a single week in September over thirty British or neutral merchant ships were sunk by two or three submarines, under 'cruiser rules', without loss to themselves, although the Channel was watched by some 600 patrol vessels of one description or another. Admiral Henning von Holtzendorff, chief of the naval staff, told the Kaiser that unrestricted submarine warfare would starve the British into submission within five months – well before the Americans could act. And even if the 'disorganized and undisciplined' Americans did intervene, he bragged, 'I give Your Majesty my word as an officer that not one American will land on the Continent' – an ill-judged echo of Admiral St Vincent's remark in the Napoleonic wars: 'I do not say the French cannot come, I only say they cannot come by sea.'

Besides, from the wings Tirpitz pointed out that the Americans were protesting increasingly against the *British* blockade. Bethmann Hollweg made the obvious rejoinder that there was a vast difference between sinking a ship and turning it back or impounding it. But Tirpitz was unimpressed: British naval prestige had been fatally damaged by the failure to replicate Trafalgar at Jutland. Indeed, the Kaiser himself boasted: 'The spell of Trafalgar is broken.'

Clausewitz seemed to be urging them from the grave: 'War is an act of force . . . [which knows] no logical limit.'

Chapter Eleven

VERDUN: THE BLOOD PUMP

'Verdun was a whole war inserted into the Great War, rather than a battle in the ordinary sense of the word . . . It was also a kind of duel before the universe, a singular and almost symbolic tourney.' So said the distinguished academician Paul Valéry in his formal reply to a speech by Marshal Pétain at the Académie Française in 1931.

The little town of Verdun – its population in 1914 was about twenty thousand – sat prettily amid hills astride the sleepy River Meuse on the old high road from Luxembourg and the Mosel to Paris. Its Roman name suggests a long acquaintance with siege warfare – Verodunum, 'strong fort'. Indeed it had been a favourite rendezvous for warriors since Caesar's day. And in August 1914 it played its part in persuading the Germans to hook through Belgium rather than hurl themselves at the border fortresses built or strengthened since 1871 (there was always a qualification with Moltke's injunction to 'build railways not forts'), for Verdun had the reputation of being, quite simply, the world's strongest citadel. But by 1916 Joffre and the *État-Major* no longer had faith in fortresses: those on the Eastern Front had been easily overcome, and so had those in Belgium – though Liège had stood barring the way of the German 2nd Army for twelve crucial days, allowing the French army and the BEF to complete their concentration, and inflicting many casualties – and Joffre had persuaded the French government to remove Verdun's classification as a fortress and let him take away its guns and garrison.

Falkenhayn could not have known for sure of its degraded status, but he decided nevertheless that Verdun was to be the bait in a cunningly laid trap. Far more subtle than Joffre (it is interesting to compare the two men's appearance – Joffre the colossal hammer, his opponent the trim screwdriver), Falkenhayn planned to use his massed artillery as a mincing-machine rather than as a ram to break through the French defences. By attacking a place of national prestige he hoped to draw the French reserves onto his guns like driven birds. 'The string [of French defences] in France has reached breaking point,' he supposedly wrote in a memorandum to the Kaiser in December. 'A mass breakthrough – which in any case is beyond our means – is unnecessary. Within our reach there are objectives for the retention of which the French General Staff would be compelled to throw in every man they have. If they do so the forces of France will bleed to death.'*

If, indeed. Plutarch wrote of just such a challenge during one of the Roman civil wars – when Pompaedius Silo, leader of the Marsi, 'who had the greatest authority and power among the enemy', goaded Gaius Marius, Julius Caesar's uncle: 'If thou art a great general, Marius, come down and fight it out with us.' Marius would not be so easily drawn however, replying: 'Nay, but do *thou*, if thou art a great general, force me to fight it out with you against my will.'†

Falkenhayn had to hope for a less circumspect adversary.

He had at first considered attacking Belfort, towards the Swiss border, but chose Verdun because it was a (French) salient and therefore cramped the defenders, and because it was close to one of the main German railway arteries, which meant that he would be able to keep his troops well supplied. There would also be the secondary effect of removing the menace to that artery which the

* Falkenhayn, *General Headquarters*.

† Plutarch, *Lives*, vol. IX, trans. Bernadotte Perrin (London, 1920).

salient undoubtedly presented. Above all, Verdun was so prominent in the French national consciousness that its loss would have a powerful moral effect; it would have to be held 'at all costs' (a flaccid concept which almost invariably reflects an unwillingness to *calculate* the costs). Falkenhayn's limited offensive would lead therefore to the destruction of the French strategic reserve in fruitless counter-attacks, and the defeat of British reserves in an equally futile relief offensive, which, he argued, would lead to the French accepting a separate peace. If they refused, his strategy would then be to attack the terminally weakened allied armies in overwhelming strength.

Some historians have doubted that this was truly Falkenhayn's advance thinking, rather than a *post facto* justification for the failure of the offensive to make any breakthrough (and at huge cost). Sir Hew Strachan, the pre-eminent British historian of the First World War, is one of those not persuaded, citing as evidence the orders issued by the German 5th Army: 'It was not seeking limited objectives and aiming to maximise French losses while minimising German. Instead, it advanced as far and as fast as it could'; and he concludes, pointing out that Falkenhayn did not regularly start using the 'vocabulary of attrition' until mid-March to explain his purpose, that 'It was a way for Falkenhayn to rationalise the failure to achieve a breakthrough, but it was a thin one.'*

Yet there are strong counter-arguments. No memorandum to the Kaiser has ever been found (there is only Falkenhayn's word for it) – although, again, absence of evidence is not evidence of absence: the Prussian military archive was all but completely destroyed in the Second World War – but there *is* evidence that Falkenhayn's thinking was picked up by Dutch military intelligence (although *how* is not known) and passed on to the British in December. Nor would 5th Army's orders necessarily reveal Falkenhayn's intention, even if he had shared it with its commander, Crown Prince Wilhelm, for besides the obvious requirement for maintaining

* *The First World War* (London, 2003).

operational security, the tactic of limited objectives – 'bite and hold', as it became known in the British army – would not necessarily have provoked French counter-attacks in the strength required. Only the threat of breakthrough, and with it the taking of Verdun, could provide the necessary provocation. But in any case, in such a ruse an element of deception has to be practised on one's own troops in order to convince the enemy, for once soldiers perceive their task to be essentially sham they will shy from the fight. Edmund Blunden, the longest-serving of the Great War poets, described this well in *Undertones of War* (1929), his memoir of service in the Royal Sussex Regiment. In the aftermath of a costly failed attack near Aubers Ridge ('the Boar's Head massacre'),

> Explanations followed. Our affair had been a catspaw, a 'holding attack' to keep German guns and troops away from the great gamble of the Somme. This purpose, previously concealed from us with success, was unachieved . . . The explanations were almost as infuriating to the troops as the attack itself (I remember conversations fiercer than Bolshevik councils against the staff concerned), and deep down in the survivors there grew a bitterness of waste.

Whatever Falkenhayn's purpose and method, at 7.12 a.m. on 21 February, only a week after Haig had met with Joffre to discuss the future allied offensive, two 38 cm railway guns, known as 'Long Max' – naval pieces served by men of the *Kaiserliche Marine* – signalled the opening of *Unternehmen Gericht* (Operation Judgement) – a bombardment by over 1,200 guns on a front of 12 miles astride the Meuse in the north of the salient. The intelligence branch at *GQG* had been warning of the buildup of troops – the Germans had concentrated more than 150 aeroplanes over the Verdun sector to prevent French aerial reconnaissance, itself an indicator that something was afoot – but Joffre was a man of the operations branch, which did his will rather than tell him things disagreeable to his own designs; and the operations branch was so preoccupied with its plans for the coming offensive that it took no notice of the warnings.

The German tactical plan involved a continuous series of limited advances each preceded by a brief (hours rather than days) but intense preparatory bombardment which would allow the infantry to take and consolidate their objectives before the French reserves could even move up to counter-attack. When eventually they did counter-attack – as doctrine required – the German infantry would be secure in the trenches and bunkers taken from the French, and their artillery could do its worst. In addition – and this is what made the plan so 'economic' – German patrols would probe the French defences *before* the main mass of infantry was launched: a tactic not seen before, and one with obvious advantages, though it required high-calibre troops, devolved command and excellent communications.

On 21 February this probing revealed that the effect of the nine hours' bombardment varied, and so the main attack was launched on only a narrow sector. The following day the bombardment was repeated to greater effect and the French line buckled in many places.

Joffre was unperturbed, however. The operations branch assured him the offensive was a feint, perhaps to disrupt preparations for his own offensive.

In a sense they were right. The attacks *were* a feint – *the* feint; it would be the artillery strike on the French reserves that would be the real blow. This is why Falkenhayn had to give every impression of trying to force a breakthrough, for only then could he rely on the French being induced to counter-attack in strength.

But in Joffre's eyes the whole assault had to be a feint. For had not he, Joffre, previously degraded the fortress? (And had there not been representations to Paris protesting, which he had indignantly repudiated? – 'I cannot be a party to soldiers under my command bringing before the Government by channels other than the hierarchical channel, complaints or protests about the execution of my orders . . .'*) He could not afford it to be anything other than a feint. And so it *was* a feint.

* Quoted in Churchill, *The World Crisis*, vol. III.

On the evening of the fourth day of the offensive, Joffre having gone to bed early as usual, Castelnau, now his chief of staff, became alarmed by the reports coming in. He had the *GQG*'s orderly officer wake *Le Chef* and ask could he, Castelnau, go to discover for himself the true situation and take whatever action was necessary? Joffre agreed and, as Castelnau set off to drive the 150 miles to Verdun, sent a typically blustering telegram to the troops in what remained of the fortress saying that any commander giving an order to retreat would be tried by court martial.

Not long after Castelnau arrived, Fort Douaumont, the largest and most elevated fort in the ring of nineteen that protected the town, though it had been left all but defenceless, fell with hardly a fight. Castelnau at once pulled the right flank back but ordered that the remaining line of forts be held, and gave Philippe Pétain, commanding 2nd Army, responsibility for the Verdun sector.

There is a story, Gallically plausible if probably apocryphal, that Pétain, a sixty-year-old bachelor, had to be brought from the bed of a favourite Parisian mistress by one of his staff. In any event, he was a good choice, if not Joffre's favourite, for as an infantryman teaching at the staff college Pétain had rejected the pre-war mantra of *offensive à outrance*, urging instead the power of the defensive with the axiom 'Le feu tue' (firepower kills). To be his deputy and also command III Corps Castelnau appointed General Robert Nivelle, conversely and paradoxically an artilleryman with a strong belief in the power of the infantry offensive.

Pétain's earlier tardy promotion as a consequence of his unorthodoxy now came to the army's aid. In August 1914 he had been a mere colonel commanding a brigade; he had therefore seen the new warfare from the ground up rather than from a headquarters where the temptation was to make the situation fit pre-conceived doctrine instead of the other way round. Only a few months before, after the failures of the autumn battles in Champagne, he had written a memorandum in which he said that it was 'impossible to carry in one bound the successive positions of the enemy', and that offensives should be limited to the reach of artillery ('material should substitute for manpower'). He would now use this appreciation in reverse to defeat the German attacks.

His immediate problem, however, was not so much defence as supply, for the German guns had closed all but two routes into the salient – a light railway and the *Chemin Bar-le-Duc*. While ordering counter-attacks to slow the Germans on what was still a narrow front, Pétain set every available pick and shovel to work on widening and maintaining this one road. Motor lorries were soon bringing forward ammunition virtually nose-to-tail – by June some six thousand vehicles a day, an average frequency of one every fourteen seconds. Auguste-Maurice Barrès, politician and man of letters, with that semi-mystical way of the French when speaking of *La Patrie*, dubbed it 'La Voie Sacrée', the sacred way, a name which defiantly stuck.*

As the road, maintained by five thousand sappers, was under constant shellfire, the bones of many a *poilu* were ground in with the crushed stone that repaired its surface. The name was indeed apt.

Falkenhayn in turn widened the frontage, on 6 March extending the attacks to the west bank of the Meuse. But the defence was now solidifying, not least through Pétain's own massing of artillery and relieving the infantry divisions before casualties and exhaustion had too great an effect on their fighting power, though this called for ever greater numbers of replacements from elsewhere in the line and, as the weeks passed, caused Joffre to become increasingly anxious that this approach (and, of course, Falkenhayn's relentless attacks) was disrupting his own planned offensive. At the end of April he had to change his intended frontage of attack (on the Somme) from 25 to 15 miles, with thirty not thirty-nine divisions, and three hundred rather than seventeen hundred heavy guns.

At no time did Joffre consider the expedient – desperate as it might have seemed – of constructing shorter and better defensive lines to the south-east of Verdun, abandoning the salient and using his

* Lloyd George himself would declare Verdun 'sacred' when at dinner below ground there in September.

artillery in precisely the same way that Falkenhayn had intended. Verdun's twenty thousand inhabitants could have been housed elsewhere, their town to be recovered in due season – as many another. Their sacrifice might have spared some of their half a million compatriots who would be killed or wounded in Falkenhayn's trap. They needed a Caterina Sforza in command, not a Jeanne d'Arc.*

But Verdun had of course become a symbol, like the medieval maiden over whose honour two knights engage in mortal combat. Somehow the German people had taken command at Verdun, willing Falkenhayn on to take the town, while the French people, as if the entire struggle at Verdun were *La Voie Sacrée* – indeed, *La Voie de la Croix* – demanded that the Germans 'shall not pass'. Indeed, when the Germans captured Fleury-devant-Douaumont on 23 June (the *commune* changed hands no fewer than sixteen times), Nivelle issued an order of the day which famously ended: 'Ils ne passeront pas!' In the Second World War the motto would be worn on the uniforms of troops manning the 'Maginot Line', named unofficially after André Maginot, the defence minister, who had all but lost a leg at Verdun.

Today, Forts Vaux and Douaumont are kept open to the public. 'Battered and crumbling', wrote Sir Alistair Horne, author of the prize-winning *The Price of Glory: Verdun 1916*, 'they stand like Shelley's statue of Ozymandias, monuments to the folly, pride and heroism that epitomized what we still call the Great War.'†

Haig now found himself having to take on a greater role in the coming offensive on the Somme, as well as fulfilling the Chantilly conference undertaking that whenever one ally came under clear

* According to legend, Countess Caterina Sforza, in besieged Forli in fifteenth-century Italy, responded to her enemies' threat to kill her hostage children by standing on the walls of the fortress, pulling up her skirts to show her gender and shouting: 'Fatelo, se volete: impiccateli pure davanti a me . . . qui ho quanto basta per farne altri!': 'Do it, if you want to: hang them well in front of me . . . I have the mould to make more!' (Elizabeth Lev, *The Tigress of Forli*, Boston, 2011). France had the mould to make many Verduns.

† *Hubris: The Tragedy of War in the Twentieth Century* (London, 2015).

threat, the others would launch attacks. On 25 February, while even Joffre was still unclear what Verdun truly portended, he had met Kitchener in London and discussed the options, which included in the worst case (as Haig put it, 'disaster') '[a] counter-attack at once close to the French'. If on the other hand a kind of stalemate developed, and yet the French had enough troops left for the planned offensive, 'then we should make our attack alongside of theirs, say, astride the Somme', in line with Joffre's original proposal.

Kitchener agreed.

The 'disaster' did not of course happen. At least, not in the sense that Haig meant – a French collapse. Instead, it was more a slow-motion disaster – cumulative catastrophe. On 26 May, Joffre came to Haig's headquarters to discuss the timing of the Somme offensive, which was now clearly linked to relieving the pressure at Verdun. For three months the French had supported the whole weight of the German attacks at Verdun, he said. 'If this went on, the French Army would be ruined.'*

He urged that 1 July be the latest date for the start of the offensive.

Haig had been counting on 15 August, by which time he would have two hundred additional heavy guns and possibly some tanks. Going six weeks early would not be without penalty in terms of materiel and training. Yet Haig felt obliged to accede to Joffre's urging – subject to London's approval. Such was the nature of coalition warfare in exigent circumstances. Yet no one appears to have tried to persuade Joffre to stop hastening the destruction of the French army in butting against the wall of fire at Verdun. At the end of March, Crown Prince Wilhelm had told Falkenhayn that the bulk of the French reserves had been exhausted and that it was now time to complete their destruction by the conventional methods of attack, using 'men, not merely . . . machines and munitions'. Falkenhayn had agreed, probably with misgivings, and the cost to the Germans began to mount, but Joffre had come to his

* Quoted in *Haig: War Diaries and Letters*.

aid by insisting that, for prestige, Fort Douaumont – the fort which had played no part in the defence, stripped of armament as it had been, and had been captured by a handful of men – should be retaken. Against Pétain's better judgement, on 3 April Nivelle's III Corps tried to do so, with a predictably bloody lack of success.

Relations between Pétain and Joffre had been steadily deteriorating, and it was not surprising that *Le Chef* ascribed Nivelle's failure to Pétain's 'pessimistic' defensive-mindedness. In May, therefore, Joffre promoted Pétain to command of the central army group, where he hoped this stubborn-minded infantryman would develop a 'broader outlook' (promotion rather than dismissal being a not unheard-of expedient, before and since, for dealing with a difficult subordinate). Nivelle was given command of 2nd Army, and at once renewed his efforts to take back the ground. The result was more slaughter for no appreciable gain. By the end of May French casualties at Verdun had reached 185,000 (and by mid-June, German losses nearly two hundred thousand).

On 4 May, as Joffre was trying to shuffle Pétain away from Verdun, Clemenceau, the former prime minister and now chairman of the Senate Military Committee, had come to Haig's headquarters 'to get me [Haig] to exercise a restraining hand on General Joffre, and prevent any offensive on a large scale from being made until all is ready, and we are at our maximum strength'. Clemenceau feared that the Russians would be able to do nothing more to defeat Germany, and that, the task thus falling to the British and French, a failed and costly attack would precipitate a change of government in Paris and with it a call for terms.

In fact the Russians were doing a good deal to honour their undertaking at the Chantilly conference. In March they had attacked in Courland and Lithuania, an offensive which collapsed with heavy loss, and on 1 June, specifically at the request of Italy to relieve pressure on her armies in the Trentino, where the Austrians, contrary to Falkenhayn's wishes, had launched an offensive, General Aleksei Brusilov would begin his long-planned attack in Polish Galicia. The Austrians would buckle under the onslaught – not least because they had withdrawn troops for the offensive in the Trentino – and the chief of staff, Conrad von Hötzendorf, in terror of imminent invasion of Silesia and Hungary, begged Falkenhayn for help. The Germans at once sent six divisions to stabilize the Galician front, and although Falkenhayn was able to renew the attacks at Verdun on 21 June, he would have no fresh divisions for the effort. Consequently Nivelle was able to hold most of his ground, and, indeed, partially restored the situation by a counter-attack on the twenty-fourth.

During these desperate months Haig had continued his planning for the Somme offensive, with considerable, if at times churlishly expressed, flexibility when it came to French entreaties. By the end of February, at Joffre's request he had taken over the major part of the French 10th Army's sector, releasing its divisions for Verdun. In May, Joffre had taken away sixteen of the forty-two divisions originally assigned to Foch for the Somme offensive and given them to Pétain for Verdun, which would now make the French secondary to the British, who had thirty-seven divisions reserved for the offensive. In other words, the success of the 'general offensive' – whatever its aim – was now dependent largely on the BEF.

Yet what precisely was the aim of the offensive? Clearly it would relieve pressure on Verdun, but Joffre had been planning it *before* Falkenhayn interrupted him. Breakthrough and then defeat of the German army in a restored battle of manoeuvre was alternately at the forefront and the back of Joffre's mind, therefore. The trouble was that even before Verdun he did not have the troops to do it, let alone the technical means. Haig himself was similarly in two minds, and perhaps even a third – for there was still the *guerre d'usure*, attrition. On 18 January, following his meetings with Joffre and after a long discussion with Kiggell, his chief of staff, and Butler, Kiggell's deputy, he had concluded that the principles on which future plans should be based were: '(1) Employ sufficient force to wear down the Enemy and cause him to use up his reserves. (2) Then, *and not till then* [emphasis added], throw in a mass of troops (at some point where the Enemy has shown himself to be weak) to break through and win victory.' He added that the wearing down would probably fall into two phases, the 'present winter activity (offensive-minded defence)' being developed into 'a series of larger attacks . . . and a more general engagement . . . with a view to drawing in the Enemy's reserves'.

For this 'series of larger attacks' he had already ordered 3rd Army (Lieutenant-General Sir Edmund Allenby) to study a scheme for a 10-mile front and report how many divisions would be required, and what frontage could be attacked and where if they had twice that number of divisions. At the same time he had told 2nd Army (Plumer) to develop schemes for attacks against the Messines–Wytschaete Ridge, Lille, and Houthulst Forest in Flanders. In mid-February, however, Joffre had given up the idea of the BEF mounting *batailles d'usure* before the main offensive, and urged Haig to concentrate instead on the combined offensive on the Somme, with just a smaller, diversionary attack, with a French corps in support, in the area between La Bassée and Ypres – at which point Falkenhayn had intervened.

Joffre's change of heart notwithstanding, wearing down the Enemy (with a capital 'E') and then, *'and not till then,* throw[ing] in a mass of troops . . . to break through and win victory' would remain Haig's military philosophy. But he was never quite able to accept the caveat *'and not till then'*, seeking always the 'break-through' in the midst of the 'wearing down'. On 5 April he studied Rawlinson's proposals for attack on the Somme by 4th Army:

> His intention is merely to take the Enemy's first and second system of trenches and 'kill Germans'. He looks upon the gaining of 3 or 4 kilometres more or less of ground immaterial. I think we can do better than this by aiming at getting as large a combined force of French and British across the Somme and fighting the enemy in the open!

This is not the same as 'break[ing] through and win[ning] victory' – arguably, the enemy could be worn down more in the open – but it is close enough to confuse the purpose at subordinate levels, and to corrupt otherwise sound plans. While Haig is on record as stating that there was no 'certainty' of 'destroy[ing] the power of Germany this year', he was clearly determined to plan in the expectation that there was.* On 27 June, just days before the attack, he was dismayed to discover that Rawlinson had 'ordered his troops to halt for an hour and consolidate on the Enemy's last line! Covered by an artillery barrage! I said this must depend on whether Enemy had reserves available and on the spot for counter-attack. I directed him to prepare for a rapid advance.'

Yet how was Rawlinson to know whether the Germans had reserves available? As the counter-attack was a German tactical precept, as the allies very well knew from the fighting at Ypres and Verdun, it would be most unusual if there were *not* troops assigned to the task. At the very least, counter-attack by artillery was a certainty. Attacking troops consolidate on the objective to prepare to defeat the counter-attack: this was the equally standard British tactical precept, and Rawlinson, for all his 'insincerity', was an infantryman of some experience.

The point would, of course, be entirely academic. Rawlinson's troops would never reach the last line – not in any sense that Haig had hoped for.

Still there were very mixed messages about the proposed action on the Somme. On 20 May, Clemenceau told Haig, through his private secretary, that the feeling was now opposed to any offensive until the allies were in a far stronger position; that the prime minister (Briand) now said there should be no offensive that year, and that Foch agreed with him. Under the impression that the attack

* Letter to Lord Bertie, British ambassador in Paris, 5 June 1916. And on 29 May, at Haig's suggestion, 'Wully' Robertson told the cabinet that in view of the small number of French and British divisions available for the offensive, far-reaching results should not be expected – which rather gives the impression that had those divisions originally assigned still been available, far-reaching results *should* be expected. It is not unheard-of for a military commander to cover his back, as it were, by warning his masters that as a result of inadequate resources his plan might not come off.

on the Somme was becoming less likely, Haig ordered Plumer to push on with plans for the Messines attack with all speed, though after his meeting with a very agitated Joffre on 26 May – the meeting at which Joffre had keened that if losses went on at Verdun at the rate currently being inflicted, the French army would be ruined – he warned Rawlinson that he might have to attack without any French assistance at all.

On 31 May another meeting took place, in President Poincaré's railway car near Amiens, attended by Haig, Briand, Joffre, Castelnau, Foch and the new French minister for war, General Pierre Roques, an engineer, 'father' of the French air arm – and independent-minded. Having first said that action must be taken to ease pressure at Verdun, and that he was hearing different things from different generals, Poincaré asked Haig's opinion. Haig found himself in a difficult position, questioned by the president of the French republic on military plans that he and Joffre had developed with varying degrees of accord. He replied that he had agreed a plan with Joffre and obtained the British cabinet's support; all he needed was a date, and Joffre had indicated early July. He also suggested that to ease the situation at Verdun and have enough divisions for the offensive, France withdraw troops from Salonika, which predictably found no favour. Joffre said the French army would give the British every assistance, and the meeting ended with Poincaré apparently more assured. Three days later Joffre wrote to Haig giving formal notice that the attack must begin on 1 July at the latest.*

* On 13 June, the head of the French mission at GHQ reported to Haig that the situation at Verdun was very serious indeed, that there was a political crisis in Paris and that Joffre wished the attack to be brought forward to 25 June. Haig reviewed the situation and reported that the best he could do was 29 June. (It was only bad weather that in the end delayed it until 1 July.) Joffre was content, however: he now knew the BEF was committed to a serious attack.

Chapter Twelve

THE SOMME: 'A SUNLIT PICTURE OF HELL'

On 5 June, just days after taking part in the Battle of Jutland, the armoured cruiser HMS *Hampshire* struck a mine off Marwick Head on the west coast of Orkney and sank in fifteen minutes with the loss of all but twelve hands. One of those drowned was the secretary of state for war, Lord Kitchener, on a 'mission of reassurance' to Petrograd. His star had been steadily in the descendant, dragged down by the 'shell scandal' and then Gallipoli; but he left the stage before it had entirely faded, in a hero's death and with what honours could still be bestowed – an effigy in a chapel dedicated to his memory in St Paul's Cathedral.*

* In May, a motion had been moved (unsuccessfully) in the Commons that his salary be reduced by £100. There is still a suggestion that Asquith sent Kitchener to Russia to get him out of the way. 'K' had undoubtedly got enmeshed in the increasing political intrigue, and his powers generally were on the wane, but this should not eclipse his earlier achievement. In 1914, such was his reputation that he had meant as much to the man in the street as Churchill did in 1940 – and even more to those in high places. He brought about a revolution in national life almost single-handed. In his first month as secretary of state for war, with no precedents, no staff and no political machine behind him, he first saw the need for and then envisaged and planned for a new army of thirty divisions, doubled the TF so that half of it could be released to serve overseas, doubled the size of the regular army in France and mustered the armies from the dominions. When he died, the army went into genuine mourning; but it was a distant, respectful mourning. He lacked perhaps any single trait or quality that could make him loveable.

His death did not augur well for Haig. Lloyd George would become war minister, and 'LG' would change his opinion of the new C-in-C. He had visited GHQ in January, writing to him afterwards: 'I have a feeling that everything which the assiduity, the care, and the trained thought of a great soldier can accomplish is being done.'

Soon, however, he would be saying that Haig was 'brilliant – to the top of his boots'.*

Falkenhayn may have regarded the French army as Britain's sword-arm, to be dashed from her hand at Verdun, but while the French had been parrying and thrusting in the great duel at the end of the *Voie Sacrée*, it was the British sword that was now to make the true riposte. It was, however, a sword of uncertain temper, and as yet unsharpened. From the summer of 1915, the 'Kitchener battalions' had begun to enter the field. By the spring of 1916, K1–5 (Kitchener's first five hundred thousand) had either seen action or were deployed and ready, mainly in France and Flanders. But the BEF's commanders had understandable reservations about their capability, not least because of Loos ('I have not got an Army in France really, but a collection of divisions untrained for the field'). To some extent the Western Front's routine of constant labour – digging, repairing, wiring, carrying forward ammunition and stores – was easy enough for the New Army battalions to cope with. In its turn in the line, a battalion would typically spend four days in the fire and support trenches, four in close reserve half a mile or so to the rear, and four resting out of range of field artillery. Out of the line the routine was training, rest and recreation. But the training of the New Army battalions had perforce concentrated on individual trench skills. Company and battalion battle drill was weak, and 'musketry' occupied nothing like its place in the pre-war army.

In short, Kitchener's men could look after themselves, but they

* According to Lloyd George's son Richard, that is. The remark, attributed to the second Earl Lloyd George, is quoted in John Terraine, *Essays on Leadership and War 1914–18* (London, 1998).

had scant practice in how to advance in the face of the enemy. And fire-and-movement seemed to be yesterday's story – the skills of 1914, before the trenches reached the coast. Now it was the bomb (grenade) and the machine gun, and occasionally the bayonet.

The routine now established on the Western Front had seemed to suppress even *thinking* about mobility. To an extent senior officers had willed this, or at least accepted it, but many were all too aware of the limitations it now imposed. The only part of the army still movement-minded (other than, of course, the Royal Flying Corps) was the cavalry, and they could only manoeuvre once the infantry had punched a hole in the defences. To the very end, Haig saw winning the war in terms of forcing the collapse of a part of the German front line so that mobile – horse-borne – troops could restore the war of manoeuvre by which the decision would be gained.

In any case, fire-and-movement was not something that could easily be taught to such green troops as the New Army battalions, however eager. There were simply not the experienced junior officers and NCOs to do the teaching. Nor were there enough officers capable of higher command and staff duties. It was no easy matter to accustom officers to whom before the war the division had been the highest level of command to directing the movements of an army of a million and a half men. Knowing this want of training in the New Army battalions, senior officers sought a simpler way of crossing no-man's-land to break open the German defences. As the last of the K5 battalions were arriving in France in the spring of 1916, the thinking in GHQ – for all that Haig looked to the cavalry for the breakthrough – had in truth become Napoleonic: 'It is with artillery that war is made.'

And GHQ was refining its thinking about artillery by studying the battle of March the previous year when Haig had had his first measure of success – Neuve Chapelle.

There, after a heavy but brief artillery bombardment, the attacking divisions (two regular British and two from the Indian Corps) made progress, though not without cost. But if the attack was in the end a disappointment – the Germans were able to recover more quickly than the British could exploit their own local success – it seemed to show what artillery could do when there was enough of it. It followed, by fairly elementary reasoning, that as great a concentration of guns (or more) firing for longer against the German line would achieve even better results.

There were two flaws in this analysis, however, the first perversely hidden. The bombardment at Neuve Chapelle had been brief – thirty minutes on the fire trenches and then a further thirty on the support lines – owing to the shortage of shells. Because that shortage was a result of the 'shell scandal', the brevity of the bombardment was seen not just as a consequence of weakness but as *the* weakness. In fact, that very brevity had achieved a degree of surprise that had contributed more to the success achieved than the actual damage inflicted by the artillery. A prolonged bombardment naturally forfeited surprise; it served notice on the defenders that they would have to stand to and repel attack, and to senior commanders that they must move reserves ready to reinforce, counter-attack, and seal any breach. The longer, too, that a battery fired, the more likely it was to be detected and put out of action by counter-battery fire. The success at Neuve Chapelle was more the result of surprise and the shock of the hurricane bombardment – 'the first true drum-fire [*Trommelfeuer*] yet heard' – than of obliteration. And resolute defenders, well sheltered, could quickly recover. If the artillery did not keep German heads down long enough, the assaulting troops would never make it across no-man's-land. Everyone had to believe, therefore, that prolonged bombardment would destroy. And it was in the way of human nature that the more the plan relied on this assumption, the stronger would be the belief in it.

The other flaw in the analysis lay in the assumption that the effect of artillery was the same on the defences across the entire front, that the Germans and their barbed wire would be as vulnerable on the Somme as they had been at Neuve Chapelle. But at Neuve Chapelle the water table was high; the German trenches were consequently built up as much as dug down, and therefore more vulnerable to artillery. In the valley of the Somme, however, the Germans had burrowed deep – 30 feet in places – into the chalk. And not only were the Germans dug in deep, in this second full year of trench warfare the barbed-wire defences in no-man's-land were thicker and deeper than ever. When the artillery bombardment lifted, it would be a straight 'race for the parapet' – the defenders up the ladders of the dugouts, the attackers through the wire and craters of no-man's-land. Neuve Chapelle was to the Somme as the English Channel is to the Atlantic.

Lieutenant-General Sir Henry Rawlinson was given a relatively free hand in planning, though with green troops and no tanks his room for manoeuvre, literally and metaphorically, was in truth limited. His plan of attack would rely on a long obliterating bombardment to destroy both the Germans in their dug-outs (the depth and extent of which had not been discovered) and the barbed wire which protected them, enabling his under-trained infantry simply to march the several hundred yards across no-man's-land and occupy what remained of the enemy trenches. And because they would not advance across no-man's-land at more than walking pace (the rate at which the artillery barrage would 'creep' – a new technique – from the fire trenches to the support trenches) they would be able to carry the extra ammunition, defence stores and rations needed before resupplies could be brought forward – a load per man of some 60 lb (27 kg).

Blunden summed up the concept of operations drily:

> Soon after this [the diversionary attack near Aubers Ridge, the 'Boar's Head massacre'] a circular appeared, which began, 'All ranks must know that the great offensive has now definitely begun,' and went on to assert the valuable creative principle that artillery and trench mortars cut the wire; infantry capture and consolidate the trenches. This promised to simplify the new warfare considerably.

There is some evidence that Haig suggested to Rawlinson that patrols might first establish the extent to which the artillery had managed to cut the wire and destroy the German fire trenches before the infantry left their own trenches en masse, as the Germans had done in the initial attacks at Verdun. If the infantry, not possessing the means to take strongly held objectives, were merely to occupy ground neutralized by the artillery, it made sense to confirm first that the artillery had succeeded (as one staff officer would say the following year, having learned the lesson: 'It is a sin to assume anything that can be verified'). Rawlinson appears to have rejected this advice, however, taking the guardsman's (as he was) preference for regular alignment in the advance over the rifleman's (as he had once been) preference for fire and movement. In fairness, Haig's final instructions, which betrayed a poor grasp of infantry tactics, ruled out the expedient of reconnaissance patrols because their use might render advancing troops in one sector vulnerable to flanking fire from German positions that were not themselves being attacked: 'The advance of isolated detachments should be avoided. They lead to the loss of the boldest and best *without result* [emphasis added – a strange essay into prophecy]. Enemy [the enemy which the artillery is supposed to have suppressed] can concentrate on these detachments. Advance should be uniform.'*

So, not so much an attack as an 'advance in review order'.

In the later (it is unclear how much later) typescript version of Haig's diary, the words 'except for reconnoitring purposes' have been added after 'The advance of isolated detachments should be avoided.' This is a significant and troubling addition. It materially alters the tenor of the instructions Haig gave to Rawlinson, for in truth what other purpose might there be for isolated detachments but reconnaissance? Did Rawlinson really ignore Haig's leave to allow recce parties to move out, before the attacking troops left the trenches, to discover the gaps in the wire and any points of German resistance – or was Haig's subsequent diary entry an attempt to distance himself from the disaster that ensued from not letting them do so, from insisting instead on a uniform advance?

Flanking fire was indeed a distinct possibility, but it was surely

* *Haig: War Diaries and Letters*, diary entry for 15 June 1916.

better to deal with the problem by laying down smoke or a machine-gun barrage, or calling for suppressive artillery, rather than presenting the breasts of brave men to draw away that fire. In any case, this was a matter for – at most – the army commander, not the commander-in-chief. Indeed, it was really a question for the level of command in contact with the enemy's fire, which was after all the ultimate arbiter of tactics. *FSR* is quite clear on the matter: 'The choice of the manner in which the task assigned to each body of troops is to be performed should be left to its commander.'

This was not Haig's finest hour. Why he should have thought himself the ultimate authority on infantry in the attack is baffling.

And his confidence in the artillery to destroy the barbed wire and trenches seemed to know no limit. The seasoned soldier's essential precautionary question in making any plan – 'What if . . .?' (What if the wire isn't cut? What if the enemy trenches and machine guns aren't neutralized?) – seems wholly to have eluded him; and, indeed, Rawlinson. At the conference with his army commanders on 15 June, Haig noted that 'The length of each bound* depends on the area which has been prepared by the artillery. The infantry must for their part, capture and hold all the ground which the artillery has prepared with as little delay as possible.'

Capture, not just 'occupy' – in other words, a fight for the ground could be envisaged, a fight contingent on the effectiveness of the artillery. In which case, said *FSR*, 'During the process of establishing a superiority of fire, successive fire positions will be occupied by the firing line.'

Just how was this to be achieved in Rawlinson's plan?

It wasn't, of course. The plan saw no need. The superiority of fire would be established by the *artillery*, not the firing line (the infantry).

The seven-day preparatory bombardment on the Somme certainly looked and sounded impressive – fifteen hundred guns firing two

* Bound: a single movement, usually from cover to cover, of troops advancing in contact (or expected contact) with the enemy.

hundred thousand rounds a day (in the end, the shell count was nearer 1.7 million, since the French added their weight on the right); but because of the length of front to be attacked (12 miles), the inadequate number of guns for the task, their varying accuracy and the failure rate of the ammunition (perhaps as many as one in three shells proved either duds or misfires), the weight of fire was proportionately only half that at Neuve Chapelle. However, Haig's diary is full of references to the various commanders' satisfaction with the bombardment: '[Pulteney, VIII Corps, 29 June] . . . also is quite satisfied with the artillery bombardment and wire cutting . . .'; '[Horne, XV Corps, 30 June] Wire very well cut, and ammunition adequate. (NB This corps expended twice as much as was allowed!)'*

That evening, 30 June, Haig wrote to his wife:

> The attack goes in tomorrow morning at 7.30 am . . . I feel that everything possible for us to do to achieve success has been done. But whether or not we are successful lies in the Power above. But *I do feel* that in my plans I have been helped by a Power that is not my own. So I am easy in my mind and ready to do my best whatever happens tomorrow.

It is not known what Haig's theology made of the first day when eventually he discovered what actually had happened. The Australian historian (albeit a *parti pris* one) John Laffin was profanely blunt about it: '[Haig] saw God in his own image.'†

In October, John Masefield, on his mission to do for the Somme what he had done for Gallipoli, looked at what he could of the old battlefield, spoke to whom he could, including Haig, and read what

* XV Corps was one of the more successful in the opening days of the battle, so perhaps the unauthorized extra shelling proves the Neuve Chapelle point. Horne, of course, was a gunner, Haig's artillery commander in I Corps in August 1914. And then, as GOC 2nd Division, he had the débâcle of his division's gas attack at Loos to live down.

† *British, Butchers, and Bunglers of World War One* (London, 1998).

he could. And of that first morning of the British army's most debilitating battle ever, 1 July 1916, he wrote:

> It was fine, cloudless, summer weather, not very clear, for there was a good deal of heat haze and of mist in the nights and early mornings. It was hot yet brisk during the days. The roads were thick in dust. Clouds and streamers of chalk dust floated and rolled over all the roads leading to the front, till men and beasts were grey with it.
>
> At half past six in the morning of 1st July all the guns on our front quickened their fire to a pitch of intensity never before attained. Intermittent darkness and flashing so played on the enemy line from Gommecourt to Maricourt that it looked like a reef on a loppy day. For one instant it could be seen as a white rim above the wire, then some comber of a big shell struck it fair and spouted it black aloft . . .
>
> In our trenches after seven o'clock on that morning, our men waited under a heavy fire for the signal to attack. Just before half-past seven, the mines at half a dozen points went up with a roar that shook the earth and brought down the parapets in our lines. Before the blackness of their burst had thinned or fallen, the hand of Time rested on the half-hour mark, and along all that old front line of the English there came a whistling and a crying. The men of the first wave climbed up the parapets, in tumult, darkness, and the presence of death, and having done with all pleasant things, advanced across the No Man's Land to begin the battle of the Somme.*

Leutnant Beck, of the 21st Reserve Infantry Regiment near Beaumont Hamel, had watched from the German trenches as the 4th Division, one of the old regular divisions that had fought in the retreat from Mons, prepared to attack:

> [From the higher ground] I could see that the British trenches were overflowing with masses of troops. They stood there laughing and joking, some groups were having a quiet smoke, sitting on the parapet

* *The Old Front Line* (London, 1917). In fact the attack began with the detonation of seventeen mines, the first, under the 'Hawthorn Redoubt', being detonated ten minutes early.

> with all their equipment on. The enemy fire increased in intensity, reaching hurricane proportions towards 8.00 a.m. Suddenly it lifted onto our rear positions and we felt the earth shake violently – this was caused by a mine going off near Beaumont. In no time flat the slope opposite resembled an ant heap. Wave after wave of assaulting British troops hurled themselves forward through the dust and smoke towards our position.*

The 'race for the parapet' had begun. But a race it scarcely was, for on the one side lines of smart new khaki advanced at a steady march, while on the other, when the bombardment shifted onto the reserve trenches, files of fossorial field grey ran up from the deep dug-outs to man the machine guns in the contest for the green fields beyond. It was – remains – the greatest set-piece attack, the greatest battle, in British history: eleven divisions in line and two more in the adjacent diversionary attack – 13 × 18,000 men.

The German 'Maxims' opened up in long raking bursts, their arcs interlocking so that just about every yard of front was swept by fire. The silent, waiting artillery batteries sprang into life, the guns laid on pre-registered lines just in front of the barbed wire so that there was no need of corrections. And into this hail of lead, high explosive and shrapnel marched that resolute infantry: pre-war regulars who had somehow made it this far, territorials toughened by a year at the front – and, only part-trained, many of them going over the top for the first time, the New Army battalions, Kitchener's men. One way or another, every man a volunteer.

To begin with, some seemed to be entering into the spirit of what was expected to be – literally – a walk-over. In the 8th East Surreys, even though – or perhaps even because – the battalion had fought at Loos, one company went into the attack dribbling footballs across no-man's-land. The game did not last long: 147 officers and men were killed and 279 wounded before they reached the German fire trench. But, as one of the few battalions to gain its

* Quoted in Ralph J. Whitehead, *The Other Side of the Wire* (Solihull, 2013).

objective that day, it reaped an impressive array of gallantry awards – two DSOs, two Military Crosses, two Distinguished Conduct Medals and nine Military Medals. The 'Football Attack' caught the imagination of the country as an example of British pluck and *sang froid*.*

The 1st and 2nd Barnsley 'Pals' (13th and 14th Battalions, York and Lancaster Regiment), attacking side by side in 94th Brigade, 31st Division, further north, got nowhere.† The 1st Pals went over the top 720 strong; by the middle of the afternoon there were but 250 of them left. The 2nd Pals fared slightly better, losing 300 before the brigade commander called them off. Both battalions were lucky, however, for besides being in the support wave their brigadier was the 34-year-old Hubert Conway Rees, a regular infantryman robust enough to stop the attack.

But too late for the battalion in front of the York and Lancasters – another Pals battalion, the 11th East Lancashires or 'Accrington Pals', 730 men from the close-knit cotton-mill towns of 'Blackburnshire'. After the first half an hour, 600 of them were dead, wounded or 'missing' (in other words, there were no remains of them after

* The 8th East Surreys, though a 'K2' battalion, and therefore supposedly with a higher proportion of former regulars than 'K3–5', had in fact been formed by a single regular captain, who sensibly asked for those who felt they could control six to eight other men to step forward, to be at once promoted corporal. Until a recent fire, the regimental museum in Clandon Park, near Guildford, had one of the balls. The only other known survivor of the attack is in the National Football Museum.

† In August 1914 Kitchener had given local grandees leave to raise battalions en bloc (often initially at their own expense) with the simple promise that those who enlisted together would be allowed to serve together. The promise of serving together proved powerful. In Liverpool the earl of Derby, the great mover and shaker of the commercial north-west (and subsequently director-general of army recruiting), called on the office workers to form a battalion: 'This should be a battalion of pals, a battalion in which friends from the same office will fight shoulder to shoulder for the honour of Britain and the credit of Liverpool.' But instead of one battalion, between 28 August (a Friday), while the BEF was in full retreat after Mons and Le Cateau, and 3 September, Liverpool raised four, the clerks of the White Star shipping company forming up as one platoon, those of Cunard as another, and so on through the warehouses of the Mersey waterside, the cotton exchange, the banks and the insurance companies – men who knew each other better than their mothers knew them, and now doing what their mothers would never ordinarily have countenanced: going for a soldier – at least 'for the duration'.

shelling, for none had got far enough to be taken prisoner). The brigadier wrote of them and the rest of his brigade:

> At the time this barrage really became intense, the last waves of the attack were crossing the trench I was in. I have never seen a finer display of individual and collective bravery than the advance of that brigade. I never saw a man waver from the exact line prescribed for him. Each line disappeared in the thick cloud of dust & smoke which rapidly blotted out the whole area. I saw a few groups of men through gaps in the smoke cloud, but I knew that no troops could hope to get through such a fire.*

Robert Graves was lucky to have missed the first day (he had been sent back to England for an operation on his nose to allow him to breathe properly in the new gas mask): three out of five of the officers in his battalion, 1st Royal Welsh Fusiliers, were killed. His fellow officer–poet Siegfried Sassoon would have been one of them, except that his company was held in reserve. Sassoon had spent a good deal of the day and night before the battle crawling about in no-man's-land trying to make wider gaps in the barbed wire with his new wire-cutters, bought on leave at the Army and Navy Stores, so that the New Army battalion of the Manchester Regiment which was to attack from their trench might have a better chance: 'It seemed to me that our prestige as a regular battalion had been entrusted to my care on a front of several hundred yards,' he wrote.† (For an action later that month he would win the MC.) Wilfred Owen, who had enlisted in 1915 and would soon be commissioned into the Manchesters, was lucky, too, to be away from the front in an officer training battalion. (It was here that he wrote much of his poetry: 'My subject is war, and the pity of war. The poetry is in the pity.')‡

* Memoirs of Brigadier-General Hubert Conway Rees, held at the Imperial War Museum.

† *Memoirs of an Infantry Officer* (London, 1930).

‡ Draft preface for a collection of poems intended for publication in 1919. Owen would be killed a week before the Armistice leading an attack with the 2nd Manchesters, notionally still a regular battalion. His MC, for a similar feat the month before, would be gazetted the following year.

Isaac Rosenberg, one of the few acknowledged greats of the war poets not to have been commissioned, was serving with the 11th Battalion, the King's Own, a 'Bantam battalion' (consisting of men under the 1914 minimum height of 5 feet 3 inches) and therefore not assigned an assault role on 1 July, employed instead on fatigue duties and burials. In the days that followed he would write what the American literary critic and Second World War infantry officer Paul Fussell called the greatest poem of the war – 'Break of Day in the Trenches'.* It is a short, stark meditation on mud, rats and poppies, with none of the spirit that had motivated men to flock to the recruiting offices in their hundreds of thousands, including Rosenberg's own 'Bantams' – pint-sized men determined to do their bit:

The darkness crumbles away.
It is the same old druid Time as ever,
Only a live thing leaps my hand,
A queer sardonic rat,
As I pull the parapet's poppy
To stick behind my ear.
Droll rat, they would shoot you if they knew
Your cosmopolitan sympathies.
Now you have touched this English hand
You will do the same to a German . . .†

And Sassoon was no doubt thinking of the men of the Kitchener battalions of Rosenberg's regiment, the King's Own – the Royal Lancasters – when he wrote:

. . . But to the end, unjudging, he'll endure
Horror and pain, not uncontent to die
That Lancaster on Lune may stand secure.‡

* *The Great War and Modern Memory* (Oxford, 1975).
† Isaac Rosenberg was killed while serving with the 1st King's Own – a regular battalion (so great had been the attrition) – on 1 April 1918.
‡ 'The Redeemer' (from *The Old Huntsman*, 1918). In fact his batman was a Lancastrian.

At the end of the first day of the battle of the Somme the casualties numbered 57,470 men, including that fearful category 'missing'. Of these, 19,240 were soon listed as 'killed in action'.

Siegfried Sassoon, who might so easily have been one of them, described the first day as 'a sunlit picture of hell'. The casualties were almost as great as the duke of Wellington's in the entire Peninsular campaign. Yet at the end of that first day's fighting no single person had a complete grasp of the scale of the disaster. The following day Haig recorded in his diary that the estimates were 'over 40,000 to date', adding that 'this cannot be considered severe in view of the numbers engaged, and the length of front attacked'. Rawlinson had expected ten thousand a day. But quite apart from the underestimating of its cost, the attack had not been successful – however success was to be measured (principally, in Haig's mind, the extent of ground captured) – and as yet Haig did not grasp this either. On 8 July he wrote in his diary: 'In another fortnight, with Divine Help, I hope that some decisive results may be obtained.' He did not in fact finally abandon ('close down' is the rather euphemistic term) the Somme offensive until the middle of November.

Yet even as the true scale of the losses became widely known, and the attacks continued, morale did not crack, as it did in the French army the following year in the wake of the failures of their renewed offensives. As the battle went on through August, however, there were some 'indications of a loss of fighting spirit', as official reports put it. On 4 September, after another failed attack, Haig recorded his dismay with the 49th (West Riding) Division, made up primarily of territorial units, who appeared to have made no gains for proportionately fewer casualties than other formations: 'The units did not really attack, and some men did not follow their officers. The total losses of this division are under a thousand!'

One of the earliest, and most instructive, failures of 'fighting spirit' occurred on 9 July, when the 11th Battalion the Border Regiment, a 'Pals' unit formed in 1914 by the earl of Lonsdale and known throughout the army as 'the Lonsdales', simply failed to carry out a night attack when ordered (or rather, what was left of the battalion failed to do so, for out of eight hundred men they had already lost five hundred killed, missing or wounded, including twenty-five of their twenty-eight officers on the first day). It was not mutiny: there was no outright refusal to obey orders, no desertions; the attack just didn't happen. There can come a stage where a sort of exhausted inertia brings activity to an eventual halt.

When the divisional commander learned of this he ordered exemplary punishment for the commanding officer (a captain who had been brought in from another battalion in the same brigade after the losses of the first day) and the few other officers left, including even the regimental medical officer (RMO). The disciplinary papers wound their way up the chain of command, gathering more and more exclamations of outrage at the acting commanding officer's failure, and that of the RMO who had reported the men mentally unfit for duty, castigating also the Lonsdales' pathetically small remaining band of NCOs. Eventually the papers arrived at Haig's headquarters where the chief medical officer, the wonderfully named Surgeon-General Sir Arthur Sloggett, pointed out one or two facts that had been overlooked in the atmosphere of scapegoating that had taken hold after 1 July: the internal cohesion of the brigade had been severely shaken; the brigade commander himself appeared unfit for duty, as indeed did the Lonsdales' acting commanding officer; and the RMO had been asked his opinion of the state of the battalion's nerves, which was not within his capability to judge. Haig, sitting outside the 'bubble' of 5th (Reserve) Army, which was commanded by the ever-certain Gough of Curragh fame and which had taken over responsibility for that part of the front, was able to agree with Sloggett, and matters were quietly rearranged. The Lonsdales were rested and reinforced, and they fought well again later in the year; by the end of the war, the officers involved had all been decorated.

The episode demonstrated that though its limits are indistinct, endurance is finite: the Lonsdales' experience was perhaps extreme, but there were other cases of battalions having lost not so much their nerve as their confidence. Still, most persevered as before, continuing to lose men, particularly young officers, in steady numbers. At Flers–Courcelette on 15 September, when tanks were used for the first time – rushed prematurely to the front and to almost no effect, for the ground was too soft – the prime minister's eldest son, Raymond Asquith, was killed leading a half-company of the Grenadier Guards. A barrister and fellow of All Souls, he had joined the army at once on the outbreak of war.

The Somme offensive was four and a half months of almost continuous attacks across the 4th Army front, with an unprecedented number of guns and supply of shells, many of them made in the United States and Canada. Yet the capture of ground was minimal, and that which was taken was frequently taken back in German counter-attacks. The fighting had become senseless, and for many almost insensate.*

Though 'the Somme' is now a byword for slaughter on an almost unimaginable scale – as Verdun is for the French – it is worth once more pondering on the figures, the statistics of the *guerre d'usure*, of attrition. The BEF's total losses from 1 July to 15 November (on the Somme and in supporting attacks elsewhere) numbered roughly half a million, which was about the same as the French losses for the whole year (including 348,000 at Verdun and 194,000 on the Somme), and by the close of the fighting that November, despite the astonishing figure of 192,000 battle-casualty replacements being sent to France – over one and a half times the number of the original BEF that had left Britain in August 1914 – Haig's army was 80,000 below strength. The French were in an even more exhausted position: on the first day of the Somme they were 92,000 below establishment, but because they had accelerated the call-up of some 78,000 of the class of 1916, they were in reality 170,000 men behind need. Replacements were increasingly difficult to find and to train. They were even calling up Catholic priests for service as

* 'We always felt that someone up above was ordering things, and that they probably knew more about it than we did,' said Captain Tom Adlam of the 7th Bedfordshire Regiment (a Kitchener battalion). 'We just carried on.' Quoted in Max Arthur, *Forgotten Voices of the Great War* (London, 2002).

combatants. It was probably only their African troops that allowed them to hang on at Verdun and to take part in the Somme.

The Germans had, of course, suffered heavily too. Exact comparisons are difficult because of how the different armies classified casualties, but it is probable that at Verdun the imperial German army's losses were around 400,000, and on the Somme 570,000.*

The impact of these figures was curiously mixed. In the French army they would lead – through asinine repetition the following year – to mutiny, but before that to the fall of Joffre.† In the German army they would lead to a hardened resolve to take whatever measures were necessary to win the war – not least that the *Kaiserliche Marine* must open unrestricted submarine warfare. Falkenhayn had been relieved as chief of staff (in effect commander-in-chief of the entire German army) at the end of August, and the two heroes of

* The first 1916 volume of the British *Official History* (published in 1932) stated that while comparisons of casualties were inexact because of different methods of calculation by the belligerents, British Somme casualties were 419,654 (out of total British casualties in France in the period of 498,054) and French 194,451; German casualties were *c*.445,322, to which should be added 27% for woundings, which would have been counted as casualties using British criteria. Anglo-French casualties on the Somme were therefore over 600,000 and German casualties under 600,000.

† Not only was Joffre's confidence in offensives on the Western Front now manifestly shown to be misplaced, his greater strategic judgement was also cast into doubt over Salonika. Romania had entered the war on the allies' side in late August, but was at once worsted by Austro-Hungarian and Bulgarian forces, who occupied Bucharest in December 1916. This not only ruled out the long looked-to Russo-Romanian attack on Bulgaria, it would enable the Central Powers to attack Salonika. Joffre had already ordered General Sarrail to cease all offensive action and instead establish a strong defence from which further offensives might be launched when opportune. To Briand's and Joffre's surprise, however, General Roques, minister of war, now returned from a fact-finding mission to Salonika recommending that Sarrail be reinforced, and that he report direct to him, not to Joffre. Briand therefore proposed that Joffre be effectively demoted to C-in-C in north-east France, although he backtracked when Joffre threatened to resign, and then (according to Joffre) promised to appoint him Marshal of France and to give him a staff of his own and 'direction of the war'. On 13 December Briand managed to form a new government, and Joffre was appointed 'general-in-chief of the French armies, technical adviser to the government [and] consultative member of the war committee', with Nivelle as C-in-C of the armies of the north and north-east. It soon became clear to Joffre that he would have neither power nor influence, however, and so on 26 December, the day he was promoted Marshal of France, he asked to be relieved.

the Eastern Front, Hindenburg and Ludendorff, now came to Berlin, Hindenburg as titular replacement and Ludendorff, as *Erster Generalquartiermeister*, his deputy and wielder of the real power. Both of them – ugly men with ugly ideas of war – lost no time strong-arming the Kaiser and Bethmann Hollweg into agreeing to unleash the U-boats. Indeed, from 1917 on they would in effect be the double head of state, Prussia once more an army with a country attached to it.

The Battle of the Somme had not been without result. Indeed, it would be one of the factors in the Germans' decision early in 1917 to withdraw several miles to better and heavily fortified ground and to shorten the front (as Wellington had done in the Peninsula with the Lines of Torres Vedras). Except for the illusory victory in 'capturing' the abandoned ground, this was hardly a benefit for the allies, who in 'the Hindenburg Line' would have a much tougher nut to crack.

Soldiers and politicians have walked ever deeper in the shadow of the valley of the Somme. The casualty lists, which filled the newspapers for months, imprinted themselves indelibly on the mind of the nation. And the lists included only the names of the officers.

Yet the Somme does not belong solely to the poets, or to the school of 'lions led by donkeys'. The battle has always had its apologists, for in the logic of the 'strategy' of attrition and nothing else it could be claimed a victory – of the sort that King Pyrrhus had eponymously lamented: 'one other such victory would utterly undo him'. On 30 June 1966, the chairman of London Transport, Sir John Elliot, who had served in the cavalry in the latter stages of the war, wrote to *The Times*:

> Sir,
>
> July 1 being the fiftieth anniversary of the Battle of the Somme, the thoughts of most people will be on the terrible casualties incurred by the new British armies, particularly on the first day, and on the oft-repeated charge against Haig of 'useless sacrifices for a few miles of devastation'. It is as well, therefore, to remember the other side of the

picture, so that those whose fathers and grandfathers died in the battle may comfort themselves that, in fact, they did not die in vain. There are sound grounds for this:–

1. The choice of the Somme as the battle-ground was Joffre's and not Haig's, the French C-in-C. insisting that here, where the Germans were strong, the greatest relief to the exhausted French at Verdun could be made. Had Haig not fought as he did, France, after her dreadful sacrifice of life, would probably have been driven out of the war, as she was in 1940.

2. British comment seldom appreciates the irretrievable damage which the Germans suffered as a result of the battle. Let Ludendorff speak for that:–

> 'The German Army was fought to a standstill on the Somme and utterly worn out . . . not only did our morale suffer, there was fearful wastage in killed and wounded . . . we had not enough men; we could not move a division from the Western Front.'

3. There can be no doubt whatever that when in 1918 the Germans finally collapsed before the Allied assault (mostly by the British under Haig in the centre) it was largely because the flower of the German armies had been destroyed at Verdun, on the Somme, and at Third Ypres and in the failure of their own great attacks of March and April, 1918. The Battle of the Somme should not, therefore, be viewed in isolation; it was a vital part of the over-all strategy of destroying the German armies in the field, a strategy which, for all its heartbreak, succeeded and finally won the war.

I am, Sir, your obedient servant . . .

Next day, the chairman of the British Committee of the European League for Economic Cooperation, Edward Beddington-Behrens MC and bar, counter-attacked furiously:

Sir,

Your correspondent Sir John Elliot writes today to justify the tactics of the British High Command at the Battle of the Somme. Those who took part in that battle at regimental level will scarcely agree with this verdict. On July 1 our division had some 70 per cent casualties on the attack on Beaumont Hamel. The tactics of the battle were based on

> the assumption that artillery, mostly field guns, would obliterate enemy wire. This proved erroneous, and when our troops 'went over the top' each man, burdened with heavy equipment, specially thought out by our General Staff, was faced with uncut wire and murderous machine-gun fire. The General Staff had obviously never tried out our artillery on an experimental ground, before basing their battle tactics on what proved to be false assumptions. When later in the Somme battle a few solitary tanks were used a great opportunity of breaking the deadlock of trench warfare was missed. Later during the Passchendaele battles, we became convinced that no generals could have visited the front in person, otherwise how could they have ordered large scale attacks over ground only a few feet above water level, where artillery fire created immense lakes to drown our attacking infantry? Such was the regimental hatred of the muddles and ineptness of British generalship that two years later I refused a staff job, sharing the feeling of front line troops that it was a dishonour to wear the red tabs of the General Staff.
>
> Yours faithfully . . .

After the Somme, in the British army – indeed, in the country as a whole – a sort of grim determination set in. Earlier in the year a French infantry officer had recorded his opinion of the BEF:

> In general, calmness and indifference. Value of their artillery, one to three of ours – but they shoot 'regardless.' At Falfemont on the 24th, they broke down. Why? They said: 'stopped by MG fire'. The fact remains that they failed. Their faults: they look on war as a sport. Too much calmness, which leads to a 'go to hell' attitude. No consistency in their work. They attack in and out of season, break down when they ought to go through; and with a certain spiritual strength say: 'Oh, well, failed today; it'll be all right tomorrow.' To sum it up, they still lack savoir faire.*

* Louis Mairet (12ème Régiment d'Infanterie), quoted in Guy Chapman (ed.), *Vain Glory: A Miscellany of the Great War 1914–1918* (London, 1937). Allies can be jealously critical of each other, perhaps more so than of the enemy. The British opinion of the French, according to Haig (15 January 1917), was that their infantry lacked discipline and thoroughness. Both these views are plausible, given the dates – the French observations before the Somme, the British after Verdun.

Not after the Somme they didn't. In those four and a half months the British army undoubtedly learned how to fight – or rather, those who were not killed or invalided out did. They learned how to fight in the same way that the duke of Wellington said he had learned in Flanders in the 1790s – observing how *not* to do it. But this is no justification for the Somme. Nor can the Somme be justified in terms of attrition, for the rough parity of losses (in proportional terms) made no real difference to the situation on the Western Front; and the Germans would soon be able to withdraw troops from the Eastern Front as Russia's capacity to resist wore away. The men in the trenches sensed this well enough. The most famous of the unofficial 'trench newspapers', *The Wipers Times*, carried a hard-edged piece in parody of the armchair advocates of attrition, notably Hilaire Belloc – 'Proof That We Are Winning The War, by Belary Helloc':

> In this article I wish to show plainly that under existing conditions, everything points to a speedy disintegration of the enemy . . . Firstly, let us take as our figures, 12,000,000 as the total fighting population of Germany. Of these 8,000,000 are killed or being killed, hence we have 4,000,000 remaining. Of these 1,000,000 are non-combatants, being in the navy. Of the 3,000,000 remaining, we can write off 2,500,000 as temperamentally unsuitable for fighting, owing to obesity and other ailments engendered by a gross mode of living. This leaves us 500,000 as the full strength. Of these 497,250 are known to be suffering from incurable diseases. This leaves us 2,750. Of these 2,150 are on the eastern front, and of the remaining 600, 584 are generals and staff. Thus we find that there are 16 men on the western front. This number, I maintain, is not enough to give them even a fair chance of resisting four more big pushes, and hence the collapse of the western campaign.

Black humour was ever the British army's safeguard. In the whole course of the war, unlike the armies of every other of the major belligerents, it never once saw wholesale mutiny and desertion. Why? Many reasons can be advanced, but perhaps none better than what

Charles Carrington MC – an infantry subaltern on the Western Front – wrote in 1968: 'We are still an initiate generation, possessing a secret that can never be communicated.'*

After the Somme the regiments were increasingly reinforced – for the first time in the nation's history – by conscripts. A Military Service Act had been passed in January 1916 making virtually all unmarried men (those unmarried by 1 November 1915) between the ages of nineteen and forty-one liable for call-up – except, controversially, men in Ireland. The grounds for the marriage exemption were in part liberal–compassionate, as the records testify, but also financial: the Treasury was wide awake to the huge war-widows' pension bill that would follow from the deaths of large numbers of married conscripts. However, in May a second Act extended liability to married men, and a third Act in 1918 extended the upper age limit to fifty-one.

This and the 'industrial scale' of the Somme offensive now changed the face of regimental soldiering. David Jones, a private soldier in a Kitchener battalion of the Royal Welsh Fusiliers, and one of the outstanding literary voices to emerge from the war, wrote:

* 'Some Soldiers', in George Panichas (ed.), *Promise of Greatness: The 1914–18 War – A Memorial Volume for the Fiftieth Anniversary of the Armistice* (London, 1968). The army was – and remains – an initiate organization. Its members honour past commanders and close ranks against outsiders.

In 1929, under the pseudonym Charles Edmonds, Carrington published his memoir of the Western Front, *A Subaltern's War*, largely written ten years earlier, in which he sought to counter the widespread view that there were no other types of men who served in the war but 'Prussian militarists' and 'disillusioned pessimists'. 'No corrupt sergeant majors stole my rations or accepted my bribes,' he wrote. 'No incompetent colonels failed to give me food or lodging. No casual staff officers ordered me to certain death, indifferent to my fate.'

The so-called 'Étaples Mutiny' in September 1917 at the BEF's notoriously tough transit and training camp south of Boulogne was in fact a case not of mutiny (even in the French sense) but of disobedience and mass disorder. Quite how mass and how disorderly is the stuff of legend – not least of 'the monocled mutineer' – but it had no influence on the course of operations. Nor indeed was that the object of the 'mutineers', theirs being a violent protest against the conditions and an at times undoubtedly brutish training regime.

> The latter [date – July 1916] marks a change in the character of our lives in the Infantry on the Western Front. From then onward things hardened into a more relentless, mechanical affair, took on a more sinister aspect. The wholesale slaughter of the later years, the conscripted levies filling the gaps in every file of four, knocked the bottom out of the intimate, continuing, domestic life of small contingents of men.*

In fact the industrial-scale slaughter on the Somme only came right home in the inter-war years, when the determination not to make the same mistakes led to over-correction into what was effectively pacifism – and in the Second World War itself, where a reluctance to press attacks or stand ground against heavy odds became a serious concern to the army's leaders.†

After the Somme, Margot Asquith would no longer be keeping her diary as the wife of the prime minister. In December her husband resigned and Lloyd George became war leader. It was not quite a case of 'gentlemen out, players in', but the change would be reflected in a marked shift in the relationship between London and the Western Front – and on the whole an unhappy one. This the Somme had wrought.

Indeed, as 1916 came to a close, with Russia on the brink of collapse, Italy staggering under the losses of her heroic but ill-judged offensives, Bulgaria and Turkey making common cause in the eastern Balkans and Black Sea, and the crushing of Romania, who had fatally delayed her entry into the war, the Germans' situation in the west was not without hope for the new brooms in Berlin.

But the Somme had, indirectly, ensured that the Germans could not now win – as long as in the meantime the allies did not entirely fall apart. For it reinforced the post-Jutland conviction that the

* Foreword to *In Parenthesis* (London, 1937).

† See, for example, Field Marshal Lord Alanbrooke's diaries, especially after the fall of Hong Kong: *War Diaries 1939–1945*, ed. Alex Danchev and Daniel Todman (London, 2001).

U-boat must be allowed to do its worst, and when the Kaiser finally conceded this in February 1917, his decision brought the United States into the war within months.

And immediately President Wilson decided to send 'doughboys' to France, the game was up for Germany. The only question was: when?

PART FOUR

1917:
The Fatal Conceit

The man of system . . . is apt to be very wise in his own conceit; and is often so enamoured with the supposed beauty of his own ideal plan of government, that he cannot suffer the smallest deviation from any part of it. He goes on to establish it completely and in all its parts, without any regard either to the great interests, or to the strong prejudices which may oppose it.

Adam Smith, *The Theory of Moral Sentiments* (1759)

Chapter Thirteen

ANOTHER SPRING OFFENSIVE

Despite, or perhaps even because of, the costly failures on the Somme and the losses at Verdun, in the eyes of the British and French high commands the Western Front remained the primary theatre of war; indeed, the only one in which decisive victory over Germany could be achieved – through the destruction of the fighting power of her army there. The Eastern Front looked increasingly like a lost cause; after the failure of the Brusilov offensive, Russia hardly looked like being able to hold out against the Austro-Hungarian army, let alone the German. Indeed, diplomats in every capital were predicting revolution – and then what? Yes, Jerusalem, Damascus and Baghdad might fall to British and Imperial armies, the Italians might sorely weaken the Austrians, the Bulgarians might perhaps be given a bloody nose out of Salonika; but these successes, argued the 'Westerners', would not end the war. For when the 'Easterners' talked of 'knocking away the props' they mistook who was propping up whom: it was not Germany's allies who were supporting Germany but the other way round. Defeat the German army in France, argued the 'Westerners', and Germany herself would be defeated – and her allies too. Yet Germany would surely be prepared to rush to the aid of an ally threatened with defeat; had she not done so for Austria several times already?

Might this therefore be a way of first weakening the German army – diverting her divisions to distant fronts?

In fact the debate was unnecessarily polarized. Defeating Germany – or defeating the German army, which in some ways amounted to the same thing – required more subtlety than a huge offensive on the Western Front. Falkenhayn had said it: armies of a million men are not destroyed.

They could, however, be hit so badly that the fight would be taken out of them. Yet as 1916 had shown, the German army, attacked head-on, was all but impossible to beat, certainly with the technology and room for manoeuvre available to the Western allies in 1917. 'The Western Front is first and foremost an engineering problem,' said Major-General John Monash, commanding the Australian 3rd Division, not a soldier by profession but a civil engineer.* Few would have disputed this, but few were ready to acknowledge the implications – that until the fortress(es) could be comprehensively breached, hurling men at the walls in modern-day 'forlorn hopes' was futile. Without thorough break-*in* there could be no break-*out*; and there could be no break-out if the break-in were not rapid and complete, for the German defences were now established in great depth – successive lines, the forward ones held lightly, capitalizing on the rate of fire of the machine gun and the lethality of artillery rather than putting men with rifles on the firestep. And they were able to seal any breaches by moving reserves with great rapidity. An old-fashioned fortress had similar lines of defence, and the attacker had to carry these in one or he would be at the mercy of the carefully sited, masked artillery within. The desire always to look to the open plains beyond the German trenches, to restore a war of movement, too often obscured this fact. The Western Front

* Monash, one of the outstanding commanders of the Western Front – and earlier Gallipoli – was the butt of both anti-Semitism and anti-Prussianism (his family were both Jewish and of Prussian descent), principally at the hands of his own countrymen, notably the journalists Charles Bean (later the Australian official historian) and Keith Murdoch, who did not believe Monash was the image of the Australian they were trying to create.

was the biggest siege in history. Yet as General Sir Ian Hamilton wrote subsequently, GHQ really seemed to be tackling it as mobile operations at the halt.

First, the German army had to be weakened, as Haig had stated ('Then, *and not till then* . . .'*), but did weakening amount to nothing more than attrition through one offensive after another – through the business of military accountancy? The blockade was having its effect directly on the army's capacity to fight by producing shortages of war materiel (not least decent rations), and indirectly by inflicting hardship on the civil population. The extent of these effects was difficult to gauge, but time was on the allies' side, although there was a justifiable concern over the corresponding U-boat campaign against British imports. As for Germany's allies, the 'props', Berlin was only too conscious of the need to contain the fighting to the Western Front, and to close down all the others as soon as possible. It followed therefore that to keep these other theatres active would be to erode German strength indirectly. And the promise of large numbers of American troops on the Western Front in 1918 meant that, again, the Entente could afford to wait. Weakening the German army was a question not just of reducing its number of men but of changing the relative strengths of German and allied forces.

From the perspective of the 'Westerners', much of this looked like evasion. Another Chantilly conference, eleven months after that which had drawn up the blueprint for 1916, now reached exactly the same conclusions for 1917: that the Western Front was the imperative theatre, and that the resources employed in the

* In his diary entry of 20 December 1916 Haig further stated: 'Our objective on the Somme was the relief of Verdun, and to wear out the Enemy's Forces with a view to striking the decisive blow later, when the Enemy's reserves are used up.' Unfortunately, the 'decisive blow' could only be judged in retrospect, as 'that blow which proved decisive' ('The owl of Minerva flies at dusk'); and as the allied forces were being weakened at the same time, and at about the same rate, as the German, it was glaringly unclear how the decisive numerical/technical advantage required to deal that blow was to be gained. Haig did, of course, have another objective, whose name could hardly be breathed – breakthrough.

others should be reduced to the smallest possible. As before, the allies agreed they would continue to press the Germans throughout the winter, and, again, if one ally were attacked, the others would immediately take to the offensive. If, however, 'the Enemy leaves the initiative to the Allies' a general offensive would be launched, the date to be settled later.*

It was to be settled sooner than expected, and for Haig – now a field marshal – in a most unsettling manner. He had cautiously welcomed Lloyd George's premiership, expecting it to herald a more ruthless prosecution of the war on the home front. But he was also wary of more interference with strategy and military operations.†

He was right to be. 'LG' immediately formed a small executive war cabinet, and soon declared his intention to strike a 'knockout blow' against Germany. Buoyed up by Briand's eulogies in Rome, he believed that at last a Napoleon had been found – Robert Nivelle. On 15 December, shortly after Nivelle replaced Joffre, an offensive by four divisions and four in reserve, planned by him and executed by Lieutenant-General Charles Mangin, had begun at Verdun. It followed a six-day bombardment by eight hundred guns firing over a million shells, directed in the latter stages with great precision by observation aircraft. The actual attack was preceded by a double creeping barrage – shrapnel from field artillery

* *Haig: War Diaries and Letters*. Chantilly also circumscribed somewhat the statesmen's conference in Rome in January 1917 to discuss Greece, though the discussions there ranged widely. When the Italian C-in-C, Luigi Cadorna, suggested a large combined offensive against the Austrians on the Italian front, 'LG' was at once enthusiastic. But Briand was certain that the coming offensive under Nivelle would lead to a breakthrough, and so Cadorna promptly backed down, apparently impressed by Anglo-French military solidarity ('Wully' Robertson being the British military representative and, Joffre having 'resigned', the new war minister, General Hubert Lyautey, acting in effect as his own chief of staff).

† To some extent Haig was reassured by the appointment as war secretary of Lord (Eddie) Derby, a Tory whose support for both Haig and Robertson was noted, though privately Haig had – or would come to have – little respect for him, in his diary likening him to a 'feather pillow, bear(ing) the mark of the last person who sat on him' and remarking that he was known in London as the 'genial Judas'.

70 yards in front of the infantry, and HE 150 yards ahead, which then switched to shrapnel along the German second line to cut off retreat and interdict reinforcements. The German defence collapsed, with over half of the 21,000 troops in the forward divisions lost and many caught under cover and taken prisoner when the French infantry arrived. By the second night Mangin had consolidated a new line half a mile beyond Fort Vaux and 2 miles beyond Douaumont, the German line having in all been pushed back nearly 5 miles. The French took 115 guns – captured guns being always a better indication of success than the number of infantrymen killed or taken prisoner.

Eleven thousand prisoners was nevertheless quite a bag for a corps operation. When German officers complained about the conditions in the PoW 'cages', Mangin replied: 'We do regret it, gentlemen, but then we did not expect so many of you.'

Mangin was a realist, though. Offensives were a bloody business, success or fail. 'Quoi qu'on fasse, on perd beaucoup de monde' ('Whatever you do, you lose a lot of men'), he said, prompting accusations of callousness. He had certainly lost men in the attack; and a million shells to support four divisions was a luxury no one could expect every time.

Briand was impressed by Nivelle, however, telling the other leaders at the Rome conference that during Mangin's attacks Nivelle had sent telegrams from various places during the advance demonstrating that his objectives were being achieved exactly according to his plan.

And now this new *chef*, who had found the key that would unlock the German defences, proposed to do the same on a far bigger scale on the Aisne: 'Nous les verrons Verdunnés,' he said – 'We shall deal with them as we did at Verdun' (though in essence, it was a return to the precepts of *offensive à outrance* – a rolling barrage and then a single rush). Lloyd George, despairing of the BEF's inability to achieve any sort of victory, let alone without staggering numbers of casualties, and increasingly irritated by what seemed to him time-wasting wrangles between the two high commands, embraced Nivelle as a man who could pull things together and push them in the right direction. He had met him briefly in Paris en route from Rome, and then invited him to London to address the war cabinet, which he did in January (in perfect English), making a strong impression. When he left, Hankey wrote in his diary: 'Lloyd George would like to get rid of Haig, but cannot find an excuse.'*

The Somme would have been the excuse, but perhaps it had been too great a failure to recognize so publicly.

At another conference, in Calais in February, Lloyd George tried a different tack: he proposed subordinating the BEF to the French for the coming offensive; in other words, requiring Haig to take direct orders from Nivelle. Haig had argued in vain for an offensive in Flanders to clear the Belgian ports of submarines and surface raiders, but as he thought the French capable of only one more big push, he had to concede the logic of giving them every support. He could not, however, accept Nivelle's being able to order him precisely how and when to do so. In the event Lloyd George backed down, with some face-saving formula for all parties, but the episode left a bitter taste in Haig's mouth and did nothing to improve Lloyd George's view of the new field marshal.

Matters then got worse. Nivelle began issuing peremptory instructions, to which Haig objected as a matter of military principle, as well as not 'believ[ing] our troops would fight under French leadership'.† Resignations loomed, both Haig's and Robertson's (Haig wrote that he 'would rather be tried by court martial'), but after the undoubted issues of military principle – as well as of *amour propre* – were settled to Haig's grudging satisfaction, things quietened down.

While all this was going on the Germans, as usual, had been making plans of their own, which, like Verdun in reverse, now upset the foundations of Nivelle's great scheme. Expecting that the allies would renew their attack on the Somme, and having nothing like the

* Hankey archive, Churchill Archives Centre, Churchill College, Cambridge.

† This is an unverifiable assertion, of course. It is however tempting to speculate on the outcome of a poll in the canteens of those who had seen the futile muddle on the Somme when compared with the latest news about French prowess at Verdun.

numbers to mount a spoiling offensive (154 divisions against 190 allied), Ludendorff had decided to forestall it by falling back to a new line of defence – the *Siegfriedstellung* ('Fortress-Position Siegfried', which the allies promptly named the 'Hindenburg Line'). 'Fortress' was no understatement, for the defences consisted not merely of trenches but of pillboxes (or, more Teutonically precisely, *Mannschafts-Eisen-Beton-Unterstände* – 'iron-reinforced concrete shelters for troops'). These in the main occupied reverse-slope positions, difficult to pin-point, and formed an altogether looser system of defence which could absorb attacks, making them more vulnerable to counter-attack. Not only was the line established on better ground to hold, by eliminating two salients that had been formed in the Somme offensive between Arras and St-Quentin, and St-Quentin to Noyon, it shortened the front by some 25 miles, releasing thirteen divisions.*

And to these would soon be added the windfall from the Eastern Front – ten divisions promptly withdrawn after the 'February' revolution (the Tsar would abdicate on 2 March; 15 March new style).

Withdrawing to the *Siegfriedstellung* was not only a shrewd defensive move, which the French might have employed at Verdun, although of course there the soil was 'sacred' (yet, equally, much of the ground abandoned in the withdrawal to the Hindenburg Line was soaked with the blood of the German defenders of the Somme), it was carried out with astonishing secrecy. Digging had begun as early as October, and RFC reconnaissance flights had reported new defences being built far behind the Somme front. On 9 November aerial photography showed a new line of defences, from Bourlon Wood north to Quéant, Bullecourt, the Sensée river, Héninel and the German third line near Arras. This in itself was not unusual; precautionary fall-back positions had been the stuff of warfare for centuries, Wellington's 'Lines of Torres Vedras' perhaps the most famous (as much a surprise to the enemy – in 1810 the French – as

* There is evidence to suggest that Hindenburg and Ludendorff, aware of Germany's diminishing manpower potential, saw this saving as a major factor in the decision.

the *Siegfriedstellung* would be to the allies). Even the forcible evacuation of thousands of French civilians (perhaps as many as 125,000, the elderly, women and children being left behind with minimal rations) was inconclusive. Deception measures and the unremarkable nature of the information gleaned from intermittent air reconnaissance (with bad flying weather in this worst winter of the war) led GHQ to interpret it as routine tactical work. Indeed, until late January it is probable that Ludendorff intended withdrawing to the new line only if there were a further British offensive (like Wellington and Torres Vedras). Above all, the allied chiefs could not believe that any soldier would willingly abandon ground, however valueless. It harked back to their historical understanding of battle – that he who was in possession of the ground at the end of the fighting was the winner. When at last, in early March, Nivelle saw that the Germans *were* retiring, he declared that 'if he had whispered orders to Hindenburg, the latter could not have better executed what he desired'. And as late as 17 April Haig would tell the DMO, Frederick Maurice, that it would be 'the height of folly for the French to stop [the Nivelle offensive] now, just when the Germans had committed the serious fault of retiring, *meaning to avoid a battle* [emphasis added], but had been forced to fight against their will.'

The Germans had retired, though, *not* to avoid battle – how could they? – but to fight on ground of their own choosing. If only Haig and Nivelle had been able to think like Ludendorff.

On 4 February, the *Erster Generalquartiermeister* gave the order to implement *Der Alberich Bewegung,* the 'Alberich manoeuvre'. This meant not just preparing to withdraw, however, but making a desert of the country abandoned. Nothing of use to the allies was to be left standing. Houses were to be destroyed, railways dug up, road junctions mined, wells fouled or filled in (some may even have been poisoned), even fruit trees cut down, and booby traps – ranging from simple pieces of duckboarding in trenches which, when stepped on, would detonate a grenade, to a huge delayed-action mine under the Bapaume town hall – laid to make the allies wary of following up too quickly.

The operation was well named: in German mythology Alberich was the malevolent dwarf who guarded the treasure of the *Niebelung,* and was eventually overcome by the hero Siegfried. Crown Prince Rupprecht of Bavaria, commanding the group of armies in the northern sector, appalled by the scale and methods proposed for this 'scorched earth' policy, contemplated resigning. He only stayed his hand because he thought his departure might suggest that a rift had developed between Bavaria and the rest of Germany.

By the end of February both GHQ and *GQG* were sure the Germans were about to withdraw, and on 4 March General Louis Franchet d'Espèrey, commanding the northern French army group, urged *GQG* to let him attack. Nivelle approved, but only a limited operation to capture the German front line.

An opportunity to upset the German withdrawal was undoubtedly lost, but it is difficult to see what serious gains might have been made, for any advance was bound to come to a halt in front of the *Siegfriedstellung,* and French casualties might well have been as great as, if not greater than, the Germans', whose artillery would have been ranged on every bridge and crossroads.

In the event, the actual withdrawal took place between 16 and 20 March. It yielded more French territory than any action since September 1914 and the counter-attack on the Marne.

The BEF, following up – as far as the aggressive German rearguards permitted – were shocked at the conditions wrought by the weather, their own artillery and the scorched earth policy.

> Trenches as such did not exist, for they had been obliterated by the concentrated fire of the guns . . . The front line was held by a series of posts and dugouts which somewhat resembled islands in a sea of mud. Shell holes pock-marked the ground, often overlapping one another and where pathways existed between them they were but a few inches wide. The holes were full of water and more than one man lost his life through slipping off the narrow pathway into the slimy mass which engulfed him.*

* Everard Wyrall, *The History of the 62nd (West Riding) Division 1914–1919* (London, 1924).

In the *Siegfriedstellung* the British (principally) were now facing a far more formidable defensive position than they had after the Somme battles, the Germans once more occupying all the higher and more tactically important ground. And the exhilaration of advancing 25 miles would soon be checked by the setbacks of the Nivelle offensive in April – an offensive which many of Nivelle's subordinates were urging him to abandon. General Joseph Micheler, commanding the army group formed to exploit the anticipated victory, argued that the Germans were simply in too strong a position on the Western Front, with more troops and artillery available for counter-attack. He urged Nivelle to stand on the defensive instead and send troops to Italy to gain a victory there before the Germans did.

But Nivelle was not deterred. 'Laon in twenty-four hours and then the pursuit,' he had said in mid-February, and he saw no reason to change that opinion: 'You won't find any Germans in front of you.'*

The more his generals voiced Micheler's concerns, the more vaunting became Nivelle's predictions. He declared he would break through 'with insignificant loss' and that in three days at most they would be in open country on their way to the Rhine.

On 23 March, Paul Painlevé, the future prime minister, replaced Lyautey as war minister.† The following day he visited Haig and 'questioned [him] closely about Nivelle' (as LG had questioned Foch rather less discreetly about the BEF's apparently poor performance – and implicitly Haig's – the previous September). Haig in his diary entry was guardedly supportive: 'I was careful to say that he struck me as a capable general, and that I was, of course, prepared to co-operate with whoever was chosen by the French government to be their C-in-C . . . my relations with Nivelle are and always have been *excellent*. The Calais Conference was a mistake, but it was not Nivelle's fault.'

Between interpreters, memory and diary there is much room for 'inaccuracy', but Haig's remarks, especially in retrospect, seem

* Quoted in Leon Wolff, *In Flanders Field* (London, 1958).

† At the Rome conference, 'Wully' had said to 'LG': 'That fellow won't last long.'

unfortunate. Clearly he blamed Lloyd George for the Calais conference, but 'LG' could not have come up with the idea of subordinating the BEF to Nivelle without Nivelle's prompting; and Nivelle should have known better, for it was neither practical nor gracious, nor even necessary. As Haig himself noted, Nivelle was confusing the *end* – unity of effort – with the *means* – unity of command. But he appears to have let his intense irritation with Painlevé, and no doubt a sense of soldierly solidarity when faced with any politician (especially, no doubt, 'an extreme socialist', as he described Painlevé in a later addition to the diary), prevent his speaking the entire truth. The offensive was only a fortnight away, and he may have thought the die to have been cast, and doubts now capable of doing nothing but harm. Whichever way, Haig's equivocation was a mistake, and one that would have dire consequences, not least in terms of many thousands more war graves.

Still Painlevé was not convinced. Having heard the discordant voices (traditionally shriller in the French army than in the British) he tried to persuade Nivelle to heed his generals – an impossible proposition, and nonsensical too, for either a commander-in-chief was to be trusted to come to the best military judgement or he was not, in which case dismissal was the only alternative. And, indeed, Nivelle threatened to resign. Painlevé, a brilliant mathematician who could have discoursed on physics with Einstein (if only Einstein had not been in Berlin), backed down. The deviser of 'the Painlevé transcendents' – solutions to 'certain nonlinear second-order ordinary differential equations' – could not find the formula or the confidence to dismiss 'the victor of Verdun'. He would count it as the costliest mistake of his long political career.*

At first things seemed to go well for the Nivelle offensive. The BEF, in its supporting role, was to make a preliminary attack along a

* Briand resigned on 20 March as the difficulties with the coming offensive – not least the unhappy inter-allied relationship – mounted. He was replaced by Alexandre Ribot.

15-mile front at Arras and at Vimy Ridge to draw German reserves away from the coming attack on the Aisne. This they began on 9 April, Easter Monday, in a snowstorm, spearheaded by 3rd Army under Allenby. Progress was encouraging. The 9th Scottish Division advanced 4 miles, and the Canadian Corps under the British Lieutenant-General Julian Byng took Vimy Ridge, the dominating heights above the Artois plain, in one of the finest feats of arms in the entire war. Vimy Ridge was no walk-over, however: in the three days' fighting to consolidate their gain, some 10,500 Canadians were wounded and 3,600 killed (the Germans, defending fiercely, suffered twenty thousand casualties). But what had given the assaulting infantry their chance was an unprecedentedly accurate three-week bombardment, during which many of them were able to shelter from the counter-fire unobserved in tunnels hewn in the chalk of Arras, and a very precise creeping barrage once the attack began. British artillery techniques had by this stage become quite sophisticated, including gas shells that neutralized much of the German artillery (the few tanks available at this stage were dogged by mechanical failure, though some proved their worth). But exploiting success was another matter, not least because of the congestion behind the British front, caused in part by the very troops who were to have been the instrument of exploitation – the mass of cavalry, which now became a target for the enemy's guns. Fighting then descended to what it had been on the Somme – a slogging match, with mounting casualties on both sides. When the battle ended on 15 May, losses in the BEF had risen to a hundred and fifty thousand. Indeed, the daily casualty rate (over four thousand) was the BEF's heaviest of the entire war.

The French attack, when it came on 16 April – delayed several days by bad weather – faltered almost at once. In the main, the German defences were on the reverse slope of the Chemin des Dames and therefore hidden from observation, except by air, and although the French had mustered a thousand aircraft, superior German fighter tactics and the bad weather negated the advantage. The Germans simply knew what the French were up to. Because of the reverse-slope positions the artillery bombardment (Nivelle had massed an unprecedented number of batteries) was much less successful than he had predicted, leaving the German machine-gunners to dominate the crest. The French infantry failed to keep up with the creeping – in fact, more a 'running' – barrage, advancing 100 yards every minute – and the attack could get no further than the top of the ridge. By nightfall the infantry had advanced just 600 yards instead of the 6 miles promised in Nivelle's schedule. Of the 132 French tanks (mainly Schneiders) massed for the attack, 57 had been destroyed and 64 had become irretrievably bogged down in the mud.

As Micheler had warned, the Germans had been able to increase the number of divisions on the Aisne – fourfold, so that the French were barely at parity, let alone with the usual superiority of three to one reckoned necessary in the attack. Nor had operational security been good, with divisional orders in some cases being copied down as far as battalion level, so that as soon as the Germans began taking prisoners they were able to piece together Nivelle's intention with little difficulty. So little, in fact, that there have been suggestions that Nivelle's critics had 'leaked' the plans deliberately – an unbelievably far-fetched suggestion were it not for the fevered state of the post-Verdun French army, which within a month would see widespread mutinies.

Yet these mutinies would 'not be a refusal to fight but a refusal to fight in a certain way'.*

The *poilus* were clearly better tacticians – and, indeed, strategists – than Nivelle.

By 26 April 95,000 French wounded had passed through the casualty clearing stations. When the offensive was abandoned a fortnight later, the total number of casualties, dead and wounded, was 187,000. Nivelle's days were numbered.

But who was to succeed him? Paris was clearly shaken, and the right answer – Pétain – seemed just too awkward. On 29 April,

* Guy Pedroncini, *Les Mutineries de 1917* (London, 1967).

Repington, who was visiting the front, wrote anxiously to Lloyd George:

> I am writing now because I hear that influence is being brought to bear on your side of the water to oppose the appointment of Pétain to the chief command on the ground that he holds certain views which, in fact, he does not hold . . . [I] ask you not to credit the silly chatter which attributes to him a want of go and resolution.
>
> He sees the situation clearly . . . He will not promise the moon as others have done. In this last French offensive our friends have lost 120,000 men, equal to two thirds of the French class of a year, *and are much depressed* [emphasis added]. Pétain foretold the failure to the War Council . . . He sees that we are practically on an equality with the enemy, and must wait until you in England, and the Americans [the United States had declared war on 6 April], provide the superiority of force necessary for victory. He is in favour of prudent offensives like that of Haig on April 9 – short-ranging attacks supported by a mass of guns. He is against trying to do much with little, and prefers to do little with much . . . He will most certainly support Haig in every way, for the arrest of this mad Rheims offensive [Nivelle's] does not at all imply quietism and want of activity . . . Believe me that he is the best general in France.*

Repington – the Playboy of the Western Front, as his detractors dubbed him – was wrong about many things during the course of the war, but not this.

In the wake of the failure of the 'mad Rheims offensive' another inter-allied conference was held, in Paris on 4 May, at which Lloyd George found himself having to put heart into the new French government, especially its head, Ribot, prime minister for a fifth time since 1892. The BEF was now in some respects co-equal with the French army, certainly in terms of fighting capability (and Britain's wider war effort – naval and economic – was now vast), but

* *The Letters of Lieutenant-Colonel Charles à Court Repington*, ed. A. J. A. Morris (Stroud, 1999).

still not strong enough to achieve any real measure of offensive success on its own. As Repington had suggested, the French now sought only to continue to wear down the Germans in the most limited fashion. Ribot gave 'LG' certain assurances, but they soon proved to be fairly hollow. The French army had serious problems of morale to put right first.

Haig saw this as a green light to switch his own effort back to Flanders, and his earlier scheme to take Ostend and Zeebrugge. Indeed, on 7 June, just three weeks after Nivelle was replaced as commander-in-chief by Pétain, the real hero of Verdun, and Foch was recalled to be chief of the general staff (a position that had remained dormant while Joffre in effect fulfilled both functions), 2nd Army under Plumer launched its long-planned operation at Messines in Belgian West Flanders – long and *meticulously* planned, and superbly executed, based for once on siege warfare principles (including colossal mines*). The object was to straighten out the Ypres salient and take the high ground that commanded the British defences and rear areas further north. From here Haig intended to launch his 'Northern Operation' – an advance to Passchendaele Ridge and thence, in conjunction with landings from the sea, including tanks, to the Belgian coast as far as the Dutch frontier south of the Scheldt.

Meanwhile the new French C-in-C, Pétain, dealt with his first task, restoring morale, by judiciously addressing the army's grievances, not least the question of leave, but also by taking exemplary action against the worst offenders among the mutineers – not shirking the firing squad – and by wagering his own high reputation

* The sappers, with help from coal-miners attached from a number of infantry battalions, had dug tunnels to lay 21 mines – more than 400 tons of ammonal explosive. All but two detonated successfully, killing instantly perhaps as many as 10,000 defenders of the ridge which the Germans had said they would have to surround and starve out. Witnesses reported clods the size of houses thrown up. When the debris settled, the 'diameter of complete obliteration' was, on average, twice that of the blast craters themselves, the largest of which measured nearly 100 yards wide and 20 deep. 'I do not know whether or not we shall change history tomorrow,' said Major-General Charles Harington, Plumer's chief of staff, the day before, 'but we shall certainly alter geography.'

with the troops. It worked. And then to Paris he proposed doing strategically what the men in the ranks had declared tactically – that they would defend the trenches but would not attack. The only rational course, he insisted, was to stand on the defensive until conditions changed in favour of the offensive, which to his mind meant more British troops, but principally the arrival of the Americans – and tanks.

Besides, there were encouraging signs that the blockade of Germany was beginning to bite: orders from the *Oberste Heeresleitung* reducing the food ration on the Western Front 'on account of the considerable shortage of cereals'; soldiers begging for food at Mons; deserters crossing the border into Holland; railway rolling stock and locomotives in poor condition. Pétain knew he could afford to sit things out for a time, like a bruised fighter regathering his strength. Haig took the signs rather *too* encouragingly, however, using them to press an increasingly pessimistic Robertson for an all-round allied effort: 'There must be no thought of staying our hand until America puts an Army in the field next year . . . We must press the Enemy now, as vigorously as possible by every means at our disposal on the Western Front.'*

Robertson was certainly cheered by the success at Messines, and, Haig noted, 'seemed to realise that the German Army was in reduced circumstances!', but he was far from convinced that the Germans were reduced far enough to justify an imminent offensive.

In any case, was the BEF really going anywhere? Haig's intention to clear the Belgian coast made sense enough – indeed, on 21 November 1916 Asquith's government had told Robertson: 'There is no operation of war to which the War Committee would attach greater importance than the successful occupation, or at least the deprivation to the enemy, of Ostend, and especially Zeebrugge';† but as A. J. P. Taylor, the controversialist and first TV historian, wrote, 'Two years of preparation and a million pounds of explosive

* *Haig: War Diaries and Letters*, diary entry for 10 June.
† *Military Correspondence of Field Marshal Sir William Robertson*.

had advanced the British front two miles. How long would it take at this rate to get to Berlin?'*

Lloyd George, though determined that the war must be won, and decisively, was equally sceptical. Indeed, his memoirs show how much in despair of Haig he was – or at least recalled that he was: 'The capture of the Messines Ridge, a perfect attack in its way, was just a useful little preliminary to the real campaign, an aperitif provided by General Plumer to stimulate the public appetite for the great carousal of victory which was being provided for us by GHQ.'

The war cabinet's instinct to avoid another major battle in 1917 was clear enough. However, with Russian resolve ebbing away by the day, the French army barely answering to discipline, the Italians increasingly hard pressed and no prospect of American relief for at least six months (and probably twelve), the British were now having to bear the burden not merely at sea and in the Middle East, but on the Western Front. How could they refuse an offensive if significant success were promised?

When Haig went to London in the middle of June to get approval for his plans, he found the war cabinet anxious that his proposed action would mean yet more heavy casualties, which besides the moral effect would be difficult to replace in the present state of manpower. At the meeting on 19 June he was told that with the submarine threat it was difficult to take more men from agriculture and shipbuilding, while taking more from the mines and factories might provoke strikes that would entail the loss of war materiel. Haig replied that he thought there were no grounds for expecting heavy casualties, but Lloyd George closed the meeting

* A. J. P. Taylor, *The First World War: An Illustrated History* (London, 1963). Meanwhile, losses to German submarines were growing alarmingly, for there was still no convoy system, the first sea lord, Jellicoe, believing it impracticable. Lloyd George wanted to remove him, but given Conservative anger at the return of Churchill, who was still blamed for the Dardanelles, as minister of munitions, it would not be until December that he could, by which time losses to U-boats had fallen considerably from their April peak (in which one ship out of every four that left the British Isles never came home), and convoys had been introduced.

by saying that he would have to consider the alternative of waiting until the French had recovered and the Americans had arrived.

Before they resumed next day, 'LG' sent Haig and Robertson a memorandum in which he stated plainly that 'a great attack which fails in its objective while entailing heavy casualties must necessarily discourage the British Army' as well as having a grave effect on public opinion in both Britain and France, and that the cabinet 'must regard themselves as trustees' for those serving and must see that they were 'not sacrificed on mere gambles'. He considered the chances of success dubious, for the Germans were superior in reserves and enjoyed 'something like equality' in other respects. Even if the French army were to pull its full weight – which he thought doubtful – the allies would be able to command only a bare superiority on the Western Front. And if the French *were* unable to pull their weight, 'we shall be attacking the strongest army in the world, entrenched in the most formidable positions with an actual inferiority of numbers. I do not pretend to know anything about the rules of strategy [a somewhat, and deliberately, disingenuous caveat], but curious indeed must be the military conscience which could justify an attack under such conditions.'

In this reluctance Lloyd George would have been joined by Foch, who on 2 June had told Henry Wilson, now chief of the British mission to the French army, that 'the whole thing was futile, fantastic and dangerous', echoing Pétain's view a fortnight before that 'Haig's attack towards Ostend was certain to fail'.*

This was the time for the British – for Lloyd George – to claim the real strategic 'say'. The French, in their albeit temporary prostration, were in no position to dictate terms on the Western Front,

* Wilson had been appointed on 17 March, with promotion to substantive lieutenant-general, which Robertson had blocked in November. Gough had written to Lord Stamfordham, the King's private secretary (i.e. for the King to see), complaining that Wilson had made little impact either as a staff officer in 1914 or as a corps commander, but had a great reputation throughout the army for intrigue and 'talk'. However, the appointment, made at Lloyd George's instigation, was welcomed by Lord Curzon (leader of the House of Lords, and member of the war cabinet), and the King urged Haig and Robertson to accept the deal.

and recognized that the war could not be won without the BEF, no matter how promptly the Americans came to the fight. Lloyd George favoured the Italian option. The Italian army, he wrote, had superiority in numbers over the Austrians: 'What they lack is guns and ammunition; these we can supply.'

When the war cabinet resumed, however, Robertson spoke strongly against any diversion from the Western Front. He 'deprecated as strongly as anyone our incurring heavy casualties without a corresponding return' but considered that Haig's plan 'should secure us against this mistake'. Haig added that he was 'fully in agreement with the Committee that we ought not to push attacks that had not a reasonable chance of success, but that we ought to proceed step by step'. He himself had 'no intention of entering into a tremendous offensive involving heavy losses' – although, as he told the cabinet, 'if the fighting was kept up at its present intensity for six months Germany would be at the end of her available manpower'.*

Still the war cabinet hesitated – but at this point Haig found an unlikely ally. Jellicoe, the first sea lord, said that nothing could be done to defeat the U-boats at sea, and that unless the army could capture their bases on the Belgian coast he considered it (according to the official record) 'improbable that we could go on with the war next year for lack of shipping' – and (according to Haig's diary), insisting: 'There is no good discussing plans for next spring. We cannot go on.'

Few but Jellicoe believed this, and Haig was not one of them, for most of the submarines were operating from bases in Germany, especially Heligoland (which in 1890 Britain had exchanged most infelicitously for Zanzibar), but he was not a one to look a gift horse in the mouth.

* *Military Correspondence of Field Marshal Sir William Robertson; Haig: War Diaries and Letters*. There was reason in Haig's assessments. In August the *Kriegsministerium* would be forced to write to the *Oberste Heeresleitung* stating that there were only 10,000 trained replacements available and that no more than 30,000 returned wounded could be expected per month for the remainder of the year. This was far fewer than the number required to cover the wastage being incurred (Jack Sheldon, *The German Manpower Crisis of 1918*, Douglas Haig Fellowship Records No. 15, 2011).

The war cabinet said it would consider the matter further, and eventually gave the go-ahead a month later after Haig promised he would halt the offensive if it became clear that his objectives could not be obtained. Yet the criteria for judging whether the objectives were being obtained were not specified. That judgement would in fact be made by the C-in-C himself – and Haig had already shown himself stubborn in the face of evidence, believing that despite casualties, failure to make progress was a sign of lack of determined leadership. Indeed, on 9 June, in the delayed aftermath of the prolonged fighting at Arras, he had sacked Allenby from command of 3rd Army, just six days after 'the Bull' had been promoted full general.*

As if to reinforce Haig in his conviction that his great 'Northern Offensive' was both practicable and necessary, on its very eve he learned that three Russian armies – some sixty to seventy divisions – were in full retreat along a 150-mile front. The terms of the Chantilly conference were at once his mandate: an attack on one ally should bring about a counter-offensive by all the others. He was thereby vindicated in rejecting the received wisdom of standing on the strategic defensive until 1918, and told a French liaison officer about to go to *GQG* 'to call Pétain's attention to the certain result of the policy advocated in Paris during the May

* Haig's diaries and letters shed little light on the affair, but self-evidently Allenby had lost the confidence of the C-in-C, whether because Haig believed he had failed to exploit an opportunity for breakthrough at Arras, or because he had overestimated the success and pressed his troops to push on. 'In the pursuit, risks must be taken,' Allenby had told his subordinate generals, and several divisional commanders complained of his handling of the fighting once it had descended into a slogging match (Allenby had told Haig that the troops had been so long in the trenches that they were like 'blind puppies', unable to make use of ground to overcome the Germans' machine guns – which has a ring of truth). Face was saved, however, and to spectacular effect, when next month Allenby was made GOC-in-C Egyptian Expeditionary Force in place of Archibald Murray, who had failed in a third appointment in a row. For by Christmas 'the Bull' would deliver a stunning victory over the Turks and enter Jerusalem (tellingly, on foot not horseback). It was fortunate indeed that Allenby had suddenly become 'available', for 'LG' had favoured Smuts for the command – and Smuts had by no means lived up to his old reputation as a Boer commander in his brief time in the campaign in German East Africa.

conference, viz. to wait and do nothing serious on the Western Front this *year* until Americans arrived!' For this, he said, would have suited the Germans perfectly, allowing them to concentrate all their reserves in the east and knock Russia out of the war before the winter. This, he proclaimed to his diary, was 'the critical moment of the war'.

Clearly therefore the offensive in Flanders would be pressed at greater cost in casualties than the war cabinet had sanctioned, for it now had a major strategic purpose as well as the questionable objective of relieving the U-boat threat. And, of course, there was the business of winning the war by defeating the Germans on the Western Front, to which Haig was single-mindedly committed.

What then *were* the objectives whose achievement was to justify continuance of the offensive in the face of heavy losses, as Haig had promised the war cabinet he would not permit? The diversion of German divisions from the Eastern Front? Killing Germans – attrition – and tying down reserves? These were by no means easy to measure in the short term, though it would be in the short term that many more of his troops might be killed – and perhaps for no gain. Haig's view of what would become known as Third Ypres would in fact be that of First Ypres, the battle in which he had made his name – that in an almost mystical way it was of supreme importance to the war overall; and therefore, as at First Ypres, the need was for sacrifice.

Besides, ever in Haig's mind was the possibility of breakthrough. He told his army commanders that 'opportunities for the employment of cavalry in masses are likely to offer'.

Chapter Fourteen

PASSCHENDAELE: 'OPPORTUNITIES FOR CAVALRY'

'One doesn't fight the Germans and the mud simultaneously,' said Pétain when Lloyd George asked his opinion as the battle got under way at the end of July. In a fortnight's bombardment, three thousand guns had fired four and a half million shells on the German defences – and on the drainage system of West Flanders. (The bombardment is calculated to have cost £22 million – in today's prices, around £1.7 billion.) Four days later, Haig's chief of intelligence, Brigadier-General John Charteris, wrote in his diary: 'Every brook is swollen and the ground is a quagmire. If it were not that all the records of previous years had given us fair warning, it would seem as if Providence had declared against us.'

'Ground' is a fundamental intelligence question. Why had no one thought to ask it?

A dozen or so years later, Gough (at the time commanding 5th Army) would describe Third Ypres – 'Passchendaele' as it is commonly, but misleadingly, called – with considerable literary power:

> Many pens have tried to describe the ghastly expanse of mud which covered this waterlogged country, but few have been able to paint a picture sufficiently intense. Imagine a fertile countryside, dotted every few hundred yards with peasant farms and an occasional hamlet; water

> everywhere, for only an intricate system of small drainage canals relieved the land from the ever-present danger of flooding . . . Then imagine this same countryside battered, beaten, and torn by a torrent of shell and explosive . . . such as no land in the world had yet witnessed – the soil shaken and reshaken, fields tossed into new and fantastic shapes, roads blotted out from the landscape, houses and hamlets pounded into dust so thoroughly that no man could point to where they had stood, and the intensive and essential drainage system utterly and irretrievably destroyed. This alone presents a battleground of tremendous difficulty. But then came the incessant rain. The broken earth became a fluid clay; the little brooks and tiny canals became formidable obstacles, and every shell hole a dismal pond; hills and valleys alike were but waves and troughs of a gigantic sea of mud. Still the guns churned this treacherous slime. Every day conditions grew worse. What had once been difficult now became impossible. The surplus water poured into the trenches as its natural outlet, and they became impassable for troops; nor was it possible to walk over the open field – men staggered warily over duckboard tracks. Wounded men falling headlong into the shell-holes were in danger of drowning. Mules slipped from the tracks and were often drowned in the giant shell-holes alongside. Guns sank till they became useless; rifles caked and would not fire; even food was tainted with the inevitable mud. No battle in history was ever fought under such conditions as that of Passchendaele.*

Why then the surprise? In December 1914 Sir John French had written of the mud at Ypres in the same terms: 'The incessant rain turned the stone-less soil of Flanders into a sort of liquid mud of the consistency of thick porridge, without the valuable sustaining quality of that excellent Scots mixture. To walk off the roads meant sinking in at once.'

If it were not that all the records of previous years had given us fair warning . . . GHQ's survey staff had collected information two years earlier, updated more recently by the Tank Corps staff, whose concern was naturally about the ability of their new machines – their

* General Sir Hubert Gough, *The Fifth Army* (London, 1931).

raison d'être – to cross the ground. Being reclaimed marshland, the Ypres area was bound to revert to swamp if the drainage system were destroyed. According to Charteris (not a wholly reliable memorialist), the records of the past eighty years showed that in Flanders 'the weather broke early each August with the regularity of the Indian monsoon'.

It was just another inconvenient truth. Planning went on regardless.

But what of Haig's assurance to the war cabinet that he would take a 'step by step' approach? Ironically, when he had discussed the coming offensive with the two commanders whose troops would take the lead, Plumer of 2nd Army and Gough of 5th, it was the solid line-infantry Plumer who, perhaps inspired by his success at Messines, urged that they should go 'all out', while Gough, the thrusting (some said 'hot-headed') cavalryman, favoured the step-by-step method – as did Haig's own staff. In fact Plumer had wanted to press on after Messines, believing the Germans had had such a shock that there was a real chance of breakthrough, but Haig had stayed his hand, not wanting to bring forward his plans so quickly. Unsurprisingly, therefore, Haig now agreed with the bolder approach, despite Plumer's having only the supporting role (a single corps) in the early stages. Besides, not only was 'the Plum' the victor of Messines, he had been the same rank – lieutenant-general – as Haig at the outbreak of the war, whereas Gough had been a mere brigade commander.

Nevertheless, at the end of the first day's fighting – fourteen divisions attacking on a frontage of 11 miles – Gough, with the support of a French corps on his left, had in fact achieved his initial objectives, notably Pilckem Ridge, while Plumer's corps on his right had not. The artillery bombardment had destroyed the drainage system – and any hope of surprise – but not the system of defence. The 'poor bloody infantry' struggled in the mud, the tanks stuck fast, the pillboxes remained, and with them the machine guns and the local reserves for counter-attack.

Still Haig reported to the War Office that evening that the results were 'most satisfactory'.

The next phase had to be postponed until 16 August, when the subsidiary battle of Langemarck saw four days of fierce fighting, with the usual (excepting Vimy and Messines) depressingly familiar results: small gains, heavy casualties. On 19 August Haig held a GHQ conference at which he said: 'Our Army's efforts this year have brought final victory near.' In the later, typescript, version of the manuscript diary, Haig amended this to 'nearer', but without resorting to logical fallacy – *post hoc ergo propter hoc* – it is difficult to reconcile Haig's view of his own generalship (for that is what he was speaking of – his direction of those efforts) with hastening the war's end, let alone bringing it close(r).

There was, however, encouraging news from the French, Pétain's shrewd leadership having nursed his wounded army back, if not to rude health then to promising convalescence. On 20 August he staged what he called 'une pièce de théâtre' at Verdun – *pour encourager les autres* (and the government and the allies). After a three-million-round bombardment, including a million heavy shells, along with a machine-gun barrage, four army corps attacked and in six days pushed the Germans back a mile on a 7-mile frontage to clear the heights north of the town, taking ten thousand prisoners, thirty guns, a hundred trench mortars and 250 machine guns. It was an emphatic statement that the French were still in the fight – and timed to perfection, as American reconnaissance parties were beginning to arrive. Haig would claim that the 'comparatively weak resistance which they [the Germans] have made to the French attack at Verdun' was due to his Ypres offensive – and that the French army 'has consequently had the quiet time desired by General Pétain in which to recover from the Nivelle Offensive'.

But all the same, Haig was dissatisfied with the BEF's progress, and he now transferred the main effort to 2nd Army under Plumer. It is sometimes suggested that Gough had suddenly become fixated on all-out breakthrough, whereas Plumer had reverted to the method of small gains – 'bite and hold' – which now suited Haig, for if he could show no spectacular gains he had to demonstrate steady progress. The evidence is sketchy, but it seems more likely that the overall superior quality of 2nd Army's staffwork, and its divisional commanders, recommended them at this stage. Since Messines they had not seen as much fighting as 5th Army, and were not as jaded.

The attacks began afresh on 20 September, in better weather, and with limited objectives, the first less than a mile from the start line – the Menin Road Ridge. 'The advancing barrage won the ground; the infantry merely occupied it,' says the *Official History*. This was followed on the twenty-sixth by the battle for 'Polygon Wood', again with such concentrated artillery support that the German counter-attacks were halted in their tracks. At a conference two days later Haig said he believed the enemy were on the point of collapse, and that tanks and cavalry could now be pushed through. On 4 October Plumer's men took Broodseinde, a mile or so north of Polygon Wood – by this stage a feature on the map only. These gains collectively gave the BEF possession of the ridge east of Ypres, a feature of tactical use, if not exactly of tactical importance, and, encouraged by what looked like a winning formula for steady progress – 'one more push, and then breakthrough' – Haig decided to continue towards Passchendaele Ridge, 6 miles north-east of Ypres.

But, contrary to his assessment that the Germans were on the point of collapse, based on the belief that their losses exceeded his own 'not improbably by a hundred per cent' (in truth their losses were much fewer than the BEF's), they were in fact strengthening their position as reserves from the Eastern Front arrived in growing numbers – while, of course, Haig's own men were nearing exhaustion, their discomfort now exacerbated by the Germans' use of mustard gas, more lethal and debilitating than the earlier chlorine or phosgene, and well suited to delivery by artillery.* On 10 October Charteris noted in his diary that 'D.H. sent for me about

* Mustard gas, an almost odourless chemical, caused serious blisters both internally and externally, and protection proved more difficult than against either chlorine or phosgene gas. It was better for purely defensive purposes, however (such as counter-battery), for it remained potent in soil for weeks after release, making capture of contaminated trenches hazardous.

10 [p.m.] to discuss things . . . He was still trying to find some grounds for hope that we might still win through here this year, but there is none.' Unwilling to concede failure to break through, however, Haig ordered three more assaults on the ridge. The eventual capture of Passchendaele village – another feature on the map only – by British and Canadian troops on 6 November finally gave him the opportunity to call off the offensive while claiming success.

The Third Battle of Ypres had cost some 310,000 British and Imperial casualties, with those on the German side in the order of 260,000.* The salient had been re-widened by several miles, but the advance had got not a yard closer to the Belgian coast. As a young brigade intelligence officer wrote at the end of the war:

> When one compares the results with the dogged tenacity of infantry, gunners and transport men under loathsome nerve-wrecking conditions and the utterly prodigal expenditure of munitions and technical resources of every kind, one feels resentful of the doctrinaire fanaticism which kept the machine driving on at top-pressure, month after month, as though the gain of each few yards of water-logged craters was worth any sacrifice. One felt at the time that the use of relief maps exaggerated the importance of contours, and the superstitious belief that every casualty we had was bound to be offset by at least one German equivalent, had fascinated General headquarters, and temporarily destroyed all sense of reality and proportion, creating a veritable madness for offensives.†

Haig would continue to argue that, notwithstanding the casualties, Third Ypres was a wholly justified success. The Germans could less afford the losses in men than the allies, who would soon be

* In *Raising Churchill's Army* (London, 2000) David French writes, in a sort of apologia, that the (British) 21st Army Group's daily loss rates in Normandy after the 1944 landings (where divisions lost up to three-quarters of their infantry) were similar to those of Passchendaele in 1917, and that average battalion casualty rates in 1944–5 (100 men per week) were similar to those of the First World War. But Normandy was a battle of supreme strategic importance, sanctioned at the highest level – and it was successful.

† D. V. Kelly, *39 Months with the 'Tigers'* (London, 1930).

reinforced by those of the United States. This is indeed the stark, undeniable logic of 'attrition'; but as a justification of generalship the logic is flawed because the premise was wrong – that even if there *was* no other front, on the Western Front there was no other way.

Lloyd George instinctively knew this. And now there was to be even more evidence, for on 24 October six German divisions – in one of which the young Leutnant Erwin Rommel was to make his name – spearheaded a huge surprise offensive on the Italian front, at Caporetto in the Julian Alps, spilling onto the plain west of the Isonzo, the high road to Venice, and opening the way to the great valley of the Po. For a while it looked as if there would be a complete collapse.

Only seven weeks before Caporetto, Haig had gone to London to oppose Foch's proposal to send a hundred guns to Italy (the Italian C-in-C, Cadorna, had asked for four hundred in order to mount yet another decisive effort), on the grounds that it would undermine his continuing offensive at Ypres. Foch argued that the political effect of success would be greater in Italy than in Flanders; Haig maintained that 'the decisive point *was* in Flanders' (emphasis added). Robertson backed him, but Lloyd George was, in Haig's words, 'anxious that some guns should be sent'. As late as 8 October Haig was still of the view that even if Russia were to quit (which he did not think likely) and Austria were therefore able to transfer all her strength to the Italian front, 'Italy should be able to hold her ground unaided'. He had not considered that the Germans would throw in their weight to try a knockout blow. But that aside, it is strange that the C-in-C of the BEF, who had not visited the Italian front or been privy to any special intelligence, should be forming strategic opinion in this way. The centre of gravity of military judgement was still – in Haig's mind at least – Montreuil (whither GHQ had moved before the Somme) rather than Whitehall.

The Austrians, statesmen and military alike, had a more realistic view of their situation, convinced that the empire – war-weary and composed as it was of disparate nationalities whose grievances seemed to be increasing – was on the brink of collapse. The new, young emperor, Charles I (Franz-Joseph had died the previous November), and his new chief of staff, Arthur Freiherr Arz von Straußenburg, persuaded Ludendorff to come to their aid, though not without difficulty, for the *Erster Generalquartiermeister* was preparing an offensive to complete Russia's defeat (though the statesmen were content simply with Russia's collapse). In the end he was probably persuaded in part by the two previous autumn knockouts of minor allies – Serbia in 1915 and Romania in 1916.

Within three weeks of Haig's confident pronouncement that the Italians – and the Russians – could hold, Venice (and much more) was in peril and the Russians were preparing to quit (the new Bolshevik government would conclude an armistice of sorts with Germany in December, though the fighting would continue intermittently for some months). And so now the crisis in Italy would force the BEF to part with more troops to help retrieve the situation than Cadorna had asked for earlier to mount an effective attack.*

Lloyd George might reasonably at this point have demanded the sword of either Robertson or Haig, or both, but Haig's assiduous cultivation of Tory and royal support was still an obstacle. Besides, who would replace them – Haig especially? In his memoirs Lloyd George says he seriously considered Arthur Currie, who since Byng's promotion to command of 3rd Army in June had led the Canadian Corps. Currie was shrewd and a fine innovative tactician, but it is inconceivable that the prime minister, whose decision it was constitutionally, could have persuaded Robertson to promote him over the heads of five British army commanders, and so he would have had to sack 'Wully' too. It is possible that the other dominion governments – South Africa, Australia and New Zealand – would also have objected. In July the previous year Repington, asked by 'LG' who could take Haig's place if there were a change, had said

* On 4 November Haig met Lloyd George in Paris to discuss, inter alia, the Italian situation, and 'urged strongly that no more troops be sent from my command' and that more effective help could be given by attacking in France/Flanders. Three days later, after 'LG' had gone to Italy to see for himself (the Rapallo Conference), Robertson ordered Haig to send Plumer with five divisions.

Allenby could, 'as he combined youth, physique and character'.* But of course by now Allenby had been sacked from command on the Western Front, and was about to take Jaffa before delivering his Christmas present to the nation – the holy city of Jerusalem. Plumer was a solid enough candidate, Byng had presence, Horne probably lacked authority; Rawlinson was lucky not to have been sacked after the Somme, and Gough had a record of prickly independence. One of the best candidates had yet fully to reveal himself – the earl of Cavan, who was about to be sent with his corps to Italy, and who in October 1918, in command of the Anglo-Italian 10th Army, would strike the decisive blow at Vittorio Veneto, the battle which brought about the end of Austrian resistance. His robust, independent judgement had shown to good effect on the Somme.

So Lloyd George would have to use more subtle methods to curb the immovable combination of Haig and Robertson – creating a complicated allied military council structure, removing Kiggell (the invisible man, as he has been called, for his lack of impression on Haig's thinking) and Charteris ('Haig's evil counsellor'), and enlisting the services of the man of intrigue and talk, Henry Wilson.

Meanwhile the allies' bacon was saved by the unexpected recovery of the feisty Italians, and by the rashness of the Austrians in trying to exploit their initial, albeit spectacular, success without the necessary resources or communications. Cadorna had beat a hasty retreat – he had little option; his troops were streaming rearwards in order not to be outflanked in the mountain valleys – and thus saved the army from complete collapse. He had first tried to rally them on the Tagliamento, and then pulled back successfully to the swollen Piave, though a quarter of a million of his troops were now prisoners of war. No army in full retreat is a pretty sight, and the stories of Italian indiscipline (and worse) are unedifying, but in truth there would be similar scenes in Gough's 5th Army in March

* Charles Repington, *The First World War*, vol. I (London, 1920). In fact Allenby was a few months older than Haig, but both were fit 55-year-olds.

1918, and the duke of Wellington's words about troops who break and run are ever instructive: 'Oh, they all do that at some time. The question is, will they rally?' The Italian army did, and largely of its own will and capability. However, the price of rushing eleven allied divisions from France to the Piave was to be Cadorna's sword (not least because he'd said that Italy might have to sue for peace). On 8 November he was replaced by Armando Diaz, a humane and respected Neapolitan who had kept his head and stabilized his part of the line on Monte Grappa, and then the Piave, and who would now very effectively play the part of Pétain after Verdun.*

Haig now needed an unequivocal and resounding victory to make his position secure, for he could hardly claim that of a few dozen square miles of Flanders mud. And fortunately the 'rude mechanicals' of the Tank Corps seemed to have the answer, despite the fact that so many of their means of victory had sunk in the mud of 'Passchendaele'. As early as 3 August, Colonel J. F. C. 'Boney' Fuller of the Tank Corps staff had proposed as a diversion a massed tank raid on the dry downland near Cambrai. The idea had at once appealed to the newly promoted Byng, whose 3rd Army held that sector, and who saw in it the opportunity for greater things – not a raid, a short operation to inflict damage before quickly withdrawing, but a breakthrough. He therefore proposed that he put his entire army into the effort, Fuller's scheme having first attracted Haig until Kiggell had pointed out that it broke the principle of concentration of effort at the decisive place – Ypres. Now, with Third Ypres 'closed down', the scheme could be resuscitated.

Byng's enthusiasm for greater things than a raid began to get the better of him. He decided to throw all his divisions into the attack, and all the allotted tanks – 380 of them – leaving himself

* It is always difficult to know what to do with C-in-Cs relieved of command, as the cases of Sir John French, Zhilinsky and Joffre had already demonstrated. Cadorna would be sent as the Italian representative to the new Supreme War Council (see chapter 15), which perhaps summed up how much faith the Italian prime minister (the tricky Sicilian professor of law, Vittorio Emanuele Orlando) had in it. Later, Joffre would be the French representative, again no compliment to its true status.

with no reserves. It is still uncertain what Haig himself expected to gain from the Cambrai action (only limited objectives, some historians claim), but he certainly expected the Cavalry Corps, which he allotted to Byng from GHQ's command, to 'pass through and operate in open country. This requires bold and determined action on the part of the subordinate Infantry Commanders.'*

Indeed, given Haig's general belief in the poor condition of the Germans, and that breakthrough was the way the war would be won on the Western Front, it would have been surprising had he not hoped for greater things than a mere raid, or even the taking of ground that was not of itself 'going anywhere'.

Be that as it may, on 20 November, in an obliging morning mist, and before a single round of artillery had been fired, the 380 tanks, less those that had broken down on the way to the start line, answered to the signal 'Driver, advance!'†

Six divisions went into the attack, on a six-mile front. The absence of the usual artillery notification coupled with quite remarkable operational security on the part of the Tank Corps, aided by the RFC's local air superiority, saw the Germans taken wholly by surprise. Tanks and infantry quickly breached the forward trenches, checked only at Flesquières, and penetrated 5 miles into the defences of the Hindenburg Line – further to date than any advance on the Somme or in Flanders. Only a half-finished fourth line stood between 3rd Army and open country, and in this there was a wide-open gap for several hours.

An advance of 5 miles, even an easy one, is tiring however. By now the tanks were crewed by exhausted men (the noise, the fumes, the concussive vibrations), or out of action, and the infantry could make no further progress without them. And if the infantry could make no progress, the cavalry certainly couldn't. A few armoured cars might have made all the difference – more agile

* *Haig: War Diaries and Letters*, diary entry for 13 November 1917.

† The engineering specification to Fosters of Lincoln, the main manufacturer, was for a mere 50 miles' mechanical endurance, the tank still being seen as a siege-breaking device rather than an instrument of mobile warfare.

than the tanks, less vulnerable than the horse, and carrying plenty of machine-gun ammunition – but there were none.

German reserves now poured into the breached line like liquid concrete. Haig sent a few more divisions, but the renewed attacks on the twenty-second and twenty-third quickly petered out. The spent troops were not relieved but told to dig in, even while victory peals were rung in England.*

Fighting now centred on Bourlon Wood, becoming heavy, and the Germans began mounting increasingly strong local counter-attacks. GHQ and 3rd Army intelligence failed to pick up the greater massing of reserves (some twenty divisions) for a counter-stroke, which, like the tanks on the first day, came out of the morning mist on the thirtieth – this time after a short, intense bombardment consisting of HE, gas and smoke. Using infiltration techniques lately developed, the Germans thrust at both flanks of the salient created by the 3rd Army's advance, and while checked in the north, in the south broke through. Disaster was narrowly averted, with considerable loss, including Brigadier-General Roland Boys Bradford VC, MC – at twenty-five the youngest brigadier of modern times, who had been commanding 186 Brigade for just three weeks – and Byng had to abandon the greater part of his original gains. The bells had rung prematurely.

German casualties in the Cambrai battle were around fifty thousand, and the BEF's forty-five thousand (of which ten thousand were deaths). Yet the BEF had nothing to show for it, just the sense that it was 'a near miss' and a demonstration of what the tank could do in attack if well handled. Curiously, and fortunately, the Germans would not draw the same conclusion. They would not develop tanks of their own in anything like similar numbers or capability.

As 1917 drew to a close, the light at the end of the tunnel was not yet even perceptible. Over the course of the year the French army

* As early as 21 November by the Caversham ringers at St Laurence's tower, Reading (504 Grandsire Caters and 880 Kent Treble Bob Royals).

had lost nearly 140,000 men killed and the BEF 190,000. Counting the Belgian war dead, the allies' total on the Western Front came to almost 350,000 men. In the same period and on the same front the German dead were a fraction over a third this number. The year was ending every bit as unpromisingly as 1916, save for the advent of the Americans. Of midnight on New Year's Eve, Edmund Blunden, now a captain in his battalion of the Royal Sussex, with an MC from the Somme, would write of 'successions of coloured lights . . . but the sole answer to the unspoken but importunate questions was the line of lights in the same relation to Flanders as at midnight a year before. All agreed that 1917 had been a sad offender. All observed that 1918 did not look promising at its birth.'*

General Émile Fayolle, who had been appointed to command the central army group when Pétain was made commander-in-chief, and sent to Italy in the wake of Caporetto, confided bleakly to his diary: 'How the devil can we finish this war?'

And on 28 December, Haig recorded his meeting with General John J. ('Black Jack') Pershing, commander-in-chief of the American Expeditionary Force. He told him that the 'crisis of the war would be reached in April'. And he had one question for his US counterpart: how might the AEF help?

* Edmund Blunden, *Undertones of War* (London, 1929).

PART FIVE

1918: More Catastrophes, Then Victory

La guerre est une série de catastrophes qui se terminent par une victoire.
(War is a series of catastrophes that ends through victory.)

Georges Clemenceau, 1918

Chapter Fifteen

UNITY OF COMMAND

It was not the first time that Haig had met Pershing. On the eve of Third Ypres, 'Black Jack' had paid him a visit – almost six weeks after first stepping ashore at Boulogne. This perhaps gave an indication of the Americans' perceptions and priorities. Yet Haig was at once taken by this fellow cavalryman, just a year older than himself: 'I was much struck with his quiet gentlemanly bearing – so unusual for an American. Most anxious to learn, and fully realises the greatness of the task before him. He has already begun to realise that the French are a broken reed.'*

July 1917 was certainly not the best of times to be seeing the French, in their post-Nivelle demoralization, but Haig's reading of Pershing here was at best faulty. The AEF's commander had an equally gloomy view of the British at this time, as his final (September 1919) despatch made only too clear:

> During three years Germany had seen practically all her offensives except Verdun crowned with success.

* *Haig: War Diaries and Letters*, entry for 20 July 1917. It is unclear how many Americans Haig had really met; he had been twice to the United States, but not since 1886 (on a polo tour). He was also impressed with Pershing's ADC, another cavalryman, 'a fire-eater, and longs for the fray' – Captain (later General) George S. Patton.

> Her battle lines were held on foreign soil and she had withstood every Allied attack since the Marne. The German general staff could now foresee the complete elimination of Russia, the possibility of defeating Italy before the end of the year and, finally, the campaign of 1918 against the French and British on the Western front which might terminate the war.
>
> It cannot be said that German hopes of final victory were extravagant, either as viewed at that time or as viewed in the light of history. Financial problems of the Allies were difficult, supplies were becoming exhausted and their armies had suffered tremendous losses.
>
> Discouragement existed not only among the civil population but throughout the armies as well. Such was the Allied morale that, although their superiority on the Western front during the last half of 1916 and during 1917 amounted to 20 per cent, only local attacks could be undertaken and their effect proved wholly insufficient against the German defence.
>
> Allied resources in manpower at home were low and there was little prospect of materially increasing their armed strength, even in the face of the probability of having practically the whole military strength of the Central Powers against them in the spring of 1918.*

It was as well that 'Black Jack' had formed that opinion, for it would mean, twelve months later, at the 'crisis of the war', that the allied strength in France would be so great that the Germans simply could not prevail.

Pershing had acted very decisively indeed: '[C]onditions made it apparent that America must make a supreme material effort as soon as possible . . . After duly considering the tonnage possibilities I cabled the following to Washington on July 6, 1917: "Plans should contemplate sending over at least 1,000,000 men by next May." '

This was a doubling of what the US War Department had originally envisaged. But unlike Haig and Robertson, and Pétain and Foch, Pershing had the full confidence of his head of state (and

* *United States Army in the World War 1917–1919, Reports of the Commander-in-Chief, Staff Sections and Services* (Washington DC, 1991).

commander-in-chief), President Wilson. By November 1918 there would in fact be *two* million American troops in France (and Italy).*

For the time being, however, Pershing had two concerns. First, that the rapidly expanding US army (which included at most perhaps 150,000 what could be called regulars) should be properly trained before arriving in France; and secondly, that the AEF should operate as a discrete force rather than placing its divisions under either French or British command, as both Haig and Pétain would have preferred. British and French instructors would be sent to America to help with training, and because of 'the tonnage possibilities' much of the AEF's heavy equipment would be provided by Britain and France, but Pershing was following Wilson's instructions by insisting on independent command, although some US divisions would serve in the line under British and French direction to gain field experience, and, indeed, find themselves under allied command during the final counter-offensive.†

Pershing also believed that the best way to end the war was to carry it onto German soil. Neither GHQ nor *GQG* would have disagreed, but Haig saw the route as being through Belgium – for Belgium (and a million Germans) was what stood between the BEF and the German border – while Pétain could as yet make no offensive plans. Pershing put his point gracefully:

> Our mission was offensive and it was essential to make plans for striking the enemy where a definite military decision could be gained. While

* Pershing had told the War Department: 'It is evident that a force of about 1,000,000 is the smallest unit which in modern war will be a complete, well-balanced, and independent fighting organization. However, it must be equally clear that the adoption of this size force as a basis of study should not be construed as representing the maximum force which should be sent to or which will be needed in France. It is taken as the force which may be expected to reach France in time for an offensive in 1918, and as a unit and basis of organization. Plans for the future should be based, especially in reference to the manufacture of artillery, aviation, and other material, on three times this force, i.e., at least 3,000,000 men.'

† On 9 January 1918 the US 1st Division took over a sector north of Toul; the 26th Division went to the Soissons front early in February; the 42nd Division entered the line near Luneville on 21 February and the 2nd Division near Verdun on 18 March.

> the Allied armies had endeavoured to maintain the offensive, the British, in order to guard the Channel ports, were committed to operations in Flanders and the French to the portion of the front protecting Paris. Both lacked troops to operate elsewhere on a large scale.

Yet there is no reason why such an offensive could not have been developed in 1917 – if the allies had not bled themselves near-white at Verdun and on the Somme, had kept the Russians in the fight and had taken a broader and longer-term view of the Western Front.

But Pershing had also drawn the conclusion that 'the long period of trench warfare had so impressed itself upon the French and British that they had almost entirely dispensed with training for open warfare'. This certainly echoed Allenby's 'blind puppies' remark. Offensive spirit in defence is not the same as preparedness for open warfare, though it is a good start. He was determined that this should be the focus of the AEF's training.

And so, with the direct approach that had characterized American military thinking for at least half a century, Pershing saw his route onto German soil as the shortest distance between two points – through Lorraine (since 1871, 'Lothringen' to the occupying Germans). This in turn made his starting place, and thus the AEF's concentration area, behind Verdun and the St-Mihiel salient. Besides, 'If the American Army was to have an independent and flexible system it could not use the lines behind the British-Belgium front nor those in rear of the French front covering Paris.'

Haig's question was – how might the AEF help in the event of a German offensive to forestall this, 'the crisis of the war'?

There were 176,665 American troops in France when Pershing called on GHQ at the end of December 1917 (although one division only had appeared at the front). Contrary to what some historians assert – that under no circumstances but for training would he subordinate American troops to British command – Pershing replied that if the situation became critical he was ready to *'break up*

*American divisions and employ battalions and regiments as draft to fill up our divisions'.**

Although Haig's diary does not say that this was a commitment to the BEF alone (there is no record of a comparable undertaking to the French) it is tempting to ponder that it might perhaps be the first tentative declaration of an Anglo-American 'special relationship'. It was certainly developing between the respective intelligence branches. The president had in effect told Pershing to keep his distance from the BEF in order to preserve operational independence, and to look to the French instead. *GQG* proved rather reluctant to share intelligence, however, and so the head of the AEF's G2 branch, Brigadier-General Dennis Nolan, turned increasingly to Charteris at GHQ, whom he found a much readier collaborator.†

However, for the time being the Americans as a force to be reckoned with seemed but a distant promise, and Fayolle's question 'How the devil can we finish this war?' was producing, again, varying answers in London depending on whether it was put to the soldiers or the prime minister. In August at Foch's prompting the French premier, Painlevé, had urged the creation of an allied general staff, but Lloyd George had been wary on two counts. First, he doubted that British public opinion – or the Tories in Parliament – would stand for it; secondly, he was wary of being faced with an even stronger military lobby than already existed. The following month he had suggested to President Wilson a much broader 'Allied Joint Council', with permanent military (and naval) representatives, as well as economic advisers, to consider all aspects of the war. Sir John French, as C-in-C home forces still a very vocal

* *Haig: War Diaries and Letters* (emphasis added).

† Nolan, who appears not to have had the same aversion to British officers as did some others of Irish immigrant descent, was especially impressed with the BEF's Sigint, commending it strongly to the founder and head of the War Department's intelligence department, Brigadier-General Ralph van Deman, who would continue in wider intelligence work after the war. In June 1918 the improbably named Colonel Marlborough Churchill (in fact a distant relative of Winston), who had been serving on the staff of the AEF, succeeded Deman, and the links with British intelligence would continue after the war, if at times tenuously, until the formalized cooperation of the Second World War and after.

and increasingly influential presence (the losses incurred in his 1915 offensives seemed to be paling into insignificance compared with the Somme and Third Ypres), strongly supported the idea; indeed, months earlier he had proposed something similar. His mistrust of Haig had grown to epic proportions, for both personal and professional reasons.* Lloyd George asked Henry Wilson's opinion too – and Wilson was enthusiastic. Doubtless there were professional reasons for his enthusiasm, and mixed motives are not necessarily bad motives, but Wilson had undoubtedly seen an enhanced role for himself in such a development. As a confidant and trusted friend of the French (as far as any British officer could be), and an exile from GHQ, to Lloyd George Wilson was anyway an obvious choice as permanent representative at such a council. In September he had been rather artfully inserted into Whitehall as GOC Eastern Command, with his headquarters in Pall Mall close to both Sir John French at the Horse Guards and the prime minister at No. 10.

Robertson, like Haig, had been fiercely opposed to the idea of the Allied Joint Council. However, Caporetto had given Lloyd George his opening, and at the emergency meeting on 5–7 November at Rapallo, on the Ligurian coast just east of Genoa – which Wilson attended, though still titular GOC Eastern Command – the French, British and Italian prime ministers had approved the creation of a 'Supreme War Council' based at Versailles to coordinate allied military strategy, initially with respect to Italy. Robertson walked out of the conference as soon as the idea was mooted, declaring 'I wash my hands of this business.'

Henry Wilson was appointed the British military representative.†

* Early in 1918 French would write a long letter to Lloyd George complaining of how Haig had intrigued against him in 1915 and how Haig and Robertson had conspired to gain supremacy over the civil power. When the Germans mounted their spring offensive he urged that Haig be sacked and replaced by Plumer.

† There is a story, perhaps in part apocryphal (notwithstanding his own diary), that when Wilson arrived at Rapallo he met Robertson, who said that (the situation being even as it was) he would not have done anything differently over the last two years – which Wilson thought 'curious', noting that 'since he has been

Robertson's increasing 'military fundamentalism' is instructive, his strategic vision focusing relentlessly on the single object of sending every last man to France. When the United States declared war he had at once begun to advocate the incorporation of American manpower in the BEF's order of battle – preferably enlisted individually into British units. It seems to have taken Repington to spell out both the practical and political impossibility of this:

> I do not agree about drafting Yankees into our Army and hope the question will not be raised. It will make America suspicious of us and I don't think that you will get the men. If you did, you would be faced with difficult questions of pay, and you would have endless trouble about discipline . . . If you shot him for disobedience of orders, as of course you would, our enemies in America, who are many, would exploit it against us. Take my advice and keep off this lay and keep others off it. Let the Yankees and the French work together. They are old pals.*

Yet Robertson had the reputation of being the cleverest man in the army. If that were indeed so (and it would be worrying if it were, for it implies a narrow definition of the adjective) then the fact that he thought he could treat American manpower as if it were British speaks volumes for how dangerously myopic the cabinet's principal military adviser had become.

Be what may, such a troubled conception and birth as the Supreme War Council's could hardly bring forth healthy issue; but initially at least the council brought improvements in the supply of munitions, shipping and food. As far as coordination of allied strategic plans was concerned, as usual the Germans had the major say.

For once, however, their action was not wholly unexpected. Any appreciation of the Germans' military situation on the Western Front could not fail to conclude that they must now see the war as

---

CIGS we have lost Romania, Russia & Italy & have gained [only] Bullecourt, Messines & Paschendal [*sic*]'.

* *Military Correspondence of Field Marshal Sir William Robertson.*

a race with the AEF. If the Anglo-French front did not collapse in 1918, and if the peace proposals which both Berlin and Washington were floating had no result (which they could not, for they amounted to effective defeat for either side respectively), a million and more Americans would be poised to decide matters in 1919. Besides, the naval blockade was beginning to cripple civilian morale in Germany, as well as constricting supplies for the front. One deserter, Heinrich Fleischer, volunteered to work for the Secret Service Bureau after going home to Berlin on leave and discovering his family 'white and emaciated, with nothing to eat but turnips and watery potatoes'.*

The Germans would therefore have to mount a knockout blow early in 1918 – or at least one that would make Britain and France sue for peace.†

Not only did logic point to this conclusion, by this stage of the war the Secret Service Bureau (SSB) was producing consistently detailed and reliable intelligence. In particular the organization known as *La Dame Blanche* (after the spectral harbinger of downfall in many a European myth), a network of train-watchers throughout Belgium and occupied France, was able to supply information on the movement of individual divisions, from which the SSB, together with the War Office's military intelligence directorate and the intelligence branch in GHQ, was able to put together a detailed German order of battle in north-west France and Flanders (the French had similar arrangements, including agents whom they actually inserted by air behind enemy lines). And all the signs of a buildup for a great spring offensive were there.

* Smith, *Six*. The legality of the blockade under international law is moot, and Britain was certainly vilified by Berlin (estimates of civilian deaths from starvation and related diseases are as high as 763,000 – figures produced by the German Board of Public Health in December 1918), but it was not London which said whether food should go to the army or the civil population.

† It is still unclear why Ludendorff thought it better to use the troops released by the Russian collapse to reinforce the Austrians for the Caporetto offensive when he himself saw the real threat as being on the Western Front. It is ironic that in doing so he forced the allies to a more cooperative stance, which paved the way for a 'generalissimo' and led to the defeat of his own principal ally, Vienna.

As R. C. Sherriff MC, former captain in the East Surreys, put it in his 1928 drama *Journey's End*, set in the run-up to that offensive, 'We are, generally, just waiting for something.'

Pétain, however, was not just waiting but looking to strengthen his defences, and in January he asked the BEF to take over a further stretch of the front – 55 miles. Haig agreed to only 25; it had been a bone of contention since October, when he had refused to take on more so that he could continue the offensive at Ypres. He believed that Pétain was constitutionally too defensive-minded, and all the more so recently because of the demoralization of the French army.

But on 16 November Georges Clemenceau had become French prime minister – for a second time, at seventy-six. Painlevé's socialists had looked irresolute, defeatist, and now 'Le Tigre' would galvanize France, and from an office in the war ministry, not the Matignon, the prime minister's traditional residence. Churchill would write that Clemenceau 'looked like a wild animal pacing to and fro behind bars' in front of 'an assembly which would have done anything to avoid putting him there, but, having put him there, felt they must obey'.

'Le Tigre' promptly told Lloyd George – a kindred spirit in terms at least of a determination to finish the job – that he would resign unless the BEF took on a more equitable share of the front. 'LG' persuaded him to submit the matter to the new Supreme War Council, for this seemed precisely the kind of question it was established to resolve.

And in due course Versailles gave a duly Solomonic judgement: the British were to take over half the distance in dispute – 40 miles in all.

Haig now threatened to resign.

It was Pétain himself who saved the day by agreeing to the original proposal after talking face-to-face with Haig. The 'Supreme' War Council prudently accepted this private settlement.

The affair was not without its strategic consequences, proving something of a blessing in disguise. As both Clemenceau and Lloyd

George recognized, if the allied commanders-in-chief had such difficulty in reaching agreement over a simple matter of frontages, how would things go in a crisis – 'the crisis of the war'?

The answer was that the council's military advisory committee should become an executive board, with Foch as chairman, controlling an Anglo-French 'general reserve' of thirty divisions.

Robertson was strongly in favour of such a reserve, but maintained that it should be controlled by the two chiefs of staff – himself and Foch. Lloyd George overruled him. 'Wully' therefore made the logical play, to take Wilson's place as the British representative on what he called 'the Versailles soviet'.

By now there was something of a Tory storm, and Lloyd George wavered. He then agreed to appoint Robertson to Versailles, making Wilson CIGS instead, albeit with reduced powers.

Robertson refused these terms (it is difficult to remember sometimes, reviewing this episode, that one of the principles of war is 'cooperation', and that there was indeed a war on). 'LG' then offered him his old post as CIGS on the same reduced terms as Wilson, which he also refused. With no more cards to play – or perhaps having played his hand superbly? – Lloyd George now removed Robertson, made Wilson CIGS and sent Rawlinson to Versailles.*

Haig does not seem to have lifted a finger to support 'Wully' in all this – for reasons that might be imagined, none of them worthy – and it clearly registered with him. At the end of December 1918 Lord Milner, who had replaced Derby as secretary for war in April, gave a dinner at the United Service Club in Pall Mall for the Army Council and the BEF's commanders. Haig made a speech in reply to Milner's, noting in his diary that it 'was very well received. I alluded to the work of the War Office during the war,

* Letters patent of 19 February 1918 included the then holder of the office of permanent British military representative, British Section, Supreme War Council of the Allied Governments, as a member of the Army Council. By an order in council of 27 February, both the CIGS and deputy CIGS were made responsible, like the other members of the Army Council, to the secretary of state for 'such business as should be assigned to them from time to time, and the special position assigned to the Chief of the Imperial General Staff in January, 1916, is thereby altered'.

Top: HMS *Audacious*, the only dreadnought to be lost to enemy action – a mine laid off the north Irish coast by the auxiliary cruiser *Berlin* in October 1914. The underwater threat – mines and torpedoes – to the Grand Fleet would force the C-in-C, Admiral Jellicoe, to adopt an increasingly cautious approach in engaging the *Hochseeflotte*.

Above: HMS *Benbow*, a 'super-dreadnought', leading the 4th Battle Squadron before Jutland, 31 May 1916, the only dreadnought fleet action in history.

Right: Admiral Sir John Jellicoe, C-in-C Grand Fleet: 'The only man on either side who could lose the war in an afternoon.' Churchill's words were no exaggeration.

Left: 'The Western Front is first and foremost an engineering problem,' said Major-General John Monash, commanding the Australian 3rd Division, not a soldier by profession but a civil engineer. Wire and machine guns posed an apparently insoluble problem for the allies, bent on attacking with (again in Churchill's words) nothing but the breasts of brave men.

Above: The litter of war: RAMC orderlies searching the packs of casualties at a dressing station for personal belongings during the battle of the Somme.

Right: Haig tries to impress a point on the new war minister, Lloyd George, during the battle, with Joffre's support. The French munitions minister, Albert Thomas, looks on somewhat blankly. By this time 'LG' had changed his mind about the new C-in-C: 'Haig is brilliant,' he said – 'to the top of his boots.'

Right: 'Ugly men with ugly ideas of war': Paul von Hindenburg and Erich Ludendorff, who took over the reins of war from Falkenhayn in August 1916 after the failure of the Verdun offensive.

Below: Voting with their feet: Russian troops being driven back to the firing line. The Russian army, critically short of war materiel, began to disintegrate after the failure of the 1916 'Brusilov offensive', just as did the country itself. 1917 would see the end of the Eastern Front.

Above: 'Lafayette we are here!' General 'Black Jack' Pershing, C-in-C American Expeditionary Force, arrives at Boulogne in June 1917. The entry of the US into the war was the certain guarantee of ultimate victory, but exactly how was to be the cause of much allied disagreement.

Above: With troops released from the Eastern Front, in October 1917 a combined Austro-German offensive at Caporetto, north of Trieste, sent the Italian army reeling, forcing at last a proper allied response to the challenge and opportunities of the Italian front.

Left: The French chief of staff, and soon to be allied Generalissimo, Ferdinand Foch, with the able new Italian C-in-C, Armando Diaz, appointed in the wake of Caporetto. Lloyd George and several French generals had believed that the Italian Front offered a better prospect for success in a grand offensive in 1917 than the Western Front, but the 'Westerners' prevailed.

Below: Ottoman machine guns in Palestine. General Sir Edmund Allenby's arrival as C-in-C in July 1917 reinvigorated the British and Imperial troops of the Egyptian Expeditionary Force, which swept north through Gaza in the autumn and took Jerusalem by Christmas.

Right: His 'Christmas present to the nation' (and to Lloyd George): Allenby entering Jerusalem on foot, the gesture of a shrewd, confident and arguably great commander.

Below: British 9.2-inch howitzer in action near Albert. All the armies on the European fronts had dramatically increased their numbers of heavy artillery – as necessary for breaking up the enemy's attacks as for supporting their own. The nimbler field batteries would come into their own once again, however, during the German spring offensive of 1918, and the subsequent allied counter-offensive.

Bottom: German troops massing for Operation Michael in the *Kaiserschlact*, 'Kaiser's battle', Ludendorff's last throw of the dice.

Left: British Mark V tanks advancing during the counter-offensive, 'the Hundred Days'.

Below: Whippet tanks, which could move at the speed of a trotting horse (on good terrain) in the restored war of movement of the closing weeks. The Tank Corps had plans to use Whippets in large numbers to disrupt command and control and play havoc in the rear areas if the war had gone on into 1919.

American troops, with British equipment (including steel helmets) and French tanks made under licence in the US, advancing in the Argonne forest during the final weeks.

Captain George S. Patton with his Renault FT. Many of the big American names of WW2 saw action in France in 1918, including Harry S. Truman and George C. Marshall.

Above: The AEF's leading ace Eddie Rickenbacker with his French-made SPAD13. The air arms of all the combatants increased exponentially during the war, in both numbers and sophistication. The Royal Flying Corps and Royal Naval Air Service together had around a hundred aircraft in 1914. By the end of the war, the Royal Air Force, formed in April 1918 from those two branches, had 22,000.

Right: Haig with Canadian troops during the Hundred Days, which mirrored the war of movement of the first months of 1914.

Left: A bridge too far (for the Germans): Brigadier-General John Vaughan Campbell VC addressing the 137th Brigade after seizing crossings on the Albert Canal to penetrate the Hindenburg Line – one of the finest divisional actions of the war, incontrovertible proof that the BEF at last knew how to fight (though no thanks to the ruinous obsession with offensives in earlier years).

Below: Armistice: the allied plenipotentiaries at Rethondes on 11 November, beside the railway carriage in which Hitler would insist the French sign the instrument of surrender in 1940.

To the victors . . . Haig with his army commanders and senior staff the day after the Armistice, Plumer to his right, Rawlinson to his left; and behind, from left, Byng, Birdwood and Horne.

To the victors . . . 'The Big Four' at the Paris peace conference, 1919: Lloyd George (*far left*) talking to Orlando; Clemenceau ('Le Tigre') facing the camera squarely; and Wilson in elegant profile.

especially of the 4 Military Members (whom I alluded to by name) . . . All were very pleased.'

Not all of those present were pleased. Haig had praised Henry Wilson, the then CIGS, whom he disliked and distrusted, but made no mention of Robertson. As 'Wully' left the club his response was: 'I'll never go farting with 'Aig again.'

Lloyd George's Versailles coup was all very well, but the immovable object – the one that really mattered – was the C-in-C. When told now that he would have to contribute nine divisions to the general reserve, Haig said he could not, having already taken over the longer frontage and made all his dispositions in expectation of the great German offensive.

There was little that Lloyd George could practicably do about this without splitting the cabinet and imperilling his own premiership (there were Liberals – Asquith's men – who would have been only too pleased to see him go). Some sort of face was saved when Haig said he had come to a further personal arrangement with Pétain, in which he had agreed to making six divisions available to him at five days' notice.

If the two commanders-in-chief were thus content, what could the politicians say?

Chapter Sixteen

THE CRISIS OF THE WAR

It would have been extraordinary indeed if neither the French nor the British armies had changed during nearly three and a half years of war. The old BEF had long been destroyed. Those who had survived First Ypres were now in staff jobs or peppered about the headquarters of the five armies in France and Flanders – brigadiers, divisional and corps commanders, staff officers – or else in New Army and territorial units, which now greatly outnumbered the nominally regular battalions; 'nominally' because conscription had changed the human landscape. There were men who had been NCOs in 1914 who were now lieutenant-colonels commanding battalions.

Generalizations are ever perilous, but the Germans had an opinion of the British soldier. In the early days of the war their field intelligence officers spoke with grudging admiration of the conduct of 'Old Contemptibles' after capture, of their resentment at being taken prisoner, of their truculent unwillingness to cooperate, and their mental and physical toughness. This was in marked contrast to reports, later, on the territorials ('not very soldierly'), the Kitchener battalions ('the finest of men, but not soldiers') and then from 1916 the conscripts, many of whom, from the lumpenproletariat, shocked their captors as specimens of debased manhood. British officers would talk of being able to lead, still, on the Somme, whereas by the end of 1917 they had to drive. And yet, somehow, in 1918 these men would in the main come up to the mark. Captain Robert Graves, convalescing in England, brilliantly conveyed the old soldiers' doubts about the new conscripts by transposition to Caesar's day and the XXIII Legion (the Royal Welsh Fusiliers, his regiment, being the old 23rd Foot):

'Is that the Three-and-Twentieth, Strabo mine,
Marching below, and we still gulping wine?'
From the sad magic of his fragrant cup
The red-faced old centurion started up,
Cursed, battered on the table. 'No,' he said,

'Not that! The Three-and-Twentieth Legion's dead,
Dead in the first year of this damned campaign—
The Legion's dead, dead, and won't rise again.
Pity? Rome pities her brave lads that die,
But we need pity also, you and I,

Whom Gallic spear and Belgian arrow miss,
Who live to see the Legion come to this,
Unsoldierlike, slovenly, bent on loot,
Grumblers, diseased, unskilled to thrust or shoot.
O, brown cheek, muscled shoulder, sturdy thigh!

Where are they now? God! watch it struggle by,
The sullen pack of ragged ugly swine.
Is that the Legion, Gracchus? Quick, the wine!'
'Strabo,' said Gracchus, 'you are strange tonight.
The Legion is the Legion; it's all right.

If these new men are slovenly, in your thinking,
God damn it! you'll not better them by drinking.
They all try, Strabo; trust their hearts and hands.

> The Legion is the Legion while Rome stands,
> And these same men before the autumn's fall
> Shall bang old Vercingetorix out of Gaul.'*

By November 1918 they had, of course, 'bang[ed] old Vercingetorix [the Kaiser] out of Gaul [France]'. For in the terrible battles of 1916 and 1917 the British army had learned how to fight; learned and been *equipped* to fight in the conditions peculiar to the Western Front. Infantry platoons were no longer upwards of fifty men with Lee–Enfields trained to fire fifteen accurate rounds a minute at 600 yards, but groupings of four or five (depending on manpower) smaller teams – 'bombing', equipped with hand- or rifle-launched grenades; 'fire', with light machine guns; and 'assault' with bayoneted rifles. These could manoeuvre in the face of resistance, the fire sections pinning the enemy while the bombing and assault sections closed with him. *Instructions for the Training of Platoons for Offensive Action, 1917,* is one of the clearest, most practical and most authoritative manuals the British army has ever produced. All it needed was for its own generals, and the Germans, to give its platoons a realistic chance of putting training into practice.

Certainly the Royal Artillery would give them better support. Not only did the new methods of 'predicted fire' increase the chance of surprise in the attack, including counter-battery (which techniques, including location, were generally much improved), the gunners' ability to respond quickly to the infantry's calls for fire, rather than the infantry having to conform to the artillery fire plan no matter what the situation, helped maintain momentum in the offensive.† As, of course, did a plentiful supply of shells, especially heavier calibre HE.

* 'An Old Twenty-Third Man' (written 1918), from *Fairies and Fusiliers* (published London, 1928).

† In his final despatch (1919), Haig said this of the artillery situation, which is not disputed: 'As regards material, it was not until midsummer 1916 that the artillery situation became even approximately adequate to the conduct of major operations. Throughout the Somme battle the expenditure of artillery ammunition had to be watched with the greatest care. During the battles of 1917, ammunition was

And there was the tank. Indeed, as long as the terrain allowed them movement and neither the enemy nor mechanical failure put them out of action, and provided the gunners silenced the enemy batteries, no defences could halt an infantry attack supported by tanks. This was a tactical watershed of strategic importance, progressively grasped, whereas the situation before the watershed had not been. The tank, in concert with improved infantry and artillery tactics, was at last the technical means of overcoming the stalemate wrought by barbed wire, machine guns and artillery – Monash's 'engineering problem'. Without them any attack was a mere gamble on how effective the artillery was in cutting the enemy's wire and keeping the Germans' heads down. 'Poor bloody infantry' – a phrase which originated on the Western Front – was an expression not so much of self-pity as of resigned despair at what had been their own tactical helplessness – what Wilfred Owen was alluding to in the first line of 'Anthem for Doomed Youth', perhaps the bleakest poem of the war: 'What passing-bells for these who die as cattle?'

But if as 'the crisis of the war' approached there were men of the 'Legion' confident that soon they would 'bang old Vercingetorix out of Gaul', what was the opinion of the Germans? For theirs was surely the most significant, possibly the most accurate, and certainly likely to be the most frank. In December 1917 the head of the operations section of the *Oberste Heeresleitung*, Lieutenant-Colonel Georg von Wetzell, in effect Ludendorff's strategic adviser, wrote a relative assessment of their two major adversaries on the Western Front:

> The artillery, like the British tactics as a whole, is rigid and stiff. The British infantry is very fully equipped with machine-guns etc. We have a strategically clumsy [i.e. at GHQ level], tactically rigid, *but tough* [emphasis added] enemy in front of us.

---

plentiful, but the gun situation was a source of constant anxiety. Only in 1918 was it possible to conduct artillery operations independently of any limiting considerations other than that of transport.'

> The French have shown us what they can do. They are just as skilful in the tactical use of their artillery as of their infantry. Their use of ground in the attack is just as good as in the defence. The French are better in the attack and more skilful in the defence, *but are not such good stayers as the British* [emphasis added]. The British are tied strategically to Flanders; the French are free.*

In the same appreciation he pointed to the essential problem of the forthcoming offensive – the *Kaiserschlacht* (Kaiser's Battle): that there would be a 'shot-to-pieces battle area' to cross, delaying the move of artillery and imposing logistical problems that would only increase as the advancing troops got further from the railheads and depots – the same problem they had encountered with the Schlieffen Plan (they had twenty-three thousand largely iron-rimmed motor lorries, whereas the allies had a hundred thousand with rubber tyres). There would therefore have to be 'operational pauses' in which the offensive could 'catch up', which would give the French and the BEF time to reorganize their defences, aided by 'the excellent railway communications behind the front'. He warned accordingly against hoping for a rapid breakthrough, and urged instead a series of coordinated simultaneous attacks, in the hope that somehow the allied line could be prised apart.

Although Ludendorff accepted these principles in theory – the appreciation went on to suggest the axes of advance for the successive attacks, in effect proposing they take the line of least resistance rather than trying to destroy the strongest or seemingly most significant points – he would in the end prove reluctant to break off attacks which appeared to be going well against apparently important objectives. And this would ultimately play to the allies' advantage.

The first of the series of attacks, Operation Michael, was to be made against the British front with the intention of completely knocking the BEF out of the fight – just as Napoleon had intended

* *Official History.*

to demolish the Prussians at Ligny at the opening of the Waterloo campaign so that he could then turn to defeat Wellington's army in detail. Ludendorff had no precise objectives other than to 'punch a hole into [their line]. For the rest, we shall see.' The idea that he wanted to drive a wedge between the allies, sending the British running for the Channel ports, has never been substantiated. 'For the rest, we shall see' was, after all, what he and Hindenburg had done so successfully in Russia in the early days.

To meet the expected attack, and to cover his lines of communication to the Channel ports, which did indeed give him very little manoeuvre room, Haig had concentrated his strength in the north. Three armies – from right to left, 3rd (Byng), 1st (Horne) and 2nd (Plumer) – covered the two-thirds of his front from Cambrai to the sea, some 46 divisions in all. Gough's 5th Army, with just 14 divisions, held the remaining third, from Cambrai to the Oise, part of it recently taken over from the French and in a comparatively poor state of defence. Haig had thus insured against the worst case, and had also strengthened Arras, which he saw as both a natural bastion and the key communications centre, but in doing so he had left the junction with the French relatively weak. Here would be the place for Ludendorff to punch a hole. And indeed there were strong intelligence indications, not least from the RFC, of a large buildup of German troops opposite Cambrai. As late as 16 March, however, GHQ was stating that 'No significant attack is expected south of the Bapaume–Cambrai road.'

In fact, and with some stealth, Ludendorff was concentrating his greatest strength opposite 5th Army. His superiority of three to one, though not overwhelming, was in conventional terms enough; and, when the innovative tactics of his attacking troops were added to the calculation, it would prove crushing.*

* On the Sunday before the blow fell there was a show-jumping competition for officers' chargers, in which Gough entered both of his, taking first place on one of them out of 120 entries. There has to be recreation of some sort in the routine of war – if only a smoke and a game of cards – and horses were there for war, not specifically for recreation, but it is a most unfortunate image, leading at least one

On 21 March the storm broke. At 4.35 a.m., without previous registration (i.e. opening fire to establish the range), six thousand guns began a torrential bombardment along 60 miles (almost half) of the BEF's, principally 5th Army's, front with HE and a great deal of gas. While the HE could destroy, gas could neutralize a far larger area. Six hours later – earlier in some areas – *Sturmtruppen*, 'storm[ing] troops' (the term *Stoßtruppe*, 'thrust troops', was also used) advanced under the cover of an obligingly thick fog. Picked men under the age of thirty-five and given better rations, they had been specially trained in infiltration tactics, bypassing strongpoints and penetrating deep into the defences, leaving the job of wiping out any pockets of resistance to the second wave of more 'legionary' infantry.

The forward zone of 5th Army was over-run alarmingly quickly. By nightfall the rearmost lines had been breached in several places – south of St Quentin the defenders driven right out. Within twenty-four hours the Germans had taken nearly 150 square miles of the Western Front. Four days later they had advanced over 20 miles and captured the important railhead of Albert.

A young officer in the 2nd Battalion the Yorkshire Regiment (Green Howards), Herbert Read, described those frantic days in a letter to his future wife:

> We were rushed up to the line in the early hours of the morning, and from then and for six days and nights we were fighting as I never dreamt I would fight – without sleep – often without food and all the time besieged by hordes of the Boche. The Colonel was wounded during the second day and I had to take command of the battalion. We were surrounded in our original position and had to fight our way through. We took up position after position, always to be surrounded. On the whole the men were splendid and there were many fine cases of heroism. But our casualties were very heavy and we who have come through may thank our lucky stars eternally.

---

historian to quip 'C'est magnifique, mais ce n'est pas la guerre' (John Grigg, *Lloyd George: War Leader*, London, 2002).

Read was a fine example of the best of the regimental officers who had emerged during the previous three years. The orphaned son of a Yorkshire tenant farmer, educated locally, he had joined the officer training corps at Leeds University 'for a free holiday in the open air'. In 1914 he had been commissioned into the Special Reserve and found himself, rather awkwardly (wrote his son), in the uniform of what regarded itself as a 'good regiment – which usually meant a higher proportion of Etonians (who appear to have looked at him – a published poet with a Yorkshire accent – rather askant)'.* He already had an MC; by the end of the *Kaiserschlacht* he would have the DSO.

No amount of determined leadership could avail, however. 5th Army had simply disintegrated, for which Gough would pay the price.†

But although Operation Michael had achieved spectacular results, and for a while it looked as if the British might indeed fall back to cover the Channel ports, and the French to cover Paris, Haig and Pétain poured in reinforcements, who dug in and fought back

* Piers Paul Read, *Standpoint* (magazine), May 2015. Sir Herbert Read, art critic and writer, is one of the thirteen war poets commemorated by name in Westminster Abbey who served in the army. In 1940 he would write of his Great War experience:

> The old guns
> barked into my ear. Day and night
> they shook the earth in which I cowered
> or rained round me
> detonations of steel and fire.
> One of the dazed and disinherited,
> I crawled out of that mess
> With two medals and a gift of blood money.
> No visible wounds to lick – only a resolve
> to tell the truth without rhetoric
> the truth about war and about men
> involved in the indignities of war.
>
> ('Ode Written During the Battle of Dunkirk', 1940)

† On 28 March, 5th Army was temporarily taken over by Rawlinson (4th Army); then on 8 April another caretaker, Sir William Peyton (Haig's military secretary), took charge of what remained, before Birdwood (Australian Corps) assumed permanent command in May to reconstitute the army. With considerable justification, Gough would later mount a strong self-defence of his dispositions and action.

aggressively, notably the Australians at Hébuterne. The offensive began to run out of steam as the Germans crossed the old Somme battlefield, not least because of the very problems that Wetzell had identified – the 'shot-to-pieces battle area', scorched earth, if not of deliberate making. And here at last the Royal Navy's presence was felt on the ground, in the fruits of blockade. So rapid was 5th Army's collapse that ordnance stores, with their abundant food and large quantities of alcohol, were abandoned across the entire front. For troops on increasingly short and unattractive rations, even the *Sturmtruppen*, it was sometimes simply too much to bypass. As more than one historian has been unable to resist asserting, the advance was slowed not for lack of German fighting spirit, but on account of the abundance of Scottish drinking spirit.

However, 'desperate times, desperate measures'. As something close to panic began taking hold in Paris, and in London too, with Pétain saying the war was as good as lost – though Lloyd George himself remained, by all accounts, supremely composed, confident that he had the men and materiel in England to make good the losses – Foch was summarily appointed 'Generalissimo'. Not as 'supreme commander' exactly, but, in the words of the memorandum, 'to coordinate the action of the allied armies on the Western Front'. Earlier, Henry Wilson had made the extraordinary suggestion that Clemenceau be made coordinator of allied armies, with Foch as technical adviser. There is nothing like a sharp dose of reality, however, to force people to take the right medicine.

Haig was content with Foch's appointment. In the circumstances there had to be complete unity of effort, and unity of command now seemed the only way to achieve it. And the appointment would have the unintended but welcome consequence of shielding him from political interference from London.

Meanwhile, Washington stepped up its mobilization: 'I am going to get the men to France if they have to swim,' declared General Peyton C. March, the US chief of staff.*

* During the *Kaiserschlacht*, Vera Brittain, serving as a nurse at the great British base

Michael had stalled; but this was to be expected at some point – hence Wetzell's concept of the series of attacks taking the line of least resistance. Operation Georgette (the Battle of the Lys), in French Flanders, would now begin (on 9 April). The original operation, St George, had counted on thirty-five fresh divisions for the offensive, but only a third of them had been moved up; so, it is said, George became the diminutive.

Georgette employed similar tactics to Michael and reaped the same initial success – including the (re)capture of Messines Ridge. The BEF held fast stubbornly in places, but overall the defence was patchy, some divisions collapsing under the sheer weight of artillery and numbers, including those of the Portuguese Expeditionary Force (corps), which, ill-led and poorly suited to the Western Front, had most unfortunately been posted in the eye of the storm at Neuve Chapelle.

On 11 April Haig issued his most desperate call to date – a 'special order of the day'. Although it was to be read out to all ranks – whose reactions (various) might be imagined, even making allowances for the passage of time – this extraordinary document is best understood as a direct communication to the officers in command of brigades, battalions and companies, on whom the burden of resistance now rested.

SPECIAL ORDER OF THE DAY
By FIELD-MARSHAL SIR DOUGLAS HAIG
K.T., G.C.B., G.C.V.O., K.C.I.E.
Commander-in-Chief, British Armies in France
To ALL RANKS OF THE BRITISH ARMY IN FRANCE
AND FLANDERS

Three weeks ago to-day the enemy began his terrific attacks against

at Étaples, saw an American contingent marching down the road – 'Tommies in Heaven . . . so god-like, so magnificent, so splendidly unimpaired in comparison with the tired, nerve-wracked men of the British Army': *Testament of Youth* (London, 1928). The French had said the same of the BEF on seeing them land in August 1914.

us on a fifty-mile front. His objects are to separate us from the French, to take the Channel Ports and destroy the British Army.

In spite of throwing already 106 Divisions into the battle and enduring the most reckless sacrifice of human life, he has as yet made little progress towards his goals.

We owe this to the determined fighting and self-sacrifice of our troops. Words fail me to express the admiration which I feel for the splendid resistance offered by all ranks of our Army under the most trying circumstances.

Many amongst us now are tired. To those I would say that Victory will belong to the side which holds out the longest. The French Army is moving rapidly and in great force to our support.

There is no other course open to us but to fight it out. Every position must be held to the last man: there must be no retirement. With our backs to the wall and believing in the justice of our cause each one of us must fight on to the end. The safety of our homes and the Freedom of mankind alike depend upon the conduct of each one of us at this critical moment.

(Signed) D. Haig F.M.
Commander-in-Chief
British Armies in France
General Headquarters
Tuesday, April 11th, 1918

Foch moved his reserves deftly, the defence again stiffened, and by 29 April Georgette was finished. Indeed, the *Kaiserschlacht*, as originally conceived, had almost run its course, though neither side knew or could admit it.

Casualties on both sides had been enormous. In five weeks the BEF (strictly, the British armies in France and Flanders) had lost some 236,000 men (20,000 dead, 120,000 taken prisoner), the French around 90,000; but the Germans an irreplaceable 348,000.

Allied appeals for US divisions, both directly to Pershing and in the Supreme War Council (President Wilson told his representative, General Tasker Bliss, who was himself in favour, as were many of the divisional commanders, that he was willing to respond), fell largely on deaf ears, though 'Black Jack' did concede two more divisions to relieve the French in a sector not under attack.*

At an emergency conference in Abbeville, Lloyd George, Clemenceau and Orlando (who had sent some Italian divisions and aircraft to fight under French command) pressed him forcefully. Bringing his fist down hard on the table, Pershing was adamant: 'Gentlemen, I have thought this programme over very deliberately and will not be coerced.'

But only weeks later US troops would be in action as the tide began to turn.†

Ludendorff was now becoming desperate, and having drawn rather too many French reserves closer to the BEF than he had expected, he decided on a further two-pronged operation (Blücher–Yorck): first a diversionary attack against the French in Champagne, and then another assault to finish off the BEF in Flanders. Though his men were tired and his materiel much reduced, the sector in which he chose to attack the French, having stronger natural defences, was relatively weakly held, and therefore offered some sort of promise. Elaborate security precautions, including the muffling of horses' hooves and the axles of guns and limbers – precautions which the Germans would use again, in the Ardennes

* These French sectors were not *entirely* quiet, however. During a sudden attack in the Vosges Mountains, American troops began to flee. Some of them were stopped by Captain (later President of the United States) Harry S. Truman of the Missouri National Guard, serving with the 129th Field Artillery. He is said to have used language so shocking, learned while working on the Santa Fe railroad, that they promptly rallied. There are leadership tricks not taught at West Point – or Sandhurst.

† John J. Pershing, *My Experiences in the World War* (New York, 1931). Pershing was of course proved right: the Entente allies managed well enough without wholesale American support, allowing him to complete the plan to form an independent army – but how could he have been so sure, with Lloyd George asking: 'Can't you see that the war will be lost unless we get this support?' The first American attack on the Western Front would take place near Montdidier, on 28 May, the second day of the German offensive on the Aisne. The American 1st Division captured the village of Cantigny and 200 prisoners, at a cost of 1,600 casualties, including 200 killed. Not a good beginning, but with US blood spilled it was a catalyst.

in 1944 – helped him gain complete surprise. On 27 May he opened the attack, between Soissons and Rheims, where there happened to be six depleted British divisions 'resting' after Michael. This whole front effectively collapsed, German troops surged towards the Marne, Paris once more looked in jeopardy, and the government began making plans to evacuate to Bordeaux again.

The gains had not come without cost, however – something like 130,000 casualties up to 6 June, mainly in the assault divisions and therefore difficult to replace. Again Foch was able to bring in reserves, and Blücher–Yorck began to lose momentum. Ludendorff, too exhilarated by the vision of Paris, now tried to regain balance by extending the offensive westward with Operation Gneisenau to draw yet more allied reserves south, and to join up with the German salient at Amiens. This attack the French were expecting, however, and the depth of their defence along the River Matz reduced the effect of the preparatory bombardment. Nevertheless on 9 June the Germans advanced 9 miles across a 20-mile frontage despite fierce French and American resistance – until a fine French counter-attack on 11 June by four divisions and 150 tanks, with no preliminary bombardment, caught the Germans by surprise and brought the advance to an abrupt halt. Ludendorff called off Gneisenau the next day.

Wetzell's concept of seeking the most promising axis of advance was now done with. Seeing it was now or never, Ludendorff reverted to the expedient of mass and bluster, though it would take him a month to garner the strength to do so. He announced the grandiloquently named *Friedensturm* (Peace Offensive), in which the 1st, 3rd and 7th Armies would draw the allied reserves south from Flanders, knock out the BEF, expand the salients and bring the Entente to the negotiating table. Given the literally threadbare state of his troops, increasingly demoralized by letters from home telling of the effects of the blockade, it is amazing that so many of them would throw their weight into it, although perhaps a growing number were motivated by the word 'peace', on any terms.

By now the allies were getting the measure of the new German tactics and way of thinking. Amply warned by air reconnaissance (lack of fuel keeping German fighters on the ground) and prisoners, once more the French were ready for the attack, having adapted the German system of what Pétain called 'a recoiling buffer defence': rather as the hydraulic railway buffer absorbs impact, the lightly held forward defences would yield to the storm troops, who, their impetus spent, would be stopped on a strong position in rear, pummelled by the artillery.

This time, too, when the Germans attacked, on 15 July along the Marne east and west of Rheims, there was no obliging fog – and, as Liddell Hart put it pithily, no 'fog of war' either. The French heavies shelled the *Sturmtruppen* even before they left their (primitive) trenches; machine guns cut them down savagely in the loose-knit forward zone, and then as they ran onto the main position – in the open, and beyond the covering range of their own guns – they were pulverized by every manner of artillery, not least the quick-firing *soixante-quinze*, tailor-made for the job.

East of Rheims the offensive stuttered bloodily to a halt, and although west of the city under cover of darkness and smoke the Germans did manage to get across the sacred Marne, by next day here, too, the attacks had petered out.

The French, with nine US divisions now fighting alongside them, counter-attacked almost at once using 'the Cambrai key' which had worked for them so well on the Matz – no artillery preparation and several hundred tanks. This time, however, the tanks were smaller, faster and more agile – the Renault FT (the letters have no meaning, merely the manufacturing designation), armed with 37 mm cannon or a Hotchkiss machine gun in a revolving turret. On 18 July the early-morning mist cloaked their advance and deadened the noise, and by evening General Mangin's rapidly assembled army had advanced 4 miles – reminiscent of the *first* triumph on the Marne. The Germans just managed to rally, nonetheless, and Mangin's attempt to push through his cavalry corps went the same way as Byng's had at Cambrai. The 'Cambrai key' was not, in fact, the tank itself, but rather the substitution of predicted artillery fire and rolling barrage for lengthy preparatory bombardment, the tanks able then to help the infantry win the 'race for the parapet' (or whatever hastily dug defences the Germans occupied). In other words, the key was the proper coordination of the all-arms battle. If only wireless communication had been developed to link the infantry, through the artillery forward observation officers, to the gun batteries, the momentum could have been kept up indefinitely, but tactical radio was the one element of battlefield technology that had not kept pace with demand. Yet Marconi had sent radio signals across the Channel in 1899, ten years before Blériot had flown it.

For the Americans, the Marne counter-attack was another sharp and salutary blooding. The Germans were still lethal, especially when cornered – even to the bravest, corn-fed 'doughboy' if his battlecraft was novice. The French, by contrast, were now perhaps too wary – or as Liddell Hart put it, in contrast with the Americans 'suffered too much from experience'.* The Germans were able to escape from the salient that Mangin had hoped to cut out, but with twenty-five thousand taken prisoner.

Ludendorff had to abandon the Flanders stroke planned for the twentieth, but he was still not persuaded that all was lost. However, his front was over-stretched and under-fortified. It ran (in places meandered) over 300 miles – 70 more than when he had launched the *Kaiserschlacht*. Instead of the formidable defences of the Hindenburg Line and elsewhere there were now vulnerable salients and primitive entrenchments. His losses since April were staggering: perhaps as many as a million dead, wounded or missing. Writing in his diary on 8 May, the chief of staff of Army Group Crown Prince Rupprecht, Generalleutnant Hermann von Kuhl, admitted the worst: 'Our supply of reinforcements and replacements is virtually exhausted . . . I doubt if further major offensives will be possible . . . The Americans are on their way. I am really doubtful if we shall be able to force a decision. We are not going to

* *World War I in Outline.*

achieve a breakthrough – and then there is the issue of horses and the supply of oats . . .'*

The allies were now presented with their long looked-to opportunity for the decisive offensive, although it was by no means clear yet how long the battle would be. Foch wrote to Clemenceau: 'The decisive year of the conflict will be 1919.'

But having gained the initiative, the Generalissimo was not going to let it slip from his hands. Besides aught else, it would almost certainly have been picked up by Pershing in 'the decisive year', for by 1919 the allies' relative strengths would be such that Pershing could not *but* be appointed Generalissimo in his place. On 20 July Foch told Haig: 'It is essential to grip onto the enemy,' and four days later, concluding that the allied armies had reached 'the turning point of the road', decided that 'The moment has come to abandon the general defensive attitude forced upon us recently by numerical inferiority and to pass to the offensive.'†

That moment was of the BEF's and the French army's making – with the help of Ludendorff's miscalculations – but it was underscored too by the Americans' entry into the field in critical strength, for on 10 August the 1st US Army (I and III Corps) would be formed; and in October II Corps.

The last act was about to begin; and fittingly – for it was the name given to Napoleon's escape from Elba and subsequent (Waterloo) campaign – it was to become known as 'the Hundred Days'.

* Sheldon, *The German Manpower Crisis of 1918*.

† *Haig: War Diaries and Letters*. The conference of 24 July was held at Foch's HQ, the Château de Bombon, 25 miles south-east of Paris, and attended by Pétain, Haig and Pershing. Foch, in a private conversation with Haig before the meeting, agreed that the operations east of Amiens should begin as soon as possible.

Chapter Seventeen

THE HUNDRED DAYS

For nearly four years the guiding principle of the allied commanders – the thrusting Foch, the cautious Pétain, the dogged Haig – had been that only offensive operations could decide matters. *Offensive à outrance,* though it had proved a costly failure in 1914, had never quite lost its hold on French thinking, in particular that of Foch. British thinking was no less resolute, asserting that 'decisive success in battle can be gained only by a vigorous offensive' and that the chief factor in success was 'a firmer determination in all ranks to conquer at any cost'. But *Field Service Regulations* also made it clear that this firm determination was not to be pursued *à outrance*: 'If the situation be unfavourable for such a course [a vigorous offensive], it is wiser, when possible, to manoeuvre for a more suitable opportunity.'

For nearly four years, however, the allies – Italy included, perhaps even Italy especially, if not for quite as long – had persevered with the doctrine of the offensive when the situation was not so much unfavourable as futile. Now, in the high summer of 1918, having lost countless hundreds of thousands of men in repeated attempts to make the situation fit the doctrine, rather than the other way round, the allies found themselves in a position where the situation really had – at last – changed to fit the doctrine.

In his memoirs, Ludendorff called Thursday, 8 August, the first day of the Battle of Amiens, 'der schwarze Tag des deutschen Heeres' – the black day of the German army. That day belonged to Haig and the BEF for their tenacity and endurance, and to Rawlinson, his 4th Army, and the Canadians and Australians especially, for their tactical flair. The high-water mark of the four-year German offensive in the west was now visible; and now would be heard its 'melancholy, long, withdrawing roar'.

After the German retreat from the Marne, begun on 20 July, Foch had been planning to reduce the St-Mihiel salient and to free the railway lines that ran through Amiens, which were critical for the movement of reserves and supplies, from German artillery fire. Meanwhile Haig had been making his own plans for an attack near Amiens, for when the BEF had at last managed to halt its retreat, Rawlinson's 4th Army had taken over the front astride the Somme – III Corps on the left, the Australian Corps under Monash on the right, forming a junction with the French to the south – and throughout June the Australians had made vigorous local counter-attacks. What these attacks showed was that the tactical doctrine developed for offensive operations in the light of the experience of Third Ypres – principally in the organization of the platoon, and well-rehearsed techniques of movement covered by fire – was indeed battleworthy; and also that the open, firm going south of the Somme was suitable for a larger offensive.

Rawlinson had put Monash's proposals for such an offensive to Haig, and at a meeting on 24 July Foch agreed to the plan but insisted that the French 1st Army (to the right and south of 4th Army) should take part. Rawlinson opposed this as the plans depended on the large-scale use of tanks, which the BEF now had in sufficient numbers, including two hundred 'Whippets', each mounting four machine guns, and which at 14 tons – half the weight of the main fighting tanks – could make 8 mph, the speed of a trotting horse.* To gain surprise he intended to use the 'Cambrai key' once more, eschewing a preliminary bombardment. The French 1st Army lacked enough tanks, however, and would be forced to bombard the German positions before the advance began, thus removing the element of surprise. The obvious compromise was reached: the French would not launch their attack until forty-five minutes after 4th Army had gone into action, so that their bombardment would not begin before 4th Army's zero hour.

The British III Corps (under Lieutenant-General Richard Butler, who had risen four ranks since commanding the 2nd Lancashire Fusiliers at Le Cateau) would attack north of the Somme, the Australian Corps to the south of the river in the centre of 4th Army's front, and the Canadian Corps (under Currie) – brought from Flanders especially for the purpose† – to the south of the Australians, with Lieutenant-General Charles Kavanagh's Cavalry Corps ready to exploit success. Extensive aerial reconnaissance and sound-ranging‡ had located nine out of ten German batteries, which could therefore be struck at zero hour without prior registration; this would be the essence of 4th Army's fire plan (using two thousand guns) – devised by Major-General Charles Budworth, another officer who had risen four ranks since 1914 – as well as providing a creeping barrage for the infantry to shelter behind in the advance. Four hundred and fifty tanks would take part, the Canadian and

* The 'star' of the BEF's new tank fleet was, however, a 6-foot longer version of the Mark V, lengthened for the purpose of crossing the broader trenches of the Hindenburg Line.

† The move was undetected by the Germans; had it been, given the corps' first-rate reputation, an attack would have been positively assumed. A detachment of two infantry battalions, a wireless unit and a casualty clearing station had instead been sent to Ypres as a bluff (a technique which would be used again in the deception plans for the Normandy landings in 1944). The last troops of the corps did not arrive in the assembly area until the day before the attack.

‡ A method of determining the coordinates of an enemy battery from data derived from the sound of its guns firing. Pairs of microphones were used to determine bearings to the source of the sound, the intersection of which gave the battery's location. The bearings were determined from the differences in the sound's time of arrival at the microphone.

Australian corps each being allocated a brigade of 108 Mark V fighting tanks, thirty-six prototype armoured personnel carriers – Mark V 'Star' tanks adapted to carry a section of infantry with Lewis-gun team – and twenty-four unarmed tanks for ammunition resupply. A single battalion of Mark V tanks was allocated to III Corps, while a hundred Whippets were attached to the Cavalry Corps and seventy to the French.* Security measures were imaginative. In 1980, as the SAS prepared to storm the Iranian Embassy in London to release the hostages taken by a group of armed militants, they covered the noise of drilling fibre-optic surveillance cables into the building by getting air traffic control to reroute passenger jets low overhead on their approach to Heathrow – a much celebrated ruse, but not a new one. The night before the attack at Amiens, the RAF's Handley Page bombers flew for hours over the front to drown the noise of the tanks coming forward.†

The battle began in thick fog, soon thickened by smoke shell, at 4.20 a.m., just after first light, the Germans taken almost wholly by surprise. In the centre the Canadians and Australians advanced quickly – 3 miles by 11 a.m. – and by the end of the day, aided by the RAF's constant 'strafing' of the roads to hinder attempts to withdraw and rally, had punched a 15-mile-wide hole in the defences south of the Somme. Rawlinson's 4th Army took thirteen thousand prisoners, the French three thousand; a further fourteen thousand Germans were killed or wounded. Infantry losses in 4th Army – British, Australian and Canadian – were around 8,800.

As at Cambrai, however, the cavalry had not been able to 'gallop through the "G" in "Gap"'. The Tank Corps staff had suggested letting the Whippets go ahead on their own, but both Haig and

* For comparison, the British army today has just 200 Challenger main battle tanks in operational service.

† The RAF had been formed on 1 April 1918 (hence the waggish 'Royal April Foolers') from the Royal Flying Corps and Royal Naval Air Service, in part to reassure the civil population of London, who had been subjected to increasing attacks by German bombers, in part to develop the concept of strategic bombing, separately from the theatre campaign, and in part also in recognition of the huge growth of the air arms. In November 1918 the RAF, worldwide, had 22,000 aircraft.

Rawlinson preferred to keep them in close support of Kavanagh's horsemen, the lesson of Cambrai being that without ready machine-gun support the cavalry would be stopped in the rear of the battle area before being able to get a gallop in open country. Nevertheless some Whippets did break through into the German rear areas, playing havoc with the artillery. One of them, 'Musical Box',* roamed at will for nine hours, shooting up a battery, an observation balloon, an infantry battalion's camp and a divisional transport column. It may not have achieved much in the greater scheme of things, but it would reinforce the Tank Corps staff in their thinking for operations if the war should continue into 1919.†

The task at hand was not about taking ground as such, however. Ludendorff called 8 August *der schwarze Tag des deutschen Heeres* not because of the ground lost, but because the morale of his troops had so evidently collapsed. *Sixteen thousand prisoners*: fighting spirit had ebbed to the point where large numbers had now begun to surrender without a fight. As with the Russians in 1917, fleeing troops shouted: 'You're prolonging the war!' at officers who tried to rally them, and 'Blackleg!' (*Streikbrecher*) at reserves moving up.

After receiving Ludendorff's report, the Kaiser said: 'I see that we must strike a balance. We are at the end of our reserves. The war must be ended.'

But how, and what favourable terms could be obtained?

The only thing that could forestall complete defeat on the Western Front was a strategic withdrawal like that of *Alberich*, to dislocate the allies' now inevitable counter-offensive. Some of Ludendorff's officers were urging this very course. But how could he ask the army to retreat over the very ground that was still wet with their blood – and when he had promised them victory; or at least *Frieden*, peace?

He could not, of course.

* Crews invariably named their machines, a nod, perhaps, to the tank's naval origins.

† See footnote p. 331.

For the allies the task was now – to use Churchill's phrase of the end of 1941 when the Americans had entered the Second World War – the 'proper application of overwhelming force'.*

But rapid and decisive victory was still not a foregone conclusion. The Amiens attack had petered out in the subsequent days: the old problem of the Germans' being able to seal the breach faster than the attackers could exploit it had still not been overcome. And being in essence a frontal assault, like all the others, it had the same drawback of pushing the defenders onto their own reserves. Foch still urged Haig on, but Haig had at last learned the lesson of the Somme and Third Ypres: not to slog away at hardening resistance. Now, too, he stayed near the front – formed a tactical headquarters – and was ready to listen to his commanders when they advised against delivering unprepared attacks against new German positions. Currie's and Monash's advice, especially, would have been almost impossible to gainsay now. Instead, and with Foch's agreement, Haig switched the main effort to Byng's 3rd Army, which had been preparing to attack at Bapaume. This effort was to be made with considerable circumspection, Haig telling Byng that 'owing to shortage of men I was opposed to doing more attacking than was absolutely necessary. Our object is to keep the battle going as long as possible, until the Americans can attack in force.'

But he was clear that at that point – with the Americans attacking in strength – the BEF too must be able to attack, 'and to have the means of exploiting victory and making it decisive'. To that end he 'wished the Cavalry Corps to be kept as strong as possible . . . ready to act vigorously when the decisive moment comes'.

With this late recognition of the art of the possible, and without the same fear of flanking fire and counter-attack that seemed to dog the planning for the battles against the linear defences on the Somme and elsewhere, both Haig and Foch had virtually stumbled on the proper application of force – in 'indirect leverage', taking the

* Winston S. Churchill, *The Second World War*, vol. II: *The Grand Alliance* (London, 1950).

line of least resistance (Wetzell's idea in essence), thereby maintaining greater momentum and spreading the Germans' problems. On 10 August the French 3rd Army had already struck on the south flank; on the seventeenth the 10th would strike even further south. On 21 August Byng's 3rd Army attacked at Bapaume, and three days later 1st Army under Horne joined in the general offensive north of Rawlinson's recuperating 4th – a sort of army-level *Trommelfeuer*, what in present-day parlance is called 'high operational tempo'.

This rash-like spread of attacks now forced Ludendorff to do what his advisers had urged earlier – withdraw to the old Hindenburg Line (as far south as Soissons). But this time there would be no opportunity for the delaying devices of *Alberich*. It was not quite *sauve qui peut*, but by the end of September the German army had abandoned almost every inch of ground taken in the *Kaiserschlacht*, harassed all the way back to their original start line by the RAF and the Aéronautique Militaire, over a thousand aircraft now flying in close support of Haig's armies on reconnaissance and artillery spotting, and in ground attack sweeps with bombs and machine guns.

And another hundred thousand of Ludendorff's increasingly ragged, half-starved troops were now at their ease and eating better rations in British and French PoW cages. Luckier still were those – fifteen thousand of them – who on 12 September found themselves eating even better rations as prisoners of the American 1st Army when Pershing took the St-Mihiel salient.

If the US 1st Army had then pushed on past Metz towards the Germans' main railway artery, as Pershing originally intended, it would have threatened to unhinge the entire front. However, as the commander of I Corps, Hunter Liggett (who would take command of 1st Army from Pershing the following month when 2nd Army formed), wrote later, such a thrust was only possible 'on the supposition that our army was a well-oiled, fully co-ordinated machine, which it was not yet'.* Luck, of course, would have been the unknown factor, and luck might indeed have gone with Pershing,

* Hunter Liggett, *A.E.F.: Ten Years Ago in France* (New York, 1928).

but there had been another counsel – Foch; and Foch was the Generalissimo. Haig had concluded, from all the evidence of the poor state of the troops taken prisoner, that the Germans could not make a stand even on the Hindenburg Line, and had therefore proposed to assault it at once. If Pershing were to attack towards Metz, he argued, this would mean offensives on diverging axes, which, while posing a real danger to the Germans, failed to concentrate the allied effort in the prescribed manner. Foch could not deny the logic of this, and so at his bidding Pershing had reluctantly agreed to limit the St-Mihiel operation and realign his axis of advance (though he would always believe it a missed opportunity). Foch in his turn conceded to pride by agreeing to Pershing's proposal for his now *converging* attack to be through the particularly difficult sector east of the Argonne forest. Unfortunately, not having time to switch his experienced divisions to this new axis, it meant he would have to use green ones. And these would pay the price. It is strange, if only in retrospect, that Haig (and, even more so, Foch) took the view that he needed to concentrate allied effort rather than disperse German force. The problem was now not one of defeating the front-line troops but of breaking out before the reserves could disrupt the exploitation – in essence the old problem, but now one that it looked possible to overcome. By concentrating the allied effort, he allowed the Germans to concentrate their reserves too.

When news of the intention to attack the Hindenburg Line reached London the cabinet evidently had a fit of *déjà vu*, Henry Wilson (CIGS) sending Haig a 'personal' telegram warning him of the feeling of the cabinet and the consequences therefore of high casualties. Haig sneered at them as 'a wretched lot of weaklings' – by implication including Wilson – and backed his own judgement. In his heart he must have *known* that this was not the situation of Third Ypres; there, in the face of all the evidence, he had continued desperately in the hope of some success, while now the evidence was staring everyone in the face. And yet high casualties without result might well spell the end for him, even now . . .

At this point, rather as the duke of Wellington had taken off his hat at the culminating point of Waterloo and waved it to signal the whole line to advance, Foch came to the rescue by issuing the simple directive: 'Everyone is to attack (Belgians, British, French and Americans) as soon as they can, as strong as they can, for as long as they can.'

London (and Paris) had appointed Foch Generalissimo; they must now live with the consequences. Haig's back was covered.

Foch's design was for a gigantic pincer attack on the great German salient between Verdun and Ypres – the ejection, no less, of the Boche from France. The right pincer was to be the Americans in the Meuse–Argonne to draw away reserves from the Cambrai–St Quentin sector and threaten the Germans' railway communications through Lorraine. The left, British pincer would, if driven deep enough, likewise threaten the lines of communication through the Liège corridor. The French would support each pincer on the inner flanks, while a further attack by a combined Anglo-Belgian force at Ypres would tie down any loose German reserves.

Pershing's expectations of progress were to prove unrealistic, however. On 28 September he was able to mass nearly three thousand guns for a three-hour bombardment of the lightly held German forward defence zone before advancing on a 20-mile front with, in theory, overwhelming odds – almost ten to one – but his green troops largely fell for the Germans' 'recoiling buffer' defence, and in the centre the advance began to falter. As his orders had been for the whole line to advance together, the rapid progress made by his troops on the flanks was soon to no avail, and the fighting developed into a slogging match until, in mid-October, he called a halt. The offensive had cost the American 1st Army a hundred thousand casualties, with (Liggett estimated) perhaps the same number of 'stragglers', a word covering a multitude of sins. No one who had seen green troops in action for the first time – at Anzac or Loos – could have been surprised. It was the *scale* of the failure that was the shock: losses on a par with the offensives of 1916 and 1917, and for equally little gain.

The BEF's pincer was rather more effective, exploiting the lines of least resistance to pierce the German front and threaten strong points from the flanks. On 27 September, after a thunderous overnight bombardment – 'Even the wurrums themselves are getting up and crying for mercy,' said a serjeant-major of the Irish Guards* – and again with the help of the early-morning mist, 3rd Army's left and 1st's right attacked on the Canal du Nord, penetrating on a narrow front and then spreading fan-like to break down the sides of the breach. By nightfall on the twenty-eighth they had reached Cambrai, beyond the northern edge of the Hindenburg Line, threatening to turn it, but here stiffening resistance brought things to a standstill.

The baton was now handed to Rawlinson's 4th Army, which had been preparing to assault the line with 3rd Army's support, but had found the roles reversed. A two-day bombardment prepared the way: sixteen hundred guns, one for every three yards, the first eight hours with gas driving the defenders to cover, the next day and a half with HE keeping them below ground without the need of further gas to hinder the attackers when they went forward on the twenty-ninth. One British and two American divisions spearheaded Rawlinson's attack, on a 9-mile front. Again, the Americans pressed bravely but without the battlefield 'savvy' that the British had learned the hard way. They gained their objectives but at much cost and had to be rescued by the Australians. Meanwhile the British division, the 46th, under cover of the smoke-thickened morning mist, used life-belts and collapsible boats to get across the St-Quentin Canal near Bellenglise, and scaling ladders to climb the bank to capture the machine-gun posts before the Germans knew what was happening. Sappers following up close behind managed to patch up several bridges only partially demolished, and then – thanks to the much improved staffwork at divisional and corps level – instead of the attacking troops continuing until exhausted, with the consequent loss of momentum, a fresh division was passed through (no

* Quoted in Kipling, *The Irish Guards in the Great War.*

small feat) and carried the advance beyond the rear line of the Hindenburg defences.

The 46th, originally a Midland territorial division, had had a poor reputation since the Somme, but had been reinvigorated in a matter of months by the arrival of the forty-year-old Gerald Farrell Boyd, 'the ranker general', who had enlisted in the Devonshire Regiment after failing the entry exam for the Royal Military Academy Woolwich. Having won the Distinguished Conduct Medal at Colenso (South Africa) as a sergeant, he was commissioned into the East Yorkshire Regiment, and in 1914 had been a captain on the staff – a promotion since the outbreak of war, therefore, of five ranks. The 46th's breaching of the Hindenburg Line was one of the outstanding divisional actions of the war. It speaks eloquently of that rare conjunction of two elusive elements in war – time and circumstance.*

By 5 October the BEF was through the Hindenburg Line and at last into open country.

Even before that, however, Ludendorff's nerve had cracked. The situation in Germany itself was becoming very ugly indeed. The *Kaiserliche Marine* was increasingly restive, there were food riots in the major cities, communist sentiment was rife and openly expressed. On the Italian front, Colonel Tullio Marchetti, General Armando Diaz's clever intelligence–propaganda officer, likened the same situation in Austria (with a fine nod to his native Roman cuisine) to 'a pudding which has a crust of roasted almonds and is filled with cream. The crust which is the army in the front line is hard to break' – but the cream was dissolving the crust.†

The inhabitants of Berlin and many another German city had not seen almonds or cream for a long time.

To forestall revolution, on 1 October the Kaiser had sent for the

* The actual assault crossing was carried out by the 137th (Staffordshire) Brigade under the 40-year-old Brigadier-General John Vaughan Campbell VC DSO, a Coldstreamer – and, by way of narrative balance to the 'ranker-general', an Old Etonian (though Boyd had joined the ranks, he had in fact been at St Paul's).

† Quoted in Mark Cornwall, *The Undermining of Austria-Hungary: The Battle for Hearts and Minds* (London, 2001).

liberal-minded Prince Maximilian of Baden, a former major-general, and a liberal, to be chancellor, and two days later the German government resigned. On the sixth, a Sunday, Haig visited Foch, who showed him one of the Paris newspapers, 'in which in large type was printed a note from Austria, Germany and Turkey, asking for an armistice at once, and stating their readiness to discuss conditions of peace on the basis of President Wilson's 14 points'.* Allenby had chased the Turks out of Palestine, and Lieutenant-General Sir William Marshall had done the same in Mesopotamia. The Italians under Diaz's judicious leadership (instead of mounting more attacks, he had put his effort

* *Haig: War Diaries and Letters*. The 'Fourteen Points' were impossibly (on the whole) idealistic terms for settling the conflict, proposed in January and promptly rejected by Berlin:

1. Open covenants of peace, openly arrived at.
2. Freedom of the seas.
3. The removal so far as possible of all economic barriers.
4. The reduction of national armaments to the lowest point consistent with domestic safety.
5. Impartial adjustment of all colonial claims.
6. The evacuation of all Russian territory.
7. The evacuation and restoration of Belgium.
8. The liberation of France and return to her of Alsace and Lorraine.
9. Readjustment of the frontiers of Italy to conform to clearly recognizable lines of nationality.
10. The peoples of Austria-Hungary should be accorded the freest opportunity of autonomous development.
11. Evacuation of occupation forces from Romania, Serbia and Montenegro; Serbia should be accorded free and secure access to the sea.
12. Autonomous development for the non-Turkish peoples of the Ottoman Empire; free passage of the Dardanelles to the ships and commerce of all nations.
13. An independent Poland to be established, with free and secure access to the sea.
14. A general association of nations to be formed to guarantee to its members political independence and territorial integrity.

This last, the genesis of the League of Nations, would be vigorously resisted by Congress during the Versailles peace conference. It was in large part the idea of 'Colonel' (the Southern states' honorific for a man of certain standing) Edward House, who had been Wilson's envoy extraordinaire since before the war, and hugely influential on his thinking – so much so that Republican (and some Democrat) detractors called Wilson 'the Jack that House built'.

into propaganda to subvert the various nationalities in the army opposite him) had defeated the Austrians' summer offensive on the Piave – dubbed by the Austrians, so critically short were they of equipment and even food, the 'bread offensive'. Now, with French, British and American help, Diaz was about to launch what would prove a knockout blow – and to launch it with exquisite theatrical timing, calculated to lift his own men and further depress the Austrians, on 24 October, the anniversary of Caporetto (the Anglo-Italian 10th Army, under the earl of Cavan, carrying out a particularly resourceful river crossing to gain surprise).

Even the apparently dormant Salonika (Macedonia) front had come to life. Indeed, it was the sudden collapse of the Bulgarian army at the end of September that had precipitated Ludendorff's breakdown. Up to that point German morale had been like cast iron – immensely strong under even pressure. When struck a sharp blow, however, cast iron can fracture, indeed shatter; and even Ludendorff's morale was not proof against the blows now raining down.

Though he had managed the Balkans reasonably well hitherto, the allies had been gaining strength there, having more than made up for the loss of the token Russian force in Macedonia after March 1918 by the acquisition of the Greek army, nine divisions, which had finally been strong-armed into the allied camp in June 1917. The manpower ratio on this southernmost front was now about three to two in the allies' favour (720,000 Serbian, French, British, Greek and Italian to 575,000 Bulgarian, German, Austrian and Turk), but two to one in artillery and ten to one in aircraft. After Amiens, with the Ottoman Empire also nearing exhaustion and the Austro-Hungarian government in chaos, the Bulgarians saw the writing on their wall and were preparing to quit Macedonia – even before General Franchet d'Espèrey, commanding the 'Allied Armies of the East', launched his two-pronged offensive in the middle of September. And so, although a breakthrough was achieved by the Franco-Serbian force at Dobro Pole, allowing the allies to surge north, the Bulgarian army managed an orderly enough retreat, though badly mauled by allied aircraft in the Kosturino and Kresna passes. Skopje, the capital of Macedonia, was retaken by the end of the month, but already Bulgarian mutineers had reached Sofia and with the Agrarian National Union proclaimed a republic. A delegation arrived in Salonika to ask for an armistice, which Franchet d'Espèrey conceded on 29 September. Now it was just the Austrians and the Turks.

The British Army of Salonika, under the shrewd Aberdonian Lieutenant-General Sir George Milne, at once struck east towards Constantinople, while the French and Serbs continued north. As there was nothing to stop Milne entering the capital, what remained of the Ottoman government (Enver Pasha and his cohort having fled for Berlin) also asked for terms.

It was at this point, with Austria's southern flank now wide open, making Diaz's job just that bit easier – and Foch's, for a new route into Germany, through Bavaria or even Bohemia, now beckoned – that Ludendorff collapsed (some accounts have him falling to the floor, foaming at the mouth). He told the Kaiser that the Bulgarian armistice had 'fundamentally changed the situation in view of the attacks being carried out on the Western Front', for to shore them up as they began to reel he had had to send east divisions that could otherwise have been kept for France – and all to no avail.*

Prince Maximilian of Baden had arrived in Berlin not a moment too soon.

His first instinct as the new chancellor, however, was to ask for time to take stock – 'even just four days' – arguing that to seek an armistice was to make any peace initiative impossible. But with Ludendorff in despair – 'I want to save my army' – Hindenburg, by now in effect the Kaiser, insisted on an immediate appeal for an

* Franchet d'Espèrey believed that with an army of 200,000 he could cross Austria and Hungary, mass in Bohemia covered by the Czechs and march immediately on Dresden. Instead his orders were to enter Romania to open up communications with Russia. By 1 November he had reached the Danube and the Serbs had retrieved their capital, Belgrade. The whole of the Central Powers' southern front had been brilliantly taken apart at the seams.

armistice. Nevertheless Baden's confirmation as chancellor (and minister president of Prussia) was delayed until 3 October, and the request for an armistice did not go out until the following day.

'Here,' said Foch, handing Haig the Paris newspaper on the sixth: 'here is the immediate result of the British piercing the Hindenburg Line. The Enemy has asked for an armistice.'

It was of course the sort of thing a generalissimo would say to the commander-in-chief of one of his armies who had pulled off a considerable tactical success which had quite evidently had its effect on the German capacity and will to continue fighting on the Western Front. Beyond that, the fall of the dominoes could not reasonably be ascribed to the 46th Division's magnificent effort at Bellenglise. And besides, having at last broken through the 'mud and blood to the green fields beyond' (as the Tank Corps' brown, red and green tricolour is said to represent), the BEF was unable to maintain the initial pressure, not least because, having for so long been geared to serving a static front, or a recoiling one, its logistics were far from agile. Certainly there was not the cavalry thrust deep into the rear areas that Haig had imagined the end days would see. In fact the German fighting line was still holding, in a sort of self-defence fashion – at least enough to check the ardour of troops who could at last scent victory and wanted to live to savour it.

Ludendorff's reaction to the Bulgarian armistice was excessive – he had not diverted *that* many troops – but it didn't matter. Defeat is ultimately in the mind of the commander – a rational one at least; and although Ludendorff's mind was knocked fatally off balance, he was essentially a rational commander.* When he learned that in fact the allies' progress on the Western Front was slowing, and the resistance of his own troops stiffening, he recovered a little. The damage had been done, however, and he continued to press for an armistice, if now with the purpose of resting his troops

* Compare with the situation in May 1945, when Hitler and his leading Nazis acted fanatically rather than rationally in not conceding or even perhaps recognizing defeat. Wars rarely end in such a way as the Second World War, with fighting on the very steps of the leader's headquarters.

so that they could withdraw in good order to shorter defensive lines on the frontiers.

Indeed, by 17 October so improved were the reports from the front that he felt able to withdraw to more secure positions without the need of an 'armistice pause'.

Berlin's strategy was now to try to separate President Wilson from the other allied leaders, to negotiate on the basis of his apparently more conciliatory stance rather than submit to what would be the Entente's far tougher terms. Wilson was not going to fall for that, however: the German army was to be eviscerated, allowing no possibility of revanchism. Ludendorff resigned on 26 October, to be replaced by Wilhelm Groener, an out-and-out *Grosser Generalstab* man who would have an insidious influence on the post-war mythology of the Schlieffen Plan.

But now came 'the stab in the back' – a phrase Ludendorff would eagerly seize on after the war to explain the defeat of his army, of his own command. Not only were there workers' risings throughout Germany, the *Kaiserliche Marine* mutinied. The *Hochseeflotte* had not made any sortie in strength since April. This prolonged inactivity while the army and submarine service were heavily engaged had done much to undermine the ratings' morale and the self-respect of the officers. Local mutinies had already resulted in executions when the naval command conceived a truly Wagnerian solution – *Tod Reit* (death ride), a desperate sortie by the entire fleet (eighteen battleships, five battle-cruisers and supporting craft) with the aim of bringing every one of the Royal Navy's ships to battle. The *Hochseeflotte* assembled in Schillig Roads (Wilhelmshaven) on 29 October to sail the following day. That evening, however, discipline dissolved when the crews became convinced they were to be sacrificed to sabotage the armistice negotiations. Admiral Hipper, who had succeeded Scheer in command in August, cancelled the operation next day and ordered the fleet to disperse in the hope of quietening things down. When the 3rd Battle Squadron returned to Kiel, however, their crews helped spark the definitive mutiny of 3 November, which in turn spurred a more widespread upheaval, and a general strike in Berlin. A Soviet Germany looked imminent.

On 9 November Groener told the Kaiser, who had bolted to army headquarters in the Belgian town of Spa: 'The army will march home in peace and order under its leaders and commanding generals, but not under the command of Your Majesty, for it no longer stands behind Your Majesty.'

The Kaiser prevaricated until learning that in Berlin Max von Baden had proclaimed a socialist republic. He abdicated, and, ever vain and frivolous, fled to Holland with a train full of his best furniture.

The leaders of the new republic at once sought an armistice.

It was signed officially at five o'clock (in fact at twenty past) on a dark morning two days later in a railway carriage at Compiègne, the ceasefire to be effective six hours later – the eleventh hour of the eleventh day of the eleventh month.

The order reached Captain Harry Truman at about ten-thirty on the eleventh. He sent at once for his battery sergeant, 'Squatty' Meisburger, who found the future president of the United States of America 'stretched out on the ground eating a blueberry pie. Where he got the blueberry pie I don't know . . . His face was all smeared with blueberries. He handed me a piece of flimsy and said between bites, "Sergeant, you will take this back and read it to the members of the battery."'*

Truman was acting like a true professional: bad news is delivered from the top; good news is passed down the chain of command.

But there was half an hour to go, and they still had a lot of ammunition. In the next half-hour they fired as much of it as they could – 164 rounds.

At 11 a.m. precisely the 15th Hussars, a regiment that like many of the cavalry had hung on to its cherished traditions throughout the war, mustered its remaining trumpeters and sounded 'Cease Fire'. It was an extraordinary moment, for the ceremonial call (all

* Robert H. Ferrell, *Harry S. Truman: A Life* (London, 1994).

calls were ceremonial, for the trumpet had long ceased to be carried in the field) had not been heard for over four years. Moreover, the regiment was mustered not a dozen miles from where they had heard the first shots fired on 22 August 1914. During that time, Britain had mobilized in all some 5,397,000 men. Over a million and three-quarters of these – army, navy and latterly air force – had been wounded; and some 703,000 killed.*

* *The Longman Companion to the First World War* (Harlow, 2001). For fuller figures, and for other nations, see annex B.

Conclusions

Quoi qu'on fasse, on perd beaucoup de monde?

The cost of victory was indeed high – high enough in blood for Britain, but twice as high for France (the cost in treasure would be recovered in punitive reparations, the peace conference decided). How could it be otherwise with so many men under arms and for so long? But need it have been *so* high?

Churchill, not an impartial witness but an experienced one nevertheless (indeed, perhaps without equal in that respect), put it thus: 'No war is so sanguinary as the war of exhaustion. No plan could be more unpromising than the plan of frontal attack. Yet on these two brutal expedients the military authorities of France and Britain consumed, during three successive years, the flower of their national manhood.'*

In war a nation is fighting for peace – at best an advantageous peace, at worst a peace that will avoid the further disadvantages brought on by a continuation of the fighting. The notion is ancient:

* Churchill, *The World Crisis*. France's 'demographic time bomb' – shortage of manpower – would in the 1930s lead her to pour all her effort into building the Maginot Line, the defences on her border with Germany (now much further east as a result of the peace treaty signed at Versailles in 1919); possibly the vainest attempt in history to rely on fortifications alone.

'Or what king, going to make war against another king, sitteth not down first, and consulteth whether he be able with ten thousand to meet him that cometh against him with twenty thousand? Or else, while the other is yet a great way off, he sendeth an ambassage, and desireth conditions of peace.'*

War – *rational* war – is only continued while peace is seen to be a worse alternative.

But the question 'Was peace a worse alternative?' is not the subject of this book. Lord Lansdowne's rhetorical demand in 1916 – what is the sense of a war of survival when, in fighting, the nation's strength does not survive? – is perhaps for another time. Britain's war, as 'Wully' Robertson had conceded to Sir Edward Grey that year, had indeed got off to a very bad start: 'Our military preparations were out of step with our diplomacy . . . the pre-war policy, which *I* think we could not have avoided, practically committed us to assist France in defeating Germany, but the bulk of our officers held the opinion that our military preparations were inadequate to carry out that policy.'

Not so, unfortunately, Henry Wilson, the then director of military operations. Under his direction (if not ultimate responsibility) the War Office had made plans for the BEF that proved strategically, operationally and tactically inflexible, and led to its destruction.† Churchill's alternative strategy, which he advocated at the meeting of the Committee of Imperial Defence in August 1911, had been infinitely more percipient, but was imperiously dismissed by Wilson and the CIGS. It would not be the last time that professional opinion expressed with unwarranted certainty and the authority of high rank would trump Churchill's surer strategic instinct. But if the quality of the staff in the War Office before August 1914 remains arguable – Wilson, for one, has his

* Luke 14: 31–2.

† It is sometimes suggested that Wilson's influence is exaggerated, because for most of his time as DMO he was a brigadier-general and could not have carried that much clout with the CIGS, three or four ranks higher. But this is fundamentally to misunderstand how the General Staff system worked (and works).

supporters – after August it was positively and demonstrably weak. Between then and the end of 1915 there was no staff 'brain' to speak of, no body of practised staff officers to help formulate and disseminate policy, transmit orders and oversee their execution – leaving Kitchener to blunder like a bull (if a brave and noble one) among china. And then Robertson, for all his robust good sense, would come to the post of CIGS as, in effect, the BEF's – Haig's – man in London, and, despite his opinion that 'no war was ever so peculiar as the present one',* perpetuate the blinkered focus on the Western Front, continuing to regard all other theatres as sideshows.

When it came to strategy, too often the centre of gravity was GHQ, not the War Office.

It wasn't as if the talent had been lacking. If Haig, an experienced and respected staff officer, had been made CIGS in August 1914 instead of going to France (there were several others who could have commanded I Corps at least as well, and probably better), he might have brought order and good sense to Kitchener's sound but unruly instincts. Haig was not 'clever' in the Robertson (astute) or Hamilton (intellectual) sense, but he was militarily educated and experienced. Likewise, Robertson himself would have brought the same disciplined staffwork to the directorate of military operations and intelligence, and while he would have been a considerable loss to the BEF as its QMG, again there were others who could have done the job. Released from the 'bubble' of GHQ, both men might have seen the larger picture in time to prevent the worst mistakes. There might, indeed, have been a good deal more trust between the 'frocks' and the 'brass hats'. There might even have been a proper understanding of the intricate interdependency of the various fronts, as vividly demonstrated by the closing months of the war. How else indeed could it have been that Ludendorff threw in the towel on hearing that the Bulgarians had collapsed?

* Robertson to Rawlinson, 26 July 1916, in *Military Correspondence of Field Marshal Sir William Robertson*.

The fundamental assumption of the 'Westerners', that the war could only be won when the German army was defeated, was correct. But the immediate deduction that the German army could only be defeated on the Western Front, because after 1917 it was the only front on which there were Germans in large numbers, led to a whole series of further faulty deductions – and to Clemenceau's 'series of catastrophes'. Before the improvements in artillery types and techniques, the introduction of the tank, the mastery of the air, the improvements in the operational staff at corps and divisional level, the better organization and tactics of the infantry battalion – advances which came very largely from the bottom up, and in many cases from men who had never before worn uniform – there had simply not been the wherewithal to break the German line, let alone exploit a breakthrough. And these developments did not reach their synergistic best – in both the British and French armies – until 1918. Not until 1919 would there have been enough light tanks – Whippets – to maintain decisive momentum beyond the line, the breakthrough that GHQ and *GQG* continually sought. Yet very probably the allied high command would have launched another huge offensive in 1918 along the same lines as before; and, notwithstanding their manpower problems, the Germans might well have been able to defeat it along the same lines as before. They had proved very adept at adjusting their defensive tactics. As Marx might have said, military history repeats itself; first as tragedy, then as farce.

Only when, in the *Kaiserschlacht* offensive, the German army obligingly abandoned their strong defences – because the Royal Navy's blockade was rapidly destroying Germany's very cohesion, and because by the end of the year American troops would give the allies overwhelming superiority – did the Entente have the opportunity to mount successful offensives.

The conditions had changed, and the military strategy of the previous years was now at last appropriate; had the conditions *not* changed, there would have been scant prospect of victory on the Western Front in 1918.

Did this matter? For in the end came victory.

'Never at any time in history has the British Army achieved greater results in attack than in this unbroken offensive,' wrote Foch to Haig after the war. 'The victory was indeed complete, thanks to the Commanders of the Armies, Corps and Divisions and above all to the unselfishness, to the wise, loyal and energetic policy of their Commander-in-Chief, who made easy a great combination and sanctioned a prolonged gigantic effort.'*

It matters when it comes to the assessment of generalship and the question: 'Need the victory have been so costly?' When Churchill wrote that 'battles are won by slaughter and manoeuvre. The greater the general, the more he contributes in manoeuvre, the less he demands in slaughter,' he drew the inescapable conclusion that 'it was because military leaders were credited with gifts of this order which enable them to ensure victory and save slaughter that their profession is held in such high honour. For if their art were nothing more than a dreary process of exchanging lives, and counting heads at the end, they would rank much lower in the scale of human esteem.'† In his *Great Contemporaries* (1935), Churchill paid tribute to Haig's personal qualities, noting that 'he was always incapable of falling below his own standards' (though the sentence which preceded this ran: 'He was rarely capable of rising to great heights). But his judgement of Haig's approach to command was melancholy:

> He [Haig] presents to me in those red years the same mental picture as a great surgeon before the days of anaesthetics, versed in every detail of such science as was known to him: sure of himself, steady of poise, knife in hand, intent upon the operation; entirely removed in his professional capacity from the agony of the patient . . . He would operate

* This was no empty praise: in the final 'Hundred Days' the BEF engaged and defeated 99 of the 197 German divisions on the Western Front, taking nearly two hundred thousand prisoners – almost 50% of the total taken by all the allied armies in France in this period.

† *The World Crisis.*

without excitement; and if the patient died, he would not reproach himself.*

Fifty years on, reflecting on the war, Charles Carrington thought the same, but concluded that in the end there was no arguing with victory:

> Perhaps his cold logistic theory of command needed the corrective that was applied in the next war, by such flamboyant generals as Patton and Montgomery. So confident was Haig, so assured of his professional mastery, that his mind, once made up, moved slowly. He lacked that brilliant, imaginative coup d'oeil which distinguishes genius from mere talent, and the plain fact that he was no Napoleon obscures what should be equally plain, that his tactics, appalling as they seem, won the war. In the dreadful campaigns of attrition, Haig at last achieved his object, whereas the German generals, who planned similar battles, could never reach a decisive victory, even when they had all the material advantages. Battles are won by margins, and there was a marginal quantum lacking in the German high command. Haig's superiority was the moral factor which always prevails in war.†

Except in the sense of *talent*, therefore, British generalship in the First World War – *allied* generalship indeed – does not (*should* not) rank highly in the scale of military esteem, to say the least. But the school of history epitomized by Alan Clark's *The Donkeys,* which asserts that the generals shared the mental capacity of that animal and (or) were callously indifferent to casualties, is facile.‡ Rawlinson's

* The fact that at Haig's funeral in February 1928, as *The Times* reported, 'Great crowds lined the streets . . . come to do honour to the chief who had sent thousands to the last sacrifice when duty called for it,' was not evidence – as *The Times* went on to assert – that 'his war-worn soldiers loved [him] as their truest advocate and friend'; nor, as others have claimed, that they regarded his conduct of the war with approval – except that he had endured, as they had, and victory had ultimately been theirs. 'We are still an initiate generation, possessing a secret that can never be communicated.' Loyalty trumps all.

† Carrington, 'Some Soldiers'.

‡ *The Donkeys* (London, 1961) is a much discredited book. Even the quote on the frontispiece ('Lions led by Donkeys'), from which the title is derived, Clark

planning for the Somme was such that Haig would (*should*) have relieved him of command were it not that to do so would have been to expose his own deficiency and acknowledge the battle a failure, at a time when Lloyd George had him in his sights. Yet it was Rawlinson who gained the victory at Amiens twenty months later, 'the black day of the German army'. And it was Haig's presiding command of the BEF as a whole that enabled that victory and what followed. Allenby, whom Haig *did* remove from command – of 3rd Army in May 1917 – subsequently outmanoeuvred the Turks in Palestine and by Christmas that year had captured Jerusalem.

'The greater the general, the more he contributes in manoeuvre, the less he demands in slaughter.' By that measure, Haig sacked a far greater general than himself.

Time and circumstance.

Whatever the individual failings – and Churchill's opinion of Haig is not unfair – there was clearly also a systemic problem. To begin with, the absolute belief in the offensive under any conditions – the British, as well as French, doctrine of 1915, 1916 and 1917 – derived from the settled principles of operations inculcated in all military officers: 'Decisive success in battle can be gained only by a vigorous offensive' (*Field Service Regulations*). But even Robertson, as early as the first weeks of the Somme, was beginning to have doubts about pre-war conceptions, writing to Rawlinson: 'Field Service Regulations will require a tremendous amount of revising when we have finished with the Boche.'

In fact they would need tremendous revision *before* they could finish with the Boche, though it would never be done. 'Principles, as we used to call them,' Robertson went on, 'are good and cannot be

---

admitted to making up – as, indeed, he did his military credentials, claiming to have 'served in the Household Cavalry', whereas he had joined the training regiment at Windsor in February 1946 while in his final year at Eton, leaving at the end of the summer half (term). *The Donkeys* inspired the Charles Chilton radio play of the same year entitled *The Long Long Trail*, which was then put on the stage by Joan Littlewood and her Theatre Workshop in 1963, and on celluloid by Richard Attenborough in 1969, as *Oh! What A Lovely War* – and, of course, the (hilarious) inanity of Richard Curtis's and Ben Elton's TV series *Blackadder Goes Forth* (1989).

disregarded, but their application is a very difficult business, and I think *we take these principles too literally* [emphasis added].'

It is not surprising that men immersed in the day-to-day uncertainty of battle with the toughest of enemies should cling to principles. That there was no organization removed from the day-to-day uncertainty that could think about the war from *first* principles – no presiding staff brain at the War Office – is as much to blame for the 'series of catastrophes' as any asinine tendency in the BEF. Instead it was always the promise of 'just one more push . . .' Indeed, on 6 July 1916, just three weeks before his letter to Rawlinson – and six days into the Somme – Robertson had written to Haig: 'We have these Germans this time for a certainty *if* we *take* the chances now offered.'*

As General Sir Ian Hamilton wrote, the BEF saw the Western Front as 'mobile operations at the halt' rather than as a variant of siege warfare.

But why did the BEF's high command cling to its 'principles' so tenaciously?

'Quoi qu'on fasse, on perd beaucoup de monde,' General Charles Mangin had said after Verdun (the Gallic shrug almost palpable): 'Whatever you do, you lose a lot of men.' It sounds so much better in French. This acceptance of casualties was a new feature of war for the professional British army, which had hitherto in colonial engagements counted its dead in hundreds. At Paardeberg, one of the major and decisive battles of the Boer War, its casualties had been 350 killed and 1,250 wounded or captured – high numbers for a country which had thought of its army in terms of an imperial police force. And in the early months of the war the French called British squeamishness over casualties 'Veldtitis'.

'Whatever you do, you lose a lot of men.' Haig himself might have said it.

And in effect he did – on the second day of the Somme, when he confided to his diary: 'The AG [adjutant-general] reported today

* *Military Correspondence of Field Marshal Sir William Robertson* (emphasis in original).

that the total casualties are estimated at over 40,000 to date. This cannot be considered severe in view of the numbers engaged, and the length of front attacked.'

In fact of course the casualties were sixty thousand; and twenty thousand of them were dead. But Haig's rationalizing would have been better rendered: '. . . in view of the numbers engaged, and the length of front attacked *by an almost parade-ground advance on the false assumption that the wire was cut and the artillery had done its job of neutralizing the defenders*'.

The mind can become numb to casualties – or else so averse to taking them as to inhibit offensive-mindedness. This is why in the Second World War Montgomery avoided visiting field hospitals – while, on the other hand, General George C. Marshall, chief of staff of the US Army, who had served with the US 1st Division in France from 1917, would daily send President Roosevelt the casualty returns to remind him of the price of war. But brigade and divisional commanders in the BEF (as, *a fortiori*, in the French army) judged too reluctant to press an attack were soon removed. Captain David Kelly, later Sir David Kelly and from 1949 to 1951 ambassador to Moscow, who had come down from Oxford with a first and joined the Leicestershire Regiment when war began, observed the effects closely. After serving with his battalion for six months he was made intelligence officer for the 110th (Leicestershire) Brigade, a newly established post for scouting and liaison to keep the brigadiers in the picture, not least about the situation of their own troops in the attack. He became indispensable to a series of brigade commanders, remaining in post throughout the war and awarded the MC. His sustained experience at the sharp end, as well as the immediacy of his journal of the 110th Brigade and the considered reflections of his later diplomatic memoir, give his opinion considerable authority: and it was his view that unrealistic orders emanated from the remote higher levels 'which the Brigadiers, naturally anxious about their own professional careers, were reluctant to challenge'.*

* Kelly's account of his *39 Months with the 'Tigers'* was written in the spring of 1919

Liddell Hart had said it: 'Their careers riveted their chains.'* Indeed, by this time the brigade had become so relatively small a cog in the vast machine of the BEF that it must have seemed to many a brigadier that his job was simply to add a few details of his own to the orders from head office. And the same could have been said of many of the divisional commanders.

But is the gibe of 'chateaux generals', levelled at the occupants of those higher headquarters – the corps and armies – fair? Command at the level of the army, five of them in all on the Western Front, tended to be static, with corps attached and detached depending on the 'operational tempo'. There were several requirements of headquarters of this size which drew them to the larger houses – 'chateaux', as they were known, no matter how small: electric light, telephone lines, stables, garages, kitchens, office space, and accommodation (hut and tentage space) for many hundreds of all ranks. A headquarters had to be at such a distance from the front that it could not be routinely shelled. It had to be 'triangulated' in such a way that the commander and his staff officers could reach their subordinate headquarters by car, and despatch riders by motorcycle; and although it was the job of army headquarters to site themselves optimally for their own subordinate headquarters, some note had to be taken of the length of front that GHQ had to cover. All this tended to pull army and corps headquarters to the rear (the Germans no less).

Did this mean that the most senior British officers and their staff became more fixed on their maps than on the actual ground? There are plenty of instances of corps and army commanders getting forward during planning, sometimes even in aircraft, as well as during offensives (as witness Haig's tactical headquarters during the 'Hundred Days'); but without radio, and with wire invariably

---

and revised – 'a very few retouches' – for publication in 1930. His later memoir *The Ruling Few* (London, 1952) repeats the assertion. (In 1940, as minister at the legation in Berne, Kelly received peace overtures from Berlin, a scene memorably portrayed in the 1969 film *The Battle of Britain* with Sir Ralph Richardson as minister.)

* *World War I in Outline.*

cut by artillery or misfortune, getting forward during an offensive could severely limit a commander's perspective. The best position of a commander in battle is that position from which he can best exercise command. That said, when communications failed, there was little alternative *but* to get forward, and some commanders were undoubtedly uncomfortable doing this – not for want of courage but because it was alien to the methods so far established. The failure to develop tactical radio was the single greatest technical omission of the war.

The debate over chateaux generalship will continue. However, once again Kelly's judgement, not untypical of officers of his experience, was unequivocal:

> They tended to lead a secluded and relatively luxurious life far behind the firing line where, immersed in office work, they had no time for personal contact with the front line troops. The result was a lack of realism and excessive optimism . . . Nothing else could explain this delusion about the 'War of Attrition' and the bull-headed persistence in counting territorial gains of a thousand yards as worth any sacrifice in lives.*

The particular danger in a commander's becoming chateau-bound, for all the good reasons of headquarters paraphernalia, is that he becomes reliant more and more on his immediate staff when forming his opinions. Haig was as keen to take the optimistic views of the situation presented to him by his head of intelligence, Charteris, and his chief of staff, Kiggell, as they were to give him news to fortify him. During planning for the Cambrai raid, for example, Lieutenant James Marshall-Cornwall, an Intelligence Corps officer at GHQ, discovered from captured documents that

* Kelly, *The Ruling Few*. There were some notable but generally unpublicized dissents by senior officers that did *not* result in dismissal. In November 1916 the earl of Cavan, commanding XIV Corps on the Somme, refused to renew the attack. 'No one who has not visited the trenches can really know the state of exhaustion to which the men are reduced,' he said, in a clear swipe at GHQ and 4th Army headquarters.

three German divisions from the Russian front had arrived to strengthen the Cambrai sector. Charteris told him: 'This is a bluff put up by the Germans to deceive us. I am sure the units are still on the Russian front . . . If the commander in chief were to think that the Germans had reinforced this sector, it might shake his confidence in our success.'*

Fine chance of that. With an admixture of suspicion for Catholicism, the commander-in-chief's selective reading of intelligence assessments could be positively Elizabethan. On 15 October 1917, as the BEF had floundered in the mud of Passchendaele, Haig wondered in his diary 'why the War Office Intelligence Department gives such a wrong [i.e. gloomy] picture of the situation except that General Macdonogh (DMI) is a Roman Catholic and is (unconsciously) influenced by information which doubtless reaches him from tainted (i.e. Catholic) sources'. It is astonishing that Haig could have thought such a casual speculation on the subconscious (or worse) of the director of military intelligence worthy of the page – and its later publication.†

The fact was that the offensives of 1916 and 1917 were too ambiguous in their objectives, impossibly ambitious in their scope,

* General Sir James Marshall-Cornwall, *Wars and Rumours of Wars* (London, 1984). Captain, later Major Sir, Desmond Morton was one of Haig's ADCs in 1917–18, and after the war a member of the Secret Intelligence Service and one of Churchill's sources during 'the wilderness years'. Haig, said Morton, 'hated being told any new information, however irrefutable, which militated against his preconceived ideas or beliefs. Hence his support for the desperate John Charteris, who was incredibly bad as head of GHQ intelligence, who always concealed bad news, or put it in an agreeable light': Gill Bennett, *Churchill's Man of Mystery: Desmond Morton and the World of Intelligence* (London, 2007).

† Brigadier-General George Macdonogh, who until August 1914 had been head of the War Office intelligence division concerned with internal security (one of the forebears of MI5), and thereafter the BEF's chief of intelligence, had been recalled to London as DMI in December 1915. Macdonogh was brilliant. He and a fellow sapper – James Edmonds, who would become the official historian of the war – had gained such high marks in the staff college entrance exam in 1896 that the results, it was said, were adjusted to conceal the margin between them and their classmates (who included Robertson and Allenby). Jesuit-educated (like, incidentally, the first VC of the war), he was deeply mistrusted by Haig and others, and although he turned the intelligence directorate into a first-rate organization, his assessments were never entirely accepted by GHQ.

and with one or two exceptions woefully badly planned. They were products of the thinking in big – not necessarily grand, but big – houses well behind the lines. The story is unsubstantiated but widely told of Kiggell's breaking down in tears when finally he visited Passchendaele in the autumn of 1917 and saw the morass in which the army had laboured: 'Good God, did we really send men to fight in that?'

His driver is meant to have said: 'It gets worse further up.'

Haig's defenders dispute the story, but in doing so they actually paint a bleaker picture: it was surely worse for senior commanders and staff to have known of the conditions and yet to have kept sending men into a literal quagmire – one in which the Germans, in Churchill's memorable phrase, 'sold every inch of ground with extortion'.

Frontal attacks: 'Quoi qu'on fasse, on perd beaucoup de monde.'

Perhaps; but all the evidence and the logic of war suggested that mounting frontal attacks with nothing but artillery and the bayonet was the certain way to lose not just 'a lot' but the *most. Field Service Regulations* had always said as much: 'If the situation be unfavourable for such a course [a vigorous offensive], it is wiser, when possible, to manoeuvre for a more suitable opportunity.'

And 'manoeuvre' did not have to be solely a literal question of physical movement, as Diaz showed in the summer of 1918 with his psychological offensive against the Austro-Hungarian army exploiting its polyglot fault-lines. Nor was 'strategic defence' until the moral and material conditions changed favourably the same as 'passivity'; and nor did it necessarily mean the loss of offensive spirit. For the most part, the British army that triumphed in Normandy in 1944 had not seen a German since 1940; they had *trained* for the offensive, however, rather than making attack after attack at great cost in learning how *not* to do things.

When Churchill wrote of 'frontal attack' he meant more than its tactical apogee at the Somme (or, indeed, Third Ypres). The insistence that the Western Front was the only place the German army could be defeated, and by immediate offensive, and therefore that every resource of manpower and materiel should be sent there at the expense of any other European theatre – the Dardanelles, Italy, the Balkans – represented the *strategy* of frontal attack.* The alternative that Churchill advocated in 1915, the Dardanelles campaign, failed because the resources were not provided; the strategy was agreed by the war council, but then schemed against in the corridors of the Admiralty, the War Office and GHQ until it had no hope of success. The strategic cost was enormous – Romania hesitating, Bulgaria throwing in with the Central Powers, Russia collapsing (recall the duke of Marlborough's nostrum that in coalition warfare the first object is to keep the coalition together). And all so that the Western Front could have more men and guns for an offensive which led precisely nowhere but to a great many graves – and at a time when in the assessment of both GHQ and *GQG* the Germans themselves had no chance of breaking through. In other words, the Western Front could have stood on the strategic defensive throughout 1915 to no disadvantage whatever.

Asquith's direction of strategic policy was fatally weak both before and during the war. He failed to develop the full potential of the CID and treated strategy as just another cabinet agenda item. The lack of cohesive strategic thinking – through cabinet, the various ministries, and GHQ in particular – meant that policy and operations were never in real harmony; certainly not where the allocation of resources was concerned. In the early years of the war, French superiority in the field meant that Paris (or rather, Joffre's headquarters at Chantilly) dominated operational thinking on the Western Front, and in turn strategy generally. Joffre's 'Miracle on the Marne' – ostensibly saving Paris when the government had fled for Bordeaux – gave him leave to dictate terms to his own political masters and to London. In the relief that Paris had been saved, his earlier poor judgement, which had allowed the Germans to gain

* '*The general strategy of the war.* We agreed that the war was only to be won by defeating the Germans. This could not be done in the Balkans but only in France. So all possible means should be sent to France, and the Enemy should be pressed continuously': Haig's minute of discussion with Robertson, 22 October 1916.

strategic surprise in their great offensive through Belgium, was overlooked. Paradoxically, as successive French governments fell, paying the price for a string of military failures, Joffre became ever more secure, the very symbol of imperturbability – indeed, immovability. France had five prime ministers during the course of the war; continuity of strategic thinking therefore rested with the *militaires*, who in seeking the answer to General Fayolle's 'How the devil can we finish this war?' proved the least willing to think beyond the notion of 'the decisive offensive'. True inter-allied coordination of strategy at prime ministerial level came only at the very end. Asquith had surrendered Britain's voice in strategy too easily. If he had played to Britain's potential – the Royal Navy, and the ability from 1917 to field as many troops on the Western Front as the French – and persuaded Paris to take 'the long view', the debilitating offensives of the war's middle years could have been avoided. We could have *trained* the New Armies rather than destroying a good half of them.

So much for the higher direction of the war. Little wonder that when Lloyd George became prime minister at the end of 1916, with so poor an opinion both of his colleagues and of the generals and admirals, he should look elsewhere for a man in which to place his faith. And cruel fate it was that led his gaze to Nivelle, for when, disappointed, that gaze subsequently fell on Salonika and later Italy, his moral authority had been lethally damaged, so that he could neither persuade nor cajole. With Salonika and Italy he had been on to something, however; if only he had had the trusted staff to give form to his instincts, to bring ideas properly into action – as Churchill made sure he had in the Second World War with his chiefs of staff committee. 'With all his faults,' wrote Maurice Hankey to Robertson in November, 'Ll.G. does get things done – munitions, compulsory service &c. I believe he is the only man who is likely to bring about the re-awakening of national enthusiasm and effort which is now so necessary.'*

Whatever and how many the reasons for the prolonged slaughter, and however facile the view that British generals were all

* *The Military Correspondence of Field Marshal Sir William Robertson.*

asinine and indifferent to casualties, nothing can acquit the high command of its failure to see beyond no-man's-land and its embrace of the 'strategy' of attrition.

And the statesmen who let them? In 1932, when at last the army undertook an investigation into the lessons to be learned from the war, the CIGS, Field Marshal Sir George Milne, who had commanded a division in France, and the army in Salonika, gave his opinion simply: 'I cannot help feeling that we must never allow it [the conduct of operations] to degenerate into what happened in the years 1915, 1916 and 1917.'*

It is a damning indictment of pre-war thinking and of his wartime superiors alike. And it is the *repetition* of those years – 1915, then 1916, and then the same again in 1917 – that is central to the indictment. Who knows? Had the Germans not miscalculated and left their secure defences, perhaps 1918 would have been added to the list. The generals were curiously unwilling to think strategically, to look beyond tomorrow and the Western Front. Nor, in the war's early and middle years, with a few notable exceptions, were they tactically or technologically very alert. Until 1918 the operational record was the very opposite of Churchill's 'proper application of overwhelming force'. Rather, it reflected the improper application of inadequate force – inadequate technologically, materially and numerically.

In *Les Misérables* (1862), Victor Hugo wrote: 'What is truly admirable in the Battle of Waterloo is England, English firmness, English resolution, English blood. The superb thing which England had there – may it not displease her – is herself; it is not her captain, it is her army.'

This was a tendentious swipe at Wellington, but a worthy tribute to British arms. Had Victor Hugo lived, he would surely have written the same – and more – of the First World War.

What the British army learned from the war is another subject.

* CIGS to Director, Staff Duties, 6 January 1932, PRO WO 32/3155.

A great part of it learned very little – witness Haig's final despatch, an apologia for attrition and a lament that the Armistice came before the cavalry could prove themselves. For many of those not necessarily convinced of the merits of attrition, learning from the war was academic: in their eyes the war, the Western Front in particular, was an aberration, Milne's 'degeneration' that must never be allowed to happen again – largely because there must be no continental war again.*

In fairness, the same could be said of the US Army. They would largely disband their tank forces and return to the old frontier mentality, which might extend into the Pacific but would certainly not see a return to the Old World. Had the war gone into 1919, victory would probably have come via a massive American thrust into Alsace-Lorraine and onward across the Rhine. How then might the textbooks of modern war, and history, have been rewritten?†

The French, on the other hand, would put their money into the

* In his final despatch, Haig explained 'Why We Attacked Whenever Possible': 'It is a view often expressed that the attack is more expensive than defence. This is only a half statement of the truth. Unquestionably, unsuccessful attack is generally more expensive than defence, particularly if the attack is pressed home with courage and resolution. On the other hand, attack so pressed home, if skilfully conducted, is rarely unsuccessful, whereas, in its later stages especially, unsuccessful defence is far more costly than attack.'

This is not in dispute, but one wonders which were the successful attacks that Haig had in mind, and what were his criteria for success. If the offensives of 1916 and 1917 are to be taken as 'successful' (they were certainly not on the whole very skilfully conducted), then it is a case of 'the operation was successful, but unfortunately the patient died'. For a fuller extract from the despatch, see annex C.

† Some in the BEF were contemplating what it needed to do differently to break the deadlock. Colonel J. F. C. ('Boney') Fuller of the Tank Corps wrote an influential paper advocating mechanized air–land operations to paralyse the German command structure (referred to as 'Plan 1919'): 'Our present theory, based on our present weapons, weapons of limited range of action, has been one of attaining our strategical object by brute force; that is, the wearing away of the enemy's muscles, bone and blood. To accomplish this rapidly with tanks will demand many thousands of these machines, and there is little likelihood of our obtaining the requisite number by next year; therefore let us search for some other means, always remembering that probably, at no time in the history of war, has a difficulty arisen the solution of which has not at the time in question existed in some man's head, and frequently in those of several. The main difficulty has nearly always lurked, not in the solution itself, but in its acceptance by those who have vested interests in the existing methods': *Memoirs of an Unconventional Soldier* (London, 1938).

heavy guns of the Maginot Line, while the Germans would seek (with eventual success in 1940) to make Schlieffen's concept of an unexpected outflanking movement workable by investing in fast-moving armoured troops supported by ground-attack aircraft.

Crucially, the man who would become Britain's war leader at her darkest hour, May 1940, had seen at first hand between 1911 and 1918 the failure that came from the lack of strategic clarity and grip. And from the outset of his premiership Churchill would be determined that there should be no repeat of that failure.

It is frequently asserted that Churchill's 'mistakes' in the First World War, in particular the Dardanelles campaign, were his making – that he learned from them and changed his tune.

This is wrong. Churchill's strategic perception both before the war – notably in the 1911 memorandum on German intentions and their implications for the BEF – and in 1915, with his recognition of the stalemate in the west and the need to turn the distant flank, was sound and far-sighted. It was the frustration of his own strategic judgement – and even more so that of the war council over the Dardanelles – by professional naval and military officers that would steel him to the task of 1940 and the years that followed.

The war also shaped decisively the man on whom Churchill would come to rely in formulating strategy after 1940 – the CIGS, General Sir Alan Brooke (later Field Marshal Lord Alanbrooke).* And it very emphatically shaped the operational outlook of the man who did the most to implement that strategy in Normandy and north-west Europe, General Sir Bernard Montgomery (later Field Marshal Lord Montgomery of Alamein). Neither general was

---

Others, notably the chemical warfare staff, were also trying to develop technical solutions.

* Alanbrooke, also co-chairman of the Anglo-US Combined Chiefs of Staff Committee from 1942, described the art of military strategy as 'to derive from the [policy] aim a series of military objectives to be achieved: to assess these objectives as to the military requirements they create, and the pre-conditions which the achievement of each is likely to necessitate: to measure available and potential resources against the requirements and to chart from this process a coherent pattern of priorities and a rational course of action' (*War Diaries*).

given to doctrines – as in 1940 the Germans and the French still were; both preferred observing the hard facts of war. In *A History of Warfare* (1968), Montgomery was unremittingly critical of British generalship in 1914–18, explaining how his perceptions of its shortcomings contributed to the formation of his own views during those later years.

It was as well that Churchill and his generals had, like Wellington in Flanders, seen 'how not to do it'; for Foch's grim prophecy in 1919 after the Versailles conference – that the treaty (*treaties*) would deliver not a peace but a twenty-year armistice – was to prove preternaturally exact.

PEACE AND FUTURE CANNON FODDER

The Tiger: "Curious! I seem to hear a child weeping!"

Annex A

JUTLAND: THE RECKONING

SHIPS SUNK

	British	German
Battleships		*Pommern*
Battle-cruisers	*Indefatigable*	*Lützow*
	Invincible	
	Queen Mary	
Cruisers	*Black Prince*	
	Defence	
	Warrior	
Light cruisers		*Elbing*
		Frauenlob
		Rostock
		Wiesbaden
Destroyers	*Ardent*	*S 35*
	Fortune	*V 4*
	Nestor	*V 27*
	Nomad	*V 29*
	Shark	*V 48*
	Sparrowhawk	
	Tipperary	
	Turbulent	

BRITISH CASUALTIES

(Figures taken from *Official History*)

	Officers			Other ranks		
Ship	**Killed**	**Wounded**	**PoW**	**Killed**	**Wounded**	**PoW**
Battleships:						
Barham	4	1	–	22	36	–
Colossus	–	–	–	–	5	–
Malaya	2	–	–	61	33	–
Marlborough	–	–	–	2	–	–
Valiant	–	–	–	–	1	–
Warspite	1	3	–	13	13	–
Battle-cruisers:						
Indefatigable (sunk)	57	–	–	960	–	2
Invincible (sunk)	61	–	–	965	–	–
Lion	6	1	–	93	43	–
Princess Royal	–	1	–	22	77	–
Queen Mary (sunk)	57	2	1	1,209	5	1
Tiger	2	–	–	22	37	–
Cruisers:						
Black Prince (sunk)	37	–	–	820	–	–
Defence (sunk)	54	–	–	849	–	–
Warrior (sunk)*	1	2	–	70	25	–
Light cruisers:						
Calliope	–	2	–	10	7	–
Castor	–	1	–	13	22	–

* Casualties sustained prior to loss of ship.

Ship	Officers Killed	Officers Wounded	Officers PoW	Other ranks Killed	Other ranks Wounded	Other ranks PoW
Chester	2	3	–	33	39	–
Dublin	1	–	–	2	24	–
Southampton	–	1	–	35	40	–
Flotilla leaders:						
Broke	1	3	–	46	33	–
Tipperary (sunk)	11	–	–	174	2	8
Destroyers:						
Acasta	1	–	–	5	1	–
Ardent (sunk)	4	1	–	74	1	–
Defender	–	–	–	1	2	–
Fortune (sunk)	4	–	–	63	1	–
Moorsom	–	–	–	–	1	–
Nessus	2	–	–	5	7	–
Nestor (sunk)	2	–	5	4	–	75
Nomad (sunk)	1	–	4	7	–	68
Onslaught	3	–	–	2	2	–
Onslow	–	–	–	2	3	–
Petard	2	1	–	7	5	–
Porpoise	–	–	–	2	2	–
Shark (sunk)	7	–	–	79	2	–
Sparrowhawk (sunk)	–	–	–	6	–	–
Spitfire	–	3	–	6	16	–
Turbulent (sunk)	5	–	–	85	–	13
Total	328	25	10	5,769	485	167

GERMAN CASUALTIES
(Figures taken from German official history, *Der Krieg zur See*)

Ship	Killed	Wounded
Battleships:		
Grosser Kuerfurst	15	10
Kaiser	–	1
Koenig	45	27
Markgraf	11	13
Nassau	11	16
Oldenburg	8	14
Ostfriesland	1	10
Pommern (sunk)	844	–
Prinzregent-Luitpold	–	11
Rheinland	10	20
Schlesien	1	–
Schleswig-Holstein	3	9
Westfalen	2	8
Battle-cruisers:		
Derfflinger	157	26
Lützow (sunk)	115	50
Moltke	17	23
Seydlitz	98	55
Von der Tann	11	35
Light cruisers:		
Elbing (sunk)	4	12
Frankfurt	3	18
Frauenlob (sunk)	320	1
Hamburg	14	25
München	8	20

Ship	Killed	Wounded
Pillau	4	19
Rostock (sunk)	14	6
Stettin	8	28
Wiesbaden (sunk)	589	–
Torpedo boats	238	50
Total	2,551	507

Annex B

THE WAR FOR CIVILIZATION: THE RECKONING

Country	Total mobilized forces	Killed
ENTENTE AND ASSOCIATED POWERS		
Russia	12,000,000	1,700,000
British Empire	8,904,467	908,371
France	8,410,000	1,357,800
Italy	5,615,000	650,000
United States	4,355,000	116,516
Japan	800,000	300
Romania	750,000	335,706
Serbia	707,343	45,000
Belgium	267,000	13,716
Greece	230,000	5,000
Portugal	100,000	7,222
Montenegro	50,000	3,000
Total	**42,188,810**	**5,142,631**
CENTRAL AND ASSOCIATED POWERS		
Germany	11,000,000	1,773,700
Austria-Hungary	7,800,000	1,200,000
Turkey	2,850,000	325,000
Bulgaria	1,200,000	87,500
Total	**22,850,000**	**3,386,200**
GRAND TOTAL	**65,038,810**	**8,528,831**

Wounded	Prisoners and missing	Total casualties	Casualties as % of forces
4,950,000	2,500,000	9,150,000	76.3
2,090,212	191,652	3,190,235	35.8
4,266,000	537,000	6,160,800	73.3
947,000	600,000	2,197,000	39.1
204,002	4,500	323,018	7.1
907	3	1,210	0.2
120,000	80,000	535,706	71.4
133,148	152,958	331,106	46.8
44,686	34,659	93,061	34.9
21,000	1,000	27,000	11.7
13,751	12,318	33,291	33.3
10,000	7,000	20,000	40.0
12,800,706	**4,121,090**	**22,062,427**	**52.3**
4,216,058	1,152,800	7,142,558	64.9
3,620,000	2,200,000	7,020,000	90.0
400,000	250,000	975,000	34.2
152,390	27,029	266,919	22.2
8,388,448	**3,629,829**	**15,404,477**	**67.4**
21,189,154	**7,750,919**	**37,466,904**	**57.5**

Annex C

THE FINAL DESPATCH OF FIELD MARSHAL SIR DOUGLAS HAIG, COMMANDER IN CHIEF OF THE BRITISH ARMIES IN FRANCE AND FLANDERS

Printed in the Fourth Supplement to the London Gazette *of 8 April 1919. Part 1 of the despatch dealt with the detail of the final days of battle, the Armistice and the advance into Germany. Part 2, 'Features of the War', contained Haig's reflections on the fighting as a whole, and the value of various arms and services, as well as appreciations of the contributions of named individuals. An extract from Part 2, Haig's principal observations, follows below.*

A Single Great Battle

In this my final Despatch, I think it desirable to comment briefly upon certain general features which concern the whole series of operations carried out under my command. I am urged thereto by the conviction that neither the course of the war itself nor the military lessons to be drawn therefrom can properly be comprehended, unless the long succession of battles commenced on the Somme in 1916 and ended in November of last year on the Sambre are viewed as forming part of one great and continuous engagement.

To direct attention to any single phase of that stupendous and incessant struggle and seek in it the explanation of our success, to the exclusion or neglect of other phases possibly less striking in their immediate or obvious consequences, is in my opinion to risk the formation of unsound doctrines regarding the character and requirements of modern war.

If the operations of the past 4½ years are regarded as a single continuous campaign, there can be recognised in them the same general features and the same necessary stages which between forces of approximately equal strength have marked all the conclusive battles of history.

There is in the first instance the preliminary stage of the campaign in which the opposing forces seek to deploy and manoeuvre for position, endeavouring while doing so to gain some early advantage which might be pushed home to quick decision. This phase came to an end in the present war with the creation of continuous trench lines from the Swiss frontier to the sea.

Battle having been joined, there follows the period of real struggle in which the main forces of the two belligerent armies are pitted against each other in close and costly combat. Each commander seeks to wear down the power of resistance of his opponent and to pin him to his position, while preserving or accumulating in his own hands a powerful reserve force which he can manoeuvre, and, when signs of the enemy becoming morally and physically weakened are observed, deliver the decisive attack.

The greatest possible pressure against the enemy's whole front must be maintained, especially when the crisis of the battle approaches. Then every man, horse and gun is required to co-operate, so as to complete the enemy's overthrow and exploit success.

In every stage of the wearing-out struggle losses will necessarily be heavy on both sides, for in it the price of victory is paid. If the opposing forces are approximately equal in numbers, in courage, in moral[e] and in equipment, there is no way of avoiding payment of the price or of eliminating this phase of the struggle.

In former battles this stage of the conflict has rarely lasted more than a few days, and has often been completed in a few hours. When armies of millions are engaged, with the resources of great Empires behind them, it will inevitably be long. It will include violent crises of fighting which, when viewed separately and apart from the general perspective, will appear individually as great indecisive battles. To this stage belong the great engagements of 1916 and 1917 which wore down the strength of the German Armies.

Finally, whether from the superior fighting ability and leadership of one of the belligerents, as the result of greater resources or tenacity, or by reason of higher moral, or from a combination of all these causes, the time will come when the other side will begin to weaken and the climax of the battle is reached.

Then the commander of the weaker side must choose whether he will break off the engagement, if he can, while there is yet time, or stake on a supreme effort what reserves remain to him. The launching and destruction of Napoleon's last reserves at Waterloo was a matter of minutes. In this World War the great sortie of the beleaguered German Armies, commenced on March 21, 1918, lasted for four months, yet it represents a corresponding stage in a single colossal battle.

The breaking down of such a supreme effort will be the signal for the commander of the successful side to develop his greatest strength, and seek to turn to immediate account the loss in material and moral which their failure must inevitably produce among his opponent's troops.

In a battle joined and decided in the course of a few days or hours, there is no risk that the lay observer will seek to distinguish the culminating operations by which victory is seized and exploited from the preceding stages by which it has been made possible and determined. If the whole operations of the present war are regarded in correct perspective, the victories of the summer and autumn of 1918 will be seen to be directly dependent upon the two years of stubborn fighting that preceded them.

The Length of the War

If the causes which determined the length of the recent contest are examined in the light of the accepted principles of war, it will be seen that the duration of the struggle was governed by and bore a direct relation to certain definite factors which are enumerated below.

In the first place, we were unprepared for war, or at any rate for a war of such magnitude. We were deficient in both trained men and military material, and, what was more important, had no machinery ready by which either men or material could be produced in anything approaching the requisite quantities. The consequences were twofold.

Firstly, the necessary machinery had to be improvised hurriedly, and improvisation is never economical and seldom satisfactory. In this case the high-water mark of our fighting strength in infantry was only reached after two and a half years of conflict, by which time heavy casualties had already been incurred. In consequence, the full man-power of the Empire was never developed in the field at any period of the war.

As regards material, it was not until midsummer 1916 that the artillery situation became even approximately adequate to the conduct of major operations. Throughout the Somme battle the expenditure of artillery ammunition had to be watched with the greatest care. During the battles of 1917, ammunition was plentiful, but the gun situation was a source of constant anxiety. Only in 1918 was it possible to conduct artillery operations independently of any limiting considerations other than that of transport.

The second consequence of our unpreparedness was that our armies were unable to intervene, either at the outset of the war or until nearly two years had elapsed, in sufficient strength adequately to assist our Allies. The enemy was able to gain a notable initial advantage by establishing himself in Belgium and Northern France, and throughout the early stages of the war was free to concentrate an undue proportion of his effectives against France and Russia.

The excessive burden thrown upon the gallant Army of France during this period caused them losses the effect of which has been felt all through the war and directly influenced its length. Just as at no time were we as an Empire able to put our full strength into the field, so at no time were the Allies as a whole able completely to develop and obtain the full effect from their greatly superior man-power. What might have been the effect of British intervention on a larger scale in the earlier stages of the war is shown by what was actually achieved by our original Expeditionary Force.

It is interesting to note that in previous campaigns the side which has been fully prepared for war has almost invariably gained a rapid and complete success over its less well prepared opponent. In 1866 and 1870, Austria and then France were overwhelmed at the outset by means of superior preparation.

The initial advantages derived therefrom were followed up by such vigorous and ruthless action, regardless of loss, that there was no time to recover from the first stunning blows. The German plan of campaign in the present war was undoubtedly based on similar principles. The margin by which the German onrush in 1914 was stemmed was so narrow, and the subsequent struggle so severe, that the word 'miraculous' is hardly too strong a term to describe the recovery and ultimate victory of the Allies.

A further cause adversely influencing the duration of the war on the Western Front during its later stages, and one following indirectly from that just stated, was the situation in other theatres. The military strength of Russia broke down in 1917 at a critical period when, had she been able to carry out her military engagements, the war might have been shortened by a year.

At a later date, the military situation in Italy in the autumn of 1917 necessitated the transfer of five British divisions from France to Italy at a time when their presence in France might have had far reaching effects.

Thirdly, the Allies were handicapped in their task and the war thereby lengthened by the inherent difficulties always associated with the combined action of armies of separate nationalities, differing in speech and temperament, and, not least important, in military organisation, equipment and supply.

Finally, as indicated in the opening paragraph of this part of my Despatch, the huge numbers of men engaged on either side, whereby a continuous battle front was rapidly established from Switzerland to the sea, outflanking was made impossible and manoeuvre very difficult, necessitated the delivery of frontal attacks.

This factor, combined with the strength of the defensive under modern conditions, rendered a protracted wearing-out battle unavoidable before the enemy's power of resistance could be overcome. So long as the opposing forces are at the outset approximately equal in numbers and moral and there are no flanks to turn, a long struggle for supremacy is inevitable.

The Extent of our Casualties

Obviously, the greater the length of a war the higher is likely to be the number of casualties in it on either side. The same causes, therefore, which served to protract the recent struggle are largely responsible for the extent of our casualties. There can be no question that to our general unpreparedness must be attributed the loss of many thousands of brave men whose sacrifice we deeply deplore, while we regard their splendid gallantry and self-devotion with unstinted admiration and gratitude.

Given, however, the military situation existing in August 1914, our total losses in the war have been no larger than were to be expected. Neither do they compare unfavourably with those of any other of the belligerent nations, so far as figures are available from which comparison can be made.

The total British casualties in all theatres of war – killed, wounded, missing and prisoners, including native troops – are approximately three millions (3,076,388). Of this total, some two and a half millions (2,568,388) were incurred on the Western Front. The total

French losses – killed, missing and prisoners, but exclusive of wounded – have been given as approximately 1,831,000.

If an estimate for wounded is added, the total can scarcely be less than 4,800,000, and of this total it is fair to assume that over four millions were incurred on the Western Front. The published figures for Italy – killed and wounded only, exclusive of prisoners – amounted to 1,400,000 of which practically the whole were incurred in the western theatre of war.

Figures have also been published for Germany and Austria. The total German casualties – killed, wounded, missing and prisoners – are given at approximately six and a half millions (6,485,000), of which the vastly greater proportion must have been incurred on the Western Front, where the bulk of the German forces were concentrated and the hardest fighting took place.

In view of the fact, however, that the number of German prisoners is definitely known to be considerably understated, these figures must be accepted with reserve. The losses of Austria-Hungary in killed, missing and prisoners are given as approximately two and three-quarter millions (2,772,000). An estimate of wounded would give us a total of over four and a half millions.

The extent of our casualties, like the duration of the war, was dependent on certain definite factors which can be stated shortly.

In the first place, the military situation compelled us, particularly during the first portion of the war, to make great efforts before we had developed our full strength in the field or properly equipped and trained our armies. These efforts were wasteful of men, but in the circumstances they could not be avoided. The only alternative was to do nothing and see our French Allies overwhelmed by the enemy's superior numbers.

During the second half of the war, and that part embracing the critical and costly period of the wearing-out battle, the losses previously suffered by our Allies laid upon the British Armies in France an increasing share in the burden of attack. From the opening of the Somme battle in 1916 to the termination of hostilities the British Armies were subjected to a strain of the utmost severity which never ceased, and consequently had little or no opportunity for the rest and training they so greatly needed.

In addition to these particular considerations, certain general factors peculiar to modern war made for the inflation of losses. The great strength of modern field defences and the power and precision of modern weapons, the multiplication of machine guns, trench mortars, and artillery of all natures, the employment of gas and the rapid development of the aeroplane as a formidable agent of destruction against both men and material, all combined to increase the price to be paid for victory.

If only for these reasons, no comparisons can usefully be made between the relative losses incurred in this war and any previous war. There is, however, the further consideration that the issues involved in this stupendous struggle were far greater than those concerned in any other war in recent history. Our existence as Empire and civilisation itself, as it is understood by free Western nations, were at stake. Men fought as they have never fought before in masses.

Despite our own particular handicaps and the foregoing general considerations, it is satisfactory to note that, as the result of the courage and determination of our troops, and the high level of leadership generally maintained, our losses even in attack over the whole period of the battle compare favourably with those inflicted on our opponents.

The approximate total of our battle casualties in all arms, and including Overseas troops, from the commencement of the Somme battle in 1916 to the conclusion of the Armistice is 2,140,000. The calculation of German losses is obviously a matter of great difficulty.

It is estimated, however, that the number of casualties inflicted on the enemy by British troops during the above period exceeds two and a half millions. It is of interest, moreover, in the light of the paragraph next following, that more than half the total casualties incurred by us in the fighting of 1918 were occasioned during the five months March–July, when our armies were on the defensive.

Why We Attacked Whenever Possible

Closely connected with the question of casualties is that of the relative values of attack and defence. It is a view often expressed that the attack is more expensive than defence. This is only a half statement of the truth. Unquestionably, unsuccessful attack is generally more expensive than defence, particularly if the attack is pressed home with courage and resolution. On the other hand, attack so pressed home, if skilfully conducted, is rarely unsuccessful, whereas, in its later stages especially, unsuccessful defence is far more costly than attack.

Moreover, the object of all war is victory, and a purely defensive attitude can never bring about a successful decision, either in a battle or in a campaign. The idea that a war can be won by standing on the defensive and waiting for the enemy to attack is a dangerous fallacy, which owes its inception to the desire to evade the price of victory.

It is axiom* that decisive success in battle can be gained only by a vigorous offensive. The principle here stated had long been recognised as being fundamental, and is based on the universal teaching of military history in all ages. The course of the present war has proved it to be correct.

To pass for a moment from the general to the particular, and consider in the light of the present war the facts upon which this axiom is based.

A defensive role sooner or later brings about a distinct lowering of the moral of the troops, who imagine that the enemy must be the better man, or at least more numerous, better equipped with and better served by artillery and other mechanical aids to victory. Once the mass of the defending infantry become possessed of such ideas, the battle is as good as lost.

An army fighting on enemy soil, especially if its standard of discipline is high, may maintain a successful defence for a protracted period,

* axiomatic.

in the hope that victory may be gained elsewhere or that the enemy may tire or weaken in his resolution and accept a compromise. The resistance of the German Armies was undoubtedly prolonged in this fashion, but in the end the persistence of our troops had its natural effect.

Further, a defensive policy involves the loss of the initiative, with all the consequent disadvantages to the defender. The enemy is able to choose at his own convenience the time and place of his attacks. Not being influenced himself by the threat of attack from his opponent, he can afford to take risks, and by greatly weakening his front in some places can concentrate an overwhelming force elsewhere with which to attack.

The defender, on the other hand, becomes almost entirely ignorant of the dispositions and plans of his opponent, who is thus in a position to effect a surprise. This was clearly exemplified during the fighting of 1918. As long as the enemy was attacking, he obtained fairly full information regarding our dispositions. Captured documents show that, as soon as he was thrown once more on the defensive and the initiative returned to the Allies, he was kept in comparative ignorance of our plans and dispositions. The consequence was that the Allies were able to effect many surprises, both strategic and tactical.

As a further effect of the loss of the initiative and ignorance of his opponent's intentions, the defender finds it difficult to avoid a certain dispersal of his forces. Though for a variety of reasons, including the fact that we had lately been on the offensive, we were by no means entirely ignorant of the enemy's intentions in the spring of 1918, the unavoidable uncertainty resulting from a temporary loss of the initiative did have the effect of preventing a complete concentration of our reserves behind the point of the enemy's attack.

An additional reason, peculiar to the circumstances of the present war, which in itself compelled me to refuse to adopt a purely defensive attitude so long as any other was open to me, is found in the geographical position of our armies. For reasons stated by me in my Despatch of July 20, 1918, we could not afford to give much ground on any part of our front. The experience of the war has shown that if the defence is to be maintained successfully, even for a limited time, it must be flexible.

The End of the War

If the views set out by me in the preceding paragraphs are accepted, it will be recognised that the war did not follow any unprecedented course, and that its end was neither sudden nor should it have been unexpected. The rapid collapse of Germany's military powers in the latter half of 1918 was the logical outcome of the fighting of the previous two years.

It would not have taken place but for the period of ceaseless attrition which used up the reserves of the German Armies, while the constant and growing pressure of the blockade sapped with more deadly insistence from year to year at the strength and resolution of the German people. It is in the great battles of 1916 and 1917 that we have to seek for the secret of our victory in 1918.

Doubtless, the end might have come sooner had we been able to develop the military resources of our Empire more rapidly and with a higher degree of concentration, or had not the defection of Russia in 1917 given our enemies a new lease of life.

So far as the military situation is concerned, in spite of the great accession of strength which Germany received as the result of the defection of Russia, the battles of 1916 and 1917 had so far weakened her armies that the effort they made in 1918 was insufficient to secure victory. Moreover, the effect of the battles of 1916 and 1917 was not confined to loss of German man-power.

The moral effects of those battles were enormous, both in the German Army and in Germany. By their means our soldiers established over the German soldier a moral superiority which they held in an ever-increasing degree until the end of the war, even in the difficult days of March and April 1918.

PICTURE ACKNOWLEDGEMENTS

Every effort has been made to trace copyright holders. Any who have been overlooked are invited to get in touch with the publishers.

Endpapers (hardback edition only):
The Schlieffen concept: map by Tom Coulson, Encompass Graphics.

Illustrations in the text
'Peace and Future Cannon Fodder' cartoon by Will Dyson, *Daily Mail*, May 1919, © John Frost Newspapers/Alamy Stock Photo.

Picture sections

(Clockwise from top left on each page/spread.)

Section 1

Kaiser Wilhelm and Count Helmuth von Moltke: General Photographic Agency/Stringer/Getty Images; Tsar Nicholas and Grand Duke Nicholas: © IWM (Q 52794); David Lloyd George and Winston Churchill, 1915: Hulton Archive/Stringer/Getty Images; French commander-in-chief Joseph Joffre with army commanders Noël de Castelnau and Paul Pau: © IWM (Q 53625).

Director of military operations Henry Wilson: Library of Congress, Prints & Photographs Division, LC-DIG-ggbain-25799; Lord Kitchener leaving the War Office, 1916: Topical Press Agency/Stringer/Getty Images; Belgian soldiers captured: Ullstein Bild via Getty Images; German siege gun at Liège, 1914: © Ivy Close Images/Alamy Stock Photo.

Russian surrender at Tannenberg: © dpa picture alliance/Alamy Stock Photo; 'Notre glorieux soixante-quinze' (French 75mm field gun): © Roger-Viollet/TopFoto; Erich von Falkenhayn: Albert Meyer/ullstein bild via Getty Images; Field Marshal Sir John French with personal staff, 1914: © Chronicle / Alamy Stock Photo; BEF retreat after Mons: © Jeanne Maze Churchill.

BEF troops resting at Ypres, 1914: Archive Photos/Stringer/Getty Images; Serbian troops surround King Peter of Serbia: Archives/AFP/Getty Images.

Austrian trenches, 1914: K. K. Kriegspressequartier, Licht/ÖNB-Bildarchiv/ picturedesk.com/ TopFoto; Admiral Robeck and General Hamilton with their chiefs of staff: © IWM (Q 13560).

'Anzacs' at Gallipoli: © TopFoto; Lord Kitchener at Gallipoli: Keystone/Staff/ Getty Images; troops crossing the Tigris: © IWM (Q 25183).

Turkish prisoners: © IWM (Q 24294); 'The gardeners of Salonika': © Chronicle/ Alamy Stock Photo; cannon being dragged through the Alps: © TopFoto.

German troops at Verdun, February 2016: © IWM (Q 23760); French reinforcements at Verdun: AFP/Getty Images; classic trench scene: Universal Images Group/Getty Images; Sir Douglas Haig and his private secretary, Philip Sassoon: © IWM (Q 23633).

Section 2

Sinking of HMS *Audacious*: © Aviation History Collection/Alamy Stock Photo; HMS *Benbow*: © IWM (SP 1885); Admiral Sir John Jellicoe: Topical Press Agency/ Stringer/Getty Images.

Wire on the Western Front: © IWM (Q 42229); RAMC searching the packs of casualties: © IWM (Q 4245); Douglas Haig, Lloyd George, Joseph Joffre and Albert Thomas: Universal History Archive/UIG via Getty Images.

Russian troops being driven back to the firing line: Hulton Archive/Stringer/Getty Images; Paul von Hindenburg and Erich Ludendorff: © Ullstein Bild/TopFoto; General Pershing arrives at Boulogne, 1917: Fotosearch/Stringer/Getty Images.

Troops at Caporetto: Hulton Archive/Stringer/Getty Images; Ottoman machine guns in Palestine: Courtesy Library of Congress, Prints & Photographs Division, LC-DIG-ppmsca-13709-00127; French chief of staff Ferdinand Foch and Italian C-in-C Armando Diaz: Photo 12/Getty Images.

Sir Edmund Allenby entering Jerusalem: Universal History Archive/Getty Images; Howitzer near Albert: © Chronicle/Alamy Stock Photo; German troops massing for Operation Michael: © IWM (Q 55480).

British Mark V tanks: Henry Guttmann/Stringer/Getty Images; Whippet tanks: Universal History Archive/UIG via Getty images; Captain George S. Patton with Renault FT: PhotoQuest/Getty Images; tanks advancing in the Argonne forest: Buyenlarge/Getty Images.

AEF ace Eddie Rickenbacker: MPI/Stringer/Getty Images; Douglas Haig with Canadian troops: The Print Collector/Getty Images; Allied plenipotentiaries beside railway carriage: Photo 12/Getty Images; John Vaughan Campbell VC addresses troops from bridge: Photo by 2nd Lt. D McLellan/IWM via Getty Images.

Douglas Haig with army commanders: © IWM (Q 9689); 'The Big Four' at Paris peace conference: Lee Jackson/Stringer/Getty Images.

Index

INDEX

INDEX

INDEX

1914: FIGHT THE GOOD FIGHT

Britain, the Army and the coming of the First World War

Allan Mallinson

It took just a month from the assassination in Sarajevo on 28 June 1914 for the huge conscript armies of Continental Europe to be on the march. By mid-August, following Germany's invasion of Belgium and responding to a treaty signed in a very different age, the one hundred thousand 'Old Contemptibles' of the British Expeditionary Force arrived in France and found themselves standing in the path of a German army many times their number. Their heroic resistance has passed into the annals of war.

In his vivid, compelling and rigorously researched new history, Allan Mallinson examines the century-long path that led to war, and the vital first few weeks of fighting – a conflict of rapid movement before the stalemate of the trenches – and speculates, tantalisingly, on what might have been had wiser political and military counsels prevailed . . .

'In the deluge of books to mark the centenary of the start of the Great War, it is refreshing to find one written by a former soldier who is also an accomplished military historian . . . with his soldier's grasp of tactics and strategy, Mallinson describes with clarity and authority the opening weeks of the war'
Simon Heffer, *DAILY MAIL*

'Compelling and rigorously researched . . . this is not dry military history. He tells the story through many eyes of those on the front line, from general to Tommy'
DAILY EXPRESS

'Mallinson writes with an exciting pen and a cool head and he understands war'
Professor Michael Clarke, *THE TIMES*

'A must-read for anyone who wants to know how Britain practically stumbled into one of the bloodiest conflicts in history'
SUNDAY EXPRESS

Shortlisted for the Duke of Westminster's Medal for Military Literature